THE DUTCH IN BRAZIL
1624-1654

JOHAN MAURITS OF NASSAU, 1647

From the print by T. Matham

THE DUTCH IN BRAZIL

1624–1654

BY

C. R. BOXER

CAMOENS PROFESSOR OF PORTUGUESE
UNIVERSITY OF LONDON
KING'S COLLEGE

ARCHON BOOKS

1973

Library of Congress Cataloging in Publication Data

Boxer, Charles Ralph, 1904-
   The Dutch in Brazil, 1624-1654.

   Reprint of the 1957 ed. published by Clarendon Press,
Oxford; with an addenda to the bibliography.
      Bibliography: p.
      1. Brazil—History—Dutch conquest, 1624-1654. I. Title.
[F2532.B7 1973]   981'.03   73-5701
ISBN 0-208-01338-5

First published 1957
Oxford, at the Clarendon Press
Reprinted 1973 with permission in
an unabridged edition and with addenda
to the bibliographical note
as an Archon Book by
THE SHOE STRING PRESS, INC.
Hamden, Connecticut 06514

Printed in the United States of America

PREFACE

IN 1896–1900 a series of articles entitled 'The Dutch Power in Brazil, 1624–1654', appeared over the signature of the Oxford historian, G. M. Edmundson, in *The English Historical Review*. Edmundson got no farther than October 1632, and the value of his work has been very differently appraised by subsequent historians. Despite the large amount of relevant material which has become available within the last fifty years, there is still no adequate account in English of this curious colonial episode. The present work is an attempt to fill this gap.

Some readers may feel that since there is already an excellent German book on the subject by H. Wätjen, *Das holländische Kolonialreich in Brasilien* (The Hague and Gotha, 1921), there is no need for one in English. Apart from the fact that Wätjen's book has long been out of print and is very hard to come by, I venture to think that the appearance of the present work is justified, for two reasons. Firstly, Wätjen made insufficient use of Portuguese (as distinct from Brazilian) sources, and at least one very important Dutch source (the Journal of Hendrik Haecxs) has come to light since he wrote. Secondly, he concentrated, understandably enough, on the governorship of Count Johan Maurits of Nassau (1637–44), and his account of the last ten years of Netherlands Brazil is in some respects both superficial and inexact. On the other hand, Wätjen's study of the financial and economic conditions of the colony is a definitive one. The reader who desires adequate information on those aspects must always go to Wätjen, since I do not claim to supersede the German scholar's work, but only to supplement it. I have tried to look at the evidence with fresh eyes, and to combine the Dutch and the Portuguese accounts to a greater extent than Wätjen was able to do.

As Robert Southey observed in the preface to his massive *History of Brazil* (3 vols., London, 1810–19), 'there are many copious and good accounts of the Dutch war', although the use which he made of this material was severely criticized by a hostile reviewer in *Blackwood's Edinburgh Magazine* (February 1824): 'His *History of Brazil* is the most unreadable production of our time. Two or three elephant folios about a single Portuguese colony! Every little colonel, captain, bishop, friar, discussed at as much length as if they were so many Cromwells or Loyolas.' I have tried to avoid this fault in the present work; but since Netherlands Brazil was at war for all save a few months of its existence, the 'old, unhappy, far-off things' related here, inevitably include a good deal about 'battles long ago' and the men who fought in them.

Southey's real fault was not, in my view, the amount of space he devoted to discussing Portuguese personalities—had they been Scots, or even English, *Blackwood*'s reviewer would doubtless have raised no objections—but his violent prejudice against the Dutch. This prejudice, deriving from the long and bitter rivalry of the two great maritime nations on either side of the North Sea, has died very hard, and is not decently buried yet. Southey's venomous observation, 'The Dutch have always been a cruel people . . . and there is no nation whose colonial history is so inexcusably and inexpiably disgraceful to human nature', was for long reflected in many English historical works, and traces of it are readily discernible today. My own object is not to whitewash the conduct of the Dutch West India Company, which was indeed subjected to the most bitter criticism in the Netherlands, and not least by its own employees, but to show that there was another side to the case. If the Company's directors were often greedy and grasping, they also included finer spirits such as the scholarly Johannes de Laet. The work of Johan Maurits, their governor-general in Brazil, can stand comparison with that of any other colonial administrator, whether East or West. Indeed, it would be difficult to name another who deserves as much credit for making available to the outside world such accurate and scientific knowledge about the country which was entrusted to his charge.

To whom is this book addressed? Primarily to those readers who are interested in the bypaths (or even in the dead-ends) of colonial history. But it may also make some appeal to those who are interested in broader themes, such as the interplay of racial and religious conflicts, or the influence of sea-power on colonial warfare. In any event, I hope that the reader, whether specialist, casual, or critical, will find here (in the words of the *Amsterdams Dam-praetje*) 'something old, something new, and something strange'.[1]

January 1956

C. R. B.

[1] *Amsterdams Dam-praetje, van wat outs en wat nieuws en wat vreemts* (Amsterdam, 1649).

ACKNOWLEDGEMENTS

SINCE I believe with Mr. W. S. Lewis that 'the collector's work is only partly done when he has formed his collection: until it is used, it is like bric-à-brac in a cabinet', this book has been written mainly from the resources of my own library. Where the help of other persons, libraries, and archives has been asked, it has been generously given, and I should like to record my indebtedness to the following. Dr. Rodrigo de Melo Franco de Andrade, Senhor Godfredo Filho and Senhor Ayrton de Carvalho, for the opportunity of visiting many of the sites and scenes connected with the history of the Dutch in Brazil on my first visit to that country in 1949. The Commission of the Congress commemorating the third centenary of the Pernambucan Restoration in 1954, for enabling me to revisit north-east Brazil in July and August of that year, and to enjoy once more the traditionally lavish hospitality of that beautiful region. His Excellency Ambassador Joaquim de Sousa Leão, Professor G. J. Renier, Professor Philip Coolhaas, and Miss Rose Macaulay, for checking some references and the elucidation of some difficult words. Professor D. Virginia Rau, for a preview of her valuable *Catalogue* of the manuscripts of Brazilian interest in the Cadaval archives, now in the press. The Royal Library at The Hague for allowing me to borrow L. Driessen's *Leben des Fürsten Johann Moritz von Nassau-Siegen* (Berlin, 1849), when no copy could be procured for my use in England. I have also to thank the University of London for a research grant which enabled me to visit Lisbon in 1953, and arrange for the copying of a number of relevant documents. But above all, I am indebted for friendly advice and stimulating discussion to three scholars who have made this field particularly their own. Dr. W. J. van Hoboken of the Amsterdam Gemeente Archief, not only furnished me with numerous transcripts from the Dutch archives, but lent me the typed copy of his richly documented thesis, *Witte de With in Brazilië, 1648-49*, which appeared while my own book was in the press. This work not only throws a flood of light on that admiral's activities in Brazil, but brings out very clearly the importance of the attitude of Amsterdam to the Brazilian problem. Dr. José Honorio Rodrigues, author of the definitive bibliography of the Dutch in Brazil, and Dr. José Antonio Gonsalves de Mello, neto, whose unrivalled knowledge of the 'Time of the Flemings' is obvious to all who have read his works, were both most helpful in every way. If my own book helps to draw attention to the work of these scholars, I shall be more than satisfied.

CONTENTS

LIST OF ILLUSTRATIONS

Maps 2–4 are based on those drawn by S. P. L'Honoré Naber on sheets 7–10 of the *Geschiedkundige Atlas van Nederland* (The Hague, 1931), by kind permission of the publisher, Martinus Nijhoff.

ABBREVIATIONS

AHU	Arquivo Historico Ultramarino, Lisbon.
BM. Add. MSS.	British Museum, Additional Manuscripts, London.
BNRJ	Biblioteca Nacional, Rio de Janeiro.
BPE	Biblioteca Publica, Evora.
HAHR	*Hispanic-American Historical Review*, Duke University Press.
JHMS	José Hygino Duarte Pereira's MS. transcripts from Dutch archives, Recife.
RIAGP	*Revista do Instituto Arqueológico e Geográfico Pernambucano*, Recife.
RIHGB	*Revista do Instituto Histórico e Geográfico Brazileiro*, Rio de Janeiro.
VOC	Dutch East India Company.
WIC	Dutch West India Company.

I

THE OPENING MOVES
1621–9

By the end of the first decade of the seventeenth century, the United Provinces of the Free Netherlands formed a prosperous and independent nation—although not a truly united one. The conclusion of the twelve-year truce with Spain in 1609 was a tacit admission of defeat by the latter power. It is true that the Spanish monarch did not formally abandon his pretensions to sovereignty over the Northern Netherlands until 1648, but those claims were no longer taken seriously by the world in general. If the fighting along the Flanders frontier had bogged down in an inconclusive stalemate, the phenomenal expansion of the Dutch overseas since 1598 clearly showed that a new and first-class power had arisen in the Low Lands by the North Sea.

Pride in the spectacular achievements of the Elizabethan adventurers (and the hot air generated nowadays about the New Elizabethan Age) should not blind us to the fact that it was the Dutch and not the English who broke the back of Iberian sea power during the first half of the seventeenth century. Tip-and-run raids against the Spanish settlements in the Caribbean might irritate and embarrass King Philip, but they did not seriously shake the power of Spain. In the year 1600 not an inch of colonial territory had been wrested from Spanish and Portuguese control, and the Iberian empire still girdled the globe intact from Macao in China to Callao in Peru. The true foundations of England's colonial expansion were not laid by the corsairs and filibusters of the Virgin Queen, but by the disgruntled Puritans who began to swarm overseas in the reign of her successor,

‘that vile Scot, the minion-kissing King’,

as a clergyman-poet accurately if uncharitably described King James the I and VI. The colonization of New England was undoubtedly facilitated by Spanish preoccupation with the menace of Dutch colonial expansion during the first few decades of Holland's Golden Century. England had dropped out of the fight against Spain in 1604, but the Dutch went on from strength to strength, destroying a powerful Portuguese fleet off Malacca in 1606, and a Spanish armada off Gibraltar in 1607. Nor did the conclusion of the truce in 1609 stop Dutch expansion and aggression in the tropical world. The chief stumbling-block in the preliminary negotiations which preceded the truce was the Dutch insistence on their right to trade in the East and West Indies. This difficulty was finally surmounted by wording the fourth clause of the treaty in such a way that it left the Dutch a relatively free hand in the East Indies, but implied that America and the West were to be regarded more strictly as a Spanish preserve.[1]

One of the principal reasons which forced the Spaniards to come to terms was the success achieved by the Dutch East India Company (incorporated in 1602) in breaking through the Iberian monopoly of the colonial world; and this success naturally suggested that similar methods could be used in the West. The moving spirit in the agitation for founding a West India Company was Willem Usselincx (1567–1647), an Antwerper by birth, and a prolific pamphleteer in the cause which he had so much at heart.[2] His ideas were in many respects original, if in some ways impracticable, and in others too far in advance of his time. His main idea was thoroughly sound, namely, that Dutch agricultural colonies should be settled somewhere in the New World, and that the development of these colonies, if intelligently fostered, would provide the mother-country with a valuable and expanding export market.

Usselincx criticized the popular conception that Spain derived her colonial wealth almost entirely from the gold- and silver-mines of Central and South America. He pointed out that the natural products of the New World, such as sugar, indigo,

[1] The text of the twelve-year truce signed in Apr. 1609 will be found in French and Dutch versions in the pamphlets catalogued by Knuttel, *Catalogus Pamphletten*, vol. i, nos. 1586–95. For an excellent succinct survey of Dutch–Iberian rivalry in the colonial world at this period see E. Sluiter, 'Dutch Maritime Power and the Colonial Status Quo, 1585-1641', in *Pacific Historical Review*, xi. 29–41.

[2] There are two well-documented biographical studies of Usselincx: J. F. Jameson, *Willem Usselincx, founder of the Dutch and Swedish West India Companies* (New York, 1887), and C. Ligtenberg, *Willem Usselinx* (Utrecht, 1915). Much relevant material will also be found in O. van Rees, *Geschiedenis der Staathuishoudkunde in Nederland tot het einde der achttiende eeuw* (Utrecht, 1868), vol. ii.

cochineal, sarsaparilla, dyewoods, hides, and pearls, &c., were even more valuable in the aggregate, while America formed a valuable outlet for the products of Spanish artisans and workers.[1] Usselincx instanced Brazil as the most striking example of his theory. That flourishing Portuguese colony produced no precious metals, but supplied sugar, cotton, Brazil-wood, &c., in abundance. These natural commodities, when marketed and sold in Portugal, almost sufficed of themselves to maintain that kingdom, which (it will be recalled) formed a dual monarchy with Spain from 1580 to 1640. Brazilian sugar alone yielded a minimum profit of 4,800,000 guilders a year, according to his calculations.

Usselincx did not necessarily advocate the seizure of Spanish or Portuguese colonies, but he urged the States-General to insist that the Spanish crown should allow Dutch trade and settlement in America during the truce years, particularly in regions such as Guiana (the so-called 'Wild Coast') and the area south of the Rio de la Plata, which were not effectively occupied by either Spaniards or Portuguese. He reckoned that the Amerindians could be won over to the side of the Dutch by fair and considerate treatment, particularly as many of them were restless under the Spanish yoke, and others were still unsubdued. Through contact with the Dutch colonists, the Amerindians would also come to need European goods and thus help to increase colonial trade with the Netherlands. Usselincx thought that even the Spanish creoles and mestizos would be glad to trade and traffic with the heretic new-comers, since they looked on America rather than on the Iberian Peninsula as their home. He argued that the Dutch could supply them with imported goods far more cheaply and efficiently than could either Spanish or Portuguese merchants.

Like all his contemporaries, Usselincx regarded colonies primarily as suppliers of raw materials for the mother-country, and as exclusive export-markets for its own manufactures and products. He therefore advised that no colonial industries or crafts should be allowed to develop, other than those which were essential for the provision of housing, &c. He urged that the emigration of agricultural labourers rather than of skilled workmen and artisans should be fostered. Germany and the

[1] Cf. B. W. Diffie, *Latin-American Civilization. Colonial Period* (Harrisburg, 1947), p. 144.

Baltic states could (he thought) supply large numbers of hard-working peasant families, whose low wages in their own home-lands deprived them of any hope of social betterment; whereas in the fertile soil of South America, a few years of honest toil would enable them to earn enough to spend their old age in peaceful retirement. He pointed out that since industrial enter-prises would not be allowed to develop in the colonies, there would be no inducement for skilled craftsmen to emigrate from the Netherlands and thus weaken their economic power.

Usselincx had never been in America, although he had lived for some years in the Azores, and he therefore underestimated the adverse effects of tropical heat on European field-labourers. He argued ingenuously that much of the heavy work (such as grinding the sugar-cane in the mills) could be done at night, or else around dawn and dusk when the strength of the sun would not be fully felt. Finally, and in this he was before his time, he stressed the superiority of free over slave labour. He deprecated the use of slaves as both uneconomical and inhuman, urging that free white labourers would work far better, when acclimatized. He also thought that voluntary Amerindian paid labour would become available in due time, when the natives of the country had become accustomed to the Dutch.

Usselincx was a fervent Calvinist, and a strong religious strain runs throughout his proposals. The idea of transplanting the 'true Christian Religion' to the New World and combating the errors of the Popish Antichrist repeatedly occurs in his pam-phlets. Although, as mentioned above, Usselincx would have preferred the peaceful colonization of unoccupied regions in America with tacit (or explicit) Spanish permission, he realized that this might not be forthcoming. He argued that in this event the truce should be limited to Europe and the war con-tinued beyond the Line, so that the Dutch could settle their American colonies at the point of the sword if necessary.[1]

Through the ambiguous wording of the fourth clause of the treaty of 1609, the truce *was* virtually limited to Europe; but the peace party, headed by the veteran statesman Johan van Olden-barnevelt, used the truce as an excuse for shelving Usselincx's ambitious plans. Oldenbarnevelt's adherents pointed out that

---

[1] The foregoing summary of Usselincx's views is mainly from his *Vertoogh hoe nootwendich, nut ende profijtelich het sy . . . te behouden de vryheyt van te handelen op West-Indien,* published anonymously in 1608.

the Dutch could now obtain all the American products which they required more easily and safely (if not more cheaply) at Spanish and Portuguese ports, than they could by, voyaging to the Caribbean. The burgher-oligarchs who supported the Advocate of Holland were not interested in founding agricultural settlements overseas, or in spreading the 'true Christian Religion' among the 'blind heathen' in the New World. They argued that the Dutch already had enough trading and fighting to do in the East Indies, where the truce was never enforced and where Dutch expansion was accelerated rather than retarded, at the cost of the tottering Portuguese 'State of India'.

But although the Dutch made their main effort in Asian seas during the years 1609–21, their activities in the Atlantic area were by no means negligible. Enterprising Dutchmen began to exploit the fur-trade of the Hudson River area, Fort Orange, near the present-day Albany, being founded in 1614. The small Dutch trading-posts which already existed in Guiana between the Essequibo and the Amazon were consolidated and even expanded. Incidentally, not only Dutch, but also English and Irish adventurers frequented various places along the lower reaches of the Amazon during this period. They obtained tobacco, cotton, and dyewood by barter from the local Indians, with whom they were on the best of terms, as the Portuguese subsequently admitted. The latter first established themselves in the Amazon region with the foundation of Belem do Pará in January 1616; but between 1623 and 1630 they succeeded in destroying all the trading-posts and the embryo settlements of the 'nations of the North' in that area.[1] Meanwhile, Dutch trade with Brazil proper made a great spurt during the truce years, for reasons which will be explained later. But it was along the Gulf of Guinea in West Africa that the traders and sailors from the Low Countries achieved their most striking success.

The figures for the earlier years of Dutch trade with West Africa have not survived; but it is clear from allusions in contemporary works and news-letters that by 1621 the Dutch had supplanted the Portuguese as the principal traders on the Gold Coast, whence they exported large quantities of gold and ivory. The Portuguese still retained their great castle of São Jorge da Mina (St. George of the Mine, or Elmina as it was more

[1] J. A. Williamson, *English Colonies in Guiana and on the Amazon, 1604–1668* (Oxford, 1923).

commonly called in northern Europe), and a number of other coastal forts, but their former trade with the Negroes had largely passed into Dutch hands. From their headquarters at Ft. Nassau or Mouree (founded 1612), the Netherlanders supplied the Negroes with Nuremberger-ware and other trade-goods at prices far more attractive than those offered by the Portuguese. When the truce began the Dutch had a yearly average of twenty ships engaged in the Guinea trade, importing over 2,000 (Amsterdam) pounds of gold a year. By the end of the truce the number had about doubled and the cargoes were proportionately more valuable, while virtually the whole of the United Provinces' gold coinage was minted with gold brought from Guinea.[1]

The execution of Oldenbarnevelt, on a trumped-up charge of high treason, in 1619 marked the triumph of Prince Maurits of Nassau and the militant Calvinist (or Contra-Remonstrant) war-party. Both the prince and the *Predikants* were anxious for a renewal of the war with Spain, although not for precisely the same reasons. The Spaniards on their side were quite ready to accept the challenge offered by the expiration of the truce in April 1621. The last twelve years had given them a welcome breathing-space in Flanders; the Thirty Years War which had just broken out in Germany was going well for them and their Austrian ally; and it was obvious that the German Protestant princes would be of little use to the Dutch. Moreover, Dutch aggression in the colonial world had proved so damaging during the truce years that the Madrid government hoped a renewal of the war in Europe would divert their heretic foes from prosecuting their overseas designs on a grand scale.[2] Events soon showed that Olivares and his councillors had miscalculated badly on this last point.

When the renewal of the war was seen to be more than likely after the death of Oldenbarnevelt, the proposals of Usselincx (and of others) for the formation of a West India Company were re-examined and earnestly discussed among the merchants and burgher-oligarchs of the northern Netherlands. The project

---

[1] 'Consideratien van handelaars over het belang van den handel op de kust van Guinea', in *Kroniek Historisch Genootschap Utrecht*, xxvii. 260–5; J. K. De Jonge, *Oorsprong van Nederlands bezittingen op de kust van Guinea* (The Hague, 1871), pp. 10–17.

[2] J. Cuvelier and J. Lefèvre [eds.], *Correspondance de la Cour d'Espagne sur les affaires des Pays-Bas au XVIIe siècle* (Brussels, 1923), vol. ii, doc. 567, p. 176. References hereafter are to pages only.

was warmly supported by the Calvinist clergy, and after much debate the West India Company was formally incorporated by a Charter dated 3 June 1621. The Company, as thus constituted, differed radically from Usselincx's dream-child, since it was not primarily a peaceful colonizing or a trading corporation, but one formed avowedly for colonization and commerce through conquest. In many ways its constitution was modelled on that of the East India Company, but the commercial side of its activities was subordinated to the naval and military. The West India Company was not, however, merely a privateering corporation, as is often alleged. Colonization and commerce were both clearly envisaged, as can be seen from the terms of the original charter, whose principal provisions may be summarized as follows:[1]

The *Octroy* of 3 June 1621 (which later received several amplifications) gave the Company a twenty-four-year monopoly of trade and navigation, conquest and commerce, in all seas and lands between Newfoundland and the straits of Magellan on the one side of the Atlantic, and between the Tropic of Cancer and the Cape of Good Hope on the other. In the Pacific Ocean the Company's sphere of action extended from the west coast of America to the eastern tip of New Guinea. The States-General, in granting this charter of 1621 after that awarded to the East India Company in 1602, had thus, in effect, made a reply to Pope Alexander VI's famous Bull which divided the non-European world between Spain and Portugal in 1493. As far as the Protestant Dutch were concerned there was now a similar division between their two India Companies. An exception was made for the flourishing trade to the salt-pans of Punta de Araya, which were left open to all traders from the United Provinces (as strongly urged by Usselincx), but this did not last long. Despite the opposition of Hoorn and other North-Holland towns which specialized in this trade, the Company's monopoly was extended to include Punta de Araya a year later. The reason for this step was to tempt hesitant investors by making the monopoly more profitable.

[1] The *Octroy* of the West India Company has been frequently reprinted since the original editions of 1621 (Knuttel, *Catalogus Pamphletten*, nos. 3229–32), but the best version is that printed by S. P. L'Honoré Naber in his edition of Johannes de Laet, *Iaerlyck Verhael van de Verrichtinghen der Geoctroyeerde West-Indische Compagnie*, vol. i, pp. (6)–(23), The Hague, 1931, which was collated with the original manuscript in the Rijksarchief.

The Company was authorized to make alliances with the natives of West Africa, America, and the Pacific islands east of New Guinea; to build fortresses; to appoint governors, officials, and justices; and to maintain troops, garrisons, and fleets. The Company was also empowered to 'colonize fruitful and unpeopled lands, and to do everything necessary for the service of the nation and for the profit and increase of its trade'.[1] Troops and war material necessary for the occupation and defence of the projected colonies would be supplied by the States-General, but paid and maintained by the Company. Naval and military personnel were to take a triple oath of allegiance to the Company, the States-General, and the stadtholder as captain-general or commander-in-chief of the armed forces. Senior civilian personnel took the oath of allegiance to the two former bodies. The Company further received a government subsidy of one million florins, for half of which sum the States-General were to participate with the other shareholders in the profits. If (as was obviously to be expected) the Company's operations should involve it in an open war, the States-General would contribute a force of sixteen warships and four yachts, fully manned, equipped, and provisioned, provided that the Company paid for their maintenance and contributed an equal force from its own resources. The Company also received a wide range of tax-exemptions and freedom from import and export duties.

The Company, as a corporate body, was divided into five regional chambers or boards (*kamers*), which held stock in the following proportions:

Amsterdam	four-ninths
Zeeland (Middelburg)	two-ninths
The Maas (Rotterdam)	one-ninth
North-Quarter (Hoorn and West-Friesland)	one-ninth
Friesland, and the district of Groningen ('Town and Country')[2]	one-ninth

Each regional board had its own directors who were selected by the magistracy of the provinces and the chief towns from among the leading shareholders.[3] The central administration

---

[1] Article II of the original *Octroy* of 1621.

[2] *Stadt en Landen*, or *Stadt en Ommelanden*, as it was often termed.

[3] Those with a minimum subscription of 6,000 florins for Amsterdam, and 4,000 florins for each of the other four chambers.

was entrusted to a board of nineteen directors (hereafter referred to as the Heeren XIX), eighteen of whom were selected from among the regional directors, in the following proportions: Amsterdam, eight; Zeeland, four; the Maas, the North-Quarter, Friesland with Groningen, two each; the nineteenth being appointed by the States-General as their personal representative. The Heeren XIX were to meet alternately at Amsterdam for six years and at Middelburg for two. The directors were to serve for six years in the first instance, and then to retire in batches of one-third at intervals of two years. They were to be replaced by other leading shareholders (minimum subscription 4,000 florins) selected in consultation with the provincial and municipal authorities.

No yearly division of profits was to be made, unless they amounted to 10 per cent. upon the capital; but every six years a general balance-sheet was to be drawn up for the information of the shareholders, wherein a clear distinction would be made between profits (or losses) derived from trading and from war. No subscriber could withdraw his subscription before the expiration of the charter in 1645, when either a general and final settlement would be made, or else subscribers would have the option of withdrawing their money if the Company's charter was renewed. In the interval, shares could be bought and sold on the Amsterdam Exchange.

Contrary to the pleas of Usselincx and his supporters, the control of the Company was not vested in the States-General, nor in the shareholders, but (as with the sister East India Company) in the directors, and more particularly in the governing body of the Heeren XIX. The provisions concerning the periodic public audit and inspection of the Company's books, and the publication of balance-sheets, were never properly carried out; and the wide powers conferred on the directors by the charter were thus further enhanced. Since the directors were selected by (or in close consultation with) the municipal authorities, this meant that the burgher-oligarchs who ruled the towns likewise effectively controlled the Company. In theory, the shareholders had more chance of seeing what was being done with their money than did those who had invested in the East India Company, and the States-General could exercise some measure of control and supervision through the director they nominated among the Heeren XIX; but in practice both of the great India Companies were really controlled by their respective governing boards, the Heeren XIX for the West, and the Heeren XVII for the East. A comparison of the names of the directors of the West India Company as given by De Laet with the list of those for the East India Company as given by Valentyn shows, as might be expected, that some well-known regent families, such as the Bickers of Amsterdam and the Lampsens of Zeeland, were represented on the governing bodies of both Companies.[1] On the whole, however, different sets of people seem to have invested heavily in the two companies, and there is not so much overlapping as might have been expected. The small investor seems to have been a more important factor in the West India Company than in the East.

Taking their cue from ignorant and prejudiced Iberian writers, other historians who should have known better for long repeated that Jewish brains, capital, and industry were largely responsible for the formation of these two great corporations which combined the use of ledger and sword in such a striking fashion. Sombart was perhaps the worst offender in propagating the legend that wealthy Marranos or crypto-Jews exiled from Spain and Portugal flocked into Amsterdam with money and resources which they placed at the disposal of the Dutch for the fight against Spain. The archival researches of Wätjen and Van Dillen have demonstrated that this assertion is grossly exaggerated; as should, indeed, have been obvious to anyone who read carefully the seventeenth-century chronicles and voluminous pamphlet-literature, or, for that matter, the standard mid-nineteenth-century works of Asher and Van Rees.[2]

Out of a total of about 3,000,000 florins which the citizens of Amsterdam subscribed to the original capital of the West India Company, the eighteen Jews who invested in the company contributed a mere 36,000 florins, and only five of these Israelites invested more than 2,000 florins. As late as 1630 there were only about a thousand Jews settled in Amsterdam, and only

[1] Cf. the lists of the directors of the two Companies printed in De Laet-Naber, *Iaerlyck Verhael*, i. (33)–(37), and F. Valentyn, *Oud en Nieuw Oost-Indiën*, i. 301–16 (Dordrecht, 1724).
[2] G. M. Asher, *A Bibliographical and Historical Essay on the Dutch books and pamphlets relating to New Netherland and to the Dutch West-India Company and its possessions in Brazil, Angola etc.* (Amsterdam, 1854–67); O. Van Rees, *Geschiedenis der Staathuishoudkunde in Nederland* (2 vols., Amsterdam, 1865–8).

twenty-one of them were really wealthy individuals. Even in 1658 a list of 169 leading shareholders (subscribers of over 4,000 florins) records only eleven Jewish names. It is true that Jewish interest and participation in the development of Dutch Brazil from 1630 onwards was quite substantial, as we shall see; but the part played by Jews in the actual formation of the two great India Companies was virtually negligible. The real change came in the sixteen-eighties, when Jewish participation in the East India Company increased enormously.[1]

A much better case can be made out for considering that the West India Company was largely the work of emigrant Calvinists from Flanders. William Usselincx indeed exaggerated when he wrote in 1627 that 'before the Brabanters, Flemings and Walloons' brought their trade to the northern Netherlands and opened up their commerce with 'East-India, West-India, Africa, the Levant and Italy', the United Provinces barely possessed the means to maintain their dikes.[2] But the fact remains that many of those most actively concerned with the origin and development of the two great India Companies were militant Calvinist refugees from the Spanish Netherlands, particularly in the case of the West India Company. Le Maire, De Moucheron, Usselincx, Plancius, De Laet, and Barlaeus are only a few of the many famous Flemings whose names come readily to mind, whereas it would be difficult to recall a single Jew in this connexion. The actual numbers of the Calvinist emigrants from the southern Netherlands may have been exaggerated by Asher, who was one of the first of modern writers to point out their importance; but it is undeniable that the influence of the merchants and intellectuals among them was very great, and out of all proportion to their numbers.[3]

Although the West India Company was formally incorporated

---

[1] H. Wätjen, *Das Judentum und die Anfänge der modernen Kolonisation. Kritische Bemerkungen zu Werner Sombarts 'Die Juden und das Wirtschaftsleben'* (Berlin, 1914), pp. 32–34; I. G. van Dillen, 'Vreemdelingen te Amsterdam in de eerste helft der zeventiende Eeuw. De Portugeesche Joden', *Tijdschrift voor Geschiedenis* (Groningen, 1935), l. 4–35. Cf. also V. Barbour, *Capitalism in Amsterdam in the seventeenth century* (Baltimore, 1950), p. 25. H. I. Bloom, *The Economic Activities of the Jews of Amsterdam in the 17th and 18th centuries* (Williamsport, 1937), is too uncritical to be a safe guide in this respect.

[2] Van Rees, *Staathuishoudkunde*, ii. 86.

[3] Cf. V. Barbour, *Capitalism in Amsterdam in the 17th century*, pp. 23–24, and the sources quoted in the footnotes there.

in June 1621, subscribers did not come forward as readily as had been hoped, and the Company did not venture to undertake any major operation until more capital had been subscribed. The States-General, so deeply committed to support the Company, made every effort to whip up subscribers, and urged the members of the provincial magistracies and municipalities to set a good example by subscribing liberally themselves. Many of them did so, but the mercantile community in general still hung back. There were several reasons for this hesitation. In the first place, many people besides Usselincx were disappointed that the shareholders had no control over the directors' policy and the handling of the ordinary investors' money. Secondly, many people thought that the Company was what would be called nowadays a racket to 'give jobs to the boys', in the form of private rake-offs and cushy posts for the directors and their relatives, at the expense of the ordinary shareholders. Other people feared that the economic and commercial ends of the Company would be sacrificed to the political and military objectives which were envisaged. Finally, the siege of Bergen-op-Zoom by the Spaniards (July–Oct. 1622) induced many people to hang on to their spare cash until they saw which way the war was going.[1]

These and other doubts concerning the prospects of the West India Company had all the more weight, because the older East India Company was then being severely criticized by a numerous and influential body of its shareholders on very similar grounds. These disgruntled subscribers were known as the *dolerende participanten*, or 'dissenting shareholders'. They complained that the Heeren XVII did as they pleased with the shareholders' money, rendering no account of the same, giving or withholding annual dividends at their pleasure, using their position to rig the market price of shares, while lining their pockets by indulging in private trade, and so forth. Another complaint of the 'dissenting shareholders' was that their directors had, at the insistence of the States-General, subscribed a million florins to the capital of the West India Company,

[1] Anonymous 'Advies tot aanbeveling van de verovering van Brazilië door de West-Indische Compagnie', d. 12 Sept. 1622, and printed in *Kron. Hist. Gen. Utrecht*, xxvii. 228–56. This proposal is often, though wrongly, attributed to Usselincx; but it has much more in common with the pamphlet of J. A. Moerbeeck, cited on p. 14, note 2, below. Cf. J. H. Rodrigues, *Historiografia e Bibliografia do domínio holandês no Brasil* (Rio de Janeiro, 1949), pp. 181–2.

without consulting their own shareholders, and regardless of the fact that the new company could, in some ways, be regarded as a rival firm.[1]

The States-General were sufficiently impressed (or embarrassed) by these allegations to order the directors of the East India Company to give some sort of satisfaction to their *dolerende participanten*, as one of the conditions for the renewal of their original charter of 1602, which was due to expire in 1621. The Heeren XVII made a grudging move in this direction by allowing some of their books to be inspected by auditors specially nominated for this purpose, although even this limited concession soon lapsed. The relief of Bergen-op-Zoom (2 Oct. 1622) gave a fillip to timid investors, and by these and other means the States-General contrived to get more financial support for the West India Company.[2] Nor did they confine their efforts to their own territory. They ordered their agents abroad to publicize the formation of the new company and to assure potential subscribers that they would be treated on the same footing as Dutch investors.[3] These efforts were not made in vain, and substantial French, Genevan, and Venetian subscriptions were received in the summer of 1623.[4] The prospect of profitable privateering also helped to bring in new investors, especially in Zeeland where the militant Calvinist or Contra-Remonstrant war-party was particularly strong, and the Zeeland subscribers seem to have been mostly of modest means. In one way and another, the Company's paid-up capital reached the total of 7,108,106 florins in November 1623, of which sum 2,846,582 florins were subscribed in Amsterdam. This total of over seven millions compared favourably with the East India Company's original capital of six and a half million florins. At this date the West India Company had fifteen ships at sea, mostly bound for West Africa and the Amazon river

[1] For the *dolerende participanten* of the East India Company, and a survey of the pamphlet-war between them and the Heeren XVII, see Van Rees, *Staathuishoud-kunde*, ii. 125, 144–72.

[2] *Gedenkschriften van Jonkheer Alexander van der Capellen, 1621–1654* (Utrecht, 1777–8, 2 vols.), i. 99, 125, 138–9.

[3] There is an English translation of the original charter of 1621 in the British Museum (Pressmark, 1029. e. 5), *Orders and Articles granted by the High and Mightie Lords the States General of the United Provinces concerning the erecting of a West-Indies Compagnie, Anno Dom. MDCXXI.*

[4] N. Wassenaer, *Historisch Verhael alder ghedenckweerdichtste geschiedenissen, die hier en daer . . . voorgevallen syn*, v (1623), pp. 102–3.

delta, and shortly afterwards its first homeward-bound ship, the *Grypende Arend*, returned with a rich cargo.[1]

The first ships which the Company sent to sea went on purely trading voyages, and the problem meanwhile arose of where to strike the first major blow. Usselincx still found adherents for his view that a start should be made by settling colonies in regions where the Spaniards had little or no control, such as Guiana or Chile, but most people had more militant views. Some advocated seizing the Panama peninsula, thus cutting the Spanish-American empire in two and facilitating the interception of the silver bullion from Mexico and Peru. Others recommended the seizure of Havana, or some other place in the island of Cuba, as better suited for the interception of the treasure-fleets in the straits of Florida and Yucatan. Others, even more daring (or more irresponsible), suggested the seizure of some port in the Iberian peninsula which could be fortified and held against all comers, thus anticipating the English occupation of Gibraltar. A proposal was also made, but rejected, that the West India Company should co-operate with the States-General and the East India Company in fitting out the 'Nassau Fleet', which attacked the Spanish settlements on the Pacific coast of South America and then sailed home by way of the East Indies.[2]

The proposal which eventually found most favour with the Heeren XIX and the States-General was, however, a plan for the conquest of Brazil. The arguments for this course of action were many and varied, but can be summarized as follows. Brazil, being colonized by the Portuguese, who were either indifferent or hostile to their Spanish kings, would be easier to conquer than any Spanish colony; particularly since the Portuguese were inferior and inexperienced soldiers in comparison with the Spaniards. Moreover, many of the Portuguese colonists were Marranos who might be expected to welcome the invaders, and there was every likelihood that the Negro slaves would revolt. Once Brazil was conquered the profits from the thriving

[1] Wassenaer, *Historisch Verhael*, vi (1623-4), pp. 38, 58, 61.

[2] This and what follows is mostly derived from the 'Advies tot aanbeveling van de verovering van Brazilië (12 Sept. 1622)', quoted on p. 12, n. 1, above, and J. A. Moerbeeck, *Redenen waeromme de West-Indische Compagnie dient te trachten het landt van Brasilia den Coninck van Spagnien te ontmachtigen, en dat ten eersten*, submitted to the States-General in April 1623, but not printed until after the capture of Bahia in 1624. Cf. also De Laet-Naber, *Iaerlyck Verhael*, i. 4–8.

sugar industry would suffice to pay for the conquest and occupation of the colony, provided that the Portuguese planters
were given no opportunity or excuse to indulge in a 'scorched-
earth' policy, but were conciliated by fair treatment. Alternatively, even if the planters fled and the *engenhos* or sugar-mills
were damaged in the fighting, they could be replaced by Dutch
colonists and time-expired soldiers from the garrisons. One
optimist calculated that the colony in Dutch hands would yield
about eight million florins yearly (of which 4,795,000 florins
from sugar alone), whereas the cost of conquest and defence
would not much exceed two and a half million.

Apart from the work and employment which would accrue
to people in the Netherlands from maintaining Brazil, much
capital would be invested in the West India Company, both
at home and abroad, for the development of the colony.
Furthermore, many people 'of modest means will try their luck
and go and live there for some years, occupying themselves with
planting and grinding sugar, growing tobacco, setting up small
shops or crafts, or doing something else which will enable them
to save something and return here to the fatherland again,
just as the emigrants from Spain and Portugal daily do, so that
the commonweal will be enriched thereby. Moreover, we will
then fully control the trade of Cape Verde, Guinea and Angola,
since we will then enjoy the Brazil slave-trade which will be
most profitable.'[1] Alternatively, the West India Company could
content itself with trading and with taxing all immigrants into
Brazil, leaving these to develop the colony from their own
resources. Possession of Brazil, or even of a part of it, would
give the Dutch an excellent base of operations, whether for
intercepting Spanish treasure-fleets or Portuguese East India-
men—or even for eventually attacking the very sources of
Spain's wealth in the mines of Mexico and Peru. Finally, the
loss of Brazil would greatly enfeeble the Spanish crown, particularly since Portugal could not exist without the resources
derived from her most flourishing colony. Either the Spaniards
would be forced to divert huge sums to support Portugal, or
else that kingdom would revolt in sheer desperation.

Opponents of the projected Brazilian expedition were not
wanting. Willem Usselincx, who disliked the bellicose character
of the new company (although he never explained how Dutch

[1] 'Advies' of 12 Sept. 1622, in *Kron. Hist. Gen. Utrecht*, xxvii. 237.

colonies could be founded in tropical America without fighting Spain), thought that the conquest of Brazil was too ambitious and beyond the Company's means. He considered that the prospect of aid from the local Marranos was illusory, and was convinced that no reliance could be placed either on Portuguese collaboration or on a Negro revolt. Other critics foresaw that Spain would react vigorously; for even if Brazil was an appanage of the Portuguese crown, it was situated in the New World. The king of Spain regarded Portuguese Asia 'as his concubine, who can shift for herself if need be, but he does not count the cost of maintaining America, which he regards as his lawful wife, of whom he is exceedingly jealous and firmly resolved to maintain inviolate'.[1]

These arguments did not weigh as heavily in the eyes of the Heeren XIX as did those of the advocates of an attack on Brazil. The latter could (and did) adduce in their favour the evidence of Dutch prisoners from Bahia who declared that the local Marrano community 'would rather see two Orange flags than one Inquisitor'.[2] Brazil was therefore selected as the scene of the Company's début, and the colonial capital city of Salvador, in the Bay of All Saints, as the first objective. Great efforts were made to keep the destination of the expedition a secret, and the fleet sailed under sealed orders which were not to be opened until the Cape Verde islands were passed. These efforts were largely futile, since in a country where the press was relatively free, speculation and discussion were rife. The government at Brussels received early warning that Brazil was the general objective, although the actual place where the first attack was to be made remained uncertain.

Brazil was indeed an appetizing prize. It is immaterial to us whether that country was first discovered by the Spaniard Pinzón or by the Portuguese Cabral in 1500; but it was the Portuguese who tried to colonize the coastal region between the Amazon and Rio de Janeiro during the sixteenth century. The Portuguese based their claim to the land of the True Cross, as it was originally called, on the treaty of Tordesillas (1494), by which, in effect, the two Iberian crowns divided the new-found

[1] *Tweede Nootwendiger Discours ofte Vertooch aan alle Lantlievende, van de Participanten der Oost-Indische Compagnie, tegens Bewinthebbers* (1622), p. 22.

[2] Dierick Ruiters' narrative of his captivity in Brazil, in S. P. L'Honoré Naber's 1914 edition of his *Toortse der Zeevaert* (1623), p. 35.

world between them, with Papal sanction. The exact where-
abouts of the line of demarcation between their respective
spheres of influence, which theoretically ran along a meridian
370 leagues west of the Cape Verde islands, was disputed on
American soil. But wherever the Tordesillas line ran, the
Portuguese pushed their undemarcated frontier steadily west-
wards during the next two centuries. When Philip II of Spain
enforced his claim to the Portuguese crown in 1580, the two
Iberian colonial empires still remained separate entities, both
in theory and in fact.[1]

Portuguese attempts to colonize the coastal region of Brazil
were originally handicapped by the mother-country's sparse
population (about one million souls), by the superior attraction
exerted by the fabled riches of the East (the *fumos da India*), and
by determined French efforts to secure a footing in the Bay of
Rio de Janeiro and elsewhere. The development of the American colony was soon (1533) entrusted to *donatários*, or lords-
proprietors, who were granted by the crown large segments of
land called *capitanias* or captaincies, in return for colonizing
and developing these regions. There were originally fifteen of
these hereditary captaincies, each of which ran for about fifty
leagues along the coast with an indefinite extension into the
unexplored interior. Most of the *donatários* had insufficient resources to settle or develop their captaincies effectively, and in
course of time some were abandoned, others reverted to the
crown, and only a few took firm root.

The establishment of a government-general at Salvador
(Bahia) in 1549 and the arrival of a band of Jesuit missionaries
marked a new and decisive stage. The French were expelled
from Rio de Janeiro after some hard fighting, and a further
impetus to the development of the colony was given by the
intensive cultivation of the sugar-cane, which had been introduced from São Thomé and Madeira about 1520. Brazil-wood
(which yielded a profitable dye and from which the country
took its name), cotton, and tobacco were other products which
deserve mention, and cattle-raising was of importance in some
districts. At the period with which we are dealing, however, it

[1] For surveys of the development of Brazil and the situation of the colony under
Spanish rule cf. B. W. Diffie, *Latin-American Civilization. Colonial Period*, pp. 633–73,
and C. R. Boxer, *Salvador de Sá and the struggle for Brazil and Angola, 1602–1682*
(London, 1952), pp. 1–39, both of which are based upon the most authoritative
Portuguese and Brazilian works.

can be said that sugar was the colony's chief product, and the steadily increasing demand for this article in Europe was reflected in the growing development and prosperity of Brazil. Over 350 *engenhos*, or sugar plantations equipped with mills for grinding the cane, were functioning in the colony in 1623.

In that year the Portuguese crown controlled the coastal region from the Amazon delta to the Bay of Paranaguá after the following fashion. The three northernmost captaincies between the island of Marajó and Cape São Roque (Pará, Maranhão, and Ceará) had just been detached from the rest of Brazil and formed into a separate colony with headquarters at São Luis do Maranhão, whence the French had been expelled in 1615. This vast region, or the 'East–West coast' as it was often called, was still very sparsely settled and of small economic importance. From Cape São Roque to Paranaguá the seaboard was divided into another twelve captaincies, whose names and positions will be found on the map at the end. The most important centres of population were those grouped around the city of Olinda in the north-east captaincy of Pernambuco; around the colonial capital of Salvador on the Bay of All Saints in the centre; and around Rio de Janeiro and on the highland plateau of São Paulo de Piratininga in the extreme south. Of these districts, Pernambuco was the most flourishing, with Bahia a good second and Rio de Janeiro a poor third; the intervening regions being all sparsely settled and mostly undeveloped. It may be estimated with some degree of probability that in 1623 there were about sixty or seventy thousand settlers of European origin (including those of mixed European blood) in Brazil and the Maranhão. Nearly half of these were concentrated in the captaincy of Pernambuco which was the richest sugar-producing region.

By this time the aboriginal Amerindian inhabitants had been either killed, enslaved, or driven away from the immediate vicinity of the principal settlements, except in places where they had been grouped together in villages (*aldeias*) under the protection and administration of the Jesuit missionaries. From the colonists' viewpoint, the Amerindians fell into two main racial divisions. The first was formed by the (for the most part) coast-dwelling Tupís, of the Tupí-Guaraní linguistic family, speaking the *lingua geral* or 'common tongue', whose various dialects were closely related, 'like Portuguese and Spanish'.

The second group was formed by the more fiercely cannibalistic Tapuyas of the interior or *sertão*, who were the sworn foes of the Tupís, and who spoke the *linguas travadas* or 'twisted tongues'. Both of these groups consisted of wandering naked savage tribes who were still in the Stone Age, and who carried on fierce inter-tribal wars in which their prisoners were usually ceremonially fattened and eaten. Those of the Tupís whom the colonists had enslaved, or the Jesuits had 'reduced' in their villages, were known as *Indios mansos* or 'tame Indians'. The Tapuyas had, with insignificant exceptions, resisted all attempts to enslave or domesticate them. Labour for the sugar plantations was mostly supplied by Negro slaves from Angola, which furnished an annual quota of about 8,000 slaves for Brazil, and nearly as many for Spanish America. The bulk of the Negro slave-trade and the Brazilian sugar-trade was in the hands of Portuguese contractors and merchants of Jewish origin.

Bahia was the seat of a governor-general, a bishop, and a colonial high court, other captaincies being ruled by governors who were sometimes appointed by *donatários* but usually by the crown. In the remoter settlements, such as São Paulo, the local *Senado da Camara* or municipal council had the principal say in local administration, and even in places like Bahia, Olinda, and Rio these councils were often very influential. The colony was thus to a large extent self-governing. The broad lines of policy might be laid down at Lisbon or at Madrid; but the methods of enforcement were inevitably left to the colonial governors acting in conjunction (or in conflict) with the municipal councils.

The Jesuits were by far the most influential as well as the most respected of the religious orders. The education of the colonists was virtually in their hands, but they were unpopular in some places owing to their opposition to the enslavement of the Amerindians. The same reproach could not be levelled by the colonists against the other religious orders, whether Franciscans, Benedictines, or Carmelites, who, with the partial exception of the first-named, concerned themselves but little with either evangelizing the heathen or educating the Christians. The Holy Office of the Inquisition had much less influence in Brazil than it had in either the mother-country or the Asian colonies. Whereas this dreaded—if in some respects popular—

institution had branches at Lisbon and Goa, it contented itself with the periodic dispatch of visiting commissioners to Brazil. Such, in briefest outline, was the state of Portugal's most flourishing colony on the eve of the Dutch assault.

The Dutch themselves were no strangers to Brazil. Their commercial connexions with the colony date back to the first half of the sixteenth century; but it was during the truce of 1609–21 that their trade with Brazil expanded greatly, despite the Spanish crown's explicit and reiterated prohibitions of foreign trade with the colony. A representation of Dutch merchants concerned in this business, which was submitted to the States-General in 1622, explains how this enviable position had been achieved. Dutch trade with Brazil had always been driven through the intermediary of 'many good and honest Portuguese, mostly living at Vianna and Oporto', who, after the first formal prohibition of Dutch participation in this trade in 1594, had spontaneously offered to continue it under cover of their names and flag. This they did with exemplary loyalty and fidelity, 'just as if they had been our own fathers and living here in our midst'. The magistrate of Vianna do Castello, in particular, had always 'tipped-off' the local Dutch Factors and their agents as to 'how they could guard themselves against damage from the Spaniards'. Three days before the expiry of the truce in April 1621 this worthy, by public proclamation, enforced payment of all outstanding debts due to Dutch merchants or their local agents, 'through which means many Netherlanders have been paid in full for debts which they had not been able to recover for many years in due course of law'.[1] Many, if not most, of these 'good and honest Portuguese' were of 'New-Christian' or Marrano origin.

Thanks to this Portuguese official complicity in breaking the laws of the Spanish king, the Dutch merchants estimated that they had secured between one-half and two-thirds of the carrying-trade between Brazil and Europe. By the end of the truce, fifteen ships were being built yearly in the Netherlands exclu-

---

[1] 'Deductie vervaetende den oorspronck ende progres van de vaert ende handel op Brasil uijt dese landen over het coninkrijck Portugael', d. 1622, and printed in J. W. Ijzerman's edition of the *Journael van de reis naar Zuid-Amerika door Hendrik Ottsen* (The Hague, 1918), pp. 98–106. For confirmation from the Iberian side cf. J. J. Andrade e Silva [ed.], *Collecção chronologica da legislação portugueza 1620–1627* (Lisbon, 1855), pp. 115, 150–1; J. Cuvelier and J. Lefèvre, *Correspondance de la Cour d'Espagne*, ii. 123, 155.

sively for use in this trade, while some 50,000 chests of sugar, besides Brazil-wood, cotton, hides, &c., were being imported by way of Portugal. Most of this Brazilian produce was shipped via Oporto and Vianna, where the duties on imports and re-exports were substantially lower than at Lisbon—and were often reduced still further by judicious bribery. Whereas in 1595 there were only three or four sugar-refineries in the Nor-thern Netherlands, there were twenty-nine in 1622, of which twenty-five were in Amsterdam. Much of the refined sugar was re-exported to France, England, and the Baltic States, at a further profit to the Dutch, while Brazil supplied a valuable export-market for Dutch linen and textiles. Needless to say, those interested in this thriving contraband trade viewed with trepidation the idea of an attack on Portuguese-American colonies or shipping, which would expose their own vessels and agents at Vianna and Oporto to reprisals. The memorial also shows that many Dutch skippers and sailors were perfectly familiar with Brazilian harbours. It affords additional evidence that the expeditions of 1624 and 1630 had no need of renegade Jews to guide them, although co-operation from the local New-Christians might well be expected.

The expedition for the conquest of Bahia, totalling twenty-six sail mounting 450 guns and carrying 3,300 men, left Dutch ports in two detachments. These sailed in December 1623 and in January 1624 respectively, and joined forces off the Cape Verde islands in the following March. The admiral was Jacob Willekens, originally a fishmonger from Amsterdam, who flew his flag in the *Zeelandia* (36). Command of the troops was en-trusted to Jan Van Dorth, an experienced soldier, but called by an unfriendly contemporary 'a man of good courage, but unversed in raiding-expeditions. I can hardly believe that he will accomplish anything durable, and I fear that jealousy is likely to arise between him and the admiral.'[1] The vice-admiral was Piet Heyn, a 'Tarpaulin' commander from Delfshaven near Rotterdam. He had served the East India Company in his youth (1608–12) and was destined to prove himself one of the greatest seamen of all time by his exploits in the West India Company's service in the next five years.

After vainly waiting for some weeks at St. Vincent in the Cape Verdes for the ship *Hollandia* (28), which was carrying

[1] Van der Capellen, *Gedenkschriften*, i. 221–2.

Colonel Van Dorth and which had become separated from her consorts, Willekens resumed his voyage with the remainder of the fleet, arriving off Bahia on 8 May. Van Dorth had actually appeared off the mouth of the bay nearly a month before, and was cruising in the offing (though not in sight) when his consorts arrived.

The governor-general at Bahia, Diogo de Mendonça Furtado, had received warning from Madrid that Brazil was the enemy's destination, and the premature appearance of the *Hollandia* confirmed his suspicion that Bahia was the first objective. On the other hand, the bishop, Dom Marcos Texeira, and the planters of the adjacent sugar-growing district (known as the *reconcavo*,) thought that the governor was being unduly alarmist. The appearance of the rest of the Dutch fleet consequently came as an unpleasant shock to them and at once lowered their morale. On the morning of 9 May, while the fleet bombarded the shipping and forts in the harbour, the Dutch troops were landed unopposed a few miles from the town. Their advance through bush and scrub could easily have been checked by a few determined men, but not even a token resistance was offered. 'The panic was such and so general', wrote a Jesuit eyewitness, 'that neither Whites nor Indians were of any use, everyone seeking a safe place, without attempting to fight.' By nightfall the Dutch soldiers had reached the Benedictine convent on the outskirts of the city, where they bivouacked for the night in drunken disorder. Meanwhile, the naval bombardment had at first given no appreciable results, but at sunset Piet Heyn manned his ships' boats and cut out or fired all the shipping in the harbour, crowning this achievement by storming the waterfront battery. The demoralization of the defenders now became general, and as soon as night fell they began to stream out of the city, despite all the efforts of the governor to stop them. When the Dutch entered the place between nine and ten o'clock on the morning of 10 May, they found it empty save for a few New-Christians, some Negro slaves, and the governor with about fifteen forlorn companions in government-house. Diogo de Mendonça Furtado at first refused to surrender, but was persuaded to do so when Piet Heyn appeared and promised the little party good quarter. The runaway defenders of Bahia later endeavoured to palliate their conduct by blaming the treachery of the New-Christians and the cowardice of the governor for the loss of the city. The former allegation was echoed in Lope de Vega's *El Brasil Restituído*, one of his most indifferent plays, but receives no support from the accounts of trustworthy Jesuit eyewitnesses nor from the voluminous Dutch narratives.[1]

The accusation against the governor was also quite untrue, as Piet Heyn himself testified in the most convincing manner to the Jesuit Provincial, Padre Domingos Coelho. This latter worthy had plenty of opportunity of finding out exactly what had happened on the disastrous 9/10 May 1624, and he wrote a few months later: '. . . the Dutch [vice-]admiral himself told me several times, when talking about this business, that the governor had behaved himself bravely and done his duty very well, and that he would testify as much if necessary. He added that if anyone affirmed the contrary, it would be to conceal the fear in which that person fled from and abandoned the city. And all the more credit is due to this observation of his, since he was very much annoyed with the governor on another occasion when some hard words passed between them, which the admiral himself told me he had only tolerated from the governor because the latter was his prisoner.'[2]

The news of the fall of Bahia caused great rejoicing in the United Provinces, and great dismay in the Iberian peninsula. Both Madrid and Lisbon for once reacted in cordial co-operation and unison. The Spaniards were seriously alarmed because they suspected that the ultimate objective of the Dutch 'was not so much the sugar of Brazil as the silver of Peru'. The Portuguese were even more worried, because they realized that if the Dutch established themselves firmly at Bahia, the loss of the rest of Brazil would inevitably follow.[3] The Dutch, on their side, knew that the enemy would make an effort to recapture the place, and that a strong fleet must be fitted out forthwith to succour and reinforce the new conquest. The news reached Lisbon a month before it did Holland; but this delay

[1] The principal sources for the Bahia campaign of 1624-5 are listed on pp. 49 and 56 of my *Salvador de Sá*, which contains (pp. 47–63) a more detailed description than that given here.

[2] Letter of the Padre Provincial Domingos Coelho, S.J., written from his prison in Holland, 24 Oct. 1624, and printed in S. Leite, S.J., *História da Companhia de Jesus no Brasil*, v. 34–48.

[3] Van der Capellen, *Gedenkschriften*, i. 312; Mathias de Albuquerque's intercepted letter printed in Wassenaer, *Historisch Verhael*, viii (1624), pp. 61–63.

would not have been fatal to the Dutch, save for the unseasonable weather during the winter of 1624–5, which kept their succour-fleet windbound in home ports, not merely for weeks but for months on end.[1]

The details of the Iberian mobilization were fully reported in the United Provinces, and the news of the Dutch preparations was similarly relayed to Madrid by the government of the Archduchess Isabella at Brussels. Spies on both sides found plenty to report, and it is amusing to observe that the intelligence services of those days functioned in much the same way as they do now. The authorities at Madrid were much impressed by the voluminous reports supplied from the United Provinces by a Portuguese Jew named Manuel Soeiro, and they frequently urged the archduchess to pay this man the large sums he demanded. This lady retorted tartly that Soeiro's reports were either rubbish, or else were common property, being derived from the news printed in the Dutch *corantos* which circulated freely throughout northern Europe. Despite her repeated protestations that money spent on Soeiro was money down the drain, and that if Madrid wanted to pay the man anything the money must be sent direct from Spain, the crown sent her a categorical order to pay him 1,000 gold ducats in November 1624. She reluctantly did so, but must have smiled wryly when Soeiro's stock slumped badly at Madrid a year later, as he gave no warning of the treacherous English onslaught against Cádiz.[2]

Writing to Isabella shortly after receiving the news of the loss of Bahia, King Philip IV urged her to keep the Dutch busy on the Flanders frontier, 'since the chief reason why we decided to renew the war with the Hollanders on the expiration of the truce, was that our army should keep them occupied on land, and so prevent them from maintaining such forces at sea as would enable them to attempt such great enterprises as this'. The archduchess replied by giving news of Spinola's commencement of the siege of Breda, which, as all admirers of Velasquez will recall, was brought to a successful conclusion in 1625. In reporting (more reliably than did Soeiro) the Dutch efforts to

---

[1] Van der Capellen, *Gedenkschriften*, i. 330, 335, 338.

[2] J. Cuvelier and J. Lefèvre, *Correspondance de la Cour d'Espagne*, ii. 191, 194, 198, 200, 226, 234, 242–3. Manuel Soeiro was born at Antwerp in 1597, son of Francisco Lopes Soeiro, a native of Loulé in the Algarve.

equip a fleet for the relief of Bahia, she added that the only thing for King Philip to do was to get his own fleet there first.[1]

This the Spanish monarch, or rather his naval commander-in-chief, Don Fadrique de Toledo y Osorio, was able to do. By dint of unprecedented efforts, and thanks to the universal enthusiasm which 'the expedition of the vassals', as it was called in Portugal, aroused among all classes and races in the Peninsula, the combined Hispano-Portuguese armada appeared off Bahia on Easter Eve 1625. This force comprised fifty-two ships, carrying 12,566 men and 1,185 guns, being the largest and strongest fleet which had yet crossed the Line. Don Fadrique de Toledo found his task much easier than he had expected. There was no sign of the succour-fleet from Holland, and the garrison was under the command of a drunken and incompetent officer named Willem Schouten, who had just succeeded his hardly more competent brother Albert, after the latter had drunk himself to death. Colonel Van Dorth, despite Alexander van der Capellen's captious criticism, was an able and popular commander, and he had taken great pains to conciliate the local Portuguese. But he had been killed in an ambush barely a month after his arrival, and demoralization soon set in under the rule of the Schouten brothers, although not to such an extent as to interfere with the strengthening and fortification of the city. The Portuguese had recovered from their panic in the previous May, and, under the leadership first of their bishop and subsequently (after his death) of a Brazilian-born *fidalgo* named Dom Francisco de Moura, they had effectively prevented the Dutch garrison from venturing beyond the range of their cannon. Moreover, the Dutch had gravely weakened their own position by sending Willekens back to Holland with eleven sail on 28 July 1624, and by sending Piet Heyn to Angola with seven sail on 5 August following. Their remaining eleven ships were in no condition to oppose the combined armada when it sailed majestically into the Bay of All Saints on Easter Day 1625.

The Dutch error in dissipating their naval strength had sprung from their otherwise correct appreciation that to hold Brazil they must control the principal slave-market in West Africa. The Heeren XIX regarded Usselincx's advocacy of employing white agricultural labourers in the tropics with understandable

[1] J. Cuvelier and J. Lefèvre, *Correspondance de la Cour d'Espagne*, ii. 176, 182–3.

scepticism. They realized that without Negro slaves to do the back-breaking field-work of the sugar plantations, Brazil, whether under Portuguese or under Dutch rule, could never prosper. On the other hand, the methods they adopted to achieve this end were curiously fumbling and inadequate.

Shortly before the departure of Willekens's fleet in December 1623, a squadron of three ships under the command of Philips van Zuylen had been sent to the coast of Angola, but this force was too small to achieve anything of importance. When Piet Heyn arrived off Luanda with his seven sail, he found Van Zuylen gone and the Portuguese on their guard, so he was likewise unable to do more than cruise along the coast and plunder a few vessels. He then recrossed the Atlantic and attacked the small settlement of Victoria in Espirito Santo in March 1625. Thanks to the fortuitous arrival of Salvador Correia de Sá e Benavides, the son of the governor of Rio de Janeiro, who was on his way north with reinforcements for the besiegers of Bahia, Piet Heyn was repulsed with the loss of over a hundred men after a week's confused river-fighting. He then returned to Bahia (18 April), but finding the combined armada in the bay, was forced to continue his voyage northwards, returning to Holland at the end of July.[1]

When Piet Heyn reached home with the news that Bahia was besieged by an enemy fleet, the directors were worried but not unduly alarmed. Despite the untoward wind and weather conditions during the winter of 1624-5, they had not done their work by halves, and by this time they had three new fleets at sea. Two of these, under Boudewijn Hendricks, burgomaster of Edam, and Andries Veron, were destined for the relief of Bahia. The third, consisting only of a few ships when finally it started under Jan Dirkszoon Lam, was destined for the capture of São Jorge da Mina, better known as Elmina, the oldest European stronghold in West Africa and the Portuguese headquarters on the Guinea coast. The Heeren XIX calculated that even if the Iberian armada had reached Bahia first, there was every reason to suppose that the Dutch garrison could hold out until the arrival of the relieving fleet, which finally sailed down the English Channel in the middle of March 1625.[2]

[1] De Laet-Naber, *Iaerlyck Verhael*, i. 30-31, 50-74, and C. R. Boxer, *Salvador de Sá*, pp. 57-60, for further details.

[2] Van der Capellen, *Gedenkschriften*, i. 366; De Laet-Naber, *Iaerlyck Verhael*, i. 32-35, 79, 85-86.

As things turned out, the demoralized and mutinous Dutch garrison capitulated on 30 April, to the great relief of the besiegers. Their commanders realized when they entered the strongly fortified town on 1 May that they could hardly have taken it by storm except at heavy cost. Hendricks and Veron arrived on 26 May with thirty-four sail, but although the rival fleets went through the motions of offering battle to each other, neither side was really anxious to come to grips. After some inconclusive skirmishing, the Dutch admirals left the Bay of All Saints, and coasted northwards to the Bay of Treason (Bahia da Traição) in Paraíba. For a time they toyed with the idea of founding a fort there, as they found the local savages very friendly, but finally decided that they were not strong enough to do so. On 4 August Veron sailed with eleven sail to join Lam in his attack on Elmina, and Hendricks left some time later with eighteen sail to attempt the capture of San Juan de Puerto Rico. Being repulsed in his attack on this place, Hendricks then cruised in the Caribbean in the hope of intercepting a Spanish treasure-fleet between Yucatan and Florida, but was again disappointed. He died off the coast of Cuba in July 1626, and his fleet then returned to Holland without having accomplished anything save the capture of some merchant ships.[1]

Lam and Veron were even more unfortunate in their expedition to the Guinea coast. They joined forces off Sierra Leone on 26 August, and two months later anchored off Elmina with thirteen sail. A force of 1,200 men was landed to attack the castle, which had only a skeleton garrison. The Portuguese governor, Dom Francisco Soutomaior, had posted a number of friendly Negroes in ambush in the neighbouring woods, promising them a substantial reward for each Dutch head which they would bring in. Shortly before sundown these Negroes rushed out upon the Dutch soldiery, most of whom were lying about on the beach resting from the heat, while their senior officers were reconnoitring the castle from a neighbouring hillock. Admiral Veron and a few others died fighting gallantly, but the great majority of the men were seized with an unreasoning panic. They made no attempt at resistance, but allowed the Negroes to cut them down like sheep. The whole force would have been annihilated, but for the fact that the Negroes coveted

[1] De Laet-Naber, *Iaerlyck Verhael*, i. 87–104.

the white men's clothes and did not want them stained with blood. They therefore picked out the best-dressed men as they shambled along, stopped them, made them strip, and then beheaded them. This procedure took so much time that many of the men were able to escape, although 442 headless European corpses were left lying on the sand when night fell.[1]

This disastrous and inglorious end to the Elmina expedition did not, however, affect the steadily increasing prosperity of the Dutch trade with the Gold Coast. Wassenaer frequently records the arrival of ships richly laden with gold and ivory from Guinea; and De Laet estimated that, between 1623 and 1636, no less than 40,461 marks of gold valued at 11,733,890 florins, and 1,137,430 pounds of ivory worth 1,178,688 florins, were imported from the same region.[2] These figures take no account of contraband imports, but are sufficient to show the value and extent of what was rightly known as 'the golden trade'.

The disasters suffered by the Dutch at Bahia, Puerto Rico, and Elmina in 1625 formed conjointly a 'nasty knock' for the West India Company, as Alexander van der Capellen noted in March 1626; but he consoled himself with the reflection that if the Dutch investors had lost their money, the king of Spain had likewise suffered severely.[3] Moreover, though thwarted in its more ambitious plans of conquest and colonization by the unexpected vigour of the Iberian reaction, the Company still had some fight left in it. At the end of May 1626 Piet Heyn was at sea again, with a fleet of fourteen sail, carrying 1,675 men and 312 guns, destined to reinforce Hendricks in the Caribbean and to help him capture a silver-fleet.

When Piet Heyn reached his cruising-station in the straits of Yucatan, he found that Hendricks was dead and his fleet had gone home; and although he subsequently met a strongly escorted and well-armed silver-fleet of forty sail in the straits of Florida on 9 September, he did not feel strong enough to attack it. His instructions envisaged the fact that he might miss Hendricks, and ordered him in such an eventuality to proceed to the coast of Brazil and cruise there until further orders. The prevailing winds made a double crossing of the Atlantic

---

[1] Wassenaer, *Historisch Verhael*, xii (1626–7), pp. 54–56; De Laet-Naber, *Iaerlyck Verhael*, i. 104–9.

[2] De Laet-Naber, *Iaerlyck Verhael*, iv. 295–6; J. K. De Jonge, *Oorsprong*, pp. 16–17.   [3] *Gedenkschriften*, i. 394.

necessary to accomplish this, and it was not until after a tedious voyage via the Azores and Sierra Leone that he appeared off Bahia on the night of 2/3 March 1627.

Despite the fierce fire of the shore batteries on the following morning, Piet Heyn sailed into the harbour and captured or fired twenty-six sail of armed merchantmen, many of which were Baltic traders. The booty amounted to 2,565 chests of sugar, apart from substantial quantities of specie, tobacco, hides, cotton, and Brazil-wood. This plunder was sent home in some of the captured ships, and the West India Company was thus enabled, as De Laet observed, to 'get their second wind and stand upright'. After subsequently cruising along the coast between Bahia and Rio de Janeiro, the Dutch admiral returned to the Bay of All Saints on 10 June. Despite the defensive precautions taken in the interval by the governor-general, Diogo Luis de Oliveira, who had shown himself 'a monster of industry', Piet Heyn made another successful attack on the shipping which had entered the harbour meanwhile. When he finally returned to Holland in October 1627, laden with cargoes of plundered sugar and tobacco, the Heeren XIX presented him with a gold medal and chain in recognition of his outstanding conduct and courage.[1]

The year 1627 had thus gone far to atone for the disasters and disappointments of 1625 and 1626. Apart from the vast profits from the 'golden trade' of Guinea, and the thirty-eight prizes taken by Piet Heyn in Brazilian waters, another seventeen Iberian ships had been taken by the cruisers of the West India Company in the Atlantic. At the end of May 1628 the Heeren XIX were thus enabled to send to sea a fleet of thirty-one sail, carrying 4,000 men and 689 guns, under the command of Piet Heyn (now promoted to 'General'), for yet another attempt on one of the silver-fleets in the Caribbean.

For the first and last time this operation, so often attempted before and since by Dutch, English, and French sailors and freebooters, was crowned with complete success. By a combination of good luck, good seamanship, and good leadership, Piet

[1] For Piet Heyn's exploits in 1626–7, cf. De Laet-Naber, *Iaerlyck Verhael*, ii. 1–16, and the original documents published by S. P. L'Honoré Naber in *Piet Heyn en de Zilvervloot* (Utrecht, 1928), pp. 1–51; Piet Heyn's report of 11 Aug. 1627, in *Bijdragen en Mededeelingen van het Historisch Genootschap Utrecht*, li; Céspedes Xeria's letters of 13 July 1627 and 23 Mar. 1629, in *Anais do Museo Paulista*, i. 167–9; ii. 18–19; Wassenaer, *Historisch Verhael*, xiv. 53–56.

Heyn cornered the silver-fleet from Mexico in the Cuban harbour of Matanzas on the night of 7/8 September 1628, and
captured it intact without firing more than a shot or two. This
fleet was worthy of its legendary name and fame. One hundred
and seventy-seven thousand pounds of silver worth 8 million
guilders formed the principal part of the booty which flowed
into the West India Company's coffers when Piet Heyn dropped
anchor off Hellevoetsluys on 10 January 1629, after a long
and stormy homeward voyage. Nor could the rest of the booty
be classified as chicken-feed. Only 66 pounds of gold are recorded in the official inventory; but a thousand pearls, nearly
2 million hides, and substantial quantities of silk, musk, amber,
bezoar 'and many other rarities' figure in the same list.[1] No
wonder the United Provinces went wild with joy and that Piet
Heyn became the most popular man in the country.

Piet Heyn's great exploit was the most spectacular as well as
the most profitable success of the West India Company in 1628,
but it was not the only one. In August of that year, Alexander
van der Capellen noted that other ships fitted out by the Company to cruise in the South Atlantic had taken so many prizes
that within a few weeks 2,178 chests of sugar, together with
large quantities of hides, tobacco, and Brazil-wood, were brought
into Dutch ports.[2] Among other prizes was a richly laden
Portuguese pinnace, *Nossa Senhora da Guia*, homeward bound
from the East Indies, which Dirck Symonsz van Uytgeest captured off Pernambuco after a hard fight in October 1628.[3]

Their ships having come home so richly laden, the Heeren
XIX evidently felt that they had money to burn. The sale of
the booty from the silver-fleet alone yielded a total of about
12 million guilders, out of which, after the Company had paid
all its outstanding debts and the cost of the expedition, some
7 millions were left. The shareholders received a 75 per cent.
dividend (in two instalments of 50 per cent. and 25 per cent.
respectively) and the prince of Orange received the princely

[1] The full itemized list of the booty taken in the silver-fleet is printed in Naber,
Piet Heyn en de Zilvervloot, pp. 128–58.

[2] *Gedenkschriften*, i. 478, 505.

[3] G. Edmundson (*English Historical Review*, xiv. 676) absurdly magnifies this
prize into 'a Portuguese fleet returning from Goa, richly laden with the products
of the East'. If this had been so, the capture would have been comparable to that
of the silver-fleet; but from the details given by De Laet (*Iaerlyck Verhael*, ii. 52–53),
and other contemporary writers, it is obvious that only this East India pinnace
and five small Brazil-traders were involved.

sum of 700,000 florins for the 10 per cent. due to him as the captain-and-admiral-general's tenth on prize money. The directors contented themselves with a modest gratuity of 1 per cent. (7,000 florins), and gave the same amount to Piet Heyn. The other officers and men received seventeen months' extra wages. Piet Heyn was evidently not very satisfied with the way that he and his men were treated, since he put forward some rather extravagant demands as a condition for renewing his contract with the Company. When these were rejected by the Heeren XIX, he left their service for that of the States-General, being appointed the real (though not the titular) commander-in-chief of the Dutch navy by the stadtholder. He at once inaugurated a number of reforms for increasing the efficiency and discipline of that service; but his career was cut short by his death in action against three Ostend privateers on 18 June 1629.

After all the tumult and the shouting about the distribution of the booty from the silver-fleet was over, the Heeren XIX had to decide what do do with the balance of the money (about half a million guilders). One thing they did was to contribute liberally with men, money, and material for the Veluwe campaign connected with the siege of Den Bosch. It was largely by virtue of their contribution that this siege was brought to a successful conclusion on 14 September.[1] They had already decided, after due deliberation, to renew their attempt on Brazil. Bahia had been lost, but this was chiefly due to the avoidable misconduct of the Schouten brothers and to the unavoidable winter weather of 1624–5. Even if the colonial capital was now too strongly fortified to be taken so easily as it was in 1624, there were other places in Brazil which were more exposed and offered equally tempting possibilities. The Heeren XIX resolved that this time their first objective would be the north-eastern captaincy of Pernambuco, which was then the richest sugar-producing region in the world and the most prosperous part of the Portuguese colonial empire.

[1] Van der Capellen, *Gedenkschriften*, i. 524–7, 530, 540.

II

THE STRUGGLE FOR PERNAMBUCO
1630–6

THE Dutch decision to attack Pernambuco was the easier to make since they were singularly well informed about the conditions prevailing in that captaincy. From letters written by the governor, Mathias de Albuquerque, which they intercepted during the Bahia campaign, they knew that the ramshackle fortifications of Olinda and Recife were in a state of disrepair.[1] Albuquerque had also stated that the local militia only amounted to about 400 untrained men, who were mostly New-Christians and could not be relied upon. The Dutch also knew that the three north-eastern captaincies contained 137 sugar-mills, which produced a total of about 700,000 *arrobas* of sugar in an averagely good year. This sugar was transported in chests containing twenty *arrobas* each, the average annual export being calculated at about 35,000 or 40,000 chests. The tithes (*dizimos*) levied on the sugar-export trade from Pernambuco were valued at between 70,000 and 80,000 *cruzados* by the Portuguese, and at 1,050,000 florins by the Dutch. The large mills, resembling small villages in appearance, owing to their numerous out-houses and workshops, employed about fifteen to twenty Portuguese and a hundred Negroes. The medium-sized mills were worked by some ten Portuguese and fifty Negroes; and the small mills (or *engenhocas* as they were sometimes called) by five or six Portuguese and twenty Negroes. Each of the larger mills produced about seven or eight thousand *arrobas* annually; the medium-sized five or six thousand, and the smaller about three thousand.[2]

[1] Printed in Dutch translation in Wassenaer, *Historisch Verhael*, viii (1624), pp. 61–63.

[2] Mathias de Albuquerque's reports to Dom Antonio de Ataide, Conde de Castro-Daire, 1627–8, in Helio Vianna, *Estudos de História Colonial* (São Paulo, 1948), pp. 240–51, from the originals in the Biblioteca Nacional, Rio de Janeiro, Secção de MSS., Codex Pernambucano, I-I-2-44; *Lyste van 'tghene de Brasil jaerlijcks can opbrengen* (n.d. n.p., but the statistics given there relate to the year 1623), an exceedingly rare Dutch pamphlet first described and reproduced by J. H. Rodrigues (*Bibliografia*, no. 720, p. 345); De Laet, as quoted by R. C. Simonsen,

All these and many other details of the sugar trade and industry in north-east Brazil were known to the Dutch, not only from their earlier contacts at Vianna, Oporto, and Lisbon, but from the contents of the numerous prizes which they had taken since the renewal of the war in 1621. Nicholas van Wassenaer noted at the end of 1626 that Vianna had only three Brazil-traders left out of twenty-nine which habitually sailed from that port.[1] A year later, Mathias de Albuquerque complained that the Dutch had taken eighty Brazil-traders in the two years 1625–6, sixty of these being lost on the homeward voyage and twenty on the outward.[2] Nor was it only the Dutch who took toll of the almost defenceless Brazil shipping. The Barbary rovers captured 'fourteen or more' sugar-ships in 1623–4;[3] and when Mathias de Albuquerque returned to Portugal in 1627, his safe arrival in a swift-sailing caravel at Caminha was recorded as an exceptional piece of good fortune.[4]

These catastrophic shipping losses naturally alarmed the authorities at Lisbon and Madrid, who made sporadic efforts to cope with the steadily deteriorating situation. Suggestions that the sugar ships should sail in well-armed convoys, after the style of the Spanish *flotas* in the Caribbean, had been made as early as 1612,[5] but nothing was done during the truce years. When losses soared upwards with the renewal of the war, and particularly after Piet Heyn's exploits at Bahia, some attempts were made to provide the Brazil-traders with means of defence. But these attempts were mostly still-born, and scarcely passed beyond the stage of paper legislation.[6] This was largely because the merchants and skippers who freighted or owned the unarmed caravels (which were the chief vessels engaged in the trade) could not afford to build bigger and better-gunned merchant-men without substantial government subsidies—and these were not forthcoming. Much of the sugar produced in Brazil in general, and in Pernambuco in particular, thus fell into the

História Económica do Brasil, 1500–1820 (São Paulo, 1944), p. 172; but I cannot find the original quotation in De Laet.

[1] Wassenaer, *Historisch Verhael*, xii (1627), p. 77.

[2] Report of 29 Dec. 1627, in H. Vianna, *Estudos de História Colonial*, p. 243.

[3] Wassenaer, *Historisch Verhael*, vi (1623–4), p. 68.

[4] Fr. Vicente do Salvador, *História do Brasil* (ed. 1931), p. 616.

[5] 'Rezão do Estado do Brasil', ed. E. Sluiter, *Hispanic American Historical Review*, xxix (1949), p. 525. Cf. also Ch. VI, pp. 206–7, below.

[6] Andrade e Silva, *Collecção Chronologica, 1627–1633*, pp. 117, 135; Varnhagen, *História Geral* (ed. 1948), ii. 50, 94–95.

power of the West India Company's cruisers. Small wonder that the sugar-planters of Brazil ruefully complained that they were virtually acting as unpaid cultivators for the Dutch.

Strangely enough, these apparently crippling losses did not ruin the prosperity of Pernambuco. On the contrary, this captaincy was, by all accounts, still in a very flourishing condition in 1630. If we compare the eyewitness description of this region by the Jesuit Father Fernão Cardim in 1584 with that of the resident Friar Manuel Calado on the eve of the Dutch invasion, we find a striking similarity between the two. Wrote Cardim of the *moradores* of Pernambuco in his day:[1]

'The local people are honourable; there are very rich men with forty, fifty, and eighty thousand cruzados of their own. Some are much indebted owing to the heavy losses they have sustained in their Guinea slaves, many of whom die, and through their own extravagance and excessive personal expenses. They themselves, their wives and children, dress in all kinds of velvets, damasks and other silks, and in this they are wantonly extravagant. The women are perfect ladies, and not very pious, nor do they often go to mass, sermons, confessions etc. The men are so gallant that they buy jennets for two or three hundred *cruzados*, and some of them have three or four valuable horses. They are very fond of *festas*. When an honourable gentlewoman married a Viannese (who are the chief people here), some of the relatives and friends wore crimson velvet, others green, and others damask and various silks of different colours; and the guidons and saddle-cloths of the horses were of the same silks as they wore. On that day there were bull-fights, horseback-fights, riding at the ring, . . . and the contestants came to show themselves off in front of the College so that the Father-Visitor could see them. You can judge from this *festa* what they will do on the other ones which are commonplace and daily events. Above all, they are given to banqueting, in which usually ten or twelve sugar-planters meet and eat together for a whole day, and taking turns in this way, they spend all they have. They usually drink about fifty thousand *cruzados* worth of Portuguese wine in a year; and some years they drank eighty thousand *cruzados* worth according to the account. In short, there is more vanity to be found in Pernambuco than in Lisbon. The Viannese are the lords of Pernambuco, and when a Viannese is involved in

[1] *Tratados da Terra e gente do Brasil* (ed. Rio, 1925), pp. 334–5.

any brawl, instead of shouting "Help here for the King", they shout "Help here for Vianna".'

Despite the depredations of the Dutch corsairs and Barbary rovers, the inhabitants of Pernambuco were no less pleasure-loving on the eve of the Dutch invasion, if Friar Manuel Calado's glowing account of their way of life is to be even half credited:[1]

'That commonwealth, before the arrival of the Hollanders, was the most delightful, prosperous, fertile, and I do not think I exaggerate much when I say the richest, of all the overseas possessions beneath the crown and sceptre of the kingdom of Portugal. Both gold and silver were beyond count, and almost disregarded. There was so much sugar that there were not sufficient ships to load it all, though great fleets of carracks, ships and caravels entered and left the port daily. These vessels came and went, meeting each other so frequently, that the pilots made gifts and treats to the planters and cultivators so as to secure their sugar-chests, and yet the vast supply was inexhaustible. The delights of food and drink were the same as all those that were available in Portugal and the Atlantic islands. The luxury and display in the houses was excessive, for anybody whose table-service was not of solid silver was regarded as poor and wretched. Ships which put into the port, evading the Peruvian duties, whether legally or otherwise, discharged there the best of their lading.[2] The women went so elegantly and richly dressed that they were not content with taffetas, camlets, velvets, and other silks, but bedecked themselves out in fine tissues and rich brocades. So many jewels adorned them that it seemed as if it had rained pearls, rubies, emeralds and diamonds on their heads and necks. There were no costly sword and dagger mountings, nor clothes of the latest fashion, with which the men did not adorn themselves. There were daily banquets, and equestrian fights and games at every *festa*. Everything was delightful, and this region resembled nothing so much as the portrait of an earthly paradise.'

[1] Fr. Manuel Calado, *Valeroso Lucideno e triumpho da Liberdade* (Libson, 1648), pp. 9–10.

[2] This refers to ships from Buenos Aires laden with silver from the Peruvian mines of Potosí, which, in defiance of all royal and viceregal edicts, persisted in visiting Brazilian ports to obtain provisions and Negro slaves in exchange for silver. Spanish ships forced by stress of weather were allowed to call at Brazilian ports for refit only, but this loophole in the laws naturally meant that *navios de arribada* (as they were termed) increased enormously. Cf. A. P. Canabrava, *O Comércio português no Rio da Prata, 1580–1640* (São Paulo, 1944), pp. 68–131.

There was, of course, another side to this idyllic picture of colonial bliss. If Pernambuco was an earthly paradise for the extravagant sugar-planters, it was also (in common with the rest of Brazil) an earthly hell for their Negro slaves, who were imported from Angola at the rate of about 4,000 a year.[1] Calado is silent on this point, but both he and Cardim agreed in denouncing the corruption of local morals and the venality of local justice. Usury, adultery, robbery, duelling, and murder alike went unpunished, as a few chests of sugar settled everything, 'and thus it was the justice of gossips'. Calado concludes his highly coloured picture of Pernambuco in its prime by quoting approvingly the prophetic threat made by a Dominican friar in a sermon preached a few days before the arrival of the Dutch. 'Between Olinda and Olanda there is nothing more than the change from an *i* to an *a*. This town of Olinda will be changed into Olanda, and it will be burnt by the Hollanders before many days are over, for since earthly justice is found wanting, divine justice will intervene.'[2]

Neither the eulogies nor the denunciations of clerical moralists need be taken too seriously, and Calado's portrait of Pernambuco is obviously overdrawn, whether he is comparing the place to an earthly paradise or to Sodom and Gomorrah. But it is also clear from other contemporary accounts that Pernambuco was really very prosperous, and that the Dutch had good reason to believe that it would prove an even richer prize than Bahia. Olinda was a well-built city, conspicuous for its fine churches, one of which alone contained 120 silver lamps.[3] Mathias de Albuquerque stated that the sugar tithes had dropped by 20,000 *cruzados* as a result of the havoc wrought by the Dutch cruisers; but if many vessels were captured, not a few escaped. Whether the Hollanders were in touch with the New-Christians is a matter of dispute;[4] but in any event these alleged fifth-columnists can have told them little that they did not already know.

---

[1] De Laet-Naber, *Iaerlyck Verhael*, ii. 139.

[2] The Portuguese wrote indifferently *Holanda* or *Olanda* for Holland, hence the pun.   [3] Wassenaer, *Historisch Verhael*, vi (1624), p. 68.

[4] Fr. Manuel Calado made this assertion in 1648 (*Valeroso Lucideno*, p. 10), but he is a most untrustworthy witness where Jews and Marranos are concerned. There is no trace of anything of the kind in contemporary Dutch records or published works. The evidence on which modern writers such as Bloom, Adler, and Roth rely, is a cock-and-bull story told to the Inquisition in 1634 by a certain Estevão Aires de Fonseca, and which the Inquisitors themselves obviously disbelieved as they made no attempt to follow up the matter.

The decision of the Heeren XIX to attack Pernambuco must have been taken late in 1628 or early in 1629, but the mobilization of the expedition was delayed by the crisis caused in Holland when the Spaniards and Imperialists burst into the Veluwe. As mentioned previously, the West India Company lent powerful and timely assistance in men and money during the critical summer of 1629, but this diversion postponed the attack on Pernambuco for a few months. Part of the expedition was able to sail in May and June, but the remainder did not leave until October and November. Command of the fleet was entrusted to Hendrick Corneliszoon Loncq, who had been Piet Heyn's second-in-command at the capture of the silver-fleet. The troops embarked for landing and garrison service were commanded by Colonel Jonckheer Diederick van Waerdenburgh, who had three lieutenant-colonels under his orders. Three civilian commissioners were nominated to act as members of the governing council which would begin to function as soon as a foothold was secured in Brazil.[1]

Loncq, who left on 27 June 1629, had to wait several months cruising off the Cape Verde islands for the remainder of his fleet. On 23 August, when only eight of his ships were in company, he fell in with a Spanish armada of forty sail under Don Fadrique de Toledo which was on its way to the West Indies. Some desultory fighting ensued, but neither side wished to engage too closely, and the armada resumed its voyage next day. By Christmas week the bulk of Loncq's fleet had arrived off St. Vincent, and he could begin his voyage across the Atlantic with a force of sixty-seven sail, great and small, carrying over 7,000 men and 1,170 guns.

The long delay in the mobilization of the Dutch expedition had naturally enabled the enemy to learn something about its destination. Due warning was received from the Infanta at

---

[1] The Pernambuco campaign of 1630 is very fully documented on both sides, as can be seen from the list of primary sources given in J. H. Rodrigues's *Historiografia e Bibliografia* (1949), nos. 387–99, 409–12, 415–19. Of the numerous secondary works, Netscher, *Les Hollandais au Brésil* (The Hague, 1853), pp. 39–51, and Varnhagen, *Historia das Lutas* (1872), pp. 45–73, both have good accounts; but for English readers the very detailed synthesis of Dutch and Iberian sources by G. Edmundson in the *English Historical Review*, xiv (1899), pp. 679–99, is the most convenient. I have relied here chiefly on Mathias de Albuquerque's official dispatches of 18 and 22 Feb. 1630; Duarte de Albuquerque, *Memorias Diarias* (Madrid, 1654; Brazilian translation, Recife, 1944); and De Laet-Naber, *Iaerlyck Verhael*, ii. 102–58.

Brussels that Brazil was the objective, but beyond instructing the governor-general to strengthen the fortifications of Bahia and Pernambuco, the government at Madrid did not do very much. Mathias de Albuquerque, brother of Duarte de Albuquerque, the donatory of Pernambuco, was in Madrid at this time, having returned two years previously from that captaincy which he had governed with conspicuous success from 1620 to 1627. In view of his local experience and ties, Mathias de Albuquerque was now appointed governor and commander-in-chief over the four north-eastern provinces of Pernambuco, Itamaracá, Paraíba, and Rio Grande. He was ordered to leave for Olinda forthwith and organize the defences of that region against a Dutch attack.

The authorities at Madrid assured him that their colleagues at Lisbon would provide him with substantial reinforcements; but his countrymen were only able (or willing) to give him three caravels laden with a few troops and munitions, most of which were to be sent on to Bahia and Rio de Janeiro. He protested strongly but in vain against the inadequacy of these reinforcements, with which he left Lisbon on 12 August, landing near Recife on 4 October 1629. As Mathias de Albuquerque is the protagonist in this chapter, a character-sketch of him by the Brazilian Franciscan friar, Vicente do Salvador, who knew him well, will not be out of place here. We know from many contemporary prints and paintings what Piet Heyn, Hendrick Loncq, and many other Dutchmen who fought in Brazil looked like. Portuguese art was singularly barren in this respect, so Fr. Vicente's pen-picture of Albuquerque is all the more welcome.[1]

'Mathias de Albuquerque, during all the time that he served as captain-major of Pernambuco and as governor-general of Brazil, which was for the space of seven years, was always very clean-handed, never accepting anything from anyone, nor taking

---

[1] Fr. Vicente do Salvador, *História do Brasil, 1627* (ed. 1931), p. 616. I can find no reliable authority for the assertion of Oliveira Lima, Helio Vianna, and other modern writers that Albuquerque had previously served under Spinola in Flanders. As he was only about fifteen years old when the twelve-year truce was signed in 1609, and was serving in Brazil from 1620 to 1627, the assertion would seem to be unfounded. Mathias was nominally acting governor-general of Brazil in 1624–6, but as he never went to Bahia to assume this function he is usually omitted from the list of governor-generals. Cf. also Lanier's dispatch of 27 July 1643 in *Miscelânea scientífica e literária dedicada ao Dr. J. Leite de Vasconcelos* (Coimbra, 1931), pp. 13–17 of the offprint.

offices from others to give them to his followers. He was always very active in time of war and on His Majesty's service, not sparing himself of work either by day or night. He would never be carried in a hammock, as is the custom in Brazil, but always went on horseback or in boats—and when he went in these last, he would not sit down, but always stood up and took the tiller himself. He had a wonderful memory and knowledge of men, even if he only saw them once. It was the same with ships, even if they had only visited the port once before; for when they came again long afterwards he would say whose they were before the master came ashore. On a certain occasion, one ship arrived with another mast, and examining it through his telescope when still a long way off, he said: "That is such-and-such a ship which came here a year ago, but she has got a new mast." And the master admitted as much when he came ashore after his arrival and was asked about it.'

Mathias de Albuquerque did his best to strengthen the local defences after his arrival in October 1629, but found that many of them had been dismantled and that the local inhabitants were largely apathetic. There were only 200 soldiers and 650 militiamen at his disposal originally, but he eventually succeeded in scraping together some 2,000 men, most of them untrained and ill armed. He found fifty-six merchantmen in the harbour of Recife, of which he dispatched eighteen fully laden with sugar to Portugal forthwith, later fitting out sixteen of the remaining thirty-eight for use as fire-ships. He tried to build batteries at some of the most exposed beaches, but he found he had neither men nor guns to man them properly. Some contemporary critics accused him of wasting time by celebrating the news of the birth of the Infante, Balthazar Carlos, with *festas* in which the pleasure-loving Pernambucans joined with more enthusiasm than in the toilsome work of drilling and digging.[1] However this may have been, no great progress had been made in strengthening the local defences, except in Recife harbour, when, on 9 February 1630, a pinnace dispatched by João Pereira Corte-Real, the governor of the Cape Verde islands, arrived with the news that the Dutch fleet had left St. Vincent and was bound for Pernambuco. Albuquerque tried to accelerate his preparations, but a few days later the Dutch ships appeared in sight and launched their attack on 15 February.

[1] Calado, *Valeroso Lucideno* (1648), p. 10.

The Dutch attack was made in two places. While Loncq, with most of the fleet, attempted to force the entrance to Recife harbour, Waerdenburgh, with the bulk of the troops, landed at the beach of Pau Amarello, six miles to the north of Olinda. Loncq's attack was repulsed, but Waerdenburgh met with no resistance worth the writing. Mathias de Albuquerque hurried back from Recife to try and stop the Dutch advance next day, but he could not induce his men to make a stand for any length of time. By the evening of 16 February the Dutch were in possession of Olinda at a cost of only fifty or sixty casualties. Realizing that the fall of Recife was now inevitable, since most of his men were completely out of control, Mathias de Albuquerque fired all the shipping and the sugar warehouses at Recife in the early hours of 17 February. Accounts differ as to the value of what was destroyed in this way, but Albuquerque claimed that he had deprived the Dutch of a booty worth '1,600,000 *cruzados*'.[1] The forts at Recife unexpectedly managed to hold out for another fortnight; but by 3 March all resistance there was over, and the Dutch celebrated the capture of Olinda, Recife, and the neighbouring island of Antonio Vaz with a thanksgiving service.

These rejoicings proved premature. As at Bahia in 1624 the *moradores* (or most of them) now rallied from their first panic, and Mathias de Albuquerque was able to organize a highly effective guerrilla campaign against the invaders. He made his headquarters in the house of a settler which was advantageously situated in swampy and well-wooded country, at a distance of about three miles alike from Olinda and Recife. Here he organized a fortified earthen camp christened the *Arraial do Bom Jesus*, which dominated the tracks and streams leading to the interior, and which was, by virtue of its natural situation, largely secure against surprise. The *arraial* was only the largest and strongest of a number of other fortified posts which Albuquerque organized round Olinda, Recife, and Antonio Vaz. The Dutch soon found that they were hemmed into these three places, and that even inter-communication between them was not secure. Albuquerque also organized *capitanias de emboscadas*,

[1] Duarte de Albuquerque, *Memorias Diarias*, under the date of 17 Feb. 1630, inflates this amount to 'four millions'. A letter of Gil Correia de Castelbranco, intercepted by the Dutch, placed the loss at about 2 million ducats. In any event, the destruction was not complete, as the Dutch found a certain amount of booty when they entered Recife (De Laet-Naber, *Iaerlyck Verhael*, ii. 132-3).

which were strong fighting-patrols led by men who knew every inch of the terrain. They lay in ambush for Dutch foraging parties, or conducted raids against their outposts and communications by night and day. Loncq himself had a very narrow escape from being killed or captured by one of these parties while traversing the sandy spit which joined Olinda to Recife, and the same experience later befell Admiral Ita. On both occasions the Dutch commanders were strongly escorted, but on each occasion their escorts were virtually wiped out before help could arrive.

So successful did these harrassing tactics prove that Albuquerque became emboldened to launch frontal attacks on the defences which the Dutch were erecting round Olinda and Recife, but these efforts were costly failures. The Dutch, on their side, had been equally unsuccessful in an attack on the *arraial* which was repulsed on 14 March. It may be added that not all the *moradores* took kindly to guerrilla fighting, or bore the hardships of bush-warfare without complaint. Men who reported for duty in the morning were apt to slink away from the scene of action at night, and it became increasingly difficult to replace the braver leaders who were killed or wounded in battle.

A stalemate thus developed in which each side was unable to overcome the other, while waiting for the arrival of substantial reinforcements from home, for which they both clamoured. The Dutch, being unused to tropical warfare, suffered severely from dysentery, and were unable to get any meat, fruit, or provisions from the surrounding country, and even their firewood had to be imported from Holland. The Portuguese had no adequate shelter and were desperately short of supplies of all kinds, Albuquerque having to take lead from fishers' nets to make bullets. Both sides suffered severely from malnutrition, the Dutch at one period being reduced to eating cats and rats, while the Portuguese soldiers received as their daily ration a single spike of maize each. Such being the situation of the combatants in Pernambuco for most of the years 1630 and 1631, we may turn our attention to the reactions in their respective homelands.

The news of the loss of Olinda reached Madrid at the end of April. Contrary to what is usually asserted, the Spanish government was seriously alarmed and made strenuous efforts to help the defenders of Pernambuco. Olivares's first reaction was to order the immediate mobilization of another combined armada of the two Iberian crowns, after the precedent of the powerful fleet which had recovered Bahia so speedily five years before.[1] But conditions had changed for the worse since 1625 in so far as Iberian power was concerned. Whereas in 1624–5 Spain was refreshed by the breathing-space given her during the twelve-year truce, the years which had elapsed since then had been full of disasters for the dual monarchy. Torrential rain and floods had devastated large areas in Spain and Portugal in the early months of 1626, and many ships of the combined armada had been sunk or damaged by storms on the homeward voyage. Early in 1627 a Portuguese armada carrying the flower of the nobility had been wrecked with great loss of life in the Bay of Biscay, together with two richly laden East India carracks. This disaster was said to be the worst that Portugal had suffered since the defeat and death of King Sebastian at the hands of the Moors on the field of Alcácer-el-Kebir in 1578. Apart from Piet Heyn's spectacular successes in 1627–8, culminating in the capture of the Mexican silver-fleet, the cruisers of the West India Company had wrought great havoc among Iberian shipping in the Atlantic. The progress of the Dutch in Asia at the expense of the Portuguese 'State of India' caused such serious concern that Olivares inaugurated a costly six-year plan for sending powerful reinforcements from Lisbon to Goa in 1628. Finally, Spinola's capture of Breda in 1625 had been offset by Frederik Hendrik's conquest of Den Bosch in 1629.[2]

When Madrid applied to Lisbon for help in mobilizing a combined armada for Brazil in May 1630, the Portuguese response was necessarily far less enthusiastic than it had been in

[1] The news of the loss of Olinda reached Madrid on 29 Apr. 1630, and orders were issued next day for the mobilization of the combined armada. Cf. *Carta régia* of 30 Apr. 1630, printed in Freire de Oliveira, *Elementos para a história do município de Lisboa*, iii (Lisbon, 1887), pp. 340–5). This letter has been overlooked by modern historians who erroneously assume (cf. Varnhagen, *História Geral*, ii. 264, 309–10) that the news first reached *Lisbon* on 29 Apr., and that the Spanish court's first reaction was the *carta régia* of 11 May, ordering public prayers and penance, and punishment of the prevailing immorality.

[2] For the reaction in Portugal to the disasters of 1626–8, cf. M. Lopes de Almeida [ed.], *Memorial de Pero Rõiz Soares* [*1565–1628*] (Coimbra, 1953), pp. 482–508. The six-year plan for reinforcing Portuguese Asia was elaborated in the *cartas régias* of 31 May and 6 June 1628, printed in Andrade e Silva, *Collecção Chronologica, 1627–1633*, pp. 132–3, 173–5. Cf. also Freire de Oliveira, *Elementos*, iii. 295–306.

1624. The Lisbon Senate, or municipal council, stated that the utmost they could do was to divert to this projected armada the money already voted for sending reinforcements to India under Olivares's six-year plan. They also suggested that the existing *consulado* tax should be raised from 3 to 4 per cent.,[1] and that the whole of the proceeds should be applied to help for Brazil. They strongly objected to the imposition of an unpopular retail tax on meats and wine called the *real de agua*,[2] and to any increase in the duties on salt or sugar, which were among the measures suggested by the Spanish government. The authorities at Madrid retorted that the municipal council's suggestions were utterly inadequate, and they insisted on the imposition of the *real de agua* and a number of other unpopular fiscal measures.

Despite the categorical and reiterated orders from Madrid, ships, men, and money were assembled only with painful slowness at Lisbon. The project of sending a powerful combined armada to Brazil had to be shelved, and only a few caravels carrying limited supplies of men and munitions left the Tagus at irregular and infrequent intervals for Pernambuco.[3] The authorities at Lisbon and Madrid wrangled obstinately about apportioning the sacrifices which their respective crowns should bear, and much time was wasted in these mutual recriminations. The Spaniards complained that the Portuguese were doing little or nothing to help themselves, but wanted to leave everything to the crown of Castile, though it was the existence of their principal colony which was at stake. The Portuguese retorted that they were already overtaxed, and that it was only their union with the Spanish empire which had drawn upon them the disastrous hostility of the Dutch. They complained that Portugal was neglected while concessions were bestowed upon

[1] The *consulado* was imposed on all imports and exports, the proceeds being theoretically applied to the cost of coast-defence fleets and convoys to protect merchant shipping. First imposed in Portugal in 1592, the proceeds of the tax were soon diverted to other uses, despite constant complaints from traders and fishers.

[2] The *real de agua*, originally imposed as a purely local tax in connexion with the water supply for Elvas, was later applied elsewhere and extended to other commodities—in the present instance it was a retail sales tax of 1 *real* on every *arratel* (16 oz.) of meat, and on every *canada* (3 pints) of wine. Cf. the 'Regimento do Real de Agua' of 31 Oct. 1636 in Andrade e Silva, *Collecção Chronologica, 1634–1640*, pp. 101–9.

[3] For the inadequacy of these supplies cf. Albuquerque, *Memorias Diarias*, 4 Mar. and 18 July 1630; Van der Capellen, *Gedenkschriften*, i. 610.

regions like Aragon and Valencia, which had not sacrificed so much for the common Iberian cause. When new taxes were imposed in Spain, the burden was to some extent lightened by the reduction or abolition of others, but in Portugal (so they complained), new taxes were constantly being imposed without any remission of the old. Finally, they pointed out that Castile was even more concerned than Portugal in recovering Pernambuco, since the Dutch looked upon Brazil only as a stepping-stone to the wealth of Spanish America which was their real and ultimate aim.[1]

The principal Portuguese spokesman was Dom Jorge de Mascarenhas, Conde de Castel-Novo, and president of the Lisbon municipal council. In October 1630 he informed the king that the imposition of additional taxation on the impoverished people of Lisbon was asking the impossible of them and would risk an open revolt. The city and its inhabitants were in such a wretched condition, he averred, that he could not describe it to His Majesty on paper. The few remaining merchants who had any money were leaving as quickly as they could, and those who were left were too impoverished to pay anything more. A year later, he wrote that the proposed increase in the price of salt, apart from being a great hardship for the poor, would induce the foreign traders to go and seek it for themselves elsewhere, 'as happened when the price of pepper and spices was increased, which was the reason why the said foreigners went and sought them by the sea-route to India, thereby depriving this crown of the trade in these commodities to our great loss, as experience has shown'. Similarly, any increase in the duties on sugar would effectively kill that trade which was already taxed to the limit.[2]

Acrimonious exchanges between the authorities at Lisbon and Madrid continued for the next decade; but although the equivalent of a capital levy and various other vexatious fiscal burdens were imposed by order of Madrid, the Portuguese were

[1] Cf. the documents printed in Freire de Oliveira, *Elementos*, iii. 344–50, 375–8, 439–42, 451–7, 460–8, 470–81; Andrade e Silva, *Collecção chronologica, 1627–1633*, pp. 176–7, 185, 202–3, 205–7, 225–6.

[2] Cf. his letters of 1 Oct. 1630 and Dec. 1631 in Freire de Oliveira, *Elementos*, iii. 375–8, 465–8, 470–81. Some of these arguments had already been adduced by the weavers of Lisbon in the remarkable remonstrance which their representative drew up on 3 June 1628, denouncing Spanish misgovernment and the diversion of Portuguese resources to serve Spanish ends (first printed in the *Archivo Pittoresco*, iii [Lisbon, 1860], pp. 147–9, 159–60, 167–8).

never able (or never willing) to find their full quota. The bulk of the money which was secured was raised by taxes such as the hated *real de agua* which bore heaviest on the poorest classes, and by forced loans from the New-Christian business community.[1] The collection of the capital levy and other subsidies was entrusted to a *junta* specially appointed for organizing the financing and dispatch of help to Pernambuco.[2] Nevertheless, and despite the allegations of Portuguese historians to the contrary, the fact remains that it was the crown of Castile which had to find the greater part of the help sent to Brazil.

Nor did the sacrifices of the Spanish crown stop here. Tentative and indirect negotiations for another lengthy truce with the United Provinces had been set afoot in 1629, and these were more seriously pressed from the Spanish side after the fall of Olinda. At first the Spanish negotiators (or rather the Flemings acting on their behalf) demanded the unconditional restitution of Olinda and Recife as a prerequisite condition for the conclusion of a truce, but they soon changed their tune. In October 1631 they were ready to offer Lingen in exchange, and a few months later they raised their bid to Breda. At the risk of anticipating matters somewhat, it may be mentioned that by the end of 1635 they were offering Breda plus 200,000 ducats for Pernambuco, in addition to conceding the closure of the Scheldt. In other words, the government at Madrid was prepared to sacrifice the vital interests of the *Provincias Obedientes* of Flanders, in order to placate their Portuguese subjects.[3]

Things were not nearly so desperate on the Dutch side, but

[1] Cf. the document published in *Revista de História*, i (Lisbon, 1912), pp. 181–3; J. L. D'Azevedo, *História dos Christãos-Novos Portugueses* (Lisbon, 1921), pp. 211–12. Helio Vianna, *Estudos de História Colonial*, pp. 298–9, misreads his own source (the papers of Dom Antonio de Ataide) when he expatiates on the patriotism of the Portuguese of all classes of society in offering money for the recovery of Pernambuco. The list he reproduces, dated 13 Nov. 1632, shows conclusively that far and away the largest contributors were the *gente da nação* (Marranos), who subscribed much more than all the prelates, Lisbon municipality, and nobles put together—and the Marranos' loan was a forced one.

[2] The 'Regimento' of this *junta*, dated 26 June 1631, is printed in Andrade e Silva, *Collecção chronologica, 1627–1633*, pp. 205–7.

[3] Cf. the correspondence between King Philip IV and the Archduchess Isabella, in J. Cuvelier and J. Lefèvre, *Correspondance de la Cour d'Espagne*, ii. 592, 603, 625, 628, 694, 701; iii. 7, 83, 90, 299. For an outline of the tentative truce negotiations in 1629–33, and the abortive efforts at reunion between the northern and southern Netherlands at this period, cf. P. Geyl, *The Netherlands Divided* (London, 1936), pp. 94–109. For the West India Company's attitude see the document printed in *Bijdr. Med. Hist. Gen. Utrecht*, xxi. 343–62.

they were very far from going smoothly. The original orders given to Loncq for the Peranmbuco expedition envisaged not only the speedy occupation of all north-east Brazil but likewise the seizure of Rio de Janeiro, and even of Bahia and Buenos Aires, if all went well.[1] The directors were consequently very annoyed when they learnt that far from conquering the whole captaincy of Pernambuco, the Dutch were hemmed into Olinda and Recife, where they could boast only of occupying 'two heaps of sand and stones'. Waerdenburgh and his colleagues explained that the Portuguese colonists and their Amerindian allies were formidable guerrilla fighters, and that substantial reinforcements must be poured into Recife if the Dutch were to extend their precariously held foothold. They also advocated the abandonment of Olinda, owing to the difficulty of fortifying the rugged and rambling hillside on which it was built, and suggested concentrating the garrison in the easily defensible strong-point of Recife. The Heeren XIX refused to allow the abandonment of Olinda, but promised to send out adequate reinforcements. They urged their commanders to take vigorous offensive action and not sit supinely on the defensive, since the Portuguese 'were not an enemy to be taken seriously'.[2]

Although Loncq and Waerdenburgh complained of the insufficiency of their reinforcements, the Dutch did in fact receive far more substantial and regular help from Europe than did the Portuguese. Mathias de Albuquerque noted that whereas two or three Dutch ships reached Recife every month, with replacements for Dutch casualties and supplies of all kinds for the garrison, the caravels which came at uncertain intervals from Portugal had to unload in harbours situated at anything between 80 and 180 miles from the *arraial*, owing to the Dutch command of the sea. Much of the material which they brought was inevitably lost on the long march through the bush and forest to the camp.[3] The long-term advantages in this war of mutual exhaustion were thus mostly on the side of the Dutch. They evidently realized this, as, although disappointed that the rich

[1] The Heeren XIX's instructions for Loncq, dated 18 Aug. 1629, were first utilized (in so far as I am aware) by J. A. Gonsalves de Mello, *Tempo dos Flamengos* (Rio de Janeiro, 1947), pp. 47–48, having been overlooked by Netscher, Wätjen, Edmundson, *et al.*

[2] Heeren XIX's letters of 17 July 1630 and 31 Oct. 1631 in Wätjen, *Das holländische Kolonialreich in Brasilien* (Gotha and The Hague, 1921), pp. 54, 58–59.

[3] Albuquerque, *Memorias Diarias*, 4 Mar. and 8 Dec. 1630.

sugar-growing district (*várzea*) still remained in the hands of the Portuguese, they rejected (after some preliminary hesitation) all the Spanish offers to exchange Olinda and Recife for some place in the Netherlands.

It seemed that the deadlock in Pernambuco would be broken when both sides received substantial reinforcements in 1631. A powerful Dutch fleet under Pater and Thijssen, which left Dutch ports in successive detachments, reached Recife between December 1630 and April 1631. Early in May, a strong Iberian armada under Don Antonio de Oquendo, a Biscayan seaman with a fine naval record, left the Tagus for Brazil. Despite constant prodding of the Portuguese by Madrid, only five small vessels out of a total of twenty-one warships were provided by the Portuguese crown; and there is no truth in the assertion of Edmundson and other historians that the whole cost of the expedition was borne by Portugal. The armada carried some 2,000 soldiers as reinforcements for Brazil, of whom 800 were destined for Bahia, 1,000 for Pernambuco, and 200 for Paraíba. Oquendo landed the reinforcements at Bahia without incident, and then steered north for Pernambuco. His fleet now consisted of 20 warships (including 16 galleons), with 12 transport-caravels and 24 sugar-ships in convoy, or 56 sail in all.

When some miles south of his destination on 12 September he was attacked by Pater, who had badly underestimated the strength of the Spanish armada and had only sixteen sail with him at the time. Less than half a dozen ships on either side came to close quarters, the remainder of the two fleets keeping well out of harm's way. Before the action began, Oquendo was urged to take some of the soldiers out of the caravels to reinforce the galleons, but he refused to do so, scornfully dismissing the enemy as *poca ropa*.[1] The action resolved itself into a homeric duel between the respective flagships, which ended in Pater's own vessel (the *Prins Willem*) and the *Provincie Utrecht* catching fire and burning to the water's edge, while the armada lost the *almiranta* and two other ships sunk and one captured. Pater, who could not swim, tried to save himself by hanging from a rope at the prow of the burning *Prins Willem*; but nobody

---

[1] He made the same mistake of underestimating his enemy eight years later, when he used exactly the same words before engaging Lt.-Admiral M. H. Tromp with a small squadron off Beachy Head on 16 Sept. 1639. Cf. C. R. Boxer, *Journal of M. H. Tromp, Anno 1639* (Cambridge, 1930), pp. 34–47, where the translation on p. 35, note (2) should be corrected.

came to his help, and he fell exhausted into the sea and was drowned.

By this time, Oquendo's flagship was no better than an unmanageable hulk, and so badly battered that she was only saved from sinking by the efforts of the Dutch sailors whom the Spaniards had picked up from the water. The Dutch had lost about 500 men, and the Spaniards rather more, Oquendo having suffered 250 fatal casualties in the *Santiago* alone. Neither side was anxious to renew the conflict, and the Dutch withdrew to Recife, thus allowing Oquendo to land his reinforcements at the Barra Grande, after first taking 300 men to help replace his casualties. Having done this, he then set sail for home and left the Dutch again in unchallenged command of the sea off the coast of Brazil.[1]

The reinforcements which eventually reached the *arraial* totalled about 700 men, 300 of these being Neapolitans under the command of Giovanni Vincenzo de San Felice, Count of Bagnuoli. If we are to believe some of their Portuguese comrades, these Italians subsequently proved to be more of a hindrance than a help, and Bagnuoli himself not merely an inefficient but a cowardly commander.[2] With these reinforcements came Duarte de Albuquerque, donatory of Pernambuco and brother of Mathias, whose *Memorias Diarias* are our chief source for the doings in the *arraial*. Some of the 'pot-bellied' planters, as Fr. Manuel Calado termed them, were disheartened when they found that relatively few reinforcements had come and that the Dutch still retained command of the sea. Nevertheless, by a

[1] There are numerous detailed accounts of the engagement between Oquendo and Pater, but I have relied chiefly on those embodied in Duarte de Albuquerque, *Memorias Diarias*, under the date of 12 Sept. 1631; De Laet-Naber, *Iaerlyck Verhael*, iii. 14–24; and C. Fernández Duro, *Armada Española*, iv. 121–8. G. Edmundson, an incurable romantic, swallows the legend that Pater, when his burning ship was on the point of foundering, 'wrapping the standard round his body, clad in armour as he was, leaped into the sea. The proud spirit of the unvanquished seaman preferred the ocean for a tomb rather than captivity in the hands of his enemies' (*English Historical Review*, xv. 44). This story is an invention of Fr. Manuel Calado (*Valeroso Lucideno*, p. 13), writing in 1645, and is explicitly contradicted by the eyewitness accounts utilized by De Laet, and by the evidence of the Dutch sailors who were picked up by Oquendo's flagship. Cf. Varnhagen, *História Geral* (ed. 1948), ii. 311–12.

[2] Fr. Manuel Calado, *Valeroso Lucideno*, is Bagnuoli's most scornful critic. His account is obviously exaggerated in some places, but accurately reflects popular opinion among the Portuguese participants in the Pernambuco campaigns. Bagnuoli had served with credit in the expedition which retook Bahia, 1624–5, and in Don Fadrique de Toledo's reconquest of Nevis and St. Kitts in 1629–30.

judicious mixture of threats and blandishments, the Albuquerque brothers contrived to keep their men in hand and to maintain the investment of Olinda and Recife. The situation in October 1631 was, therefore, very much what it had been a year previously, with the Dutch in full command of the sea and with the Portuguese holding the upper hand on shore.

Since 14 March 1630 Olinda and Recife had been governed by a political council (*Politiek Raad*), in accordance with the regulations drawn up by the Heeren XIX in 1629 for the government of their projected colony. This council was originally composed of three civilian commissioners, who were later joined by two others. After the departure of Loncq in May 1630, the command of the land and sea forces devolved on the senior military officer, Colonel Diederick van Waerdenburgh. He was given the title of governor, and the second seat and vote in the political council, but he was not allowed to assume the chairmanship, which devolved upon each of the civilian commissioners in monthly rotation. Waerdenburgh also had an advisory military council to assist him, and the civilian and military elements seem to have worked fairly smoothly together on the whole.[1]

They both finally agreed that Olinda was indefensible and that it would be better to concentrate their strength in Recife. This was done in November 1631, when a general muster showed a total ration-strength of nearly 7,000 men fit for service, including soldiers, sailors, and Negroes. The Dutch territory in Pernambuco was now limited to Recife, Antonio Vaz, and a little islet off the southern tip of Itamaracá which they had occupied seven months previously. Here they built a fort named Oranje, which was held by a garrison of 366 men under the command of a Polish captain, Crestofle d'Artischau Arciszewski, a man of exceptional intelligence, courage, and initiative.[2]

---

[1] The regulations of 13 Oct. 1629 for the *Politiek Raad* and government of the colony were printed by Aitzema, *Saken van staet en oorlogh, 1621-1632*, p. 1055, and in the *Groot Placcaet-Boeck* of 1658. S. P. L'Honoré Naber makes one of his very rare blunders when he writes (De Laet-Naber, *Iaerlyck Verhael*, iii, p. xix) that Waerdenburgh had the title of commander-in-chief and governor 'zonder zitting in den Raad!' The relevant passage in the original instructions states categorically that Waerdenburgh 'sessie ende stem in de politique raedt soude hebben'.

[2] Arciszewski (1592-1656) was a Polish nobleman who had killed a shyster lawyer for ruining his family's fortune. He thereby incurred sentence of perpetual banishment from Poland, although this sentence was revoked in 1625. He served in the Netherlands and France as a soldier of fortune from 1624 to 1629, when he

One of the council's reasons for evacuating Olinda had been to free many of the men from garrison duty, and thus enable them to undertake offensive operations elsewhere. They tried to enlarge their foothold by sending expeditions successively against the fort of Cabedello in Paraíba, and against the Rio Grande, the Rio Formoso, and finally Cabo de Santo Agostinho. In each case the Portuguese were on the alert, and Mathias de Albuquerque was enabled to forestall or frustrate them by the timely dispatch of reinforcements from the *arraial*. It seemed as if this stalemate would continue indefinitely, each side being powerless to eject the other from its chosen positions, when an event occurred which completely transformed the situation.

On 20 April 1632 a Mulatto named Domingos Fernandes Calabar deserted to the Dutch. He was not the first deserter by any means, and the Dutch already had several hundred Negroes in their service, who were mostly runaway slaves of the Portuguese planters. But Calabar was someone far more important' and influential than these. Born at Porto Calvo, he knew every inch of the country and he had distinguished himself in the defence of the *arraial*, where he had been wounded. He was a most active and intelligent man, and the Dutch could have found no better guide or adviser to indicate their enemy's weak spots. He was as strong as the proverbial ox, many stories being related of his feats of physical strength in cattle-punching and other tests of endurance. The reasons for his desertion are uncertain, and the Dutch naturally did not trust him very far at first, but he soon proved his worth.[1]

At his suggestion, and personally guided by him, Waerdenburgh led a column through muddy and unfrequented bush-paths on the night of 30 April, which fell upon the little town of Iguaraçu on the morning of May Day. The Portuguese were taken completely unawares, and the Dutch secured a substantial amount of booty besides inflicting heavy casualties on their opponents. Before the sack of the place began, Waerden-

enlisted in the service of the West India Company. Cf. J. C. M. Warnsinck's sketch of his career and his quarrel with Johan Maurits on pp. xxv–lxxiii of the introduction to De Laet-Naber, *Iaerlyck Verhael*, iv. His name also appears in such forms as Artichewski, Arquixofle, Artichoke, &c.

[1] For Calabar cf. De Laet-Naber, *Iaerlyck Verhael*, iv. 171, and the works quoted in J. H. Rodrigues, *Bibliografia*, nos. 962–5. Fr. Manuel Calado's allusions to Calabar are not necessarily trustworthy, although the friar has been accused (and not without apparent reason) of violating the seal of confession in his description of Calabar's last hours (*Valeroso Lucideno*, pp. 14, 21–22).

burgh took care to stave in 200 pipes of wine which he found there, so as to prevent his men getting drunk and disorderly as they had done on the capture of Olinda. He also collected all the womenfolk, among whom were many pretty girls, in the church and placed a guard on the door to prevent them from being molested. This success, which was the forerunner of many others similarly planned and guided by Calabar, encouraged the Dutch as much as it disheartened the Portuguese. The latter now realized that their fighting patrols could no longer prevent Dutch penetration of the *várzea*, and in fact the days of the defenders' moral ascendancy were soon over.

At the turn of the year 1632 substantial reinforcements arrived from the United Provinces, and with them came two of the nineteen directors, Mathias van Ceulen of the Amsterdam chamber and Johan Gijsselingh from Zeeland, to take over the direction of affairs from Waerdenburgh at his own request. The new leaders lost no time in initiating a more vigorous offensive policy by exploiting Calabar's unrivalled knowledge of local conditions and terrain. In rapid succession, and mostly under the guidance of Calabar, Dutch raiding parties and flying columns fell upon the Portuguese in widely separated areas, and regions hitherto immune from attack were now ravaged. In February 1633 a redoubt on the Rio Formoso was carried by storm after its small garrison of twenty men had literally fought to the last man. In March the Dutch took the Portuguese post in the Afogados, building a fort on its site which outflanked the *arraial* and facilitated the entry of Dutch raiding parties into the *várzea*. In June the island of Itamaracá was occupied by Sigismund von Schoppe, who gave his name to the small settlement that was promptly founded there. Apart from several other subsidiary operations, the Dutch scored another important success in December when Van Ceulen captured the strongly situated fort of Reis Magos at the entrance to the Rio Grande, which was rebaptized with his own name.[1]

The Dutch had made several previous attempts to get in touch with the savage cannibal Tapuyas who lived in the hinterland of Ceará, and who were the most dreaded of all the

---

[1] Detailed accounts of the operations in 1631–3 will be found in Duarte de Albuquerque, *Memorias Diarias*, and De Laet-Naber, *Iaerlyck Verhael*, iii. Cf. also G. Edmundson's article in the *English Historical Review*, xv. 38–57, although this last only goes as far as Oct. 1632.

Portuguese colonists' Amerindian foes. After the capture of Rio Grande close contact was established with these savages whose principal chief, Nhandui, did indeed co-operate heartily with the invaders, responding to their overtures by massacring some of the local *moradores* forthwith. However, not all of the Tapuyas were equally friendly. A number remained faithful to their old acquaintance, Martim Soares Moreno, who was one of the most celebrated Indian-fighters among the Portuguese. He had lived among the Tapuya tribes as a youth, and not only spoke their 'twisted tongues' fluently, but on occasion fought alongside them stark naked except for his war-paint. He had led a contingent of these savages, whose fearsome aspect duly impressed the Dutch, against the French invaders of the Maranhão in 1613–15, and another to the help of the defenders of the *arraial* in 1630. But on the whole it can be said that the bulk of the Tapuyas were henceforth active allies of the invaders, whereas most of the Tupís continued to support the Portuguese, largely owing to the influence of a Petiguar chieftain named Poty or Potí, known to the Portuguese as Dom Felipe Camarão, who was granted a knighthood in the coveted Order of Christ for his outstanding services.[1]

The Dutch did not have matters entirely their own way, and the Portuguese fought back valiantly. Two attacks on the *arraial* were repulsed in March and August 1633, respectively, as was a second expedition against the fortress of Cabedello at Paraíba in February 1634. The Dutch atoned for these reverses by repulsing a well-planned but ill-executed night-attack on Recife (1 March 1634), and by securing a foothold at the 'Pontal' of Cabo de Santo Agostinho in the same month. This was the key to the best and safest roadstead used by the caravels coming from Portugal with men and supplies for the *arraial*, and the most convenient place for taking on board the sugars with which they returned. Mathias de Albuquerque at once counter-attacked vigorously, but was unable to dislodge the Dutch from their position. The most he could do was to maintain a close watch on the Pontal from the makeshift fort of Nazaré which

[1] For the interesting career of the hard-fighting Martim Soares Moreno (1586–1650?), who was among other things the founder of Ceará, see the works quoted in J. H. Rodrigues, *Bibliografia*, nos. 991–3. There is an extensive literature concerning the Amerindian chief, D. Antonio Felipe Camarão (1601–48), for which see the definitive biography by J. A. Gonsalves de Mello, *D. Antonio Filipe Camarão* (Recife, 1954).

crowned a neighbouring height, and where he remained for nearly a year; but the use of the roadstead was henceforth denied to the Portuguese and available to the Dutch. The latter had a great advantage in all these operations, because they could move their forces from one point to another speedily and easily by sea. The Portuguese, on the other hand, had to march to all the threatened points overland, through bush, scrub, swamp, and forest, wading across numerous rivers and creeks. Moreover, under the guidance of Calabar, the Dutch were now becoming better at bush-warfare. Two of their leaders, the Pole Arciszewski and the German Von Schoppe, were fully a match for the best that the Portuguese could produce.

Van Ceulen and Gijsselingh left for Holland in September 1634, leaving the direction of affairs in Brazil entrusted to a council of five members: Servatius Carpentier, Willem Schotte, Jacob Stachouwer, Balthasar Wyntgens, and Ippo Eyssens. Colonel Sigismund von Schoppe assumed the command of the land forces, as the senior field-officer, Arciszewski, who had been promoted to the same rank during a short visit to Holland, unselfishly waived his claim after his return in favour of his German comrade. Having received strong reinforcements in the course of the year, the Dutch leaders decided to make a third attempt on Paraíba, and this time they were successful. After a short siege, the fort of Cabedello surrendered six days before Christmas, followed by the provincial capital a few days later. Meanwhile, Mathias de Albuquerque had dispatched Bagnuoli with a relieving column; but if the malicious Fr. Manuel do Salvador is to be trusted, the Italian commander 'took eleven or twelve days on the way and did not arrive in time; although when he returned to our camp after the loss of Paraíba he took only three days to cover the same ground, being told by some of those who were with him that the enemy was in pursuit'.[1]

The position of the Portuguese was now desperate, as the Dutch controlled the whole coastline from Rio Grande to Cabo de Santo Agostinho. The few caravels which escaped the Dutch cruisers could no longer find an unfrequented bay or creek in which to unload what scanty supplies they did bring. Many of

---

[1] Fr. Manuel do Salvador, *Valeroso Lucideno*, p. 15. Detailed accounts of the Paraíba campaign will be found in Duarte de Albuquerque, *Memorias Diarias*, 7 Nov.–30 Dec. 1634, and De Laet-Naber, *Iaerlyck Verhael*, iv. 71–92, 119–27.

the *moradores* began to despair of a successful end to the war, and rather than be left to the tender mercies of the Tapuyas, decided to come to terms with the invaders. Shortly after the surprisal of Iguaraçu, the Dutch had issued a manifesto addressed to 'the plantation-owners and *moradores* of Pernambuco', pointing out the hopelessness of their position, and promising them (among other things) liberty of conscience, freedom of property, and a reduction in their taxes if they would submit.[1] This had little effect at the time; but after the capture of Paraíba better terms were offered to the local colonists in January 1635, and these had the desired result. In exchange for taking an oath of loyalty to the new government, the *moradores* were now granted freedom of worship and not merely liberty of conscience, being allowed to retain some priests and friars to administer the church services. Advantageous terms regarding security of property, permission to bear arms, and other concessions being granted at the same time, most of the *moradores* of Paraíba now submitted, and their example was soon followed by those of Rio Grande and Goiana.[2]

The steadily deteriorating position of the defenders of Pernambuco was reflected in Mathias de Albuquerque's repeated appeals for help; but although (contrary to what is often asserted) the authorities at Madrid and Lisbon were well aware of his critical situation, there was little they could do about it. Brazil was not the only headache for Olivares and his advisers. The progress of the Swedish armies in Germany, the loss in a West-Indian hurricane of the richest silver-fleet which ever left Mexico (November 1631), the defeat and death of Constantino de Sá in Ceylon, and three successive years of drought and famine in Portugal (1630–2), were but a few of the disasters suffered by the vassals and allies of the Most Catholic King. It was not only from Pernambuco that urgent appeals for help came, but from the West Indies, from India, from Flanders, from Italy, and from Germany. It was these manifold commitments on other fronts, and not Spanish indifference or lethargy, which prevented adequate help from being sent to Pernambuco for so long.

---

[1] This manifesto (in Dutch translation) is printed in De Laet-Naber, *Iaerlyck Verhael*, iii. 101–4. On this occasion the Dutch granted only liberty of conscience, and not, as Edmundson wrongly states (*English Historical Review*, xv. 36), liberty of worship.

[2] The terms granted to the *moradores* of Paraíba are printed in De Laet-Naber, *Iaerlyck Verhael*, iv. 132–4.

The official correspondence between the authorities at Lisbon and Madrid clearly reveals the difficulties with which they had to contend. In December 1631 the king wrote to Portugal, stressing the contributions which the crown of Castile had made, was making, and would continue to make in ships, men, and money for Brazil, deploring the fact that the Portuguese were still hopelessly in arrears with their quotas. The king announced his intention of dispatching Don Fadrique de Toledo with an armada composed of whatever warships were available, and ordered the Portuguese to prepare an armada of twenty galleons by Midsummer Day 1632 at the latest. He left it to the Portuguese to decide how they could best find the money, but find it they must.[1]

Nothing came of this grandiose scheme. In April 1632 Don Fadrique de Toledo reported that the men of Oquendo's armada were still unpaid after all their sufferings and sacrifices since their mobilization in 1629. At the time of writing he could not even find them their daily rations. The governor of Portugal, Dom Antonio de Ataide, Conde de Castro-Daire, reported that there was not a *maravedí* in the royal treasury for him to pay these starving sailors[2]—let alone find and equip twenty galleons. Being unable to fit out another high-seas fleet, the crown then ordered that 1,400 men should be sent to Pernambuco in caravel-transports at the rate of at least two caravels a month. Even this modest programme was not fulfilled at Lisbon, and on 24 June 1633 the king wrote again in a mixture of anger and despair seldom found in official documents. He pointed out (correctly enough) that none of the leading gentry in Portugal had volunteered for service in Pernambuco—in striking contrast to the enthusiasm with which they had enlisted in 1624 for the recovery of Bahia. He now ordered that henceforth no promotions or rewards for services rendered would be made or even considered unless those services had been rendered either in India or in Pernambuco. If any *fidalgo* was excepted from this rule, it would only be on payment of a lump sum of 1,000 cruzados to provide for a substitute (or substitutes) in those theatres of war. The crown also promulgated various other

[1] *Carta-Régia* of 1 Dec. 1631, in Andrade e Silva, *Collecção chronologica, 1627–1633*, pp. 231–2; Freire de Oliveira, *Elementos*, iii. 471–3.

[2] Original correspondence between D. Fadrique de Toledo and D. Antonio de Ataide in April 1632, preserved in the Codex Castel Melhor, I–1–2, no. 45, Biblioteca Nacional, Rio de Janeiro.

edicts for raising more money and collecting the arrears of contributions which still remained unpaid in whole or in part. On 16 September 1633 the crown again circularized all the local-government organs in Portugal, bitterly complaining of their backwardness in contributing to the cost of equipping a powerful fleet 'which is the one and only remedy for the preservation of the conquests'. Neither these nor many other appeals produced better results than previously, and the Portuguese countered with protestations of extreme poverty and consequent inability to pay what was demanded of them.[1]

The war of exhaustion in north-east Brazil was therefore being slowly but surely won by the Dutch. Apart from the submission of the *moradores* of Paraíba, Goiana, and Rio Grande, they had other encouragements to persevere with their policy of 'frightfulness' in ravaging the sugar-plantations, coupled with offers of generous treatment to the colonists who surrendered. They knew all about the state of affairs in the *arraial* from intercepted letters, which also informed them that many of the planters disliked the Albuquerques' rule, while some of the soldiers were suspicious of Bagnuoli. Deserters provided another, if usually less reliable, source of information, but these did not go in one direction only. Catholic soldiers in the Company's service sometimes came over to the Portuguese, and at one time both sides were scattering leaflets written in English and French to seduce men of these nationalities in the opposite camp. Some of these men changed sides more than once, and Albuquerque hung an English deserter who was captured for the second time.

The Dutch grant of freedom of worship to the submissive *moradores* of Paraíba provoked a counter-move by the bishop of Brazil at Bahia. Apparently at the request of Mathias de Albuquerque, he ordered the withdrawal to Portuguese territory of all Roman Catholic clergy who had taken advantage of the Dutch offer to remain with their flocks in occupied districts. When the episcopal decision was referred to the authorities at Lisbon for confirmation, the Board of Conscience and Orders (*Mesa de Consciencia e Ordens*), which acted, as its title implies, as the keeper of the crown's conscience, strongly condemned the Bishop's action.

[1] Andrade e Silva, *Collecção chronologica, 1627–1633*, pp. 361–6, 369; Freire de Oliveira, *Elementos*, iv. 2–4, 63–65; Varnhagen, *História das Lutas* (Lisbon, 1872), pp. 97–106.

The Board considered that the *moradores*, if deprived of their spiritual pastors, would take this as a tacit admission that the home government despaired of reconquering the lost territory, and they would thus more readily submit to the Dutch. In point of fact, although the Board naturally did not know it, the exact reverse had happened at Paraíba. De Laet tells us that after the surrender of Cabedello, two monks who were in the fort strongly advised the Dutch to ship away the garrison to the West Indies, assuring them that they would then find the *moradores* much easier to handle and readier to co-operate. The Board reminded the king of the vast sums spent on subsidizing Roman Catholic missions in heretic and heathen countries, pointing out that priests in the occupied districts could work, if necessary, in disguise. Reasons of Church and State alike demanded that 'far from withdrawing those that are there, new ministers of the Church should be sent to them. If these suffer hunger, thirst and other hardships, there are none nor could be none in which they would be better employed, and which are more in their line of duty . . . forasmuch as much greater perils and hardships are endured by the missionaries in China and Japan for the sake of increasing the Faith.' The crown cordially agreed with this spirited exhortation to martyrdom by the Lisbon bureaucrats, and the parish priests were ordered to stay at their posts in occupied territory.[1]

The Dutch offer of toleration did not extend to the Jesuits, whom they declined to admit on any terms. The Society of Jesus was anathema to Protestants in general and to the Calvinists in particular. Moreover, those doughty representatives of the Church Militant had given the Dutch particular trouble in Brazil by leading, or at least encouraging, the Amerindians of their *aldeias* to fight against the heretic invaders. While tolerating, at any rate from 1635 onwards, the presence of secular parish priests, and even Franciscan friars and Benedictine monks on occasion, the Dutch deported all the Jesuits on whom they could lay their hands. This differentiation was likewise reflected in the attitude of the Roman Catholic clergy. Many of the parish priests, friars, and monks stayed with their flocks in occupied territory; and there were some, like Fr. Manuel

---

[1] 'Consulta da Mesa de Consciencia e Ordens', 5 Sept. 1635, and *Carta-Régia* of 17 Oct. 1635, in Andrade e Silva, *Collecção chronologica, 1634–1640*, pp. 66–67. For the collaborating monks of Paraíba see De Laet-Naber, *Iaerlyck Verhael*, iv. 84.

Calado, who actively collaborated with the invaders. The Jesuits, on the other hand, decided that the lesser of the two evils would be to avoid compromising themselves under any circumstances. Their Provincial ordered the evacuation of all members of the Society from occupied territory in May 1635, and this attitude they maintained even when the crown reversed the Bishop of Brazil's original order that all of the Roman Catholic clergy should leave.[1]

There are, of course, exceptions to every rule, and even the Jesuits fell from grace occasionally. When they did, as is usually the case with people of very high standards, great was the fall thereof. In Brazil the classic example was the notorious Padre Manuel de Moraes. A native of São Paulo, son of a Portuguese father and a Paulista mother, he had taken the three ordinary vows of the Society, and was an ordained priest in charge of some of the Amerindian mission villages when the Dutch invaded Pernambuco. For nearly four years he led his flock against the heretic invaders, distinguishing himself in many guerrilla skirmishes. All the more surprising was it, therefore, when in January 1635 he voluntarily surrendered to the Dutch at Paraíba. Having gone this far, he evidently decided to go the whole hog. Numerous witnesses subsequently testified that he actively helped the heretics in many ways against his compatriots, apart from associating freely with Calvinists, attending their services, and eating meat during Lent, &c. Fr. Manuel do Salvador, admittedly no friend of the Society of Jesus, went so far as to imply that the renegade Jesuit's assistance to the Dutch was more valuable to them than that of Calabar. This was an exaggeration, but it is quite certain that he gave them much valuable information about the country and the people.[2]

In March 1635 the Dutch attacked Porto Calvo at the instigation of Calabar, who was a native of that district, and also because they were informed that many of the *moradores* would welcome their arrival. Bagnuoli, who commanded the

---

[1] Letter of the Padre Provincial Domingos Coelho, S.J., to Mathias de Albuquerque, dated Bahia, 14 May 1635, in *Anais da Academia Portuguesa de História*, vii. 127–8. Cf. also S. Leite, S.J., *História da Companhia de Jesus no Brasil*, v. 371–3, 375–6, 379 n.

[2] De Laet-Naber, *Iaerlyck Verhael*, iv. 128–31, and the evidence of the witnesses in the proceedings of the Inquisition against Manuel de Moraes, printed in the *Revista do Instituto Histórico e Geográphico Brasileiro*, hereafter referred to as *RIHGB*, lxx (1907), parte i, pp. 1–165. Cf. also S. Leite, S.J., *História*, vi. 363–9, 581–2, and Appendix I, pp. 267–9, below.

defenders of that region, was routed after offering only a feeble resistance and fled southwards to the Alagoas. The Dutch made great efforts to win over the local *moradores*, granting them even better terms than those given to the inhabitants of Paraíba; and thanks to the ready co-operation of Fr. Manuel do Salvador, their overtures met with a favourable response. According to the friar's own account, the Dutch commander, Admiral Licht-hart, had lived some time in Lisbon and spoke good Portuguese. Calado also alleges that the admiral declared that he was a crypto-Catholic. This assertion cannot be credited, but it is clear that Lichthart went out of his way to conciliate the local *moradores*, summarily executing three soldiers who had stolen an ox.[1]

It was now the turn of the *arraial*, which was closely invested by Arciszewski and capitulated on 8 June after a siege of three months, endured with great fortitude by the starving defenders. By the terms of surrender, the garrison was embarked for the West Indies; but the *moradores* in the camp were forced to ransom themselves for a large sum of money before being allowed to go their several ways. According to Arciszewski this ransom money was not distributed among the Dutch soldiers, as was ostensibly intended, but divided between the civilian councillor Stachouwer and his cronies. The Pole also accused Stachouwer of embezzling the treasure belonging to a wealthy Portuguese Jew named Pantaleão Monteiro. The latter had buried this hoard in the bush, but the cache was given away by his secretary, a Madeira-born Mulatto named João Fernandes Vieira, of whom we shall hear much more. Impressed by this man's unscrupulous ability, Stachouwer employed him as his confidential clerk.[2] The two soon made their fortunes by combining Fernandes Vieira's knowledge of local conditions with Stachouwer's authority to exploit it.

The fall of the *arraial* was followed nearly a month later by that of Fort Nazaré at Cabo de Santo Agostinho, whose garrison capitulated on similar terms after repulsing several assaults. The *várzea* was at last firmly in Dutch hands, and there was

---

[1] Fr. Manuel Calado, *Valeroso Lucideno*, pp. 18–19. Cf. De Laet-Naber, *Iaerlyck Verhael*, iv. 150–7.

[2] De Laet-Naber, *Iaerlyck Verhael*, iv. 142–50; 'Memorie door den Kolonnel Artichofsky bij zijn vertrek uit Brazilië in 1637 overgeleverd etc.', in *Kroniek van het Historisch Genootschap Utrecht*, xxv. 253–349, especially pp. 330–5; *RIHGB*, lxxv. pt. ii (1912–13), pp. 37–38.

a great rush to buy derelict sugar-plantations by speculators who hoped to make their fortunes when the mills could be got working again. Many of the local *moradores* now submitted, but many others followed Mathias de Albuquerque to the south, the total number of emigrants in this exodus being reckoned at over 7,000 persons of both sexes and of all ages, races, and colours. The Portuguese commander had stayed at Serinhaem for as long as the *arraial* and Nazaré held out, although he was not able to do much to help the besieged, since Von Schoppe was masking him with a larger force.

His position was now untenable, and he had no option but to retreat to the swampy region known as Alagoas in the southernmost limits of the captaincy of Pernambuco. The only track practicable for ox-carts led through Porto Calvo, which was held by some 500 men under Major Picard and Calabar, so Albuquerque had perforce to attack this place. Thanks to the treachery of a local *morador* named Sebastião do Souto, who was implicitly trusted by the Dutch and who reported all their moves to Albuquerque, the latter was able to storm a key-position in the defences, thus compelling Picard to ask for terms. The latter made some efforts (strenuous according to his own account, but half-hearted according to that of Fr. Manuel do Salvador) to secure a categorical assurance that Calabar's life would be spared, but Albuquerque would only promise that the Mulatto would 'remain at the disposal of the king' (*ficar à mercê del Rey*). This proved to be a short shrift. A summary court martial decided that Albuquerque in his capacity as commander-in-chief represented the person of the king, and Calabar was thereupon sentenced to be garrotted, drawn, and quartered as a traitor. This sentence was carried out at dusk on 22 July, and a few hours later the Portuguese evacuated the town and continued their retreat southwards, taking with them some 300 Dutch prisoners.

When the combined forces of Von Schoppe and Arciszewski reoccupied Porto Calvo on 24 July they were infuriated to find Calabar's quarters impaled on the fortifications. After giving these mangled remains a funeral with full military honours, their first reaction was to take summary vengeance on the remaining *moradores*. From this they were dissuaded by the ubiquitous Fr. Manuel do Salvador, who convinced them that a generous policy of forgiveness would conciliate the local inhabitants and so redound to their own interests in the long run. In addition to being on friendly terms with Lichthart, the friar also got on very well with Arciszewski, whom he regarded as a 'very good Latinist, who spoke Latin very discreetly and eloquently'. The Polish colonel returned the compliment by reporting that Fr. Manuel 'seems to be a rather intelligent politico and a polite man, also one who is well affected towards us'. This induced him to believe a pack of lies that the Portuguese friar told him about the existence of rich silver-mines in the interior.[1]

Socorro de España ó llega tarde ó nunca. 'Help from Spain comes late or never' says the Spanish proverb, which was once more verified in the present instance. Admittedly, there were strong reasons for the delay in mobilizing the 'Grand Armada for the Restoration of Brazil' which the government at Madrid had been trying to assemble in the Tagus ever since May 1630. The victory of Nördlingen gained by the Spaniards and Imperialists over the Swedes and Protestant Germans in September 1634, which threatened to restore Spanish preponderance in Europe, induced Richelieu to bring France into the war against Spain in February of the following year. The Spaniards henceforth had to fight on two fronts in Flanders, and to contend with the French fleets in the Atlantic and Mediterranean as well as with those of the Dutch on the seven seas. As noted previously, Don Fadrique de Toledo had been designated as the commander-in-chief of the projected expedition after Oquendo's return. This was a wise choice, in view of his triumph in 1625, and his popularity in Portugal through allowing Dutch ships to bring corn to Lisbon during the famine years of 1631–2. Finding that neither men nor ships were forthcoming on what he considered an adequate scale—he asked for an expeditionary corps of 12,000 men—he declined to assume the command. He was promptly disgraced by Olivares, who was in any event jealous of his superior abilities, and thrown into prison where he died.[2]

[1] Fr. Manuel do Salvador, *Valeroso Lucideno*, pp. 19–25; De Laet-Naber, *Iaerlyck Verhael*, iv. 161–72; Duarte de Albuquerque, *Memorias Diarias*, 25 June–23 July 1635; *Kron. Hist. Gen. Utrecht*, xxv. 343–4.
[2] 'Cartas de algunos PP. de la Compañía de Jesús sobre los sucesos de la Monarquía entre los años de 1634 y 1648', in *Memorial Histórico Español*, xiii (Madrid, 1861), pp. 79–81, 105–6, 108, 110, 114–15; Antonio Rodriguez Villa, *La Corte y Monarquía de España en los años de 1636 y 1637* (Madrid, 1886), pp. 82–83,

Command of the reinforcements for Brazil was eventually given to Don Luis de Rojas y Borgia, a veteran of the wars in Flanders who had recently been governor of Panamá. He left the Tagus in September 1625, in an armada commanded by Don Lope de Hoces y Córdoba, consisting of thirty sail including transports. These ships carried a total of 2,500 soldiers between Spaniards, Portuguese, and Italians for Pernambuco, and a new governor-general, Pedro da Silva, to relieve Diogo Luis de Oliveira after his ten-year tenure at Bahia. This armada appeared off Recife on 26 November, at a most unexpected and awkward moment for the Dutch, since most of their men and ships were away in the south. Had De Hoces and Rojas risked an attack on Recife, as some of their officers urged them to do, they might well have succeeded, since the neighbouring *moradores* were ready to revolt the moment that the Iberian soldiers landed. The Spanish commanders decided not to take the risk, greatly to the relief of the Dutch, and sailed down the coast to disembark their men at Jaraguá in Alagoas. Having landed Rojas with his men, Don Lope de Hoces then went on to Bahia, where he landed the new governor-general, returning to Lisbon with the sugar-fleet in the following year.

Don Luis de Rojas now took over the command from Mathias de Albuquerque, who retired to Bahia before embarking for Portugal. Although neither he nor his brother was popular with many of the *moradores*, his departure was sincerely regretted by most of his compatriots. He was not a great commander, but he had done a good job in singularly difficult and dis-couraging circumstances. Nothing is more demoralizing for even the best-trained troops than a continuous retreat or a series of withdrawals in the face of a more powerful enemy who scores one success after another. This was essentially Mathias de Albuquerque's situation ever since the loss of Paraíba in January 1635, and his force of Iberian and Italian soldiers, Amerindian and Negro auxiliaries, Portuguese and Brazilian colonists was not an easy one to control under any circum-stances. It speaks highly for his soldierly qualities that he could always get his men to face the enemy again after each

115, 124, 175; Andrade e Silva, *Collecção chronologica, 1627–1633*, pp. 251, 258–306, 314, 361–9; ibid., *1634–1640*, pp. 40, 51, 63, 64; Freire de Oliveira, *Elementos*, iii. 469–81, 527–9, 563, 571–6, 580–2; ibid. iv. 2–4, 63–65, 66–70, 75–85, 107–10, 116, 135; C. Fernández Duro, *Armada Española*, iv. 128–9, 141–3.

successive reverse, and that after the loss of the *arraial* and Nazaré he could win such a decided victory at Porto Calvo.

Contrary to the advice of the cautious (or cowardly) Bagnuoli, Don Luis de Rojas lost no time in assuming the offensive. Early in January 1636 he advanced on Porto Calvo with a column of 2,600 men, including Amerindian auxiliaries, leaving the Italian general at Santa Luzia with the remainder. Von Schoppe evacuated Porto Calvo at his approach, Don Luis reoccupying the town with a garrison of 1,000 men before continuing his advance. Arciszewski, who was not aware of his superior's withdrawal, moved from his position at Peripueira, and blundered into the advancing Spaniards on the night of 17 January. Battle was joined next day at the Mata Redonda, the short but sharp action which ensued ending with the defeat and death of Don Luis de Rojas and the precipitate flight of his troops. Arciszewski did not follow up his victory, as he was short of supplies and encumbered with too many wounded, so the result was of greater moral importance than anything else. 'The sun again shone rather brighter', as the Pole himself put it; but even after he had joined forces with Von Schoppe, the Dutch commanders did not feel strong enough to attack Porto Calvo, or even to hold the Barra Grande, and so they fell back upon Serinhaem.[1]

Both sides remained inactive for the next three months, and although Arciszewski kept on urging an expedition against Porto Calvo, it was the Portuguese who first took the offensive in mid-April. Bagnuoli, who had assumed command after the death of Rojas, did not venture to challenge Von Schoppe and Arciszewski in the open field, but he renewed and intensified the guerrilla warfare which had been so successful in the previous years. Flying columns and strong fighting patrols under the leadership of veteran guerrilla leaders such as the Portuguese Francisco Rebelo (nicknamed Rebelinho on account of his small size), the Indian Felipe Camarão, and the Negro Henrique Dias ravaged the occupied territory far and wide, even venturing as far north as Paraíba. The Dutch were occasionally able to catch their enemy unawares, as when Rebelinho was surprised

---

[1] For the expedition of Don Luis de Rojas and the battle of the Mata Redonda, cf. Fr. Manuel do Salvador, *Valeroso Lucideno*, pp. 26–34; Duarte de Albuquerque, *Memorias Diarias*, 20 Oct. 1635–19 Jan. 1636; De Laet-Naber, *Iaerlyck Verhael*, iv. 176–81, 207–21; *Kron. Hist. Gen. Utrecht*, xxv. 274–5; Fernández Duro, *Armada Española*, iv. 129–31.

and routed by Stachouwer on 23 April, and Camarão by Arciszewski on 21 August, but as a rule the guerrillas were far too elusive for their slower-moving opponents.

The Dutch had made great progress in bush-fighting during the last five years, but they still could not compete on level terms with men who had been born and bred in a tropical country. The Dutch casualty-rate from disease was much higher, and they needed much better and more varied provisions than their spartan opponents. Even such an old campaigner as Arciszewski complained that he did not feel fit without a daily ration of wine,[1] which was difficult to get in the Brazilian bush. The enemy, on the other hand, could subsist on a handful of *farinha* (manioc flour) and a little water. Both sides used Amerindians as scouts and guides; but the guerrilla leaders could usually count on getting much better co-operation and intelligence from the *moradores* than could the Dutch. The guerrillas had another great advantage in the use they made of Negro slaves as carriers of munitions and supplies. They were thus able to move farther and faster than the Dutch, whose radius of action was limited by the fact that their soldiers could only carry eight days' rations in their knapsacks. Arciszewski severely criticized the civilian councillors at Recife for selling the hundreds of Negroes captured in Portuguese slave-ships voyaging from Angola to Brazil, instead of using them as carriers for the Dutch punitive columns.

The worst sufferers in this bitter guerrilla warfare were the luckless *moradores*. They were liable to be treated as traitors by both sides if they tried to remain neutral; whereas if they remained faithful to one side they exposed themselves to savage reprisals at the hands of the other. At first the guerrillas only attacked Dutch-occupied sugar-plantations, but they soon spread their scorched-earth tactics more widely, sacking and burning the properties of anyone whom they suspected of having dealings with the invaders whether under compulsion or not. Many of the *moradores* now trekked southwards through the bush to join their compatriots with Bagnuoli in Porto Calvo and Alagoas. Those who remained behind suffered increasingly from this war of reprisals which was conducted (as Fr. Rafael de Jesus

---

[1] '. . . den mage sonder wijn sijnde (sulcx tractement ongewent), helpt oock niet weynich daertoe', Arciszewski wrote to the Heeren XIX on 4 Nov. 1635 (De Laet-Naber, *Iaerlyck Verhael*, iv, p. xlii). Cf. also Arciszewski's 'Memorie' of Mar. 1637, in *Kron. Hist. Gen. Utrecht*, xxv, especially pp. 278–311, 315–17, 325–6 for the hardships of campaigning in Brazil.

wrote in his *Castrioto Lusitano*) 'as if each side aspired to be lord of a desert empire'.

Colonel Arciszewski repeatedly pointed out to his superiors that the efforts of the heavily equipped Dutch soldiers to corner and destroy their far more mobile guerrilla opponents were virtually hopeless. He urged that the only way to stop these damaging raids was to reoccupy Porto Calvo and to drive the enemy south of the river São Francisco. His proposal was ostensibly accepted by the councillors at Recife, but excuses were always found for postponing the projected expedition. Lack of sufficient stores and supplies was the usual reason advanced; but Arciszewski, who made a thorough inspection of the magazines at Recife in July 1636, considered that this excuse was inadequate. He found sufficient stocks of most things on hand, and stated that a few provisions which were lacking could be replaced by others which were available in the country. He estimated that there was a total ration-strength of 10,000 men and a fleet of forty-seven ships, but many ships and soldiers were being diverted from purely naval and military duties to mercantile and commercial activities.[1]

The main trouble, however, was divided control and the lack of a co-ordinating head at the seat of government in Recife, for Von Schoppe's title of governor was purely nominal. One of the five civilian commissioners of the political council always accompanied the forces in the field to assert the principle of civilian control. Another supervised the sugar export trade and the provision of supplies to the troops, usually concentrating on the former to the detriment of the latter. The other three councillors supervised the administration of different regions in the captured captaincies; one of them, Ippo Eyssens, governor of Paraíba, being killed by Rebelinho's men in a guerrilla raid on 14 October.[2] These councillors were therefore very busy, and could only occasionally meet for joint deliberation at Recife. As Arciszewski wrote, when anything was suggested, 'there were ten conferences and twenty exchanges of letters', and in the end usually nothing was done. He had clamoured for the appointment of a supreme governor with extensive powers ever since

---

[1] Arciszewski's 'Memorie' of Mar. 1637, in *Kron. Hist. Gen. Utrecht*, xxv. 280–4, 313–19.

[2] De Laet-Naber, *Iaerlyck Verhael*, iv. 248–9; *Kron. Hist. Gen. Utrecht*, xxv. 296–7, 328, 338.

1631, and recent events had brought many people round to his way of thinking, including Von Schoppe and the civilian commissioners themselves.

The Heeren XIX had other reasons besides those advanced by Arciszewski for deciding to make a drastic change in the government of their Brazilian colony, or New Holland as it was officially called. Although the war was now going favourably for the Dutch on land as well as at sea, the financial position of the West India Company was bad. Between 1623 and 1636 their 806 sail had taken 547 Iberian ships valued at nearly 7 million florins, and booty worth over 30 million florins. But the cost of the fleets, troops, and supplies which they had to maintain during the same period totalled over 45 million florins, quite apart from the occupation costs. These last surpassed the income derived from the sale of sugar, Brazil-wood, and other colonial products, although the receipts from these sales were by no means inconsiderable. The fact remained that the Company was now indebted to the tune of some 18 million florins, and that the annual subsidies due from the provincial governments were falling increasingly into arrears.[1]

The directors realized that if their war-torn colony was to be consolidated and made to pay its way, the control of its affairs must be entrusted to a governor-general with powers somewhat similar to those of the man who directed the Dutch East India Company's operations so successfully from his headquarters at Batavia. We do not know how many people the Heeren XIX considered in this connexion before they made their final choice; but we do know that after consultation with the States-General and the stadtholder, their choice fell on Johan Maurits, count of Nassau-Siegen.

[1] De Laet-Naber, *Iaerlyck Verhael*, iv. 280–97; Netscher, *Les Hollandais au Brésil*, pp. 80–82.

III

THE CONQUESTS OF JOHAN MAURITS

1637–41

WHATEVER the reasons which influenced the Heeren XIX in their choice of Johan Maurits as their first (and as it proved their last) governor-general in Brazil, subsequent events showed that they could hardly have made a better selection. It is true that he had no colonial experience, but he was a scion of one of the most famous families of Europe, and had received as sound an education as the troubled times afforded and his early initiation into a military career allowed. His father 'Jan de Middelste', so called to distinguish him from his own father and eldest son of the same name, was the prolific count of Nassau-Siegen (1561–1623), a zealously Calvinistic nobleman who had twenty-three children by his two wives. Johan Maurits was Jan de Middelste's eldest son by his second wife, Margaretha, princess of Holstein-Sonderburg (1583–1638). His paternal grandfather, Jan de Oudste (1536–1606), was the elder brother of William the Silent, and head of that branch of the Nassau family whose seat was the picturesque castle of Dillenburg, where Johan Maurits was born on 17 June 1604.[1]

The boy went to school successively at Herborn, Basle, and Geneva, where he evidently showed a greater aptitude for humanistic learning than for the dry husks of Calvinist theology, although he remained a convinced Protestant all his life. His studies were interrupted by the outbreak of the Thirty Years War, when he was sent to join his uncle, Willem Lodewyck, the stadtholder of Friesland. Two years later he volunteered for

---

[1] Of the various biographies of Johan Maurits of Nassau-Siegen (1604–79) the two best are probably the earliest and the most recent: L. Driessen, *Leben des fürsten Johann Moritz von Nassau-Siegen* (Berlin, 1849), and D. J. Bouman, *Johan Maurits van Nassau, de Braziliaan* (Utrecht, 1947). For others cf. J. H. Rodrigues, *Historiografia e Bibliografia*, pp. 431–4. Wätjen is also very illuminating on Johan Maurits's governorship of Brazil in *Das holländische Kolonialreich in Brasilien*, *passim*.

service in the States-General's army and fought in many subsequent summer campaigns with increasing distinction. He
passed the winters in the cultivated and cosmopolitan court of
the stadtholder Frederik Hendrik at The Hague, where his
strongly developed aesthetic sense was further stimulated by
close contact with artists, poets, and men of letters. He spoke
Dutch, French, and German with equal facility, and could carry
on a conversation in Latin.

His military career gave him several opportunities of distinguishing himself, and his successive promotions owed as much to
his own merits in the field as to his family and courtly connexions.
He took a prominent part in the siege of Den Bosch in 1629, and
at the capture of Maastricht in 1632, when he repulsed a determined attempt by Pappenheim to relieve the beleaguered stronghold. The recapture of Schenckenshans in April 1636, after a
long and arduous siege, was principally his work and gave him a
European reputation. He was now in the prime of life, the pos-
sessor of an exceptionally fine physique and of a jovial disposition
which made him popular with all classes of society. We do not
know whether he hesitated to accept the offer of the governor-
generalship of Netherlands Brazil, but the probability is that he
did not. Always a lavish spender, and already a generous patron
of architects and painters, he had begun to build a costly house
and lay out a garden at The Hague which was proving a heavy
drain on his purse. The prospect of a well-paid colonial post with
even more attractive emoluments may have made him jump at
the offer, which in any event he formally accepted in August
1636.

The conditions offered by the West India Company and the
States-General were certainly attractive. The appointment was
to be provisionally for five years, with the title of governor-,
captain-, and admiral-general, or in other words governor and
commander-in-chief of the Company's possessions in Brazil.
Johan Maurits was also to be president of the newly established
'High and Secret Council' (*Hooghen en Secreten Raad*) consisting
of three other members besides himself. These other members
were Van Ceulen and Gijsselingh, who had given such a good
account of themselves in Brazil in 1632–3, and Adriaen van der
Dussen, an able but unscrupulous man who had been discharged
by the East India Company. The high and secret councillors
were to share the supreme executive responsibility with Johan

Maurits; but the latter's predominance was assured by his being given two votes in council, so that even if only one of the other councillors voted with him on any given occasion his views would prevail. He was given the princely salary—for the times— of 1,500 florins a month, together with a lump sum of 6,000 florins for immediate expenses, and table-money for himself and certain members of his suite. The Company was also responsible for paying the salaries of his personal chaplain, physician, and secretary. In addition to all this, Johan Maurits was to retain his rank and pay as a colonel in the States-General's army, and he would further receive 2 per cent of all prize-money in Brazil. The existing political council at Recife was to be reinforced with new members from Holland, but would henceforth function primarily as a court of justice with civil and criminal jurisdiction. Two financial experts from the political council were to assist the governor-general in financial matters with the title of treasurers.[1]

In the first flush of enthusiasm at this 'new deal', the directors talked of sending out Johan Maurits with a fleet of thirty-two sail and an expeditionary force of 7,000 or 8,000 men. This scheme proved to be too costly, and they soon scaled down their estimates to the more modest figures of twelve ships and 2,700 men. The Heeren XIX have often been blamed by historians for their allegedly parsimonious and cheese-paring conduct towards Johan Maurits, but in truth the financial position of the Company left them no option but to shelve their ambitious plans. We saw in the last chapter that the Company was indebted to the tune of over 18 million florins, but this was not the whole story. The province of Holland alone owed the Company nearly a million florins on account of unpaid annual subsidies due for the years 1633–5, and the other provinces were much further in arrears with their respective quotas, some of them having paid nothing at all. With the provincial governments thus defaulting on their obligations, the directors found it not only impossible to equip a fleet of thirty-two sail but even had great difficulty in fitting out the projected twelve.

Tired of waiting for all his ships, Johan Maurits left the Texel with four sail on 25 October 1636, reaching Recife with two of

---

[1] The original instruction for Johan Maurits and the new form of government for Brazil is preserved in the archives at The Hague (WICOC, no. 48) and is summarized by Wätjen, *Holländische Kolonialreich in Brasilien*, pp. 184–6.

them on 23 January 1637.[1] He fell in love with Brazil from the moment he stepped ashore. In his first letter to the directors, written on 3 February 1637, he described the country as '*un de plus beaux du monde*', and he never wavered subsequently in his affection for the tropical New World. He reported that he found the garrison and local affairs '*en estat assez bon*', and that he was resolved to lose no time in dislodging Bagnuoli from his base at Porto Calvo.[2] The chief difficulty was in the adequate provisioning of his force, which comprised some 3,000 white soldiers, 1,000 sailors, and 1,000 friendly Amerindians. The north European races which supplied the bulk of the Company's mercenary troops required far more solid and substantial rations than those which sufficed for men who came from poor and rugged countries such as Portugal and southern Italy, where congenital under-nourishment was accepted as a necessary evil.

The supply difficulty having been surmounted by a mixture of bluff and ingenuity, Johan Maurits marched down the coast with the bulk of his force, the artillery and supplies going by sea to Barra Grande in twenty-four sail under Admiral Lichthart. Bagnuoli was advised to delay the Dutch advance by laying ambushes in the intervening wooded country, but he rejected this advice and preferred to offer a set battle in front of Porto Calvo. When Johan Maurits launched his attack on the morning of 18 February the Italian commander completely lost his head and 'rode up and down on horseback without giving any proper orders', as Fr. Manuel do Salvador (admittedly no friendly eyewitness) avers. Not unnaturally, the defenders soon became demoralized and broke and fled southwards in confusion, losing some 400 men in the process. They were not followed very far, as Johan Maurits recalled his men to invest the fort of Povoação, which capitulated after a fortnight's siege. The Dutch casualties in this fighting were few, but among them was a young nephew of Johan Maurits, who was killed by a cannon-ball on 25 February, when directing the fire of the besieging batteries.[3]

    [1] Barlaeus-Naber, *Nederlandsch Brazilië onder het bewind van Johan Maurits Grave van Nassau, 1637–1644* (The Hague, 1923), pp. 38–41, for a full account of the voyage to Brazil. I have used this work throughout in preference to the original Latin edition of C. Barlaeus, *Rerum per octennium in Brasilia*, &c. (Amsterdam, 1647).
    [2] Johan Maurits's letter of 3 Feb. 1637, printed in full in Netscher, *Les Hollandais au Brésil*, pp. 86–87.
    [3] Barlaeus-Naber, *Nederlandsch Brazilië*, pp. 42–43. For details of the Porto

Johan Maurits now resumed the pursuit of Bagnuoli, but just failed to catch the latter's forces before they crossed the river São Francisco. Fr. Manuel Calado, who clearly disliked the 'pot-bellied' planters, as he repeatedly termed them, maliciously relates how many of them fled southwards with Bagnuoli, their pretty Mulatto mistresses riding pillion behind them while their neglected wives struggled dishevelled and barefoot through swamp and scrub.[1] After sacking the little township of Penedo, Johan Maurits founded a fort there bearing his name, some eighteen miles from the mouth of the river ('as broad as the Maas in Holland at Delfshaven'), where the stream narrowed. The district on the southern bank was laid waste, and the in-habitants ordered to remove themselves and their cattle to the north of the river. Good relations were established with the local Tapuyas, although nobody was found who could understand their language. 'By means of miming and drawing sketches, however, we were able to convey our meaning to each other, and the chief thing was that they should prevent the Portuguese from crossing over from the other side of the river and kill them if they tried to do so. They understood our terrible orders and signified their agreement therewith.'

The whole of the captaincy of Pernambuco was now cleared of the enemy, who had retreated into that of Sergipe, where Johan Maurits did not attempt to follow them. The failure to follow up his success by attacking Bahia is usually ascribed to lack of sufficient supplies and men. In his official report to the prince of Orange, however, Johan Maurits makes no such asser-tion but plainly states that he was fully satisfied with what he had already achieved. He thought that the broad river São Francisco with its depopulated southern margin would form an effective and easily defensible boundary between Portuguese and Netherlands Brazil.[2]

The more Johan Maurits saw of the country the more he liked it. His report to the prince of Orange from Penedo stressed the existing fertility and the alluring potentialities of this part of the colony. 'I do not think that a milder and more temperate climate

Calvo campaign cf. ibid., pp. 43–48; Albuquerque, *Memorias Diarias*, 21 Jan.–31 Mar. 1637; Calado, *Valeroso Lucideno*, pp. 35–41; Varnhagen, *História das Lutas*, pp. 165–70.

[1] Calado, *Valeroso Lucideno*, pp. 39–40.

[2] Lengthy quotations from this dispatch in Barlaeus-Naber, *Nederlandsch Brazilië*, pp. 52–55, whence the extracts in the text are translated.

can be found anywhere. As a rule, the heat of the day on the march is no more severe than the cold at nights, although occasionally we shivered a little. Smooth plains watered by flowing brooks and leisurely rivers extend for over ten miles one after another, and here and there herds of 500, 5,000, or 7,000 cattle can be seen grazing. I was astonished at the sight, and would not have believed it had I not seen it with my own eyes. The soil needs nothing but inhabitants and cries out for colonists to people and till this solitude. I have written to the Heeren XIX to send us here German refugees driven from their fatherland and deprived of their property;[1] they will find a fine country to cultivate and come under a mild rule. I commend the same idea to the sympathetic consideration of Your Excellency, because without colonists these districts will be of no use to the Company, nor will we be able to prevent the enemy's raids. If this project should not succeed, I wish that the Amsterdam workhouses would be opened and the galley-slaves released so that they could here till the soil with the mattock, be diverted from misconduct, and honourably atone for their former disgrace by proving themselves useful and not harmful members of the commonwealth.'

With the advent of the rainy season in April, Johan Maurits returned to Recife, where he found more than enough to occupy him. Barlaeus, who was inordinately fond of classical allusions and comparisons, made the inevitable observation about the state of the Augean stables[2] at Recife and the Herculean task involved in cleansing them, but his cliché was not very wide of the mark. A start had been made by Johan Maurits's three civilian colleagues during his absence in the south, but he continued and expanded their good work. The atmosphere at Recife was that of a boom-and-bust town which attracted swarms of adventurers and shady characters as well as respectable and enterprising traders. The Company's mercenary troops inevitably included rough-and-ready individuals who were apt to run riot when off duty; and many of the local Portuguese inhabitants who had submitted to the invaders were not conspicuous for loyalty and integrity to either side.[3] Barlaeus

---

[1] i.e. during the Thirty Years War.

[2] Barlaeus-Naber, *Nederlandsch Brazilië*, p. 59.

[3] Salvador Correia de Sá e Benavides wrote of the *moradores* who had submitted to the Dutch: 'a gente de Pernambuco não he da mais escolhida deste Reyno e

assures us that the prevailing spirit was that 'there were no sins beyond the Equator', thus anticipating Kipling's aphorism about there being no ten commandments east of Suez. Perhaps the strictures of Calvinist preachers need not be taken too seriously, but Johan Maurits's predecessors had complained that Recife was apparently regarded by the directors as a close-stool for voiding the dregs of Dutch society.[1] Moreover, although the West India Company paid its employees better (generally speaking) than did the East India Company, yet the salaries of the junior grades were totally insufficient. Apart from anything else, houses at Recife cost from 5,000 to 14,000 florins, and rents were six times as high as those at Amsterdam, while the monthly pay of an ordinary employee was only about sixty florins. Bribery and corruption were therefore not only inevitable but widespread, although this was nothing new in the colonial world. Similar conditions prevailed, *mutatis mutandis*, at Goa, Batavia, Havana, or Bombay.

Johan Maurits soon made his presence felt, and by all accounts he effected a notable improvement in a remarkably short space of time.[2] Discipline was restored and drastically enforced, some of the worst offenders being shipped back to Holland. Regional magistrates and bailiffs were appointed to deal summarily with petty crimes, and the administration of justice was overhauled and improved. The local Portuguese were subjected to Roman-Dutch law, but were guaranteed equal rights under this law with the subjects of the United Provinces, and were taxed at the same rates as they. All those *moradores* who took the oath of allegiance to the Company's rule were allowed to wear sidearms as a protection against bandits. They were further allowed to reoccupy their land and to rebuild their houses in dismantled Olinda, although this concession was later revoked. Johan Maurits formally assured the *moradores* that their welfare was his chief

ainda dessa se retirou a melhor no tempo da guerra e a que ficou com os olandezes hé amiga de novidades' (*Parecer* of 17 Feb. 1647, in *RIHGB*, lxxv, pt. ii [1912–13], p. 48). Cf. also Arciszewski's observations quoted on p. 75, below.

[1] Political Council to the Chamber of Zeeland, 20 Dec. 1635, in Wätjen, *Holländische Kolonialreich in Brasilien*, p. 250. For details concerning the cosmopolitan population of Recife at this period and its reactions to the Brazilian environment, see J. A. Gonsalves de Mello, *Tempo dos Flamengos*, pp. 56–59, 64, 144–9.

[2] A detailed (and over-optimistic) description of Johan Maurits's reforms is given in Barlaeus-Naber, *Nederlandsch Brazilië*, pp. 58–64, whence the following account is summarized.

concern, and promised them that his council would devote two days a week to hearing their petitions for justice. Food-rationing was enforced upon all the Company's civil and military employees, and although this move was most unpopular it did make for fairer distribution. All derelict sugar-mills were declared forfeited to the Company and were sold at auction to the highest bidders, long-term payments being arranged in sugar or cash. The receipts on paper from these sales totalled over two million florins, but many purchasers defaulted on their payments and most of this sum was still outstanding when the revolt broke out in 1645.[1] Nevertheless, a great fillip was given to business in this way, and the sugar industry was put firmly on its feet in the years 1637–9. The fortifications were thoroughly inspected, all surplus works being demolished and the others strengthened and improved.

Exceptionally tolerant for his day and generation, Johan Maurits allowed both Roman Catholics and Jews freedom not only of conscience but of worship, despite the opposition of the *predikants* and other Calvinist zealots. He did not, indeed, allow the *moradores* to receive a delegate of the bishop of Bahia, but he allowed some French Capuchin friars to enter the colony, and Roman Catholic church services and religious processions were explicitly permitted. This enlightened attitude contrasts strongly with the short-sighted intolerance displayed by the States-General to the Roman Catholic inhabitants of Den Bosch and the Meierij after their surrender in 1629, and it went a long way towards conciliating the local Portuguese. It may be added that the French friars were most scathing in their denunciation of the ignorance and corruption of the local friars and clergy; but they admitted that this did not seem to undermine the ardent Catholicism of the *moradores*.[2]

Johan Maurits showed an unusual flair for dealing with the Amerindians, whose trust he set out to win and whose loyalty he was remarkably successful in retaining. Nor was he unmindful of the lowest but most essential class of all, the Negro slaves, on

---

[1] For the sums nominally paid for each *engenho* in 1637, and the amounts still outstanding in later years, cf. the documents edited (in Portuguese translation) in *RIAGP*, no. 34 (1887), pp. 197–8, and J. A. Gonsalves de Mello, edition of Adriaen van der Dussen, *Relatório sobre as capitanias conquistadas no Brasil pelos Holandeses* (Rio de Janeiro, 1947), pp. 157–63.

[2] Letter of Fr. Colombe de Nantes, O.F.M.Cap., 25 Aug. 1643, in *Brasilia*, ix. 89.

whom, in the last analysis, the welfare of the colony depended. In reply to representations by the planters, he consented that fugitive slaves who had deserted their masters *after* the latter had made their submission to the Dutch, would be handed back to their former owners if they were apprehended; but he flatly declined to return those who had deserted to the Dutch earlier and helped them in their campaigns.

All these varied measures, and still more his obvious determination to see justice done to all sorts and conditions of men, produced an excellent effect. Barlaeus indeed exaggerated when he wrote that Johan Maurits 'through the melting together of several races, Netherlanders, Portuguese and Brazilian, made as it were a homogeneous nation, and laid firm foundations for the flourishing of a rising community'. Things had not progressed quite that far even by the time Johan Maurits left the colony seven years later. But there is no doubt that he was working on the right lines; and if his policy of mutual tolerance and respect for the rights of all races and classes had been continued and developed unhindered, it might eventually have had more lasting results. Arciszewski, who left for Holland at the end of March 1637, sent Johan Maurits a lengthy *aide-mémoire*, in which he wrote: 'We have certainly found the Portuguese nation to be of a hard, treacherous and obstinate character, but likewise we gave them no small reason to behave like this'.[1] If Johan Maurits achieved nothing else, he could at least boast that he had done his best to remove this reproach, and given victors and vanquished the chance of mingling on equal terms.

One of Maurits's major preoccupations at this time, and one of the principal reasons for the boom-and-bust atmosphere of Recife, was the struggle between the advocates of free-trade and the upholders of the West India Company's monopoly. This monopoly had been breached on 16 October 1630, when the trade to Olinda and Recife was provisionally thrown open to all inhabitants of the United Provinces, and also to all the inhabitants of Brazil who would submit to Dutch rule; on condition that all traders used only Company's ships to carry their cargoes, and paid freight, convoy-tax, and other dues to the Company. Intending emigrants were promised a free passage with all

---

[1] 'Missive van den Kolonnel Artichofsky aan graaf Maurits en den hoogen raad in Brazil, Amsterdam, 24 Juli, 1637', *Kron. Hist. Gen. Utrecht*, xxv. 222–48, whence the quotations in the text are taken.

found to Brazil, where they would be granted suitable lands on favourable terms. An emphatic assurance was given that nobody would be interfered with on account of his (or her) religion, provided that no public scandal or provocation was given by word or deed. Shareholders in the West India Company were granted certain preferential trading terms, such as a reduction of 5 per cent. on the freight rates, as compared with those traders who were not.[1]

Despite these tempting conditions, relatively few private traders engaged in the Brazil trade for the first four years after the capture of Olinda, since the savage guerrilla warfare round Recife afforded no scope for peaceful commerce. With the capture of Paraíba and the clearing of the *várzea*, the outlook improved. The Company's revised declaration promising a limited form of free-trade, which was promulgated on 9 January 1634, eventually met with a better response. The chief difference between the edicts of 1630 and 1634 was that under the new arrangement the export of provisions and munitions to Brazil was reserved to the Company, as was also the dyewood monopoly. Intending emigrants were now expected to pay for their own food and drink on board ship, although they were still given free passage-room. On the other hand, the freight rates from Brazil were substantially lowered, and the guarantee of religious toleration was repeated.[2] Arciszewski noted that just before the promulgation of this last edict, nobody would pay 2,000 florins for the best house in Recife, whereas a few months later a good house could not be bought for ten times that sum. The feverish boom atmosphere at Recife impressed all new arrivals and returning old-timers.[3]

Fortunes were made by merchants who imported European provisions and manufactured goods which they sold or exchanged for sugar; but these fortunes were made by private traders for the most part, although some of the Company's employees continued to amass wealth 'on the side'. Complaints poured into the Heeren XIX about the profits made by the 'free-people' (*vrijluiden*) or free-traders, as the independent merchants were

[1] *Articulum . . . over het open ende vry stellen van den handel en negotie op de stadt Olinda de Pernambuco, ende custen van Brasil* (Amsterdam, 1630).

[2] *Narder Ordre ende Reglement . . . over het open ende vry stellen van den handel ende negotie op de Stadt Olinda de Pernambuco ende custen van Brasil* (The Hague, 1634).

[3] *Kron. Hist. Gen. Utrecht*, xxv. 236–7. Cf. also the testimony of Lichthart and Gijsselingh in Gonsalves de Mello, *Tempo dos Flamengos*, pp. 59, 63, 84, 93.

called, at a time when the Company was being steadily ruined by the costly war it was waging against Portuguese and Spaniards. The advocates of a monopoly urged that the Company, having expended such a vast amount of blood and treasure in conquering north-east Brazil, was entitled to reap the exclusive profits now that the profit-making stage had been reached. Why should the West India Company bear all the costs of the war and the occupation while the free-traders and interlopers reaped all the profits? They saw no reason to honour the promise given to the *moradores* who had submitted on condition of being allowed to trade as freely with the United Provinces as they had formerly done with Portugal. This would be favouring treacherous Papist Portuguese planters at the expense of loyal Protestant Dutch investors. As for potential emigrants to Brazil, they did not believe that private individuals 'intent only on their own profit' would cultivate the land properly for the benefit of the Company. The advocates of a monopoly were particularly vocal and influential in Zeeland, where Calvinist feeling was strong and anti-Catholic feeling correspondingly bitter; but similar sentiments prevailed among the directors and shareholders of the chambers of Rotterdam and Groningen.[1]

The arguments for free-trade were championed by the chamber of Amsterdam, and their principal points can be summarized as follows: the Company could not in any event supply all the imports required for north-east Brazil, or buy up all the sugar for export, since it had not got sufficient working capital. If the limited free-trade system were continued, the Company would soon derive much more profit from the fees, dues, taxes, tolls, &c., which it exacted, than it could ever hope to gain by trading on its own account with insufficient resources. Netherlands Brazil would only attain lasting prosperity if it were adequately colonized; and colonists would never emigrate to a region where they could not trade freely but were at the mercy of a harsh and all-embracing monopoly. Pending adequate colonization by Dutch and Germans, the existence of the sugar industry

---

[1] The monopolists' case is given in the petition of the Utrecht shareholders (10 Feb. 1637) in *Kron. Hist. Gen. Utrecht*, xxv. 197–9; the Zeelanders' arguments in J. P. Arend, *Algemeene Geschiedenis des Vaderlands, 1581–1795*, Deel iii, stuk 5, p. 48. Cf. also the pamphlet-literature cited in Knuttel, *Catalogus*, nos. 4425, 4515; J. H. Rodrigues, *Historiografia e Bibliografia*, nos. 725, 728; Aitzema, *Saken van staet en oorlogh, 1633–1644*, p. 445.

depended on the co-operation of the Portuguese *moradores*. This could only be secured by honouring the terms on which they had surrendered, allowing them to sell their sugars to whom they chose and at prices mutually agreed on, and not at those imposed by a monopolistic company.[1]

Amsterdam's case was weakened in the eyes of her opponents and in those of the States-General by the close connexion of most of the free-traders with that city, and by the notorious readiness of the Amsterdamers to trade with the enemy. These activities were naturally resented by investors who had retained their shares and seen all hope of dividends steadily dwindle.

Their High Mightinesses took the side of the monopolists, and on 27 December 1636 the States-General passed a resolution authorizing the West India Company to resume and enforce its original monopoly forthwith. All ships other than those of the Company which were bound or were being laden for Brazil were to be confiscated with their cargoes. This draconic resolution naturally provoked a storm of protest from the aggrieved shippers and merchants, who demanded that ships and cargoes laden for or *en route* to Brazil prior to 27 December 1636 should be allowed to complete their voyages under the terms and charter-parties originally arranged. The States-General rejected this request, but ordered the West India Company to take over the ships and cargoes at a fair valuation. The Heeren XIX, belatedly realizing that they had neither money to pay such a vast sum, nor any possibility of speedily arranging sufficient imports for the colony on their own account, were compelled to ask the States-General to agree to the free-traders' demand. Their High Mightinesses again refused, but they were eventually persuaded by the provincial states of Holland to give a reluctant consent to this proposal, as otherwise the Company would find itself involved in endless and costly litigation with the disgruntled parties.[2]

The struggle between monopolists and free-traders continued throughout the year 1637, and is reflected in the pamphlet literature of the time. An impartial committee appointed by the States-General to consider and report on the problem

[1] Correspondence of the Amsterdam Chamber with the Utrecht shareholders (Jan.–Mar. 1637), in *Kron. Hist. Gen. Utrecht*, xxv. 191–7, 200–3; Knuttel, *Catalogus*, no. 4514; J. H. Rodrigues, *Historiografia e Bibliografia*, no. 727.

[2] *Resolutien* of the States-General, 27 Dec. 1636, and 3, 5, 6, 7 Jan. 1637, *apud* Arend, *Algemeene Geschiedenis*, Deel iii, st. 5, p. 47.

gave conflicting advice, and confusion was made worse confounded by the contradictory reports received from Brazil. Arciszewski, who reached Holland when the dispute was at its height, wrote a full and interesting account of the situation to Johan Maurits at Recife, in the course of which he observed: 'Two separate letters were received here on the same day from Mr. Van der Dussen. In the general letter which he had signed, he wrote that the trade should be left open for all comers, and in the private letter addressed to his own Chamber [Rotterdam] he wrote that the trade should be reserved to the Company alone. This makes the people here not only ill-disposed but also confused and discouraged. Some of the directors and shareholders, angry at such confusion, told me with heartfelt bitterness that the Company and all its conquests were not worth tuppence.'[1]

The chamber of the North-Quarter now came out on the side of Amsterdam (Hoorn had never forgiven the West India Company for monopolizing the salt trade to Punta Araya in 1622), at least to the extent of recommending that a final decision should be postponed until the opinion of Johan Maurits had been obtained. Meanwhile, the States-General again resolved (30 March and 14 April) that the abolition of the free-trade system should go through; but the states of Holland sided with Amsterdam and held up the enforcement of the reiterated resolution by delaying tactics. Arciszewski, an ardent supporter of the free-trade system, was not given an opportunity of stating his views to the States-General, but he developed them at length in his above-quoted letter to Johan Maurits.

He reminded the governor-general that the scorched-earth policy applied by both sides in Brazil had resulted in the ruin of most of the *engenhos*. Although the pro-monopoly chambers were calculating on an annual sugar production of 14,000 chests, he averred that the actual production was only about 2,000. Pending the arrival of agricultural emigrants from northern Europe (for whom there was plenty of room in the interior 'as far as the Cordilleras of Peru'), the Company must needs conciliate the local *moradores* and keep faith with them. 'I blushed with shame on reading the allegation of the Chambers that we need not keep faith with them since they had sometimes proved

---

[1] 'Missive' of 24 July 1637 in *Kron. Hist. Gen. Utrecht*, xxv, 222–48, whence the quotations in the text are taken.

faithless to us. It is true that most of them were often faithless, but by no means all; and some of them always remained loyal to us and never gave us any reason to complain, for they never sinned but were often useful to us. It is not fair to ask now for the first time whether the councillors[1] were authorized to make such oaths and conditions. They were sent there by the West India Company, and they have done what they did in the name of the West India Company. If they sinned therein, the Company must take the consequences, since it was responsible for sending those who sinned. There can never be any jesting with Holy Writ: "Thou shalt not take the name of the Lord thy God in vain." '

The advantages of a free-trade system, Arciszewski argued, were evident not only from the boom which Recife enjoyed after the edict of 9 January 1634, but above all from the shining example of the United Netherlands themselves. 'What power, what means, would the Netherlands have from their land and public capital alone, and how could they pay such notable and wondrously heavy expenses as they do, except for the multitude of private traders? What has made the town of Amsterdam so splendid among so many others? Is it not the multitude of private traders, and these not Netherlanders alone, but likewise those of all nations in the world who can move and trade freely in the town according to their good liking?'[2]

The monopolists argued that the West India Company should follow the example of the older East India Company in maintaining a profitable monopoly, but Arciszewski easily demolished this argument. He observed that if the East India Company would allow private trade it would be ten times as strong as it was, adding that a great part of its wealth was derived from competing freely with other nations in the interport trade of Asia. Moreover, the East India Company could effectively maintain its monopoly of the spice trade, which was concentrated in a few small islands of the Moluccas, whereas the West India Company could never hope to do the same with its sugars. If this Company tried to charge monopoly prices, 'then the Netherlanders will go and import sugars from Spain, from the Portuguese captaincies in Brazil, from the island of

---

[1] Of the *Politiek Raad* or political council at Recife. Cf. p. 49, above.
[2] *Kron. Hist. Gen. Utrecht*, xxv. 237. Cf. V. Barbour, *Capitalism in Amsterdam in the 17th century*, pp. 17–42.

São Thomé, or from the East Indies, and they will sell them here, or at Hamburg or at Danzig, so that the West India Company will be left whistling for its money'.

Arciszewski's report evidently impressed Johan Maurits, who made use of many of the same arguments in his dispatch to the Heeren XIX dated 16 January 1638.[1] He likewise stressed the advantages of free-trade, the need to encourage immigration on a large scale, and the necessity of treating the *moradores* fairly and abiding by the promises which had been given them. He warned the directors that the enforcement of the monopoly would be 'the road to ruin' for the Company. He pointed out that the idea of taking over existing stocks in the hands of free-traders was quite impracticable, as was an alternative suggestion that the Company should confine itself to wholesale trading and leave the retail trade to the private merchants. In May 1637 the *moradores* of Pernambuco had written to Johan Maurits protesting against the proposed enforcement of the monopoly as a breach of faith, and they threatened to abandon their sugar plantations if it was carried out.[2] Johan Maurits now warned the directors that the *moradores* were not bluffing, and that they would leave the country 'rather than work for others under a closed trade, and toil for the Company in a slavery like that of their Negroes who work in the sugar-mills for them'.

This dispatch of Johan Maurits seems to have tipped the balance in favour of the free-traders. At any rate, after over a year of vacillation, negotiation, and argument between the various chambers, the Heeren XIX, and the States-General, a compromise agreement was reached and promulgated on 29 April 1638—the chamber of Zeeland still strongly dissenting. The essence of the new arrangement was that the trade with Brazil in Negro slaves, dyewoods, and munitions should be reserved to the Company, but that otherwise free-trade would be allowed under licence to all inhabitants of the United Provinces who were shareholders in the West India Company. The *moradores* of the conquered captaincies would also be allowed to trade on equal footing with those subjects of the United Provinces, although they were not shareholders in the Company, since it was realized that they had sunk all their capital in their sugar-mills and had nothing left to invest. On the other hand,

[1] *Kron. Hist. Gen. Utrecht*, xi. 62–70.
[2] *Moradores'* petition of 8 May 1637 in *Kron. Hist. Gen. Utrecht*, xxv. 203–5.

the directors of the Company and its employees (as distinct from shareholders) were strictly forbidden to participate directly or indirectly in this private trade. All imports to and exports from Brazil by private traders had to be declared, inspected, weighed, and registered in the presence of the Company's representatives, for the payment of customs dues, freight, wharfage, &c. An *ad valorem* duty of 10 per cent. was levied on all imports by private merchants to the colony, and they likewise had to pay 20 per cent. on all Brazilian products exported, with an additional tax of half a stiver on each pound of sugar. Taxes, freight, and anchorage dues, &c., could be paid either in cash or in sugar, in the latter event at the Recife market-rate. Elaborate arrangements were drawn up to check smuggling, and offenders were threatened with dire penalties, but these proved largely ineffectual in practice. Most of the Company's personnel were easily suborned, and the skippers and crews of the ships proved themselves adepts at the game of defrauding the customs. Nevertheless, the edict of 29 April 1638 was a beneficent move, and gave a great impetus to the general trade with Netherlands Brazil by ending the uncertainty as to the Company's ultimate intentions.[1]

Although the clearing of the *várzea*, the sale of derelict sugar-mills, and the suppression of the guerrillas combined to encourage commercial activity at Recife in 1635–7, there was still one major obstacle to the complete recovery of the sugar industry. This was the lack of sufficient labour in the form of Negro slaves, for the Dutch had not yet entered the slave-trade in a big way. As early as 1596 an enterprising trader had brought a cargo of a hundred Negroes to Middelburg, but the city fathers insisted that they should be freed unconditionally and immediately.[2] It will be recalled that in 1608 Usselincx also opposed the use of Negro slaves in his projected South American colonies, although on economic rather than on religious grounds (p. 4, above). We have seen that Dutch trade flourished exceedingly along the Guinea coast during the truce years, but it was gold and ivory which formed the staple of

---

[1] *Reglement byde West-Indische Compagnie . . . over het open-stellen vanden handel op Brasil* (The Hague, 1638). A more detailed summary of the various provisions will be found in Wätjen, *Holländische Kolonialreich*, pp. 296–8. For Zeeland's stubborn opposition cf. Aitzema, *Saken van staet en oorlogh*, ii. 527, 538–9.

[2] J. K. de Jonge, *Opkomst van het Nederlandsche gezag in Oost-Indie*, i. (1862), 38–39.

Dutch exports from West Africa. Very few slaves were exported, if only because there was no market for them in Dutch-controlled territory. The conquest of Paraíba and Pernambuco in 1634-6 radically changed this state of affairs, as there was now a great demand for slaves in north-east Brazil. Johan Maurits at first toyed with the idea of using free white labour in the sugar-mills, but he was speedily disillusioned in his hope that the home authorities would arrange for a constant flow of hard-working German emigrants. He likewise, therefore, came round to the prevailing view that 'it is not possible to effect anything in Brazil without slaves . . . and they cannot be dispensed with upon any consideration whatsoever: if anyone feels that this is wrong, it is a futile scruple'.[1]

The Heeren XIX were early aware of the lucrative potentialities of the West African slave-trade, but their Calvinist consciences were not entirely at ease, and they appealed to the *predikants* to tell them whether this trade in human flesh was permitted by biblical authority. The Protestant theologians proved as accommodating on this point as did their Roman Catholic rivals, although there were a few exceptions on both sides. Prominent among these latter was the Spanish Padre Alonso de Sandoval, rector of the Jesuit College at Cartagena de Indias, who published a violent denunciation of the slave-trade which went through two editions before it was (apparently) suppressed.[2] The slave-trade also had its critics among Protestants, and some Dutch divines roundly denounced it as wholly wrong and unlawful. But the majority-view was that expounded by the Reverend Godfried Udemans, who stated that it was lawful on certain conditions, one of which was that slaves should not be sold to Spanish or Portuguese masters, thus exposing them to the perils of Popery. He also said that slaves should be instructed in the principles of the 'true Christian religion', and released after years of faithful service. He even went so far as to claim that slaves who were ill-treated could lawfully run away from their cruel masters and should not be returned to them.[3] As things turned out these restrictions and

[1] 'Sommier Discours over den staet vande vier geconquesteerde Capitanias' (Jan. 1638), in *Bijdr. Med. Hist. Gen. Utrecht*, ii. 292-3.

[2] For the importance of Sandoval's *De Instauranda Aethiopium Salute*, published under slightly different titles and in very different forms in 1627 and 1647, respectively, cf. C. R. Boxer, *Salvador de Sá*, pp. 237-9.

[3] G. Udemans, '*T geestelick Roer van't coopmans schip* (Dordrecht, 1655), pp. 313-19,

reservations either were never put into practice or else very soon ceased to be operative. The Dutch entered the slave-trade belatedly and rather reluctantly in the sixteen-thirties, but they soon made up for their late start. Their behaviour in Brazil was not unduly severe, but their later record in Surinam is as foul as that of any other slave-holding nation anywhere at any time.

Shortly after their capture of Bahia the Dutch had attempted to seize Elmina and Luanda; but the loss of Bahia and the failure of these attempts discouraged them from renewing their efforts against those strongholds for another decade. When the demand for slaves in north-east Brazil became crucial in 1635, the Heeren XIX wrote to their 'general', or commander at Mouree on the Gold Coast, to arrange for a regular supply of slaves for Pernambuco as soon as possible. In the same year they also began to consider the possibility of another attack on Elmina, since the reports which they received from the Gold Coast stressed the weakness of the Portuguese garrison there, although the strength of the old castle of São Jorge was still regarded as formidable. Soon after his return to Recife in March 1637 Johan Maurits resolved to send an expedition to attack Elmina. The expedition, commanded by Colonel Coen (or Koin) and including a number of Brazilian Indians, accomplished this task with unexpected ease. A preliminary attack by pro-Portuguese Negroes on the Dutch vanguard at one moment threatened to repeat Veron's débâcle in 1625, but this time the Dutch main body stood firm, and the onslaught was repelled with heavy loss to the attackers. The fortress of São Jorge capitulated on 28 August after a few days' bombardment, greatly to the surprise of the besiegers. Coen found that the fortress was very strong and well supplied, and had the garrison done their duty the place might never have been taken.[1] About 1,000 slaves were imported from Guinea to Pernambuco in 1636; and in 1637, with the capture of Elmina, this figure rose to 1,580, but they were not found to be of a very suitable type, for reasons which will be explained in the next chapter.

for a contemporary Calvinist justification of the slave-trade which was first printed in 1638. Cf. also Van Rees, *Staathuishoudkunde*, ii. 321–5; K. Ratelband, *Vijf Dagregisters van het kasteel Elmina, 1645–7* (The Hague, 1953), p. lxxx n.

[1] Barlaeus-Naber, *Nederlandsch Brazilië*, pp. 66–77; K. Ratelband, *Vijf Dagregisters van Elmina*, pp. lxvii–lxix; J. Gonsalves de Mello, *Tempo dos Flamengos*, pp. 204–9.

While Coen was engaged in the capture of the Castle which Johan Maurits correctly described as 'the key to the Gold Coast', the Dutch forces did not remain idle on the other side of the Atlantic. The governor-general had previously detached Lichthart to cruise along the coast of Portuguese Brazil in order to harry the enemy's trade and shipping. In the course of his operations the Dutch admiral raided the little township of São Jorge de Ilhéus, south of Bahia, although he did not actually sack it. Bagnuoli, on his side, gave signs of recovering from his disastrous defeat at Porto Calvo, and sent several guerrilla bands across the river São Francisco to raid the Alagoas district of Pernambuco. In order to cope with this renewal of the guerrilla menace Johan Maurits dispatched Colonel Von Schoppe to invade Sergipe in November 1637. The German commander devastated this captaincy with traditional *furor teutonicus*, although it is not clear whether this was done with Johan Maurits's approval. On Von Schoppe's approach Bagnuoli beat another of his precipitate retreats, this time as far as the tower of Garcia d'Avila, a prominent landmark some forty miles north of Bahia, which he reached on 29 November. At the invitation of the local Tapuya tribes, Johan Maurits ordered the occupation of the northern captaincy of Ceará, which was reputedly rich in amber and salt. The occupation of this region was effected without any difficulty in December 1637, since the scanty Portuguese garrison of Fortaleza was unable to offer more than a token resistance to the Dutch invaders and their savage allies. With the acquisition of Sergipe and Ceará, the Dutch now controlled half the captaincies of Brazil; but these new conquests proved disappointing economically, as they were found to produce little of any value save some herds of cattle.[1]

Johan Maurits was seriously ill at the turn of the year 1637, probably from malaria. His strong constitution pulled him through, and after making a trip of inspection on horseback to Paraíba and Rio Grande do Norte, he was ready for fresh exertions in April 1638. Several of the directors of the provincial chambers in Holland and Zeeland—although *not* the Heeren XIX themselves as is usually alleged—had been urging him in private correspondence to attack Bahia, and this he finally

[1] Barlaeus-Naber, *Nederlandsch Brazilië*, pp. 78–83; Albuquerque, *Memorias Diarias*, 5 May–31 Dec. 1637.

decided to do. It was by now pretty obvious to both sides that as long as Recife remained in Dutch hands, or Bahia in those of the Portuguese, neither nation could feel completely secure in its own half of Brazil. The Dutch knew from letters which they had captured in Portuguese shipping that preparations for the mobilization of a combined armada were still going on at Lisbon; but they also knew that things were going extremely slowly, and that many people in the Peninsula doubted the armada would ever be ready. 'While our King goes a-hunting, the French and the Flemings hunt his towns and lands away from him', discontented people were muttering in Spain and Portugal, according to the reports which reached Johan Maurits.[1] The Dutch also knew from other intercepted letters that the situation at Bahia itself was going from bad to worse. Bagnuoli was generally despised and disliked; no love was lost between Italians and Iberians, or between his troops and the citizens; and the governor-general at Bahia, Pedro da Silva, was hardly on speaking terms with his Neapolitan military colleague, whose behaviour he scathingly denounced in his correspondence with Lisbon and Madrid.

It seemed to observers on both sides of the Atlantic that a determined Dutch attack on Bahia, which was daily expected, would most likely be successful. Lord Aston, the English ambassador at Madrid, reported to his government on 17 June 1637: 'There is a great fleet preparing in Lisbon, which the conde de Linhares[2] is to command; it is designed for the settling their affairs in Brazil, and is to carry 24,000 land soldiers. The conde de Linhares is to settle in la Bahia; but it is here generally thought he will find the Hollanders masters of it when he arrives.' The count was most anxious to hire English ships and gunners to serve in this expedition, but nothing came of his earnest endeavours to secure them.[3] As was usual in such circumstances, the Iberian authorities eventually fell back on the expedient of freighting Scandinavian and Hansa shipping to

---

[1] Johan Maurits to the Zeeland Chamber, 19 Mar. 1638, in J. C. M. Warnsinck, *Van vlootvoogden en zeeslagen* (Amsterdam, 1940), p. 135. This receives striking confirmation from Quevedo's sonnet complaining of the royal indifference to 'El Brasil en poder de luteranos', printed in L. A. Marín (ed.), *Obras completas de Don Francisco de Quevedo Villegas. Edición crítica. Obras en verso* (Madrid, 1932), p. 138; *Kron. Hist. Gen. Utrecht*, xxv. 171–88, 663.

[2] Dom Miguel de Noronha, viceroy of Portuguese India, 1629–35.

[3] *Clarendon State Papers* (ed. Oxford, 1767), i. 763–7.

supply the deficiencies of their own. The intercepted letters and dispatches afforded so much first-hand and apparently reliable evidence of Spanish sloth, Portuguese procrastination, and downright demoralization at Bahia, that Johan Maurits cannot be blamed for risking an attempt on that place, even though the substantial reinforcements for which he had repeatedly asked (and been repeatedly promised) had not yet arrived from Holland.

He left Recife on 8 April 1638 with a force of 3,600 Europeans and 1,000 Amerindians, embarked in thirty sail. The troops were landed without opposition, and the outlying forts were taken without difficulty; but the city, as Johan Maurits wrote later, proved 'not the kind of cat to be taken without gloves'. Bagnuoli and Pedro da Silva sank their personal differences 'like Herod and Pilate on a former occasion', as Johan Maurits observed rather irreverently, and co-operated effectively in the defence. The garrison was superior in numbers to the besiegers, who soon found that they could not invest the place effectively nor prevent the entry of supplies and reinforcements. Finding that the city could not be starved into surrender, and having only an inadequate siege-train, Johan Maurits decided to risk everything in a desperate assault. This attack was made with great determination on the night of 17–18 May, and it came very near to succeeding. The defenders had been forewarned by a deserter, but they barely managed to hold their own, and they made no effort to counter-attack when the Dutch finally withdrew exhausted after several hours of savage hand-to-hand fighting. Luckily, the Portuguese did not realize the extent of their success and granted the Dutch a brief armistice next day, so that both sides could bury the slain. One of the defenders noted in his diary of the siege: 'We counted their dead when we handed them over—237 of the finest-looking men who ever were seen; they looked like giants and they were undoubtedly the flower of the Dutch soldiery.' Johan Maurits effected a masterly withdrawal, embarking all his troops on the rainy night of 25–26 May, unhindered by the besieged who did not discover until daylight that their enemy had gone.[1]

---

[1] The Bahia campaign of 1638 is very well documented. For the Dutch side, I have relied principally on Johan Maurits's own dispatches as summarized in Barlaeus-Naber, *Nederlandsch Brazilië*, pp. 92–106, and printed in Portuguese translation in the 'Cartas Nassovianas', *RIAGP*, x. 35–49. For the Portuguese side

Although chagrined by his severe reverse, and particularly by the loss of so many of his best officers and men, Johan Maurits did not show himself unduly depressed when he returned to Recife early in June. He even contrived to help Admiral Jol with ships, men, and provisions for an expedition intended to repeat Piet Heyn's exploit of 1628 in the Caribbean. The attempt failed, but even before he knew this, Johan Maurits began to regret having parted with men and supplies which he could ill spare. Intercepted Iberian correspondence, as well as other news from Europe, revealed that a powerful armada was being mobilized in the Tagus, although there was some doubt as to its ultimate destination in the summer of 1638. Johan Maurits and his council thought that it was bound for Brazil, but the Heeren XIX wrote him that the Spaniards were far too preoccupied with French attacks in Flanders and Navarre to think of sending a powerful fleet to South America.[1]

In point of fact, the Catholic king and Olivares had never wavered in their determination to wrest Pernambuco from Dutch control, cost what it would in money and blood. The trouble was that for a long time neither of these essentials was forthcoming in sufficient quantities. In vain King Philip complained that Portugal had never produced her quota of men, ships, and money for the reconquest of Pernambuco since 1630, whereas the crown of Castile had spent 'over a million and a half' for that purpose. The Portuguese retorted that Castile was bleeding them white to serve purely Spanish ends in Flanders and Italy, thus leaving them powerless to help their own colonies in India and Brazil. Spanish difficulties were increased by the fact that the tide of war was everywhere flowing against the forces of the *Rey Planeta*. But despite the loss of Breda to the prince of Orange in October 1637, and the siege of Fuenterrabia by the French in the summer of 1638, King Philip and Olivares did not divert to the North Atlantic the combined armada which was being so painfully assembled in the Tagus.[2]

Fuenterrabia was unexpectedly relieved by the Admiral of Castile's spectacular victory over the prince of Condé on the

---

I have relied principally on the *Relação Diária do cerco da Baía de 1638 por Pedro Cadena de Vilhasanti* (ed. S. Leite, S.J., and M. Murias, Lisbon, 1941).

[1] Barlaeus-Naber, *Nederlandsch Brazilië*, pp. 111–19; Johan Maurits's dispatch of 18 Feb. 1639, in *RIAGP*, x. 49–52; J. C. M. Warnsinck, *Van vlootvoogden en zeeslagen*, pp. 136–42.

[2] Freire de Oliveira, *Elementos*, iv. 302–10, 323–5, 338–40, 342–3, 347–51.

6 September; but on that very date, and thus before the fate of Fuenterrabia was known, the combined armada in the Tagus received orders to sail for Brazil. The conde de Linhares, having quarrelled with Olivares, had been deprived of the supreme command, and this eventually devolved upon Dom Fernão de Mascarenhas, conde da Torre, a former governor of Ceuta and Tangier. His sole qualifications appear to have been his aristocratic birth and the fact that nobody else wanted the post. The armada consisted of forty-six sail, including twenty-six great galleons, carrying about 5,000 soldiers in addition to their crews. There was some reason for Olivares's boast to the Cardinal-Infant that despite all the disasters recently suffered by Spain, her naval forces were stronger than they had ever been before, even at the time of the Invincible Armada. Unfortunately for him, this comparison was to prove apter than he had intended.[1]

The Heeren XIX had thus miscalculated badly when they assured Johan Maurits that the Spaniards were so preoccupied with the French that they could not worry about Brazil. Johan Maurits himself was not quite so confident, and in any event he needed strong reinforcements to fill the gaps caused by battle and disease, to say nothing of the 600 men whom Jol had taken with him to the West Indies. 'We have crossed here not merely the Rubicon but the Ocean', he reminded the directors on one occasion; and again, 'for a long time now we have been staring out to seaward daily with expectant eyes, but in vain, and we know not what to think'. The Portuguese of Pernambuco, who hoped for the coming of the 'new Messiah of the Spanish fleet' were being convinced that the Dutch were losing the mastery of the seas, 'to the great discredit of our nation'. A plot among the *moradores* to rise in arms upon the appearance of the armada was discovered at this time, but the government at Recife was able to nip it in the bud. This naturally added to Johan Maurits's anxieties, and it was only with great difficulty that he succeeded in fitting out a squadron of ten sail which

---

[1] *Correspondance de la Cour d'Espagne sur les affaires des Pays-Bas au XVIIe siècle*, iii. 195–6; 'Cartas de algunos PP. de la Compañía de Jesús sobre los sucesos de la monarquía entre los años de 1634 y 1638', in *Memorial Histórico Español*, xiii. 79–81, 105–15, 200–1, 275, 350, and xiv. 366–417; A. Rodriguez Villa, *La Corte y monarquía de España en los años de 1636–37* (Madrid, 1887), pp. 83, 115, 124, 175; Cánovas del Castillo, *Estudios del reinado de Felipe IV* (Madrid, 1888), i. 168; Fernández Duro, *Armada Española*, iv. 132–3, 190.

he dispatched southwards to cruise off Bahia in November 1638.

The conde da Torre's armada wasted much time and lost some 3,000 men from disease at the pestilential Cape Verde islands; but on 10 January 1639, Johan Maurits saw thirty-two sail of this fleet steering southwards past Recife, and there could no longer be any doubt of the deadly seriousness of the threat to Pernambuco. He dispatched some yachts to shadow the armada, and himself mounted horse and rode southwards along the shore with as many men as he could muster in order to oppose the expected landing. As with De Hoces and De Rojas in 1635, however, the conde da Torre refused to take the advice of many of his officers to land his men somewhere on the coast of Pernambuco, but continued on his course for Bahia, where he hoped to recruit men to replace those he had lost at Cape Verde.[1]

After following the armada as far as Porto Calvo, Johan Maurits realized that no immediate attack was intended, and returned to Recife. Arciszewski appeared with the first detachment of the long-awaited reinforcements (about 1,200 men in seven ships) on 20 March, but Johan Maurits and his governing council soon fell out with him. The reasons for the governor-general's intense dislike of Arciszewski have not been fully explained, but Johan Maurits deliberately picked a quarrel with the latter and sent him packing back to Holland, 'like a dog through the sea', a bare two months after his arrival. On his return to The Hague in July 1639 Arciszewski tried to obtain satisfaction for his ignoble dismissal, but although he was partially successful he was not re-employed by the West India Company. He remained in Holland until 1646, when he re-entered the king of Poland's service as commander-in-chief of the artillery. He served in several campaigns against the Cossacks with his usual courage and conduct before retiring to Danzig, where he died in 1656.[2] Although Johan Maurits had got his way and broken Arciszewski's brilliant career in Brazil, this episode did neither himself nor the Company any good in

[1] Barlaeus-Naber, *Nederlandsch Brazilië*, pp. 105–6, 120–4, 219–21; *Kron. Hist. Gen. Utrecht*, xxv. 295; J. C. M. Warnsinck, *Van vlootvoogden en zeeslagen*, pp. 137–43.

[2] Barlaeus-Naber, *Nederlandsch Brazilië*, pp. 126–48; Arciszewski's lengthy 'Apologie' of Aug. 1639 in *Kron. Hist. Gen. Utrecht*, xxv. 351–92. The definitive secondary account is J. C. M. Warnsinck's essay, 'Christoffel Artichewsky, Een proeve tot eerherstel', in De Laet-Warnsinck, *Iaerlyck Verhael*, iv, pp. xxv–lxxiii.

the long run. Even though Arciszewski's friends in Holland did not criticize Johan Maurits publicly, it was probably this incident rather than the failure at Bahia which originated the mistrust between the Heeren XIX and their governor-general. On the other hand, camp-gossip in Brazil muttered that if Arciszewski had been present at Bahia in 1638 the expedition would probably have been crowned with success. This may have been one of the reasons for Johan Maurits's unworthy jealousy of the Polish colonel.

Strengthened by the reinforcements which had arrived with Arciszewski, Johan Maurits and his council sent their Admiral Loos southwards on 25 May with a fleet of thirty sail. Loos was ordered to cruise off Bahia and try to intercept the supplies and reinforcements for the armada which were expected to arrive from the Azores, Rio de Janeiro, and Buenos Aires. In this he was not very successful, as all these contingents managed to slip into the Bay of All Saints at different times, but he did capture an outward-bound caravel with many official dispatches and private letters on board. From this intercepted correspondence, the Dutch learnt that conditions in Bahia were about as bad as they could be. There was general dissatisfaction with the conde da Torre's behaviour, and he was freely called a coward for his failure to attack Recife in January. Food supplies were extremely short, and the half-starved and ill-clad soldiers were dying or deserting in shoals. Those who were left were behaving in the traditionally brutal and licentious fashion, and the Portuguese commander was either unable or unwilling to maintain discipline. No woman was safe in the streets, and some were even violated in their own houses. In order to fill the gaps in his ranks caused by disease and desertion, Torre was trying to recruit men locally and from the southern captaincies of Brazil, where the governor of Rio de Janeiro, Salvador Correia de Sá e Benavides, was busy collecting men and supplies for the expedition.[1]

If provisions were very short at Bahia, things were not much better at Recife, where Johan Maurits claimed that the very rats in the warehouses were dying of hunger. In his correspondence with the directors at this critical time, the governor-general wrote that the need for food supplies was even more acute than the want of ships and soldiers, for his men could not

[1] C. R. Boxer, *Salvador de Sá*, pp. 116–20, and sources there quoted.

fight if they were not fed. 'Speed and promptitude is necessary', he wrote on 10 July, 'here the proverb applies: "he who gives quickly gives twice". If your honours send us men without provisions, that is the same as cutting their throats. Someone from the Spanish council of state could not give you better advice on behalf of his king. . . . Our magazines are quite empty, and your honours send us nothing, so that we have nothing wherewith to supply our forts and enable us to keep our ships at sea.' Despite the critical situation at Bahia, he knew that the conde da Torre hoped eventually to muster a force of over fifty ships and 8,000 men for a combined attack on Pernambuco. 'In short,' wrote Johan Maurits, 'we must expect a blow which is not a little to be feared, although we will not fail to quit ourselves like men.'[1]

The conde da Torre on his side sought to atone for his previous irresolution by initiating a policy of 'frightfulness'. During the months of July to September he dispatched overland to Pernambuco and Paraíba strong contingents of guerrilla fighters under such veteran leaders as André Vidal de Negreiros, D. Felipe Camarão, and Henrique Dias. These bands had orders to take up positions in the hinterland of Pernambuco, whence they could harry the Dutch from the rear and induce the *moradores* to rise in rebellion, while the armada landed troops from the sea. They were not to expose themselves by attacking the Dutch garrisons prematurely, but were to content themselves with ravaging Dutch-owned sugar-plantations and wait until the armada was in the offing before commencing major operations. Then, however, it was to be war to the knife. 'Give the Indians and the Dutch no quarter', wrote one of Torre's most senior commanders, Luis Barbalho Bezerra, 'but hand them all over to the [cannibal] Tapuyas.' All the sugar-mills and plantations were to be 'burnt and razed to the ground, without leaving one stone on another'. The only exception to this scorched-earth policy was inspired by the need to secure Negro slaves for the sugar-plantations of Bahia. 'I want no pillage in money or goods, but Blacks and more Blacks', wrote Luis Barbalho on the eve of the armada's sailing. Johan Maurits learnt of the tenor of these orders from prisoners, but he did

---

[1] Johan Maurits's dispatches of 1639, in *RIAGP*, x. 49–52; Barlaeus-Naber, *Nederlandsch Brazilië*, pp. 211–22; J. C. M. Warnsinck, *Van vlootvoogden en zeeslagen*, pp. 141–6.

not at first believe them, as he thought that Torre would not wantonly devastate the rich sugar-plantations which he hoped and expected to recover for his king. Later on, however, the Dutch realized from captured dispatches that this was indeed the case, and consequently the fighting became more embittered than ever.[1]

Thanks to the arrival of strong contingents and supplies from the Azores, Rio de Janeiro, and Buenos Aires, the conde da Torre succeeded in virtually doubling his armada during his ten months' stay at Bahia. When he finally put to sea on 19–20 November 1639, his force consisted of eighteen Spanish and twelve Portuguese galleons, together with thirty-four armed merchantmen fitted out as troop-transports, and twenty-three smaller vessels such as yachts, caravels, and galliots. The armada was rumoured to have 11,000 or 12,000 troops on board, but these last figures were evidently circulated with a view to deceiving the Dutch, as in point of fact there were less than half that number. Nevertheless, this armada of eighty-seven sail was the strongest which had as yet appeared in Brazilian waters; and hopes of victory ran high at Bahia, despite the known incompetence of the commander-in-chief.[2]

It must be admitted that the conde da Torre was not entirely responsible for the fiasco which followed, since it seemed as if 'God from the beginning was against this Spanish fleet and on our side', as a contemporary Dutch pamphleteer noted. To begin with, a most unseasonable northern wind made the armada's voyage to Pernambuco inordinately slow. Then, in the first days of January 1640, the wind suddenly veered round to the south, and in conjunction with a strongly flowing current to the north, drove the armada past Recife, as far as Paraíba. Here Torre collected his vessels and worked back slowly against wind and stream towards Recife. Meanwhile, Admiral Loos, who had been forced to break off his blockade of Bahia and

---

[1] Many of Torre's original papers connected with this armada and its stay at Bahia are now in the library of the Brazilian Foreign Office, Itamaratí, Rio de Janeiro, where I was able to consult them in 1949, thanks to the courtesy of H.E. Joaquim de Sousa Leão, *filho*. Cf. also the compromising orders printed in *RIAGP*, no. 34 (1887), pp. 33–40, from the originals in the Rijksarchief at The Hague, and the dispatches of Johan Maurits for 1639–40, printed in Portuguese translation in 'Cartas Nassovianas', *RIAGP*, x. 49–52, and xii. 533 ff.

[2] Barlaeus-Naber, *Nederlandsch Brazilië*, pp. 222, 229–30; J. C. M. Warnsinck, *Van vlootvoogden en zeeslagen*, pp. 144–6; Torre's correspondence cited in the last note.

return to Recife for provisions a week before the armada sailed, was kept informed by scouting vessels of the armada's movements and was prepared to offer battle at the first opportunity. The Dutch fleet totalled some forty-one sail manned with 2,800 men, including 1,200 soldiers whom Johan Maurits had spared from his scanty garrison, realizing that it was on the sea that the fate of the colony would be decided.

On 12 January 1640 the two fleets came up with each other off Itamaracá, and a series of running fights ensued with the contending ships drifting slowly northwards during the next five days. A great deal of gunpowder was expended by both sides, but casualties were not particularly heavy, although Loos was killed on the first day. The armada lost one large ship and nine or ten small vessels, whereas the Dutch lost one ship sunk and one driven ashore. Several of the Dutch captains were court martialled for cowardice after their return to Recife, one being publicly executed and others cashiered with ignominy or heavily fined, so that neither side could claim a glorious victory.

Strategically, however, the advantage was wholly with the Dutch. When the two fleets parted off the Rio Grande, Torre had given up all thought of attacking Recife, or even getting the bulk of his fleet back to Bahia. The armada drifted confusedly to the vicinity of the shoals of Cape São Roque, where two galleons and a merchantman went ashore. There was no hope of his lubberly galleons and transports being able to weather Cape São Roque in face of the prevailing winds and tide, and many of his ships were already desperately short of food and water. In these critical circumstances, Luis Barbalho volunteered to be set ashore with the bulk of the expeditionary force and make his way back overland to Bahia through Dutch territory as best he could. Torre, having accepted this offer, embarked in a small vessel to return to Bahia with some of his principal officers, leaving the rest of the armada to its own devices. Some ships steered for the Maranhão, some for the Azores, and others set their course for the Caribbean where they scattered among the various Spanish ports and islands. Such of them as did eventually reach Lisbon or Cádiz again, arrived in a most lamentable condition after losing many of their men from hunger, thirst, and disease.[1]

[1] For the naval actions of Jan. 1640 and the subsequent dispersal of the armada,

Luis Barbalho had been put ashore near Cape São Roque with some 1,200 or 1,300 men. On their way south, they were successively joined by the forces previously sent overland from Bahia to ravage Dutch territory, under André Vidal, João Barbalho, Camarão, &c., which apparently comprised another couple of thousand men. The march of this column from the Rio Grande to Bahia, a distance of about 1,200 miles, through difficult country dominated by Dutch garrisons, has often been compared to the celebrated retreat of the 10,000 Greeks under Xenophon from the Tigris to the Bosphorus. Soon after beginning this epic march, Luis Barbalho wrote a 'very humble and courteous' letter to Johan Maurits, asking the Dutch governor to give quarter to his sick and wounded who were incapable of marching and had perforce to be abandoned by the wayside. Johan Maurits replied 'by sending him an authentic copy of the letter which he, Luis Barbalho, had written, and copies of the instructions signed by the conde da Torre and addressed to Camarão and João Lopes Barbalho, in which they ordered that no quarter should be given to anybody, and that all prisoners should either be killed out of hand or delivered to the Tapuyas to be slaughtered; His Excellency adding that Luis Barbalho's own letter decided the kind of quarter which he might expect'.

Even before this incriminating Portuguese correspondence had been captured in a skirmish on 3 February, Johan Maurits and his council had decided to refuse quarter to their enemies, for reasons which they explained in their dispatch to the directors written on 2 March 1640. After narrating the defeat of Torre's armada and the capture of the Portuguese vice-admiral, Antonio da Cunha de Andrade, with over 200 men in the hired English ship *Chagas*, they observed: 'These prisoners are a great embarrassment to us. We regret that our men gave quarter to all those who were trapped like rats, particularly as we cannot see any means of feeding them. We have not yet decided what we should do with these prisoners, nor do we

cf. Johan Maurits's lengthy dispatches of 26 Feb. and 2 Mar. 1640, in *Copye ofte cort ende waerachtige verhael*, &c. (Amsterdam, 1640); *Kron. Hist. Gen. Utrecht*, xxv. 515–29; *RIHGB*, lviii. 2–56. Cf. also Barlaeus-Naber, *Nederlandsch Brazilië*, pp. 222–8, where the dispatch of 26 Feb. is likewise printed, but erroneously ascribed to a P. van der Maersche, who was evidently only the copyist or courier. By far the best secondary account of the campaign is by J. C. M. Warnsinck, *Van vloot-voogden en zeeslagen*, pp. 147–59. Bibliographical information in J. H. Rodrigues, *Historiografia e Bibliografia*, nos. 472–83.

know if we are obliged to respect the quarter given, for we knew then from rumours which have since been confirmed by intercepted letters that the Spanish armada brought orders not to give quarter to anyone, with no exceptions whatsoever.'[1]

The fact that Barbalho was able to reach the river São Francisco with the bulk of his men was mainly due, as Johan Maurits wrote, to the co-operation which they received from the *moradores* in Dutch territory. 'The Portuguese, disloyal to this State, were their principal salvation. If they had not helped the enemy troops and at the same time deceived our own men, the enemy would not have got so far. The remote and unfrequented paths which they followed through the bush, and the incredible speed with which they marched, abandoning without a backward glance those who fell by the wayside, were the reasons why they escaped our hands. They did not get away scatheless, however, for they lost several hundred men (including nine captains, several lieutenants, and an ensign), between those who could not endure the hardships of the march and those who left the route in search of food and were found and cut down by our men.'

The Dutch on their side lost over 150 men in this bitter campaign, but they were very pleased with the loyalty shown by their Amerindian allies, who 'well knew that the enemy did not give quarter either to them or to us'. The Portuguese, on the other hand, were temporarily embarrassed by the atittude of the invaluable Camarão, who at one moment seemed inclined to give up the struggle and retire into the interior with his Petiguar Indians. This mood did not last long, and Dutch efforts to bring about a split between him and the Portuguese failed in 1640, as they had done two years previously.[2] During his march, Barbalho's men burnt several sugar-plantations, but Johan Maurits and his councillors claimed that the damage thus inflicted was not so great as some pessimists had reported to Holland. About this time several friars were caught in what the Dutch naturally regarded as treasonable correspondence with

---

[1] For the guerrilla warfare of 1639–40, and Barbalho's march through Dutch territory, see Johan Maurits's dispatches of 2 Mar. and 7 May 1640 in *RIHGB*, lviii. 19, 26–28, 54–58; Barlaeus-Naber, *Nederlandsch Brazilië*, pp. 238–49; Varnhagen, *História Geral* (ed. 1948), ii. 352–7, 388–90.

[2] For the abortive negotiations between Camarão and the Dutch, cf. Barlaeus-Naber, *Nederlandsch Brazilië*, pp. 119–20, and J. A. Gonsalves de Mello, *D. Antônio Filipe Camarão* (Recife 1954), pp. 33–36.

Bahia. This resulted in about sixty Carmelites, Benedictines, and Franciscans being assembled on Itamaracá, whence they were subsequently deported to Europe via the West Indies.[1]

In March 1640 Admirals Jol and Lichthart arrived at Recife with the bulk of the long-awaited reinforcements from Holland, comprising twenty-eight ships with 2,500 men. They brought dispatches from the directors advocating another attack upon Bahia, but Johan Maurits felt that this should not be attempted with less than 6,000 men. Instead of a direct attack upon the city of Salvador, Johan Maurits and his colleagues decided to send an expedition under Lichthart to ravage the sugar plantations of the *reconcavo*, by way of reprisal for the damage done by Vidal, Barbalho, and Camarão on the plantations in Dutch territory. Lichthart destroyed twenty-seven sugar-mills in the district round Bahia and might, perhaps, have risked an assault on the city itself had not Luis Barbalho arrived with his veterans of the long march. The Dutch also raided other places along the littoral, but they were not equally successful everywhere else. A column under Major Van den Brande which ventured too far inland along the Rio Real was badly cut up and the commander himself captured. An attack by Colonel Coen on Espirito Santo was also repulsed, and in July Jol and Lichthart left with the bulk of the fleet for the West Indies, where they made another futile attempt to emulate Piet Heyn's exploit of capturing a silver-fleet.

The reinforcements which reached the Dutch in March 1640 were to a large extent counterbalanced by the arrival of Dom Jorge de Mascarenhas at Bahia in June, with a fleet which prisoners reported (probably with exaggeration) as consisting of eighteen sail carrying 2,500 men. Dom Jorge had been given the title of marquis of Montalvão, and he came out with the rank of viceroy (the first so styled in Brazil) to supersede the conde da Torre who was recalled home in disgrace. This double promotion was presumably made with the idea of making the governor-general of Portuguese Brazil the better able to compete with Johan Maurits in days when rank and social precedence counted for so much.

[1] Barlaeus-Naber, *Nederlandsch Brazilië*, pp. 248–9. Fr. Manuel Calado, *Valeroso Lucideno*, pp. 45–46, 51–52, gives a somewhat highly coloured version of the arrest and deportation of the friars, which in any event was not so sweeping as is usually stated.

The war of reprisals which was now raging in Brazil threatened to bring the entire economy of the country to a standstill, and both sides began to realize that in destroying each other's sugar plantations they were exposing their own to the same ruin. The chief sufferers were (as in 1633-6) the *moradores* in Dutch-occupied territory. The conde da Torre's original orders had envisaged only the destruction of Dutch-owned *engenhos*, or of those occupied by collaborators with the invaders. In practice, however, the plantation-owners of Pernambuco were liable to be treated as traitors or collaborators by the soldiers of both sides, apart from being harassed by bands of armed deserters, fugitive Negro slaves, and other bandits who roamed the countryside. The denial of quarter which was the official policy of both sides was also somewhat repugnant to Johan Maurits and Montalvão, both of whom were essentially humane men, although the former at least could be ruthless on occasion.

In October 1640 the vicar-general and the regular Roman Catholic clergy who were left in Pernambuco after the expulsion of the friars, submitted a petition to Johan Maurits and his councillors, begging them to rescind the orders given to refuse quarter (24 February) and destroy all enemy *engenhos*. Contemporary Portuguese writers alleged that this move was inspired by Johan Maurits himself, whereas the Dutch chronicler Barlaeus claimed that Montalvão was the originator of this idea. Subsequent developments tend to indicate that the former supposition was the correct one, and in any event Johan Maurits received the petition favourably. He forwarded it under a flag of truce to Montalvão at Bahia, with a covering letter to the effect that he was prepared to revert to more civilized methods of warfare if the viceroy would reciprocate. He pleaded that the Dutch had only inaugurated their policy of 'frightfulness' with great reluctance and as an unavoidable reprisal for the pitiless orders promulgated by Torre and Luis Barbalho in 1639. He claimed that the Dutch had not burnt the *engenhos* of the *reconcavo* when they besieged Bahia in 1638; and if they had done so two years later, it was only in revenge for the devastation wrought by Vidal, Barbalho, and Camarão in Dutch territory.[1]

Montalvão replied through the bishop of Bahia (to whom he

---

[1] For the negotiations between Johan Maurits and Montalvão in 1640, see their correspondence printed in *RIAGP*, no. 35 (1888), pp. 53-77; Barlaeus-Naber, *Nederlandsch-Brazilië*, pp. 261-3.

submitted his correspondence with Johan Maurits) that during the siege of 1638 the Dutch had slaughtered many innocent civilians of both sexes in cold blood. He added that if the Dutch had not burnt the *engenhos* on that occasion it was only because they were forced to raise the siege in such haste and secrecy that they had no time to do so. He also pointed out that the Portuguese had frequently given quarter to the Dutch in recent months, as was evidenced by the number of Dutch prisoners he held, and stated that he would be willing to receive Dutch emissaries at Bahia and discuss the matter further. Johan Maurits, in his answer to Montalvão's observations, admitted that some excesses had occurred during his siege of Bahia; but he claimed they were committed by Amerindian auxiliaries or by undisciplined soldiers, without his knowledge or consent, whereas the written orders of Torre and Barbalho to give no quarter to the Dutch were as categorical and official as they could be. By and large, however, Montalvão's answer was deemed satisfactory, and Johan Maurits and his council decided to send a commission to negotiate an agreement at Bahia.

The commissioners selected were Codde van der Burgh, a member of the governing council, Colonel Coen, and a couple of political councillors. Their instructions authorized them to agree that quarter would normally be given in future, without reserve and exceptions, to all 'women, children, clergy, old people and persons incapable of bearing arms, as also to the sugar-planters (*senhores de engenho*), merchants, and all inhabitants and natives of the country, of any race, colour, or quality whatsoever, including Brazilian Indians, Mulattoes and Negroes'. Soldiers and sailors would also be given quarter if they asked for it, and these military and naval prisoners would then be eligible for exchange or ransom in accordance with their rank and category. The wanton destruction of sugar-plantations, churches, convents, and private houses would be stopped; and the fruits of the earth were likewise to be spared by both sides from the date of the signing of the projected agreement.

These humane and liberal provisions were, however, only to be granted on one essential condition, whose importance was impressed on the commissioners in the following paragraph of their instructions. 'They will negotiate principally and above all for stopping the burning of the sugar-mills and the cane-fields, because this is the sole end which we have in view in arranging this treaty, and, provided this is agreed upon, the other articles concerning the granting of quarter to combatants et cetera can be discussed and decided as the delegates may agree among themselves; and it would be most advantageous if we could obtain the end of incendiarism without giving quarter, unless it is asked for, as this in itself is of little use to the Company, and is only convenient because it will be easier to obtain in this way an end to the incendiarism.' The Dutch commissioners were accordingly instructed that they were on no account to sign any article concerning the granting of quarter unless an agreement to spare the sugar-plantations had been reached previously, or at least the two things could be secured conjointly. The governor-general and council stated frankly that they were thinking primarily of saving the next sugar crop rather than of sparing human lives.[1]

On the eve of the departure of the Dutch commission under a flag of truce for Bahia, a caravel arrived at Recife bearing a dispatch from Montalvão dated 2 March which contained startling news. The viceroy reported that a revolution had broken out in Lisbon on 1 December 1640, when the duke of Braganza was proclaimed the rightful king of Portugal with the title of Dom John IV, and the whole country had unhesitatingly followed the example of the capital. When the news reached Bahia on 15 February 1641 the marquis of Montalvão contrived to disarm the Spanish and Neapolitan regiments in the garrison, and then proclaimed King John IV with the enthusiastic adherence of the clergy, populace, and Portuguese troops. It may be added that almost all the Portuguese possessions in three continents subsequently gave their adherence to the new dynasty with little or no hesitation. Only in Terceira did the Spanish garrison hold out for any length of time, and Ceuta was the only Portuguese possession which remained permanently loyal to Spain.

There can be no doubt of the genuine enthusiasm with which the vast majority of the Portuguese in Brazil, as elsewhere, welcomed the news of the overthrow of the Spanish régime in the motherland. Two years earlier, the ecclesiastical administrator of the bishopric of Rio de Janeiro, Dr. Lourenço de Mendoça, had warned the government at Madrid that many of

[1] The instructions for the Dutch commissioners are printed (in Portuguese translation) in *RIAGP*, no. 35 (1888), pp. 70–77. Cf. especially p. 75.

the local populace were bitterly hostile to the Spanish connexion. He ascribed this feeling largely to the numerous immigrants of Azorean origin, who were mindful how their forefathers had held out for the Pretender Dom Antonio in 1580, and who had never forgiven their bloody subjugation by the marquis of Santa Cruz. Nor is there any reason to think that he was exaggerating. The commander of the Spanish garrison at Terceira in 1623–4 wrote to his king that the sullen hatred of the local population was more to be feared than open Dutch aggression. He reported that the news of the capture of Bahia in 1624 had been received with ill-concealed satisfaction by the islanders. They believed that the Dutch were acting on behalf of Dom Antonio's grandson, who, as claimant to the Portuguese crown, would speedily be acknowledged by the whole of Brazil.[1]

Anti-Spanish feeling was not, of course, limited to the Azoreans and their descendants in Brazil, but was prevalent among all classes of Portuguese society, particularly among 'the common people, who are eternal enemies of the Castilian nation'. Nor was this feeling unrequited. Castilian contempt for and dislike of the Portuguese was seldom concealed in official and private correspondence, although the numerous flattering references to Lusitanians in the literature of Spain's golden age may give another (and wholly misleading) impression.[2] Above all, the Portuguese were closely associated with the Jews in the minds of contemporary Spaniards, as exemplified by their coarse proverb 'A Portuguese was born of a Jew's fart'.[3] Throughout Spain and her American colonies, the terms 'Jew' and 'Portuguese' were virtually synonymous, and the above-mentioned Dr. Lourenço de Mendoça submitted a lengthy memorial to the crown in 1630, indignantly protesting against this widespread practice.[4]

[1] Dr. Lourenço de Mendoça's printed memorials to the Consejo de Estado at Madrid in 1638–9, in the British Museum (Pressmark 1324. i. 9 (14)–(15); 8042. c. 31; 4745. f. 11 (12); 1324. i. 2 (24)); Letters of D. Pedro Estevam de Avila from Terceira in 1622–5, quoted in F. Mendes da Luz, *Boletim do Instituto Historico da ilha de Terceira*, vi (Angra do Heroismo, 1948).

[2] M. Herrero Garcia, *Ideas de los Españoles del siglo XVII* (Madrid, 1928), pp. 125–68; A. Zamora Vicente, 'Portugal en el teatro de Tirso de Molina', in *Biblos*, xxiv (Coimbra, 1948).

[3] J. Howell, *Epistolae Hoeliane, Familiar Letters, Domestic and Foreign* (London, 1645), vi. 25–26.

[4] Lourenço de Mendoça, *Suplicacion a su Magestad Catolica del Rey, ante sus Reales consejos de Portugal y de las Indias, en defensa de los Portugueses* (Madrid, 1630), especially pp. 25–26, 35, 42–43, 51–53.

Although the allegation that Portuguese Jews ('Christãos Novos' or 'Marranos') monopolized the trade of Spanish America 'from the vilest African Negro to the most precious pearl' was obviously exaggerated, it was an undoubted fact that Portuguese merchants (whether of Jewish origin or otherwise) were very active throughout the viceroyalties of Mexico and Peru. This activity, which provoked repeated protests from Mexico City, Lima, and Buenos Aires, was in defiance of the terms of the Cortes of Tomar in 1581, which had legalized King Philip II's (of Spain) seizure of the Portuguese crown on condition that the two colonial empires should remain separately administered entities, and that vassals of the one crown should not be allowed to travel or reside in the overseas dominions of the other. Spanish resentment at the penetration of their Atlantic colonies by the Portuguese was not lessened by the knowledge that the latter were much more vigorous and successful in keeping their own colonial empire free from any important penetration by the Spaniards. National pride, anti-Semitic feeling, and the monopoly theory of empire all combined to exacerbate mutual bitterness between Spaniards and Portuguese to a point where the explosion of December 1640 split the Iberian world-partnership permanently asunder.

Relations and reactions between the Portuguese and Dutch in 1641 were more complicated. The first news of the accession of King John IV was received in the United Provinces with astonished delight by all classes of society, since it was obvious that Spain, the hereditary enemy, would be greatly enfeebled by this wound in her side. The shares of the West India Company rose from 105 to 128, and in February 1641 the States-General published proclamations forbidding their subjects to make war on the Portuguese in Europe or to seize their ships. Nor was the news at first less enthusiastically received in Netherlands Brazil, where one of the councillors at Recife wrote that it was worth more than the capture of a silver-fleet. But this diplomatic honeymoon did not last long.[1]

Tristão de Mendonça Furtado, who arrived as Portuguese envoy at The Hague in April 1641, brought instructions to

---

[1] *Kron. Hist. Gen. Utrecht*, xxv. 395-7, 664-7. What follows is derived mainly from Aitzema, *Saken van staet en oorlògh, 1633-1644*, pp. 754-9; E. Prestage, *Embaixada de Tristão de Mendonça Furtado á Holanda em 1641, com documentos elucidativos* (Coimbra, 1920).

secure a truce for ten years, during which time a treaty of peace and alliance would be negotiated, and to ask for the restitution of Netherlands Brazil on payment of suitable compensation by the crown of Portugal. The directors of the East and West India Companies, on thinking over the situation, opposed the conclusion of a truce, and suggested either a continuation of the war outside Europe, which would enable them to extend their conquests at the expense of the Portuguese, or alternatively the speedy conclusion of a peace which would enable them to consolidate their present gains and to economize by drastically reducing their overseas garrisons. Their influence was sufficiently powerful in the provincial states of Holland, where the town of Amsterdam was strongly represented, to ensure that the Portuguese proposals for the restoration of north-east Brazil were rejected out of hand. But the prince of Orange and the representatives of five of the other provinces were eager to conclude a truce with King John IV, since they realized that by giving active support to Portugal they would divert Spanish strength from Flanders. Moreover, the valuable salt-trade with Setúbal, continued under licence even during the war with Spain, was one of the mainstays of the flourishing Dutch herring industry, and an additional inducement to keep on friendly terms with Portugal.[1]

After prolonged triangular negotiations between the States-General, the provincial states, and the Portuguese envoy, a compromise was reached whereby a ten-year truce between Portugal and the United Provinces was signed at The Hague on 12 June 1641.[2] This truce was to begin in Europe forthwith (in practice it was already operative), and in Brazil, Africa, and the East Indies when the public proof of the ratification by both sides reached those regions. Other provisions were made for the granting of naval and military aid to Portugal against Spain, for the commencement of negotiations for a permanent peace-treaty within eight months, and for mutual trade and intercourse. The last article provided that ratifications should be

[1] Cf. V. Rau, *A exploracão e o comércio do sal de Setúbal. Estudo de história económica* (Lisbon, 1951), pp. 151–77.

[2] For the text of this treaty see the editions listed in J. H. Rodrigues, *Historiografia e Bibliografia*, nos. 606, 614, 621–4. Oddly enough, Aitzema, who twice prints the text in full (*Saken van staet en oorlogh, 1633–44*, pp. 756–9, and *Verhael vanden Nederlandsche Vredehandeling*, pp. 149–52), each time misdates it as 22 instead of 12 June.

exchanged at The Hague within the next three months, but for some inexplicable reason King John IV delayed his ratification until 18 November. The States-General, whether of malice aforethought or otherwise, delayed their own ratification for another couple of months, so that the Dutch Companies thus had a legal excuse for continuing hostilities against the Portuguese colonies until well into the year 1642. Even this belated cessation of hostilities was regarded as disadvantageous to the interests of the East and West India Companies, whose shares fell respectively from 500 to 400 and from 128 to 114 during the months of negotiation.[1]

When Johan Maurits received the news of the Portuguese Restoration from Montalvão on 14 March 1641, this naturally facilitated the negotiations which had already begun for the humanizing of the conduct of the war and the sparing of the sugar-plantations and crops. Montalvão was deposed by a misunderstanding (or an abuse) of secret orders received from Lisbon at Bahia in June; but the junta which succeeded him pending the arrival of the new governor-general, Antonio Telles da Silva, carried on with the negotiations. Hostages were exchanged between Recife and Bahia, prisoners were returned by both sides, and the guerrillas were withdrawn from the hinterland of Pernambuco. No formal truce was actually signed, but fighting virtually ceased in Brazil while the agreement for humanizing the conduct of the war was being discussed at Bahia. Although such an agreement was eventually signed, Johan Maurits and his councillors were disappointed in their hope that they would thereby secure a record sugar harvest and so content the directors in the United Provinces. Unseasonable rain and floods, and a smallpox epidemic among the Negro slaves, did almost as much havoc as the guerrillas could ever have done, and the harvest was a disappointingly small one.

Meanwhile, Johan Maurits celebrated the news of the accession of King John IV with magnificent *festas*, including theatrical performances of some French comedies, and by equestrian sports and contests which lasted for several days in the grounds of his palace near Recife. All the principal Portuguese planters were invited to these festivities, in which the count himself naturally took a leading part. Fr. Manuel Calado, who was an eyewitness

---

[1] Aitzema, *Saken van staet en oorlogh, 1633–1644*, p. 754.

and chronicler of these junketings, assures us that nearly all the prizes were carried off by the Portuguese contestants, prominent among whom was João Fernandes Vieira, no longer a needy Mulatto adventurer but one of the wealthiest (and best mounted) men in the colony. But if the Portuguese were the better horsemen, the Northerners proved themselves the better trenchermen in the gargantuan banquets which followed the distribution of prizes, and of which Fr. Manuel gives us a vivid description.[1]

The abstemious Portuguese records with horrified fascination how these lengthy repasts were punctuated by 'the drinking of numerous toasts, as is the custom of their country, and with some playful ceremonies in which the losers had to pay a forfeit of drinking three successive toasts. And every time that a toast was drunk to the health of Dom John the fourth of this name king of Portugal, all those who were present had to rise to their feet with their hats in their hands, and they could not sit down again nor cover themselves until the toasts had been honoured round the whole table; and while the toasts were being drunk, the trumpets (which were many) did not cease to play, nor was the sound of martial music silenced. And if the banquet was a dinner[2] the drinking-bout lasted until night, and if it was a supper until dawn. The most beautiful and elegant Dutch, French, and English ladies living in Pernambuco attended these banquets, in which they drank deeper than their men-folk, explaining that such was the custom in their countries.'

These convivialities in honour of the new Portuguese monarch did not, however, prevent Johan Maurits from planning the further prosecution of the war against King John IV's vassals in Africa and Brazil. He politely rejected Montalvão's request for a temporary local truce pending the negotiation of a definitive one in Europe, pleading that he could not cease hostilities without authorization from the States-General and the directors. These two bodies, far from telling him to refrain from further hostilities, urged him to fish in troubled waters and to make what further conquests he could, before the conclusion of a truce or a peace with Portugal should prevent further hostile action.[3] The

---

[1] Fr. Manuel Calado, *Valeroso Lucideno*, pp. 108–11.

[2] 'Dinner' then began, of course, at any time after noon.

[3] Barlaeus-Naber, *Nederlandsch Brazilië*, pp. 264–5; Varnhagen, *História Geral* (ed. 1948), ii. 361–3; *Bijdr. Med. Hist. Gen. Utrecht*, iii. 358–60.

directors were above all anxious for the conquest of Bahia, for the reasons cogently expressed by Adriaen van der Dussen in his report of 10 December 1639:

'Experience has taught us that our dominion in Brazil is continually harrassed by those of Bahia de Todos os Santos, and, so long as the Spaniard remains master of Bahia, he will always have great opportunities of molesting us, whether by sea or land. . . . Therefore, in my opinion, the capture of Bahia is absolutely essential for the completion of the conquest of Brazil and the consolidation of the Company's rule there. Only then will that ants-nest be broken up, whence so many vexatious bandits come continually to disturb our territory and keep everything in turmoil.'[1]

Even before he had received his orders to intensify the war against the Portuguese, Johan Maurits had decided to do so on his own responsibility, particularly since his hands were much freer with the withdrawal of the guerrillas from the hinterland of Pernambuco. He considered that Bahia was still 'not the kind of cat to be taken without gloves', and he did not feel strong enough to make a second assault on that stronghold. His first move was to reoccupy the captaincy of Sergipe del Rey which had been abandoned after its devastation by Von Schoppe in 1637, but which would (he hoped) support large herds of cattle and thereby ensure adequate meat supplies for Recife. This operation was effected without difficulty, since the region was a virtual no-man's-land. Not content with this easy victory, Johan Maurits resolved on the conquest of the great slave-depot of São Paulo de Luanda on the other side of the Atlantic Ocean.

Elmina had proved rather disappointing as a slave-market, mainly because the Negroes from the Guinea coast (and especially the Hausa from the hinterland) were harder to control in bondage than were the more tractable Bantu from the region of Congo and Angola. The conquest of Luanda would not only give the Dutch access to the best and most populous breeding-ground for Negro slaves, but would (so Johan Maurits speciously argued) deprive the Spaniards of the port whence they secured

---

[1] Barlaeus-Naber, *Nederlandsch Brazilië*, pp. 150–99, from the original in the archives at The Hague. Cf. also the carefully annotated Portuguese translation of A. van der Dussen, *Relatório sobre as capitanias conquistadas no Brasil pelos holandeses (1639)*, pp. 137–8.

about 15,000 slaves yearly for work in the mines of Mexico and Peru.[1] Johan Maurits deliberately brushed aside the possibility that the Portuguese in Angola might declare (as indeed they did) for King John rather than for King Philip, but in any case the delay in the ratification of the ten-years' truce gave him the technical excuse which he needed. A strong expedition for the conquest of Angola, Benguela, and São Thomé was assembled at Recife during the months of April and May. It was commanded by Admiral Jol and Colonel Henderson, who had under their orders a force of twenty-one ships carrying some 3,000 men including 240 Brazilian Indians. Johan Maurits's character again appears in a decidedly unfavourable light on this occasion. When the Portuguese envoys from Bahia, whom he was entertaining so hospitably at government-house, asked him whither this expedition was bound, he unblushingly replied that it was going to cruise against the Spaniards in the Caribbean.

Jol and Henderson left Recife on 30 May 1641, and anchored off Luanda on 23 August. The occupation of the city was effected without difficulty three days later, the governor, Pedro Cezar de Menezes, and the citizens having fled northwards to the river Bengo after offering only a token resistance. The conquest of Luanda was followed by the occupation of Benguela, and by the capture of the islands of São Thomé and Anobom in October. Only the castle of São Sebastião at São Thomé offered a serious resistance, but the deadly climate of that island soon claimed the lives of Admiral Jol and many of his men. The Dutch offensive in West Africa was rounded off by the capture of Axim, the last of the Portuguese forts on the Guinea coast, in February 1642.[2]

[1] This was an exaggeration, as the figure of 15,000 was an (optimistic) average for the total annual export of slaves from Luanda to the whole of Iberian America. Cf. C. R. Boxer, *Salvador de Sá*, p. 225. Nevertheless, the number of Negroes imported for work in the mines of Mexico and Peru was larger than is generally realized, 'por ser dichos Negros de naturales robustos y fuertes son necessarios para dichas minas y ingenios de açucar etc.', as the procurator of Mexico City stated in 1644, when stressing the vital importance of the Negro slave-trade. See his *Memorial* (British Museum, Pressmark 1324. i. 9 (30), cap. 24, fols. 20–21), and cf. those of Juan de Ibarra Guetzasaen on behalf of Potosí (about 1615), Fr. Pedro de Sosa, O.F.M., and Captain Juan Gonzalez de Azevedo, all bound up together in B.M. Pressmark C.62.i.18 (1–100).

[2] For details of this expedition, cf. Barlaeus-Naber, *Nederlandsch Brazilië*, pp. 266–7; Varnhagen, *História Geral* (ed. 1948), ii. 363–4; K. Ratelband, 'De expeditie van Jol naar Angola en São Thomé, Mei–October 1641', reprinted from the

Johan Maurits's final conquest in America was the occupation of São Luis do Maranhão in November 1641. This was achieved by Lichthart and Coen with the aid of Trojan Horse methods combined with the ineptitude of the old governor, Bento Maciel Parente. The shameless way in which these conquests had been effected naturally disillusioned and infuriated the Portuguese on both sides of the Atlantic. King John IV and his ministers warmly protested that they were a breach of the truce, but, as Caspar Barlaeus wrote, this was 'preaching to deaf men's ears'. Legally, Johan Maurits had considerable justification, for the official news of the ratification of the truce did not reach Recife until 3 July 1642, being solemnly proclaimed there two days later. Morally, however, the Dutch position was indefensible; for at the time when Johan Maurits was organizing these conquests, a Dutch fleet was actively co-operating with the Portuguese armada in European waters, and Dutch troops were serving with the Portuguese army in the Alemtejo. Small wonder that the cynical way in which the Dutch maintained an alliance with Portugal in Europe, while plundering her finest colonial possessions (for the East India Company was equally aggressive in Ceylon), laid up a legacy of hatred and bitterness which was to cost them dear before long.

For the moment, however, it seemed as if everything was going in their favour. With the acquisition of the Maranhão, Johan Maurits now ruled over seven out of the fourteen captaincies into which Portuguese America had been divided. Contrary to his advice, the Dutch possessions on the west coast of Africa were not placed under the administration at Recife, but were directly controlled by the Company at home through a 'General of the Coast' residing at Elmina, and a senior factor as director at Luanda. The West India Company's Atlantic empire had now reached its zenith. It included the fur-trading establishments along the Hudson River, some posts in Guiana, and the Caribbean islands of Curaçao and Aruba; but all the profits from those areas and from West Africa could not compensate for the amount which the Company was spending on Brazil, where its writ ran for a distance of over a thousand miles along the coast. It was on Brazil that the Company's energies

West-Indische Gids, xxiv (1943); D. Pedro de Alcega, 'piloto y cosmografo-mór de Cantabria', in the *Memorial* of his services (B.M., Pressmark 1324. i. 2 (116)). Cf. also *Anais do Museu Paulista*, v. 152–3.

were concentrated, and it was on the fate of Brazil that its own solvency and existence ultimately depended.

Most modern historians consider that the West India Company was unsound from the beginning, and that its Brazilian enterprise in particular was doomed from the start. Professor Geyl, for instance, dismisses the possibilities of establishing a lasting Dutch colony in Pernambuco as 'altogether chimerical'.[1] I hesitate to differ from so distinguished an authority, who probably knows more about his country's history than does any other man living, but I cannot help feeling that there is a good deal of 'hindsight' involved in this assertion. At any rate, that was certainly not how the situation looked to contemporaries on both sides of the Atlantic in 1640–1. The Dutch position in Brazil was admittedly not without grave weaknesses, as we shall see in the next chapter, but the prospects for Portugal and her sorely tried Brazilian colony seemed much more dubious to most people in those critical years.

We have already had occasion to observe the strong strain of frustration and defeatism which runs through the correspondence of the court of Madrid with their subordinates at Lisbon and Brussels in so far as efforts for the recovery of north-east Brazil were concerned in 1630–40, and it would be easy to multiply such quotations.[2] The increasingly gloomy view taken on the other side of the Atlantic is also evident from the tenor of the correspondence from Bahia which had been captured by the Dutch, and to which allusion has already been made in passing. This pessimistic feeling, which was crystallized in the common saying 'God does not wish the Restoration of Brazil', is most strikingly exemplified in the famous sermon delivered by Padre Antonio Vieira, S.J., at Bahia on the eve of the Portuguese Restoration. This sermon, inspired by the psalmist's verses beginning 'Awake, why sleepest thou, O Lord? Arise, cast us not off for ever', has been rightly described by the Abbé Raynal as 'the most vehement and extraordinary ever heard in a Christian pulpit'. The preacher, addressing God as much in anger as in sorrow, bitterly denounces the Deity for favouring the heretic Dutch at the expense of the Catholic

---

[1] P. Geyl, *The Netherlands Divided, 1609–1648*, p. 198.
[2] Freire de Oliveira, *Elementos*, vols. iii and iv *passim*; Cuvelier and Lefevre, *Correspondance de la Cour d'Espagne sur les affaires des Pays-Bas au XVIIᵉ siècle*, vols. ii and iii *passim*.

Portuguese, and urges God to change His mind before it is too late.[1]

'If You were resolved to give these same lands to the pirates of Holland, why did You not do so when they were still wild and uncultivated, instead of now? Has this perverse and apostate people rendered You such services that You first sent us here as their harbingers, so that we might cultivate the lands and build the cities for them, and after we had cultivated and enriched the same, hand these over to them? Must heretics and enemies of the Faith thus enjoy the fruits of the work of Portuguese and of the sweat of Catholic brows? *En queis consevimus agros?* Behold for whom we have worked for so many years.[2]

'But since You, O Lord, wish and ordain it thus, do whatever seems good to You. Give Brazil to the Dutch, give them the Indies, give them the Spains (for the results of the loss of Brazil will be no less perilous), give them whatever we still have and possess (as You have already given them so much), and place the World in their hands; as for us, we Portuguese and Spaniards, abandon us, repudiate us, destroy us, finish us. But I cannot forbear to tell and remind Your Majesty, O Lord, that it may chance one day that You will need these same whom You now spurn and cast from You, and You will then no longer have them. . . .

'Burn, destroy, consume us all, but it may chance one day that You will need Spaniards and Portuguese, and that You will not be able to find them. Holland will give You apostolic conquerors who will carry through the world the standards of the cross; Holland will give You gospel preachers who will sow the Catholic doctrine in savage lands and water it with their own blood; Holland will defend the truth of Your Sacrament and the authority of the Roman Catholic Church; Holland will build temples, Holland will raise altars, Holland will consecrate priests and will offer the sacrifice of Your most Holy Body; Holland, in short, will serve You and will venerate You as religiously as they do daily in Amsterdam, Middelburg and

---

[1] 'Sermão pelo bom successo das armas de Portugal contra as de Holanda, pregado na igreja de N. S. da Ajuda da cidade de Bahia no ano 1640.' Quotations are from the edition by A. Sérgio and H. Cidade, *Padre António Vieira. Obras Escolhidas*, x. 42–79.

[2] A modified version of Virgil's *Bucolics, I*, lines 71–72 ('See for whom we have sown our fields'), as my colleague, Prof. W. S. Maguinness, kindly informs me.

Flushing, and in all the other colonies of that cold and watery hell!'

If this was done in the green tree, what could be expected in the dry? If the united efforts of Spain and Portugal could not drive the Dutch from Pernambuco in 1630–40, what prospect had the Portuguese of doing so alone, at a time when they had need of all their resources to defend themselves against Spain? Their difficulties were further increased by the loss of Luanda and São Thomé, for only a thin and intermittent trickle of slaves could henceforth be expected from West Africa, and without an ample supply of 'black ivory' the sugar-plantations would decay and die. If an impartial observer had been asked to forecast the future of Brazil when the truce was belatedly declared there in July 1642, he might well have put his money on the dynamic young colony in the north-east rather than on the older and apparently declining settlements around Bahia and Rio de Janeiro.

IV

A HUMANIST PRINCE IN THE NEW WORLD

1637-44

JOHAN MAURITS has been called 'the most remarkable man ever connected with the sugar industry',[1] and an outline of his record as governor-general of Netherlands Brazil shows that this estimate is not an exaggerated one. He was not only a capable general and a first-class administrator, but a ruler who was in many respects far in advance of his time. We have seen that he fell in love with Brazil on the day that he landed at Recife, and he wrote of that country in nostalgic terms a twelvemonth before his death as 'ce beau Pay de Brasil, lequel n'a pas son pareil sous le ciel'. During the seven years of his rule he spared neither his own energy nor the Company's money in his efforts to develop the colony. He improved and enlarged the existing city of Recife with new (and paved) streets, roads, and bridges. He laid out a new town named Mauritia, or Mauritsstad, on the adjoining island of Antonio Vaz, the site of which forms the heart of the modern city of Recife. Here he built two spacious country-seats, one of them complete with a well-stocked aviary and zoological and botanical gardens, where he indulged his taste for growing exotic fruits and transplanting tropical trees on a lavish scale. He also erected the first astronomical observatory and meteorological station in the New World where regular wind and rainfall records were kept. He even envisaged the foundation of a university which would be frequented by Protestant Dutch and Catholic Portuguese, although this particular project never got beyond the paper stage.

During his stay in Brazil Johan Maurits gathered around him a carefully selected entourage of forty-six scholars, scientists, artists, and craftsmen from the Netherlands, all of whom had their own special functions and assignments. Piso studied tropical diseases and their remedies, Marcgraf made scientific

[1] N. Deerr, *The History of Sugar* (London, 1949), i. 106.

collections of the fauna, flora, and geography of Brazil and Angola, in addition to astronomical and meteorological observations; while half a dozen painters, including Frans Post and Albert Eckhout (the latter possibly a pupil of Rembrandt), filled their portfolios with sketches of every aspect of local life and culture. Only a part of the material amassed by these men was published in Johan Maurits's lifetime; but the sumptuous folio volumes of Barlaeus, Marcgraf, and Piso, printed at the count's expense after his return to Holland, are among the finest examples of seventeenth-century book production. For over 150 years they remained the standard works on Brazil in any language, being only displaced by the publications of Maximilian of Neuwied, Spix, and Martius in the first half of the nineteenth century.

'La belle, très belle et bellissime maison' of the Mauritshuis at The Hague,[1] well known to all art-lovers and visitors to the Netherlands, was originally built for Johan Maurits to the design (or at least under the supervision) of his friend, the celebrated architect Pieter Post, whose brother Frans had accompanied him to Brazil. This 'sugar-house', as the disgruntled directors of the West India Company sarcastically called the new palace, was largely furnished with Brazil-wood sent home by Johan Maurits during his tenure of office, and it was no wonder that his countrymen nicknamed him 'Maurits the Brazilian'. The museums of Berlin, Copenhagen, and Paris still contain valuable ethnographical and artistic collections which form only a fraction of those which he and his helpers methodically amassed in Brazil. No such systematic and intelligently directed scientific work by white men in the tropics was seen again until the great expeditions of Captain Cook and his successors. With every justification did Johan Maurits choose for his motto the Latin phrase *Qua patet orbis*, 'As wide as the world's bounds'.

Nor was Johan Maurits less enlightened in his treatment of the local Portuguese. He fully understood the importance of reconciling the planters and the *moradores* to Dutch rule, and his efforts met with a considerable degree of success, at any rate outwardly. A staunch Protestant himself, and in an age when Calvinists and Catholics regarded each other as inevitably doomed to hell-fire, he deliberately tolerated the local

---

[1] *Briefwisseling van Constantijn Huyghens*, iii, no. 2996.

Roman Catholic priests and friars (the Jesuits alone excepted), despite the opposition of the colonial Calvinist ministers and their supporters at home. In an endeavour to avoid the evils of monoculture and to make the colony self-supporting in foodstuffs, he fostered the cultivation of manioc and other crops besides sugar. He reduced taxation and allowed liberal credit-terms to the planters to help them rebuild their ruined *engenhos* and to buy Angola slaves. He gave them a form of representative local government, through the creation of municipal and rural councils on which both Portuguese and Dutch colonists could serve, although his efforts to induce the two races to co-operate whole-heartedly met with no lasting success.

On leaving the colony in 1644 he observed that the secret of ruling Pernambuco was to remember that the Dutch merchants attached more importance to their money and goods than to their lives, whereas the Portuguese inhabitants valued courtesy and politeness more than property or pelf. The planters (he said on another occasion) were mostly 'as poor as Job and as proud as Braganza'. Those of the Portuguese who were pro-Dutch should only be favoured secretly, he advised, so as to avoid arousing the suspicion and resentment of their compatriots. He stressed the unreliability of evidence extorted under torture, even when this was duly sanctioned by law; and he emphasized the importance of maintaining strict discipline among the garrison, while paying them punctually and feeding them well. All in all, it is not surprising to learn from Fr. Manuel Calado, who was a frequent and welcome guest at government-house, that the Pernambuco Portuguese called Johan Maurits their 'Santo Antonio' after the most popular saint in their calendar. His departure was sincerely mourned by the whole colony, Calvinist Netherlanders, Catholic Portuguese, and cannibal Tapuyas alike.[1] The total production of sugar during his tenure of office was estimated at 218,220 chests valued at 28 million florins, and the sugar industry was well on the way to complete recovery when he left. It was also during his rule that improved methods of cultivating sugar and tobacco were introduced from Pernambuco into the Antilles, thus giving a great impetus to the economic development of the English and French possessions in the Caribbean.

---

[1] Cf. the so-called 'political testament' of Johan Maurits (6 May 1644) in Barlaeus-Naber, *Nederlandsch Brazilië*, pp. 373–83; Calado, *Valeroso Lucideno*, pp. 42, 129.

Such, in barest outline, is a summary of the achievements of Johan Maurits during his seven years in Brazil, and we must now consider in more detail how far they were likely to last, and how far they were offset by other factors in the daily life of the colony. There is no doubt that the greatest single asset which the West India Company possessed in Brazil was the personality and character of the governor-general, who was locally styled the prince of Nassau, for reasons which Fr. Manuel Calado explains with his habitual infusion of sly malice: 'Because the Dutch styled and called him thus, and the Portuguese, in order to avoid incurring his displeasure, and to curry favour with him, would have given him even higher titles if he had accepted them, on account of their subjugation as captives, and he being their lord and master.'[1] Johan Maurits was, as a Brazilian historian recently observed, a true *grand seigneur* who only felt at home in a spacious palace or on an extensive estate.[2] He constructed two country-seats on the island of Antonio Vaz, where he laid out the new city of Mauritsstad, one being called by a Dutch name, 'Vrijburg', and the other by a Portuguese, 'Boa Vista'. Fr. Manuel Calado gives us an entertaining account of Johan Maurits and his princely tastes in the graphic pages of the *Valeroso Lucideno*.

'The Prince-Count of Nassau was so preoccupied with the construction of his new city, that to induce the *moradores* to build houses, he himself went about very carefully plotting the measurements and laying out the streets, so that the town should look more beautiful. And by means of a dike or levee through the middle of it, he brought the water of the river Capivaribe from the entrance of the bar. Canoes, boats and barges entered by this dike for the use of the *moradores*, underneath wooden bridges which crossed over this dike in some places, as in Holland, so that the island was completely surrounded by water. He also made there a country-seat which cost him many *cruzados*, and in the midst of that sandy and barren waste he planted a garden stocked with every kind of fruit-tree which grows in Brazil, as well as with many others brought from different parts; and by bringing in much other

[1] Calado, *Valeroso Lucideno*, pp. 46, 123. Johan Maurits became a genuine *Fürst* in Nov. 1652, when the Emperor Ferdinand III made him a prince of the Holy Roman Empire.
[2] Gonsalves de Mello, *Tempo dos Flamengos*, p. 95.

fruitful earth from outside in lighters, together with a great quantity of manure, he made the site as fertile as the most fruitful soil. He planted in this garden two thousand coconut-trees bringing them there from other places, because he asked the *moradores* for them and they sent them to him in carts. He made some long and beautiful avenues of them, like the Alameda of Aranjues, and in other places many trellised vine-arbours and garden-beds of vegetables and flowers, with some summerhouses for gambling and entertainment. Hither came the ladies and his friends to pass the summer holidays, and to enjoy their convivial gatherings, picnics and drinking parties, as is the custom in Holland, to the sound of musical instruments. The Prince liked everyone to come and see his rarities, and he himself delighted in showing and explaining them. And in order to live more at his ease, he left the buildings where he stayed originally, and moved to this country-seat with the greater part of his household.

'He also brought thither every kind of bird and animal that he could find; and since the local *moradores* knew his taste and inclination, each one brought him whatever rare bird or beast he could find in the back-lands. There he brought parrots, macaws, *jacijs*, *canindes*, wading-birds, pheasants, guinea-fowl, ducks, swans, peacocks, turkeys, a great quantity of barnyardfowls, and so many doves that they could not be counted. There he kept tigers, ounces, *cissuarana*, ant-bears, apes, *quati*, squirrel-monkeys, Indian boars, goats from Cape Verde, sheep from Angola, *cutia*, *pagua*, tapirs, wild boars, a great multitude of rabbits—and in short there was not a curious thing in Brazil which he did not have, for the *moradores* sent him these with a good will, since they saw that he was kindly and well-disposed towards them. And thus they also helped him to build these two establishments, both the country-seat Vrijburg where he lived, as well as Boa Vista on the bank of the Capivaribe, where he spent many days strolling around and enjoying himself. For some sent him wood, others tiles and bricks, others lime, and in short they all helped him in what they could. And he showed himself so grateful and favoured the Portuguese so much, that it seemed as if they had a father in him, and he greatly lightened the pain and grief they were in at seeing themselves captives.'[1]

---

[1] Calado, *Valeroso Lucideno*, pp. 52–53. I have left in their original Brazilian forms the names of some birds and animals which I cannot identify with certainty.

Fr. Manuel Calado did not exaggerate the popularity of Johan Maurits with the Portuguese of Pernambuco, and not for nothing did they term the heretic but humane and humanist prince their Santo Antonio. As indicated above, Johan Maurits's guiding principle in dealing with the *moradores* was his conviction that if they were treated with courtesy and consideration, they would be more amenable and obedient to the Company's rule than were the Dutch colonists themselves. 'I know by experience', he wrote in his so-called 'political testament' of 1644, 'that the Portuguese are a people who value courtesy and consideration more highly than they do money and goods.'[1] In this he was not far wrong, and his policy certainly succeeded so long as he was at the helm. Nor were the Portuguese unmindful or ungrateful. Shortly after the restoration of Portuguese independence, but before news had been received at Lisbon of the treacherous capture of Luanda, King John IV seriously contemplated asking Johan Maurits to become commander-in-chief of the Portuguese forces and their allied auxiliaries against the common Spanish foe.[2] Even after Johan Maurits's departure from Brazil, and at a time when a real and a paper war was raging between Portugal and the United Provinces, no criticism was voiced of his behaviour by scurrilous pamphleteers who otherwise pulled no punches, Calado's innuendos against his financial integrity aside—and financial integrity was not seriously expected of any colonial governor in those days—the references to Johan Maurits in contemporary Portuguese works are very favourable, apart from his treacherous seizure of Angola and the Maranhão.

Nowhere is Johan Maurits's policy of conciliation seen more clearly than in the proceedings of the legislative assembly which was convened on his initiative in August 1640, and in the so-called 'political testament' or injunctions which he left to his successors on his departure for Holland in May 1644. From these sources, as well as from the minutes of the meetings of the Calvinist consistory in Brazil, we can trace the development

---

[1] Barlaeus-Naber, *Nederlandsch Brazilië*, p. 378; *RIHGB*, lviii. 230. Portuguese punctilio made a similar impression on other contemporary Northerners. Cf. the comments of the English East India Company's factors at Surat, in W. Foster [ed.], *The English Factories in India, 1637–1641*, p. 204; ibid., *1642–1645* (Oxford, 1912–13), p. 210.

[2] Marquis of Montalvão to Johan Maurits (12 Mar. 1642) in Barlaeus-Naber, *Nederlandsch Brazilië*, pp. 306–7; *RIAGP*, no. 34 (1887), pp. 54–55.

of Johan Maurits's enlightened policy of racial and religious toleration, and ascertain to what degree he was successful.

An outline of Johan Maurits's preliminary reforms and his administrative measures for cleansing the Augean Stables of Recife was given on pp. 72–74, but the result was not so successful as Barlaeus and other panegyrists imply. A report which was made to the Heeren XIX in 1640 shows that many of the abuses rampant in 1636 were far from extinct four years later.[1] Indeed, Quelen's denunciation of the venality of Dutch justice at Recife has striking affiliations with Calado's comparison of Olinda with Sodom and Gomorrah in the previous decade. Quelen is careful to exculpate Johan Maurits from any share in these abuses. He states expressly that the Portuguese *moradores* and the Dutch soldiers were sure of obtaining justice tempered with mercy, if only they could get direct access to him. The difficulty was that corrupt magistrates, bailiffs, and jacks-in-office interposed between Johan Maurits and the *moradores* on the one hand, while the Dutch senior officers strove to prevent him from mitigating the rigour of the court-martial procedure against their men on the other. One of the reforms suggested by Quelen was that the leading planters and other *moradores* should be assembled in conclave at Olinda once a year, under the presidency of the governor-general, when their grievances could be discussed and remedial measures adopted. Whether this was Quelen's own idea or (as seems more probable) derived from Johan Maurits, I do not know; but Johan Maurits did convene a legislative assembly composed of the *moradores'* elected representatives from the captaincies of Pernambuco, Itamaracá, and Paraíba, from 27 August to 4 September 1640.[2]

In his opening address, Johan Maurits observed that the victory of January 1640, obtained 'without harm to the people', had brought peace to Pernambuco. Nevertheless, the colony was still plagued by 'some abuses, unnatural customs, oppressive insolencies, ravages of robbers, misbehaviour of the soldiery, and disobedience of the *moradores*. All of which, we suppose, is chiefly due to the little love which the Portuguese have towards the Netherlanders'. Johan Maurits went on to say that he and

[1] A. van Quelen, *Kort Verhael vanden staet van Fernambuc* (Amsterdam, 1640). In the French edition of the same year, the author's name is given as De Guelen, but I have retained the other form, as all my quotations are from the Dutch.

[2] The proceedings of the assembly are printed in full (in Portuguese translation) in *RIAGP*, v. 173–238; cf. *RIHGB*, lvi. 117–39.

his councillors, on the contrary, earnestly wished to show their good will towards the Portuguese. They had therefore convoked this assembly of the leading notables to discuss their existing grievances, 'and to provide them with the most efficacious remedies with your approval and pleasure'. He concluded by urging them all to speak their minds with the utmost freedom and as God inspired them.

This the representatives proceeded to do, and the deliberations of this body—the first (and for a long time the only) legislative assembly in South America—were marked by a frankness and reasonableness which does credit to both sides. For instance, it was agreed that the *moradores* would be given back the weapons which had been confiscated from them at the time of Torre's armada, so that they could defend themselves and their plantations against marauding bands of military deserters and revolted slaves; but they would not be obliged to use these weapons against the Portuguese guerrillas, despite the harm that these were doing to the Dutch. Arrangements were also made for mutual aid to be given by the outlying Dutch garrisons and Portuguese plantation-owners against the assaults of bandits, and for the apprehension of runaway slaves. The Dutch authorities also promised to establish standing patrols (partly paid and fed by the *moradores*) to deal with unauthorized foraging by their own soldiers, and to ensure that these did not oppress the planters. We know from other sources that the Dutch soldiers, with their pay and rations usually in arrears, often committed such excesses as killing an ox merely for the sake of eating the tongue—a particularly aggravating crime in a community which depended on the labour of oxen only slightly less than on that of Negro slaves.[1]

Johan Maurits and his councillors also took cognizance of the numerous complaints made against the minor Dutch officials, such as the bailiffs and sheriffs (*schouten*) who were very prone to abuse their powers over the *moradores*, and whose venality was a byword. Remedial measures were proposed and adopted to curb these petty tyrants, although their enforcement proved another and a more difficult matter. Decisions were also taken to speed up the administration of justice in the local courts, and to

---

[1] Quelen, *Kort Verhael*, p. 13. For the association between Negroes and oxen cf. G. Freyre, *Nordeste. Aspectos da influencia da canna sobre a vida e a paisagem do Nordeste do Brasil* (Rio, 1937), pp. 89, 101-8.

facilitate appeals to the higher tribunals at Recife. These resolutions included the reduction of legal fees, and permission for Portuguese litigants to plead in their own language. Other resolutions were adopted with a view to simplifying the collection of imposts and taxes, and preventing abuses in the fiscal administration.

It is true that many of these reforms, although explicitly stated by Johan Maurits to have legal sanction as from that date, were enforced either half-heartedly or not at all; and others had to be referred to the Heeren XIX for confirmation, which was not always forthcoming. But there is no doubt that the position began slowly to improve, particularly after the cessation of guerrilla activity on orders from Bahia in March 1641. In any event, the oppression and extortion of which the *moradores* complained in the judicial, fiscal, and administrative spheres were little if any worse than the corresponding abuses which riddled the officialdom of Portuguese Brazil. Seventeenth-century colonial administrators had very different standards and ideas from those of the present day; and a comparison of the planters' complaints from the records of Portuguese and Dutch Brazil shows clearly enough that it was a case of six of one and half a dozen of the other. Anyone who doubts this should read some of Padre Antonio Vieira's sermons denouncing the rapacity of the crown officials and lawyers at Bahia, or glance through that satirical masterpiece, the *Arte de Furtar* (*Art of Thieving*), usually attributed to the same Jesuit, but almost certainly the work of Dr. Antonio de Sousa de Macedo.[1] The *moradores* of Pernambuco felt that in Johan Maurits they had a governor-general whose concern for their welfare could hardly have been greater had he been a Brazilian-born Portuguese. There is little reason to doubt the spontaneity of the petition which they addressed to the Heeren XIX during the historic conclave of 1640, asking that his tenure of office might be extended indefinitely.

Official corruption and administrative incompetence were not necessarily, therefore, a permanent bar to the acceptance of the Dutch yoke; although it is doubtless true that (other things being equal) people would rather be oppressed by their

[1] 'Sermão da visitação de Nossa Senhora' (1640), and 'Sermão da dominga vigesima segunda, post pentecosten' (1653), in *Obras Escolhidas* (ed. Sergio-Cidade), x. 104–10, 130–1; A. Pena Junior, *A Arte de Furtar e o seu autor* (2 vols., Rio, 1946). Cf. also *Atas da camara da cidade do Salvador, Bahia, 1625–1659* (3 vols., Bahia, 1944–9), *passim*.

own nationals than by foreigners. A much more serious problem was posed by the difference in religion. This formed a dividing line between Portuguese and Dutch which not even Johan Maurits's tolerance and tact could obliterate, although he probably came nearer to success than any other man living could have done. There was inevitably a great gulf fixed between Catholic Portuguese and Calvinist Dutch; but Johan Maurits's position was made still more difficult by the fact that the West India Company was essentially a creation of the militant Calvinist or Contra-Remonstrant party, whose adherents regarded any toleration of Popery as pandering to the Great Whore of Babylon.

It is true that the original charter of the West India Company, as also the solemn declarations made to the *moradores* of Brazil in 1624, 1630, and 1635, emphasized that liberty of conscience, and latterly a certain degree of liberty of worship, would be allowed to Roman Catholics. But these concessions had always been regarded askance by many Calvinist zealots, particularly in Zeeland where the votaries of the 'true Christian religion' were strongly represented. One of the most influential of these self-appointed sentinels on the watch-towers of Zion, the Reverend Godfried Udemans, argued in his *Spiritual Rudder* that it was sinful and illegal for the Dutch to promise liberty of worship to Roman Catholic Portuguese in the colonies which had been wrested from the Lusitanian crown.[1] It was indeed ironical that the most rigid Calvinist extremists in the United Netherlands should have found themselves in control of a large and equally fanatical Roman Catholic population in Brazil.

Fr. Manuel Calado records many instances of Johan Maurits's personal kindness to the Roman Catholic priests and friars in Pernambuco, and the Dutch records likewise show how he rejected or evaded the Calvinist consistory's repeated demands for the more effective curbing of 'Popish superstition and idolatry'. Johan Maurits even invited Calado to live in his palace; and when the friar politely declined, the prince insisted that he should live near him and visit him frequently, which Calado duly did. The friar was also allowed to say mass behind closed doors in the precincts of government-house. Equally striking testimony to the tolerant and understanding religious policy of Johan Maurits is given by Calado's pet aversion, the

[1] G. Udemans, '*T Geestelick Roer* (Dordrecht, 1655), pp. 311–13, 375 ff.

vicar-general Gaspar Ferreira; by the Jesuits (even though these were normally excluded from his favours); and by the French Capuchin friars. One of the latter wrote to the College of the Propaganda Fide at Rome: 'Blessed be God who has made the prince who rules this country so well-disposed and benevolent that he encourages us with his kindness, and not only does not hinder our plans, but on the contrary tries to forward them in so far as he can. He is a prince indisputably adorned with all the natural virtues, very compassionate and generous to all. He does not demolish churches nor utter mortal threats against the Catholics, but is peaceful and mild; we find that he lacks only the light of the true faith to make him a perfect man.'[1]

Johan Maurits naturally had an uphill task in defending the Catholics against the zeal of the *predikants*, who continually tried to whittle down the amount of religious freedom which the *moradores* had been formally granted. The consistory could not very well refuse to allow liberty of conscience, since this much was guaranteed by the terms of the Company's charter and was enjoyed by Roman Catholics in the United Netherlands; but liberty of public worship was something which they were ill disposed to tolerate. In 1638, for example, the consistory complained of 'the great liberty allowed the Papists, even in places which had surrendered unconditionally'. The *predikants* pointed out that monks and friars were 'allowed to live in their cloisters, draw their incomes and revenues unhindered, and officiate at the marriages of Netherlanders', &c. They petitioned Johan Maurits to stop these practices, as no such liberties were allowed to the Roman Catholics in the Seven Provinces.

Johan Maurits adopted a policy of masterly inactivity towards all these complaints, as he explained in his 'political testimony' of 1644. He gave the *predikants* fair words, and promised to see that all unauthorized Roman Catholic activities were duly curbed; but in fact he deliberately refrained from doing so, and continued to give aid and comfort more or less secretly to Calado and the Capuchins. It is therefore not surprising

[1] Calado, *Valeroso Lucideno*, pp. 42, 47–49, 51–52, 62–64, 133; Fr. Colombe de Nantes, O.F.M. Cap., to the Propaganda Fide, 25. viii. 1643, printed by Fr. F. Leite de Faria, O.F.M. Cap., in *Brasilia* (Coimbra, 1954), ix. 63–64; Gonsalves de Mello, *Fr. Manuel Calado do Salvador* (Recife, 1954), pp. 63, 87–93, 105–7; S. Leite, S.J., *História*, v. 394–5.

to find that complaints of the excessive freedom allowed the Portuguese in celebrating the rites of their religion continually recur throughout the years of Johan Maurits's rule.[1] The government often promised to adopt stern measures but it very seldom did so. One such rare occasion occurred in 1640. Johan Maurits had given the *moradores* permission to rebuild one of the ruined chapels at Olinda, although they already had the use of one church and two convents there. When the work was finished the Calvinist ministers forcibly seized the building for Protestant use, apparently with the tacit support of some members of the governing council.[2]

Johan Maurits's religious toleration was even extended to include the Jews, although hatred, ridicule, and contempt for Jewry was the one point on which the *predikants* and the friars were united. Fr. Manuel Calado asserts that the Jews publicly congregated for worship in two synagogues at Recife; and the Calvinist consistory remonstrated against the toleration of Jewish religious practices almost as frequently as they did against 'Popish idolatry'. The preachers complained that the local Jews were allowed to marry with Christians, convert Christians to Judaism, circumcise Christians, employ Christian servants in their houses, and keep Christian women as their concubines. The consistory considered it the bounden duty of Johan Maurits and his council to stop these unauthorized activities which gave great scandal to Protestants and Catholics alike. Only in Pernambuco, they complained, did the Jews enjoy unlimited freedom; being subjected to some sort of restrictions in every other country in the world. Johan Maurits ignored both these and subsequent protests; although when individual Jews occasionally overstepped the mark by publicly criticizing the Christian religion, such offenders were severely dealt with. Jewish appreciation of Johan Maurits's attitude was convincingly expressed in 1642, when their representative informed the Heeren XIX 'that if His Excellency could be paid to stay in this land by the purchase of anything in the world, that they would find no price too great to pay, even if it were their own blood, if only they might retain him'.[3]

[1] 'Classicale Acta van Brazilië, 1636–1644', in *Kron. Hist. Gen. Utrecht*, xxix. 328, 331–3, 343, 347–8, 361, 363, 375, 393–4, 400–1, 403, 410–11.
[2] 'Classicale Acta Brazilië', op. cit., pp. 347, 363; Quelen, *Kort Verhael*, p. 17.
[3] 'Classicale Acta Brazilië', op. cit., pp. 329, 343, 348, 361, 386, 400; A. Wiznitzer, *The Records of the earliest Jewish community in the New World* (New York,

Since the religious beliefs of the Negroes and the Amerindians (such as they were) were likewise left virtually undisturbed by the authorities, it can be asserted that a greater degree of religious freedom was allowed in Netherlands Brazil during the years of Johan Maurits's rule than anywhere else in the Western world.[1] For this alone his name and fame are deserving of lasting remembrance. Unfortunately, he was too far in advance of his time; and although he kept the peace between the warring factions of Christianity for seven years, even he could not permanently heal the breach made by the Reformation between Catholic and Protestant. If he had stayed longer, or if he had been succeeded by a man of the same calibre, greater results might have been achieved, although even this is doubtful. The efforts of the Calvinist ministers to convert the local *moradores* failed completely, as they themselves admitted, and the Portuguese never came to regard the religion of the heretic intruders with anything else but loathing. The friars, on the contrary, were much more successful in converting a number of the Netherlanders of both sexes. Dutchmen who married local women, and there were quite a number of them despite the alleged unattractiveness of most of the Pernambucan ladies, usually adopted their wives' religion.[2] Many of the West India Company's mercenaries were also Roman Catholics, or crypto-Roman Catholics, and the friars had no difficulties as regards these; while Dutch Catholics were more numerous at this period than is commonly supposed. Nevertheless, the gulf remained between the adherents of the two militant and mutually exclusive creeds. John Maurits himself bridged it, but with his departure in May 1644 the bridge was removed, leaving the rift as wide and deep as ever.

Another barrier between Portuguese and Dutch was formed by their widely differing social habits and customs. Take, for example, their respective attitudes to wine and women. Although Portugal was a wine-producing country, the Portuguese

1954), pp. 23–24; P. J. Bouman, *Johan Maurits*, p. 74; letter from the leaders of the Jewish community, d. 1 May 1642, reproduced in facsimile by A. Wiznitzer in *Aonde Vamos? Semanario Judaico independente do Brasil*, no. 589 (Rio de Janeiro, 7 Oct. 1954).

[1] Most Asian countries compared more than favourably with European nations in this respect. Cf. S. Sen [ed.], *Indian Travels of Thevenot and Careri* (New Delhi, 1949), pp. xli–xlii.

[2] For some concrete instances see Gonsalves de Mello, *Tempo dos Flamengos*, pp. 166–70.

were (and still are) noted for their abstemiousness. The chaplain to the English factory at Lisbon in the last quarter of the seventeenth century justly observed: 'I believe there is no people in Europe less addicted to that most inexcusable vice of drunkenness than they are, . . . the people of this country, persons of quality more especially, and indeed all who have the least regard to their credit, being very shy of drinking wine.'[1] Holland, on the contrary, produced no vines, but wine was cheaper, more plentiful, and better appreciated there than in many wine-drinking countries.[2] A famous Dutch colonial governor wrote of his countrymen in the East, 'our nation must drink or die'; and a much-travelled contemporary of his observed that most of the officials of the West India Company 'knew nothing but how to drink themselves drunk'.[3] We have seen how Fr. Manuel Calado watched with fascinated horror the drinking-bouts over which Johan Maurits jovially presided, although prowess with the bottle was not the only art which was cultivated in Netherlands Brazil.

As for women, the attitude of the Portuguese towards the fair sex was thought to be unduly jealous and restrictive even by the Spaniards, who, like their neighbours, had perhaps inherited their ideas about the seclusion of women from the centuries of Moorish occupation.[4] On the other hand, women in the United Provinces probably enjoyed more freedom than anywhere else in contemporary Europe. Foreign observers frequently noted that most Dutchmen not only discussed matters of business and of state with their wives in private, but drank freely with them in public.[5] This was, of course, the

---

[1] J. Colbatch, An Account of the Court of Portugal (London, 1700), i. 4–5.

[2] Aenwysinge dat men van de VOC en WIC een compagnie dient te maecken (The Hague, 1644), pp. 8, 12. Cf. V. Barbour, Capitalism in Amsterdam in the 17th century, pp. 92, 96.

[3] '. . . want onse natie drincken ofte sterven moeten' (H. T. Colenbrander [ed.], Jan Pieterszoon Coen. Bescheiden, i. 459); 'sulcke narren in't Landt stuerden, die niet en wisten als van droncke drincken' (D. P. de Vries, Korte Historiael, Hoorn, 1655; ed. Linschoten Vereeniging, p. 178).

[4] Cf. the lines from Tirso de Molina, Amor Médico, quoted in Biblos, xxiv (Coimbra, 1948), p. 28; Thomé Pinheiro da Veiga, Fastigimia (ed. Porto, 1911), pp. 37–38, 44, 82–83, 143–7, 153, 268; D. Francisco Manuel de Mello, Carta de Guia de Casados (ed. Lisbon, 1651), pp. 76–77, 79–80, 99–100.

[5] Noted by such contemporary observers as Fr. Manuel Calado, Francisco de Sousa Coutinho ('. . . seguindo a maxima framenga em todos os tempos de dar muita mão à mulher', Correspondência diplomática, ii. 59), and Sir William Temple.

strongest possible contrast to Portuguese practice. The chronicler Duarte Nunes de Leão assures us in his *Descrição do reino de Portugal* (Lisbon, 1610) that women who drank wine were regarded as being in the same category as those who committed adultery. Johan Maurits and his council wrote in 1638 that the local *moradores* jealously secluded their womenfolk, 'thus recognizing that the men of their own race are prone to covet their neighbours' wives. As a rule, the women, even when young, lose their teeth; and owing to their sedentary way of life they are not so active as the Dutch, walking on their *chapins* [high-heeled cork shoes] as if they had chains on their legs. They only go out covered, and are carried in a hammock with a carpet slung over the top, or hidden in a sedan-chair, so that they adorn themselves only to be seen by their intimate friends. When they go out to pay visits, they first send a notification of their intention; the lady of the house then seats herself on a beautiful Turkish carpet on the floor and awaits her friends, who also squat down on the carpet at her side, cross-legged like tailors, keeping their feet covered, as it would be a great shame to let anyone see their feet.'[1]

The difference between the Dutch and the Portuguese attitude to women emerges clearly from the following story related by Fr. Manuel Calado. A deputation of planters' wives came to beg on bended knees before Johan Maurits for the life of Dona Jeronima de Almeida, 'mother of nine girls who were almost grown women and of three sons', who had been condemned to death for sheltering guerrillas. 'The Prince Johan Maurits Count of Nassau received these ladies with a smiling countenance (which he had for everyone), and he asked them very courteously to rise up from the ground, telling them that if he had realized he was to have such beautiful and honoured guests, he would have prepared a banquet such as they deserved; but that since they had taken him unawares, he could only invite them to join him at his ordinary dinner. They kissed his hand for this grace and favour, replying that the banquet which they came to seek at his house was that, finding grace in his eyes, His Excellency would be pleased to stop so great a cruelty

---

[1] 'Somier Discours over de vier geconquesteerde capitanias, 14 Jan. 1638', in *Bijdr. Hist. Gen. Utrecht*, ii. 257–317. Cf. pp. 173–4 of the Portuguese translation in *RIAGP*, no. 34 (1887), which is preferable to the original Dutch text disfigured by numerous misprints.

and pardon Dona Jeronima. And that as for dining at his table, they would take this favour as received; for it was not usual nor customary among the Portuguese for women to eat with anyone other than their husbands, and they would not even sit down at table with them if anyone else was present save a father or a brother; nevertheless, that favour which His Excellency had offered them, they would keep in the intimacy of their hearts. The Prince was satisfied with their courteous and honourable answer, and he dismissed them with the assurance that he would do everything he could to favour their petition, accompanying them to the top of the staircase on their way out. He forthwith signed a decree commuting Dona Jeronima's death-sentence, by virtue of the power and authority he possessed as governor and captain-general of Pernambuco and the other captaincies conquered and subdued by the Dutch.'[1] Fr. Manuel slyly adds that the ladies' petition was reinforced by ninety chests of sugar, most of which were apparently retained by Gaspar Dias Ferreira, the 'contact-man' who had arranged the interview.

Although a considerable number of Dutchmen married Pernambucan women, Fr. Manuel Calado assures us that there was not a single instance of a Portuguese man having a love-affair with a heretic woman, let alone marrying one. The nineteenth-century Brazilian historian, Manuel de Oliveira Lima, gallantly comments that he trusts the friar did his countrymen an injustice in this respect; but however that may have been, it remains true that most of the Dutchmen who married local women tended to identify themselves with their wives' religion and country rather than with their own. We cannot tell how far this process would have continued, or which side of the family the children would eventually have chosen, as the colony had only three years of uninterrupted peace in the whole of its existence. It seems probable, however, that these mixed marriages would have increased and multiplied if the revolt of 1645 had not abruptly stopped the process. It may be added that Johan Maurits, although he carefully avoided the yoke of matrimony,[2] did not remain fancy-free in Brazil. If the gossip retailed by Fr. Manuel Calado is to be trusted on this point, he jilted his first mistress, Margaret Soler, for the

[1] Calado, *Valeroso Lucideno*, p. 63.
[2] 'Mauritius nooit vast aen't juk der vrouwen', as Vondel sang in 1660.

daughter of the local garrison-commander, with the result that the unfortunate Margaret died of a broken heart.[1]

As may be imagined, Johan Maurits had a difficult task in conciliating the interests of the Portuguese planters and *moradores* with those of the Dutch invaders, whether these latter were officials, merchants, settlers, or soldiers. Since the colony was virtually an occupied territory, and the bulk of the population was latently or overtly hostile, Johan Maurits stressed that it was essential to keep the garrison well paid, well fed, and up to strength. He pointed out that if this was done, the soldiers would have no excuse for plundering the *moradores*, and could be kept in their garrisons under strict discipline. Unfortunately, the directors had not sufficient money to pay their troops punctually or to ration them adequately; and they sought to economize by reducing the strength of the garrison, and by sending out insufficient replacements. Their payments were slow and the arrears consequently piled up; although this was not necessarily their own fault, but mainly due to the fact that they did not receive the provincial subsidies on time or in full.

They tried to induce time-expired men to remain in Brazil as settlers, instead of returning to Holland to take their discharge, with the double object of obtaining colonists who were inured to a tropical climate and of saving money on return-passages. A fair number of men did so, and more would have done so if they had been paid what was due to them, which was seldom the case. It was the Company's system to withhold a proportion of the men's pay, as a security for their good behaviour and as a precaution against desertion, until the time of their engagement (usually three years) had expired, when they were supposed to receive the balance. In practice, the soldiers' accounts were often 'cooked' by their own paymasters, or by the Company's officials who issued them with clothing and other necessaries which were charged to their accounts at fictitious rates. Consequently, many soldiers who expected to return to Holland with a good credit-balance after long and faithful service in Brazil,

---

[1] Calado, *Valeroso Lucideno*, p. 128. Margaret's father, Vincent Joachim Soler, was originally a Valencian Augustinian friar who had renounced Catholicism to become a Calvinist convert and minister. His *Cort ende sonderlingh verhael* (Amsterdam, 1639) is one of the most curious accounts of the colony. Cf. Gonsalves de Mello, *Tempo dos Flamengos* (index *in voce* Soler), and J. H. Rodrigues, *Historiografia e Bibliografia*, no. 436.

found that on their discharge they received little or nothing.
Naturally, those who did return to Europe were often exceedingly embittered, and they put off potential recruits with their
complaints, warning all and sundry not to go to Brazil. The
Dutch colonial court martial procedure was also exceedingly
rigorous, and it was alleged that before the arrival of Johan
Maurits these military tribunals 'made no more difficulty about
sentencing a soldier to death than they would a hen'. Johan
Maurits strove with some success to mitigate these and other
abuses; but although the soldiers realized that 'his goodness and
diligence keeps their lives and honour', the Company's precarious financial situation never allowed the directors to pay and
maintain their troops on a really satisfactory basis.[1]

Johan Maurits was very careful of the welfare of his men,
but if he was not a harsh martinet, neither was he a lax disciplinarian. He was particularly anxious to prevent them from
plundering and outraging the *moradores*, which they were very
apt to do if not forcibly restrained. The soldiers knew that
most of the *moradores* had given aid and comfort to the guerrilla
bands from Bahia whenever they could, and the former consequently felt justified in helping themselves to livestock or even
more valuable things on occasion. Johan Maurits never coun-
tenanced these unofficial reprisals, and punished them severely
when they came to his notice.

All the nations of northern Europe were well represented
among the Company's soldiery. Pierre Moreau claimed that
Frenchmen were the most numerous; and in 1642 Johan
Maurits wrote that the majority of the men were 'English, Scots,
or Frenchmen', when he was ordered to discharge all those not
of German, Dutch, or Scandinavian origin.[2] At one time the
garrison at Paraíba included over 150 English soldiers under
the command of their compatriot, Captain John Goodlad.
The West India Company's soldiers were recruited by voluntary enlistment, although the crimps who enlisted recruits often
virtually kidnapped unsuspecting foreigners or country lads.
The botanist and naturalist, E. Rumphius, who later achieved
great fame in the East Indies, enlisted as a young man for service in sunny Italy (as he thought) but found himself on board

[1] Quelen, *Kort Verhael*, pp. 4–5, 7, 16–17.
[2] P. Moreau, *Histoire des derniers troubles du Brésil entre les Hollandois et les Portugais*
(Paris, 1651), p. 14; Gonsalves de Mello, *Tempo dos Flamengos*, p. 195.

a ship bound for the still sunnier Brazil.[1] Disbanded mercenaries from the campaigns of the Thirty Years War were also
another perennial source of recruits. But the Portuguese soldiers
were recruited by even more dubious methods, jail-deliveries
being the usual way of scraping together some cannon-fodder
for the colonial battlefields.

Many of the Dutch soldiers stationed in Pernambuco married
local women, and despite (or perhaps because of) their sedentary
habits, those ladies evidently made better wives and mothers than
did their Dutch sisters. These latter (it was freely alleged) were
apt to take to drink, cuckold their husbands, and neglect their
children. A similar state of things prevailed in the East Indies,
where it was found that Macaonese women and other Eurasians
made better wives and mothers than did the adventurous but
bibulous wenches who came out from the Netherlands.[2]

Frederick the Great once remarked that the spirit of an army
depends on the officer-corps, and the same principle was
enunciated a little later by Lord Cornwallis, who wrote home
from India to his commander-in-chief: 'Your Royal Highness
well knows that all troops are good or bad according to the
merit and exertion of their officers.' From this point of view,
the West India Company did not lack good commanders who
were capable of getting the best out of their men. Apart from
Johan Maurits himself, Arciszewski was quite outstanding; and
even after the premature removal of the Polish colonel from
the Brazilian scene, the Heeren XIX could still count on some
first-rate officers with a decade of experience in this field. The
German Von Schoppe, the Englishman Henderson, and the
Dutchman Van den Brande were opponents worthy of any
man's steel; while the Company's naval service was still more
fortunate in the possession of great fighting seamen such as
Lichthart and Houtbeen. Future events were to show that the
Portuguese commanders on land were more than a match for
their opposite numbers, but this was not yet apparent in the
years 1637–44. The Portuguese leaders might excel in guerrilla
warfare and raiding tactics, but they could hardly meet and
beat their opponents in the open field. In this as in so many
other vital spheres, the directors of the West India Company

[1] S. P. L'Honoré Naber, *De West Indische Compagnie in Brazilië en Guinee* (1930), p. 22.
[2] Cf. P. Coolhaas [ed.], *Jan Pietersz. Coen. Bescheiden omtrent zijn verblijf in Indië*,
vii. 336; cf. Gonsalves de Mello, *Tempo dos Flamengos*, pp. 145–7.

seemed to be better served than the recently re-established but still highly insecure king of Portugal.

As regards the civilian elements, the Dutch in Brazil could be divided into two catagories: those who were employed by the West India Company (*dienaaren*) and those who were not (*vrijluiden*). The personnel of the High and Secret Council, the Political Council or Council of Justice, and the Financial Council were all drawn from salaried officials of the Company. These officials were not supposed to engage in private trade or to operate sugar plantations for their own account, but many of them did so. Lower down the administrative ladder were the regional or municipal councils which Johan Maurits substituted for the Portuguese *camaras* in 1637. They were organized on the metropolitan Dutch model, but were composed of leading Dutch and Portuguese delegates, selected by the governor-general and council from regional electoral lists which were submitted to them annually. These local bodies had both municipal and judicial functions, but these latter were limited to litigation involving a maximum of 120 florins. Litigants had the right of appeal to the Council of Justice at Recife.

The conquered captaincies were subdivided into administrative districts, of which Pernambuco, being the largest and most populous, comprised six. Each of these contained a *schout* (bailiff, sheriff), who was a salaried Company official, and who was supposed to keep an eye on the Company's interests in his district and to investigate all misdemeanours and abuses. These worthies were heartily detested by the *moradores*, who complained that they used their authority solely to extort money by threats and blackmail.[1] It was also alleged that they embezzled practically everything which they confiscated in the Company's name. Calado gives chapter and verse for many of their misdeeds, and although some of his allegations may be exaggerated, Johan Maurits himself admitted on more than one occasion that these functionaries grossly abused their powers. These petty tyrants formed the weakest link in the governmental system; and although the governor-general and his

---

[1] As did their namesakes with the Roman Catholics in the United Provinces. Cf. Barlaeus-Naber, *Nederlandsch Brazilië*, pp. 171, 379–80, 386, 404; Quelen, *Kort Verhael*, p. 22; P. Geyl, *The Netherlands Divided*, p. 81. For their excesses in Brazil cf. also Calado, *Valeroso Lucideno*, bk. iii, ch. 1.

council made sporadic efforts to make them more honest and efficient, no lasting results were achieved. Their intolerable behaviour was indeed one of the principal causes of the rising in 1645. Finally, the Calvinist ministers, chaplains, and lay readers (*krank-bezoekers* and *ziekentrosters*) were also paid by the West India Company which was, as previously noted, essentially a Contra-Remonstrant or militant Calvinist organization.[1]

The Dutch merchants, settlers, and artisans who were not directly employed by the Company were known as *vrijburghers* or *vrijluiden* (free-burghers or freemen). Many of them were time-expired soldiers who had married and settled down as shopkeepers, retail-traders, or smallholders who worked plots (*partidos*) of sugar-cane with the aid of a few slaves. All the burghers were organized into militia companies which could be mobilized to reinforce the garrison in emergencies. Some of the traders were merchants who had come out from Europe to trade on their own account, and others were the agents of individual Dutch merchants or of trading firms. Others again were people who had emigrated from the Netherlands to seek their fortunes in Brazil, whether as sugar-planters, manual labourers, or artisans. Skilled workmen, such as smiths, masons, builders, and cobblers, could be sure of a good living at Recife, where in 1639 a master carpenter could earn six florins a day and his assistant three or four.

On the other hand, efforts to encourage the immigration of skilled agricultural labourers failed almost entirely, for reasons which will be mentioned later. The great bulk of the immigrants did not go to (or at least did not remain in) the rural districts where they were wanted to replace the Portuguese; but they settled in or near Recife, which was grossly over-crowded and where the cost of living was inordinately high. There was a fair number of prosperous merchants among the free-burghers, but Johan Maurits and his council complained that too many of the immigrants were penniless ne'er-do-wells. These latter were merely a burden on the Company, since they were unwilling to work at anything save such parasitic occupations as tavern-keeping.[2] Nevertheless, the free-burghers

[1] For details of the administrative set-up in Netherlands Brazil cf. Barlaeus-Naber, *Nederlandsch Brazilië*, pp. 169–73, 390–4; Wätjen, *Holländische Kolonialreich in Brasilien*, pp. 179–215; Gonsalves de Mello, *Tempo dos Flamengos*, pp. 71–77, 135–40.
[2] Barlaeus-Naber, *Nederlandsch Brazilië*, pp. 157, 159; Gonsalves de Mello,

and traders were the economic mainstay of Recife, which owed much of its development to their industry and activity. Most of the trade passed through their hands, the Company's revenues being mainly derived from the dues, tolls, taxes, and freights which it levied on all shipping and cargoes, in addition to its monopoly of the commerce in Negro slaves, dyewood, and munitions. But for the houses which the burghers had built at Recife, the place would still have been a heap of sand, ex-claimed Quelen in 1640, apparently forgetting Johan Maurits's contribution. The flourishing condition of the free-burghers and traders at Recife formed a striking contrast to the situation at Batavia, where the corresponding class was completely over-shadowed by the East India Company's employees and never achieved a comparable position.

The Jewish community in Netherlands Brazil was also of two kinds. There were practising Jews who had emigrated from Amsterdam, and there were the local crypto-Jews, New-Christians or Marranos, who were already in Pernambuco in con-siderable numbers under Portuguese rule. Many, but by no means all, of this last category renounced their Catholic religion when the Dutch conquered the colony, and formally adhered to the Jewish faith, after submitting to circumcision and other requisite ritual practices. A number of New-Christians con-tinued to conform at least outwardly to Catholicism, since they doubted whether the Dutch dominion would last. Both kinds of Jews were disliked and despised by their 'Old Christian' neighbours, whether Catholic Portuguese or Calvinist Dutch; but the numbers and influence of the Jewish community, though relatively considerable, have been greatly exaggerated by contemporary pamphleteers and modern historians.

Quelen claimed in 1640 that the Jews were nearly twice as numerous as the Christians at Recife; but the recent researches of Dr. A. Wiznitzer have conclusively shown, from census-returns and other trustworthy sources, that the number of Jews in Dutch Brazil reached its highest point with a total of about 1,450 souls in 1644. The total white civilian population of *vrijluiden* was then just under 3,000; so that although the Jews

Tempo dos Flamengos, pp. 155–6. Similar complaints were voiced of time-expired soldiers and others who became free-burghers in the East Indies, where tavern-keeping was their favourite occupation. Cf. E. Reimers [ed.], *Selections from the Dutch records of the Ceylon government. Memoirs of Ryckloff van Goens, 1663–1675* (Colombo, 1932), pp. 24, 34, 54.

formed a relatively large section of the community, they were certainly not in a majority. The bulk of these Israelites were Sephardic Jews, although a few of those who had emigrated from the United Provinces were Ashkenazim. Contrary to what prevailed in the Jewish communities at Amsterdam and elsewhere, the statutes drawn up for the regulation of the Jewish community at Recife made no discrimination whatever against non-Sephardic Jews—a significant innovation for this period, as Dr. Wiznitzer has pointed out.[1]

Contemporary Portuguese and Dutch writers explained that the Jews succeeded in monopolizing much of the retail trade and many other branches of business, because they knew both languages and so became the indispensable middlemen. Relatively few of the Dutch ever learnt to speak Portuguese fluently (Johan Maurits became tongue-tied when he tried, states Calado), and there is no recorded instance of an 'Old Christian' Portuguese of Pernambuco having troubled to learn Dutch. Incidentally, their mutual ignorance of (and unwillingness to learn) each other's language was one of the chief reasons for the unsatisfactory way in which the mixed municipal and rural-district councils functioned. It may be added that the Jews of Recife were not all wealthy 'monopolists and engrossers', as one might easily imagine from reading the anti-Semitic effusions of their Catholic and Calvinist critics. If some arrived in Brazil, as Fr. Manuel Calado wrote, 'with nothing but the little torn garment which they wore', and subsequently made their fortunes, many others achieved only a modest competence at the most, while some remained in abject poverty.

As indicated previously, the Amerindians with whom the Dutch came into contact were likewise of two kinds. The first (usually called 'Brazilians') were those who had been more or less domesticated by the Portuguese, and were grouped together in *aldeias* or village communities. Each village had a native headman who was supervised by a European overseer. These Indians lived in primitive thatched huts on a communal basis, forty or fifty families in a hut. Their worldly possessions were limited to a hammock, a few dishes and calabashes, a shift or

[1] Gonsalves de Mello, *Tempo dos Flamengos*, pp. 266–311; A. Wiznitzer, *Records*; idem, 'The number of Jews in Dutch Brazil, 1630–1654', reprinted from *Jewish Social Studies*, xvi (New York, 1954), pp. 107–14.

shirt of cotton cloth, and their bows and arrows. They planted a few allotments of manioc and beans around their villages, but were very negligent about cultivating them, chiefly relying on the products of the chase and forest fruits for their sustenance. They were very loath to work either on their own account or for the Europeans, but would make considerable exertions for the sake of brandy and other strong drink, which they prized above all else in the world. Some of them knew the rudiments of Roman Catholic Christianity, and the Dutch made sporadic but serious efforts to convert them to the Calvinist faith. A number were sent to Holland for their education, and some of them became so europeanized that they forgot their own language. Others relapsed into semi-savagery on their return to Brazil, and at one time the Calvinist ministers thought of abandoning their proselytizing efforts in despair. Despite these set-backs, however, the High Council at Recife reported in February 1645 that these efforts were still continuing, 'and that with fair progress'.

The second kind of Amerindians were stark-naked savages in the stone-age stage of culture. Many of them were cannibals, and they all led a wandering life in small bands in the forest, living entirely by hunting and fishing and eating fruits and wild honey. Savages of this type were grouped together under the generic term of Tapuya. They consisted of many different tribes, speaking the so-called *linguas travadas* or 'twisted tongues', most of which are now extinct. The detailed accounts of their nature and habitat given by Dutch and German adventurers who lived among them, or associated closely with them (Baro, Herckmans, Rabbe), are still of the greatest interest to anthropologists, as are the remarkable paintings and sketches of them made by the artists of Johan Maurits's entourage. These cannibals would never consent to be educated or civilized by the Dutch; but they were perfectly willing to co-operate with them against the Portuguese, and proved themselves valuable if at times embarassing allies. The Tapuyas treated the Dutch, and were treated by them, on a footing of perfect equality. Johan Maurits gladly accepted from them the title of 'brother', and he had a life-size portrait painted with himself in the middle of a group. In fact he showed himself as sympathetic and understanding as any twentieth-century anthropologist could have been. A party of Tapuyas voluntarily accompanied him on his return to

Holland in 1644, and for years afterwards he continued to send gifts and letters to their chiefs in Brazil.[1]

It is often said that the Spaniards and Portuguese were more intelligent and successful in their dealings with the Amerindians than were their Dutch and English successors, but this is certainly not true of the period with which we are concerned. On the contrary, the more perspicacious among the Portuguese and Spaniards freely admitted that 'the nations of the North' handled the Amerindians much more tactfully and successfully than did the *conquistadores* and the *encomenderos*. A Franciscan friar with long experience in the American mission-field told the Council of the Indies in 1621 that Spanish mistreatment of the New World Indians had greatly facilitated the progress of the better-behaved Hollanders in the borderlands of the Caribbean. 'We have given the heretics a pretext and an argument to enhance their heresy and evil way of life, and to defame our Gospel, by telling the Indians, as they usually do, that we are the heretics and the breakers of God's laws and commandment, as they can very well judge for themselves by the difference in the deeds of the one and the other.'[2]

Padre Antonio Vieira, S.J., wrote of the Indians of the Amazon estuary in 1654: 'They have conceived such hatred and aversion for the Portuguese nation that they wish to have neither peace nor trade with us, whereas they usually have both with the nations of the North who frequent this region, because they say that they find them more truthful and that their freedom is safe with them.' When Vieira visited the Indians of the Serra of Ibiapaba a couple of years later, he found that many of them had 'been born and bred among the Dutch', and had fled to the interior after the loss of Netherlands Brazil in 1654. They had Dutch books which they could read, Venetian paper on which they wrote elegant letters sealed with red wax, and some of them were dressed in silks and cloth which the Hollanders had given them. He adds: 'In this way the politicos of Holland knew how to purchase the good-will and submission of these people, and transfer them from our obedience to their own. We

[1] Barlaeus-Naber, *Nederlandsch Brazilië*, pp. 161–3, 323–32; P. Moreau, *Relation du voyage de Roulox Baro . . . au pays des Tapuies dans la terre ferme du Brasil* (Paris, 1651); Gonsalves de Mello, *Tempo dos Flamengos*, pp. 231–65; *RIAGP*, no. 31 (1886), pp. 278–88; High Council to Heeren XIX, 13 Feb. 1645 (JHMS).

[2] Juan de Silva, O.F.M., *Advertencias importantes acerca del buen govierno y administracion de las Indias* (Madrid, 1621).

could have stopped this by the same means, at much less cost, but through not giving a little voluntarily, we end by losing everything involuntarily.' Vieira averred that these Protestant Indians had turned the Serra de Ibiapaba into a local Geneva, where 'many of the inhabitants were as Calvinist and Lutheran as if they had been born in England or in Germany'.[1] Even allowing for some exaggeration in Vieira's exuberant pen, it is obvious that the results of the Dutch religious propaganda and education in 1625–45 were greater than the ministers at Recife realized.

I do not mean to infer that there were no excesses nor mistakes committed by the Dutch in their dealings with the Brazilian Indians. There were, particularly in the Maranhão, where some natives were kidnapped and enslaved, in defiance of the West India Company's regulations which prohibited the enslavement or forced labour of the Amerindians in the most categorical terms. But as compared with Portuguese and Spanish methods, the Dutch attitude in the days of Johan Maurits was (generally speaking) more humane, more sensible, and more successful. It may be added that a similar state of affairs prevailed in Angola, where the Portuguese admitted that the Dutch treated the Negroes (other than slaves) far more kindly and considerately than they did themselves.[2]

Although both Portuguese and Dutch governments legislated for the freedom of the Amerindians, and the Dutch at least observed these laws reasonably well, both races were agreed on the necessity of exploiting the sons of Ham if the colony was to survive. 'Without Negroes and oxen nothing can be expected from Pernambuco', the Heeren XIX were authoritatively told in 1640; and Padre Antonio Vieira wrote eight years later: 'Without Negroes there is no Pernambuco, and without Angola there are no Negroes.'[3] This last observation was not pedantically accurate, as the Dutch could also obtain Negroes from Guinea, but slaves from Angola were preferred for reasons explained below.

Neither Dutch nor Portuguese slave-traders could distinguish

[1] *Cartas de Antonio Vieira, S.J.* (ed. Azevedo), i. 393, 478, 569; *Obras Escolhidas* (ed. Sergio e Cidade), v. 77–82, 89, 114–15. Cf. also the discussions in the Conselho Ultramarino on a proposal to settle Irish emigrants from St. Kitts in the Maranhão in 1644–7 (AHU 'Consultas Mixtas', Cod. 13, fol. 79, and Cod. 14, fol. 93).

[2] Letter of Bento Teixeira de Saldanha, Luanda, 10 Apr. 1653 (AHU, 'Angola, Papeis Avulsos', 1653). Cf. C. R. Boxer, *Salvador de Sá*, p. 270.

[3] Quelen, *Kort Verhael*, p. 13; Vieira, *Cartas* (ed. Azevedo), i. 243.

between the numerous tribes from which the West African slaves were drawn, but they grouped them into four main divisions, named after the respective coastal districts where they were secured. These were the Ardras, Minas, and Calabares from Upper Guinea, and the Angolas from the Congo and Angola. At this period the Bantu Angola slaves were the most esteemed; partly because they were the most numerous, and so it was easier for the old field-hands to instruct the ignorant new-comers in their own language, or at least in a language which they both understood. They were also more tractable and more easily domesticated than most other slaves. Moreover, the mortality in the slave-ships from Guinea was usually much higher than that in the vessels which sailed from Luanda, whose crossing of the Atlantic was not so liable to be delayed by calms. The Ardras, who seem to have been mainly tribesmen of Sudanese origin from the hinterland of Upper Guinea, were often sullen and rebellious, nor could the Bantu slaves understand their language. On the other hand, when the Ardras *did* work willingly, they worked much harder and better than any others, being more intelligent and of finer physique. The Negroes from the region between Sierra Leone and Cape Verde were described as being rather lazy, 'but clean and vivacious, especially the women, for which reason the Portuguese buy them and use them as household slaves'.[1]

The Negro slave-trade was one of the Company's main sources of profit, although some critics alleged that it would have been still more profitable if it had been better conducted. Quelen reported to the Heeren XIX in 1640 that 'the fruits of the land can never be secured or garnered save through their work; and consequently there is not the smallest doubt that the more slaves are imported, the better will the land be cultivated, and the greater will be the Company's profits, which in these last years would have been twice as great if more slaves had been imported'. He alleged that the Company's officials kept the imports down in order to keep prices up, which was a very short-sighted policy. In the years 1636–45 a total of 23,163 Negroes were imported into Recife, and sold for a total

---

[1] Barlaeus-Naber, *Nederlandsch Brazilië*, pp. 77, 164; Ratelband, *Vijf Daghregisters van Elmina*, pp. lxxix–lxxxii. The first serious attempt at a systematic tribal identification was made by Alonso de Sandoval, S.J., *Naturaleza de todos Etiopes* (Seville, 1627), liv. 1, cap. 16, and the latest known to me is that by R. Ribeiro, *Cultos Afrobrasileiros do Recife* (Recife, 1952), pp. 14–20.

of 6,714,423 florins.[1] On paper this represented an enormous profit for the Company, since for much of this period slaves were obtainable in Guinea and Angola for trifling goods worth from twelve to seventy-five florins a head (? or a *peça*), and they were sold in Brazil at prices ranging from 200 to 800 florins, according to their age, sex, and condition. But the planters were accustomed to buy slaves on credit, paying only at the next harvest and then in sugar, and many of them defaulted in whole or in part. The amount of money which came into the Company's coffers was therefore considerably less than this paper total, although it is difficult to say how much less. An estimate drawn up shortly after Johan Maurits's departure in 1644 gives a figure of 840,000 florins as the Company's annual income from the profits of the West African slave-trade, but the reliability of these figures is doubtful.[2]

To avoid incurring bad debts, the Heeren XIX decreed in 1644 that slaves could only be sold for ready money. Since the planters had none, this resulted in most of the slaves being bought by Jewish speculators for very low cash prices. Johan Maurits complained that this move, far from increasing the Company's profits, led to slaves being sold at Recife for less than what they had cost at Luanda. This was not much of an exaggeration, as the High Council at Recife writing in March 1645 stated that the Heeren XIX's untimely insistence on slaves being sold for spot cash meant that prices had dropped to between thirty and fifty *patacas*. Meanwhile, the Jews resold the slaves to the planters for three or four times the price they had paid, although they had to accept payment in instalments (at higher interest rates) and in sugar. The planters, on their side, complained that the slaves had often been compelled to drink sea-water during the Atlantic crossing, and so died soon after they had been bought, thus being worthless to their purchasers. This was particularly liable to happen in the slave-ships from Guinea, which were often inadequately provisioned and supplied with insufficient fresh-water casks.[3]

[1] Quelen, *Kort Verhael*, p. 12; Wätjen, *Holländsche Kolonialreich in Brasilien*, p. 311, where Guinea is misprinted as Genoa. I also suspect that the Negroes were not sold *per capita* as he implies, but by the *peça*, which might include two Negroes, or three Negroes for two *peças*, according to sex, age, and condition. Cf. C. R. Boxer, *Salvador de Sá*, p. 231.

[2] Cf. Appendix II below.

[3] Barlaeus-Naber, *Nederlandsch Brazilië*, pp. 401, 403, 407 (where the figure of

The miserable lot of the Negro slaves in Brazil has been too often described elsewhere for detailed repetition here. The bulk of them were sold to Portuguese planters, who (if Pierre Moreau is to be trusted) used them much more harshly than did their Dutch owners. This may be doubted, and it is alleged by others that the slaves often preferred to work for Portuguese masters, as they then had holidays on the numerous Catholic Saints' feast-days as well as on Sundays. From this standpoint, slaves working for Jewish masters were even more fortunate, as their owners had to let them rest on the Jewish Sabbath and did not dare to work them on the Calvinist Sunday. Despite the urging of Udemans and other devout 'servants of God's word', the Dutch did not try very hard to convert the Negro slaves to Protestant Christianity. The matter was often discussed in the Brazilian Calvinist consistory, and even sanctioned by the Heeren XIX in Europe, but nothing concrete was ever achieved, partly for lack of a qualified preacher in Portuguese.[1]

During the years of turmoil and warfare before 1641, many Negro slaves who fought for either Portuguese or Dutch were given their freedom, and many others escaped into the forest. These fugitives founded communal agricultural settlements known as *quilombos*, where they lived 'in the same way as they did in Angola'. They periodically raided outlying plantations in order to get new recruits, women, and provisions, although they grew most of their food in well-cultivated allotments. Some of these *quilombos* were broken up by the Dutch or by their Tapuya allies, but the largest one survived for many years after the Portuguese reconquest of Pernambuco. A major military campaign was necessary to destroy it in 1694, after numerous previous attacks had been repulsed.

Slavery and sugar being the two pillars on which the existence of Pernambuco depended, let us take a glance at the sugar industry in the days of Johan Maurits. The *senhor de engenho*, or sugar-plantation owner, usually leased out most of his land to smallholders known as *lavradores*, in exchange for an agreed proportion of their crop, depending on whether this was planted

64,000 slaves imported in eighteen months should be corrected to 6,400); Calado, *Valeroso Lucideno*, pp. 125–6; Gonsalves de Mello, *Tempo dos Flamengos*, pp. 211–12; letter of High Council to Heeren XIX, d. 26 Mar. 1645, in JHMS.

[1] P. Moreau, *Histoire* (1651), pp. 40–43; Gonsalves de Mello, *Tempo dos Flamengos*, pp. 204–30. I have not seen M. Goulart, *Escravidão Africana no Brasil* (São Paulo, 1949), which is apparently an authoritative work.

with or without the help of the *senhor de engenho*.[1] The cane, once planted, lasted for many years if properly weeded and tended, although Pernambuco suffered severely for most of this period from natural and man-made disasters. The *lavrador* had his cane cut by his own slaves, and transported in his own (or hired) ox-carts to the mill where it was processed. The resultant sugar was divided with the *senhor de engenho* in the agreed proportion. This usually varied from one-third for the *lavrador* and two-thirds for the *senhor de engenho*, to two-fifths for the *lavrador* and three-fifths for the *senhor de engenho*, this last being the more common ratio. Smallholders who owned their own land usually divided the sugar with the *senhor de engenho* on a fifty-fifty basis.

In leasing land to the *lavradores*, calculations were based on how much cane a mill could grind in the space of twenty-four hours. This amount, called a *tarefa* ('task'), was reckoned at between twenty-five and thirty-five cartloads of cane for a mill driven by oxen, and at between forty and fifty cartloads for one driven by water-power. The land which the *lavradores* leased from the *senhor de engenho* was called a *partido*, and the average *partido* apparently produced about forty *tarefas* in a year. For this purpose, the *lavrador* needed at least twenty able-bodied Negro slaves, and from four to eight ox-carts, according to the distance of his *partido* from the mill. *Partidos* were divided from each other by wide lanes to lessen the risk of fire. The *lavrador* had to supply his Negroes with tools and utensils, and to arrange for the packing and transportation of the sugar after his share had been handed over to him at the mill. The harvesting season began early in September and finished in April.

The sugar-cane was passed through the mill (*engenho*), which operated on the principle of the clothes-wringer, although the rollers or cylinders forming the press were vertical instead of horizontal. The juice squeezed out was then channelled by troughs to the adjacent boiling-house. Here it was boiled in a series of great copper cauldrons, with certain agents added to bring the impurities in the juice to the surface, where they were skimmed off. The juice was then ladled into a set of smaller cauldrons, where it was allowed to cool off somewhat and become semi-crystallized, though still mixed with molasses. It

---

[1] Who was not, therefore, necessarily a planter himself in the strictest sense of the term; but since he usually owned all the land, his social position corresponded to that of the plantation-owners in the Antilles and Virginia.

was then ladled or poured into cone-shaped clay tile forms or moulds with a small hole in the bottom. These cones, each of which contained about an *arroba* (32 lb.) of sugar, were taken to the purging-house next day after their contents had become quite crystallized. They remained for about a week in the purging-house, where fine wet clay was placed on each cone. Water from this clay filtered slowly through the sugar, washing out most of the molasses and whitening the remaining sugar. This process was repeated two or three times in the case of the better grades. The white sugar freed of molasses was then placed out in the sun to dry, and the sugar which was still mixed with the molasses adhering to the inside of the teat of the cone was placed in a separate heap. This brown-coloured sugar was called *muscavado*. The planter, the *lavrador*, and the sugar-tithe contractor then came along and divided the sugar, whether white or *muscavado*, in the agreed proportions. The drainings were boiled into a low-grade sugar called *panela* which was a perquisite of the *senhor de engenho*. The sugar, after being weighed and packed, was then sent to Recife or some other port for shipment to Europe, either for sale or for further refining into pure white sugar.[1]

A sugar-mill and plantation was a costly investment, needing a large initial outlay of capital. The *senhor de engenho* had to acquire much heavy equipment and engage a number of skilled technicians to operate it, apart from the slaves. He required a minimum of forty or fifty able-bodied Negroes, a dozen carts and twenty yoke of oxen, but many of the larger plantations had several hundred slaves, with other personnel and equipment in proportion. The *casa-grande* or 'great house' in which the planter and his family lived, the *senzala* or slave-quarters, and the chapel completed the plantation set-up, familiar to us from the paintings of Frans Post. The Dutch do not seem to have introduced any innovations into the Luso-Brazilian rural architecture, or, what is perhaps more surprising, into the technical process of the manufacture of sugar.

If we are to believe Gaspar Dias Ferreira, an able and unscrupulous Portuguese planter who was Johan Maurits's evil

[1] The foregoing is mainly derived from A. van der Dussen's description of the Pernambuco sugar industry in 1639 in Barlaeus-Naber, *Nederlandsch Brazilië*, pp. 165–8. For further technical details and comparison with procedure elsewhere cf. N. Deerr, *History of Sugar*, i. 108–10; M. Ratekyn, 'The Early Sugar-industry in Española', *HAHR*, xxxiv. 1–19.

genius, the Hollanders never mastered even the elementary techniques of the industry. 'It is certain', he wrote in 1645, 'that God created the various nations among men, and endowed each one with a different disposition and ability for various occupations, so as to foster mutual distribution and intercourse in the world which he gave them for a dwelling-place, and that as regards the Dutch nation he gave them no aptitude for Brazil. If this observation seems unjustified, show me the Hollander who up to the present day in Pernambuco was a workman in making sugar, or who wished to learn it, or any other position in a sugar-mill; whereas each mill has four white workmen merely for making the sugar—the master, the *banqueiro* who is the assistant, the skimmer, and the purger besides some others. . . . There are but few Flemings who devote themselves to the sugar industry or to the maintenance of the mills in Brazil, and only rarely do they own them, and thus both the Negroes and the sugars have to pass through the hands of the Portuguese.' This may sound (and perhaps is) an exaggeration, but Quelen wrote in 1640: 'Although there are at present many Dutch owners of sugar-mills, yet they cannot dispense with the Portuguese factors and smallholders for the management and overseeing of the same.' Dutch dependence on Portuguese planters and technicians in the Brazilian sugar industry was also attested by Van der Dussen and by Johan Maurits in almost identical terms.[1]

Admittedly, there were those who thought otherwise, but they seem to have been a small minority. One of them, Mathias Beck, writing in 1654, claimed that as good white sugar was made in Barbados as had ever been made in Brazil, 'without a Portuguese hand having touched it'. He in his turn seems to have been exaggerating. It is fairly certain that the improved methods of sugar-manufacture which were introduced into Barbados about the years 1636–50 were due to island planters who had gone to Pernambuco to study Brazilian methods and conditions on the spot.[2]

---

[1] 'Cartas e pareceres de Gaspar Dias Ferreira' in *RIAGP*, no. 31 (1886), no. 32 (1887); Barlaeus-Naber, *Nederlandsch Brazilië*, pp. 161, 308; Quelen, *Kort Verhael*, p. 18; Gonsalves de Mello, *Tempo dos Flamengos*, pp. 155–8. Thirty years later it was said of Surinam that 'the Dutch have not the skill of making sugar, but hire the very raggedest English' (*Calendar of State Papers. Colonial Series. America & West Indies, 1675–1676*, no. 405, p. 154.)

[2] Ligon, Beck, and other contemporary authorities quoted by A. P. Canabrava,

In any event, it is undeniable that the functioning of the sugar-plantations of Pernambuco depended primarily if not entirely on the local Portuguese and their Negro slaves, although there were a few Dutch planters and even some Dutch colonists among the smallholders. But most of the Dutch who bought plantations in the 1637–8 boom apparently sold out later to Portuguese or Jews. It will be recalled that these plantations (and the slaves and equipment to operate them) were supposed to be paid for on the instalment system by deliveries of sugar at harvest-time. As most of the buyers defaulted in whole or in part, due to a succession of bad harvests, floods, droughts, and other natural calamities, apart from guerrilla activities before 1641, neither the Company nor individual Dutch creditors received much in the way of repayment. The result was that the rural civilization of the *várzea* continued to be dominated by the Portuguese planter and smallholder, whereas the Dutch officials, burghers, and merchants dominated the urban civilization of Recife and Mauritsstad.

Modern Brazilian historians never tire of contrasting the failure of the Dutch to settle themselves in the countryside with their success in developing a distinctive urban civilization in the colonial capital. From this they draw the conclusion (or at least they imply) that Gaspar Dias Ferreira was right when he wrote that God did not give the Dutch any aptitude for Brazil, and that the failure of the heretic colony was therefore a foregone conclusion. It may be so, but here again I cannot help feeling that there is too much 'hindsight' in their line of reasoning. It is true that the Dutch never did succeed, with a few but noteworthy exceptions, in integrating themselves with the rural life of the colony, and so they lost virtually everything outside their fortified coastal towns when the revolt broke out in 1645—except in the northern districts where they were supported by the Amerindians. But their failure to secure effective control of the countryside was due, at least in part, to the fact that they had only a bare three years (July 1642–June 1645) in which to do so. For seventeen out of the twenty-four years in which Netherlands Brazil existed, fighting in the *várzea* never entirely ceased and was at times

'A influência do Brasil na técnica do fabrico de açúcar nas Antilhas francesas e inglesas no meado do século XVII', on pp. 63–76 of the *Anuário da faculdade de ciências econômicas e administrativas, 1946–47* (São Paulo, 1947).

very severe. In these circumstances, a methodical settlement by agricultural workers from northern Europe, as was repeatedly advocated by Johan Maurits, was rendered prohibitively expensive if not altogether impracticable. If the Dutch had been granted a few more years of peace under the rule of Johan Maurits, or of someone else equally enlightened, it is possible that rural emigration from northern Europe could have been arranged on a large scale. This is admittedly arguable, and it is equally possible that under a continuance of Dutch rule Pernambuco would have become nothing more than another Surinam, a slave colony of the most repugnant kind.

However this may be, no blame for this failure can be attached to Johan Maurits. We have seen that he urged the immigration of Dutch and German agricultural settlers from the start, and he and his council more than once stressed that this was 'the sole means of securing this conquest for us'.[1] Nor were the Heeren XIX so blind to the necessity of encouraging this type of immigrant as is often alleged. On the contrary, they frequently legislated in favour of such potential settlers, although their policy in this respect was not always consistent. In October 1641, for example, the Heeren XIX agreed in principle that 'the welfare of the Company depended on peopling the land', and discussed measures for attracting soldier-settlers in Brazil. At one time they went so far in their endeavours to encourage north European emigrants who would supplant the Portuguese, that Johan Maurits protested. He argued that it would be unfair to drive out the planters and the *lavradores* who had contrived to produce sugar under such difficulties in the war-torn years 1635–40, and who therefore deserved more consideration at the Company's hands.[2] His own policy was rather one whereby a constant stream of agricultural emigrants from northern Europe would gradually fuse with the existing Portuguese population and so create a new race attached to the soil, in which the ethnic strain of the former would increasingly predominate and thus automatically ensure their loyalty to Dutch rule. He was still trying to arrange for the immigration of Dutch agricultural settlers into Sergipe and

---

[1] Letters of Johan Maurits and council to Heeren XIX, d. 15 Jan. 1638, 31 May 1641, 24 Sept. 1642. Cf. Gonsalves de Mello, *Tempo dos Flamengos*, p. 141 n.

[2] Barlaeus-Naber, *Nederlandsch Brazilië*, pp. 307–8. The same point was made by Quelen in his *Kort Verhael* of 1640. Cf. also *Bijdr. Hist. Gen. Utrecht*, iii. 356.

Alagoas in 1642–3, but the directors were in an economical mood and his projects came to nothing.

The directors had some reason to insist on making drastic economies, since the financial position of the Company was worse than ever; but this insistence came at a singularly inopportune time, having regard to long-term Dutch interests in Brazil. The basic trouble was that the Heeren XIX wished Johan Maurits to send them large and ever-increasing shipments of sugar, from the profitable sale of which they could later supply Pernambuco with the money and goods so badly needed. Johan Maurits, on the other hand, argued that no great increase in the sugar production could be expected until the colony was thoroughly secured from all fear of invasion or insurrection; and this, of course, involved the maintenance of a large garrison. Both sides had a good case, but that of Johan Maurits was the stronger, since it was rash of the Heeren XIX to insist on drastically reducing the garrison after they had given the Portuguese such intolerable provocation in the Maranhão, São Thomé, and Angola. A preliminary warning came with the revolt of the Maranhão in October 1642, and the local Dutch garrison was finally withdrawn after a year of desultory fighting. Another revolt took place at São Thomé, but this was suppressed to the extent that the Dutch garrison retained control of the port and castle of São Sebastião. The outbreak of these rebellions provided the Dutch at Luanda with an excuse to make a treacherous attack on the nearby Portuguese camp (*arraial*) on the river Bengo in May 1643. This was successful in its immediate outcome, the local Portuguese governor being taken prisoner; but in the upshot it merely served to antagonize the Portuguese still further, and strengthened their resolve to pay the Dutch in the same coin when opportunity offered.[1]

In view of the West India Company's chronic indebtedness, and the directors' insistence on reducing the garrison in Brazil, it is surprising that they organized an expedition to Chile in 1642–3, with which Johan Maurits was ordered to co-operate. This he did, contributing (in January 1643) a force of five ships and 400 men under the command of the sailor-poet, Elias

---

[1] For details of the trouble in Angola cf. A. da Silva Rego, *Dupla Restauração de Angola 1641–1648* (Lisbon, 1948), pp. 31–85; *Arquivos de Angola*, 2nd series, i. 99–104; *Kron. Hist. Gen. Utrecht*, xxv. 530–4; A. de Oliveira de Cadornega, *História Geral das Guerras Angolanas*, ii. 295–343.

Herckmans. Apparently, the old mirage of gold-mines was what induced the directors to throw good money after bad on this occasion. Nevertheless, it is conceivable that the Dutch might have got a firm footing in southern Chile if the expedition had been better led, since they made contact with the unsubdued Araucanian Indians, who, according to the Spaniards' own admission, had done them more harm than all the other races in the New World put together. The greed and brutality of Hendrik Brouwer, the ex-governor-general of the East Indies who was the original leader of the expedition, aroused the mistrust of the Araucanians and spoilt a promising start in May 1643. Brouwer died soon after, and although the more tactful Elias Herckmans effected a temporary reconciliation, the Araucanians' suspicions were again aroused by his renewed inquiries after the gold-mines. Having fallen foul of their native allies, without whose co-operation success was hopeless, the Dutch re-embarked in their ships and returned to Recife, where Herckmans died shortly after his arrival in December 1643.[1]

Johan Maurits had previously conceived the far more feasible plan of seizing the strategically important but unfortified port of Buenos Aires. He envisaged the occupation of this place as opening the back door of the long and difficult road to the silver-mines of Potosí in High Peru. Preparations for this expedition were well advanced when they had to be cancelled in November 1642, owing to the necessity of reinforcing Brouwer's expedition to Chile and the Dutch garrisons in the Maranhão and São Thomé.[2]

Although these abortive expeditions were not the only ones inspired by a desire to find gold- and silver-mines which the Dutch could exploit in South America, both the Heeren XIX and Johan Maurits realized that sugar was the key to the economic welfare of Netherlands Brazil. Unfortunately, we have no completely reliable figures for the total value of the sugar exported from the colony during the time of Johan Maurits, although Wätjen has published some valuable statistics.[3] De

[1] For the Dutch expedition to Chile cf. J. H. Rodrigues, *Historiografia e Bibliografia*, nos. 194, 499–501, 982–3. Herckmans was the author of *Der Zeevaart-lof* (Amsterdam, 1634), a poem in praise of the United Netherlands' maritime achievements which is one of the classics of Dutch literature.

[2] Cf. the 'Secrete Notulen' of Johan Maurits and his council, 21 Aug.–25 Dec. 1642, translated in *RIHGB*, lviii. 296–304.

[3] Wätjen, *Holländische Kolonialreich*, pp. 316–23. Cf. also Appendix II below.

Laet, who after all was in a good position to ascertain the facts, gives the following totals for the years 1637–44:

	(a) Amount exported by the WIC	(b) Amount exported by private traders
White sugar	332,425 arrobas (32 lb.)	1,083,048 arrobas
Muscavado	117,887 ,,	403,287 ,,
Panela	51,961 ,,	71,527 ,,
Total	502,273 ,,	1,557,862 ,,
	Valued at 7,618,498 florins.	20,303,478 florins.[1]

thus showing that roughly one-third of the total export was for the account of the Company, and two-thirds for the private traders. The Company, of course, got a substantial rake-off from the latter in the form of taxes, freight, &c. Wätjen considers the second category a reasonably accurate estimate, but he believes the first to be a gross under-statement. Deerr, on the other hand, thinks that Wätjen's own figures are far too low, and he accepts another estimate, that of Barlaeus, as being nearest to the truth.[2]

To my mind, it is doubtful if these or any other figures make sufficient allowance for the great amount of smuggling, fraud, and embezzlement which was admittedly carried on by methods such as those described in Quelen's pamphlet of 1640. One of the sources of this leakage was the extensive smuggling practised by the crews of homeward-bound West-Indiamen which touched at English Channel-ports. It was, perhaps, with a view to curbing this particular practice that the Heeren XIX ordered quantities of sugar conserves to be prepared for presentation to English port officials—or was this literal *douceur* intended to facilitate the smuggling of Brazilian sugar into England by the agents of the West India Company?[3]

Other products exported from Pernambuco to Europe included dyewoods, building-timber, tobacco, and hides. The dyewood trade, like the slave-trade, was a monopoly of the Company, and the export of tobacco and hides was not very important at this period. Such export statistics as are available for these commodities will be found in Wätjen's book, together

[1] De Laet-Naber, *Jaerlijk Verhael*, iv. 298.
[2] Wätjen, *Holländische Kolonialreich*, p. 330; N. Deerr, *History of Sugar*, i. 110. Cf. p. 114, above.
[3] Quelen, *Kort Verhael*, pp. 10–12, 14–16; Gonsalves de Mello, *Tempo dos Flamengos*, p. 172.

with the available figures for the imports of European goods and raw materials to Recife. The erudite German professor rightly observes: 'It is certain that the import and export trade of New Holland, even in its best years, could not vie with that of the East Indies. Nevertheless, it is undeniable that in the time of Johan Maurits the Brazil trade constituted an important factor in the economic life of the Seven Provinces.'[1]

The difference between the trade of the two Companies was reflected in the value of their respective shares on the Amsterdam market. In July 1645 the West India Company's shares of 100 florins were quoted at 46 florins, partly because the Company had only paid out two or three dividends in the whole course of its existence. The 100-florin shares of the East India Company, which was now paying substantial dividends with fair regularity, were quoted at 460 florins. There was also a great difference between the regions where the two Companies respectively operated, which told heavily in favour of the older organization. The East Indies were largely self-supporting in the matter of provisions; meat, rice, arrack, and other necessaries of life being freely available in most places at cheap rates. In Netherlands Brazil, on the other hand, many provisions had to be imported from the United Provinces at excessive cost. The concentration on sugar-planting, the insufficiency of the manioc crop, and the destruction of cattle and livestock in the years 1630–40 meant that meat, flour, butter, wine, &c., had to be exported in much larger quantities to Brazil than to the East Indies. Johan Maurits made every effort to minimize the evils of monoculture by ordering the planters and *lavradores* to plant a certain proportion of manioc for each slave they possessed. The Heeren XIX also tried to encourage the planting of rice and other food-grains by legislative enactments. These efforts bore relatively little fruit, in view of the stubborn opposition of the planters and *lavradores* who preferred to concentrate on sugar as the most valuable cash-crop.[2]

When ships from Europe were overdue, prices of essential foodstuffs at Recife rose to astronomical heights, provoking repeated complaints that Netherlands Brazil was the most expensive place in the world, even in the relatively prosperous

---

[1] Wätjen, *Holländische Kolonialreich*, pp. 303–31.
[2] The evidence is carefully collected by Gonsalves de Mello, *Tempo dos Flamengos*, pp. 175–82.

years of 1642–3.¹ This state of affairs enabled many of the Dutch and Jewish private traders to make their fortunes, but it did not benefit the Company, whose local representatives often had to replenish their depleted stocks from the private traders' stores at the prevailing high prices. Although these imports were primarily for the consumption of the Dutch inhabitants of the colony, they also had a considerable sale among the Portuguese in the interior, cloth and cheese being two of the items that were in great demand.²

The fact that Recife was one of the most expensive places in the world naturally made the Heeren XIX resentful of Johan Maurits's lavish expenditure. The 'Prince of Nassau' had incontestable merits as a governor, statesman, and general, but none as an economist or a financier. He was a free spender of his own and the Company's money, but he never bothered about casting accounts, and he ostentatiously ignored the members of his financial council with whom he seldom deigned to speak.³ A princely patron of the arts, a keen amateur architect and landscape-gardener, he gave his inclinations full rein, whether in the erection of his costly seat at Vrijburg, in building the bridge between Recife and Mauritsstad, in sending home valuable timber for the Mauritshuis, and in maintaining a galaxy of artists and scientists around him in Brazil. It is true that part of this expenditure came from his own pocket, but most of it was a charge on the Company in one form or another.

The outstanding name among Johan Maurits's entourage is that of the young German scientist, Georg Marcgraf of Liebstadt (1610–44), who was educated at Rostock and Leiden, and who died from fever in Angola at the age of thirty-four and the height of his powers. A modern American scientist has remarked that if he had lived to publish more of his work he might well have become the greatest naturalist since Aristotle.⁴ Much of his work has been lost, but what survives is impressive enough. Apart from the botanical and zoological collections which he

---

¹ Wätjen, *Holländische Kolonialreich*, pp. 206, 308.
² Gonsalves de Mello, *Tempo dos Flamengos*, pp. 183–5.
³ Wätjen, op. cit., pp. 205–8.
⁴ E. W. Gudger, 'George Marcgrave, the first Student of American Natural History', *The Popular Science Monthly* (Sept. 1912), pp. 250–74. For a detailed appreciation of Marcgraf's work by a number of Brazilian scientists see A. Taunay [ed.], *Jorge Marcgrave. Historia natural do Brasil. Edição do Museo Paulista* (São Paulo, 1942), which also contains (pp. i–xxxvi) the fullest bio-bibliographical account of Marcgraf published hitherto.

sent to Europe in 1644, and which continued to be studied down to the nineteenth century, some of the copious notes on natural history which he left were edited and published by his friend Johannes de Laet in the *Historia Naturalis Brasiliae* (Amsterdam and Leiden, 1648). This work contains the first truly scientific study of the fauna and flora of Brazil, a description of the geography and meteorology of Pernambuco, including daily wind and rainfall records,[1] and an ethnographical survey of the local Amerindian races. The illustrations include 200 woodcuts of plants and 222 of animals, birds, insects, and fishes, most of which had never been described before.

Another version of this work appeared in 1658, in which Marcgraf's contributions were mostly embodied with the observations of his colleague, Dr. Piso, and suffered somewhat in the process.[2] In compensation, this edition contains a few of Marcgraf's pioneer astronomical observations in the southern hemisphere, including the eclipse of the sun in 1640. It may be added that Johan Maurits helped Marcgraf by building an observatory for him in one of the towers of Vrijburg, and by ordering all ships' captains to take careful observations of solar and lunar eclipses as well as other celestial phenomena. In addition to being a naturalist and astronomer, Marcgraf was also an accomplished mathematician, surveyor, and cartographer, many of the maps in Barlaeus's truly monumental work being based on his own. He was not the only cartographer on Johan Maurits's staff, and the remarkably accurate charts and maps drawn by these men were not wholly displaced until within living memory.[3]

Even more celebrated, although not so outstanding a scientist, was Marcgraf's Dutch medical colleague, Dr. Willem Piso of Leiden (1611–78). A year younger than Marcgraf and educated at Caen, he followed Johan Maurits to Brazil as his personal

---

[1] 'These are, perhaps, the first official records anywhere, as the earliest known in Europe are those made in 1653 by the order of Ferdinand II of Tuscany' (N. Deerr, *History of Sugar*, p. 106 n.).

[2] *De Indiae, utriusque re naturali et medica Libri quatrodecim quorum contenta pagina sequens exhibet* (Amsterdam, 1658).

[3] Cf. Rio Branco's comment in 1891: 'It is sad to say it, but even today whoever wishes to study the coastal zone from Rio Grande do Norte to Sergipe, finds valuable geographical information in the map of the illustrious Marcgraf, which he would vainly seek in even the most recent Brazilian maps, all of which are drawn on a much smaller scale' (quoted in Taunay, *Jorge Marcgrave, Historia Natural*, p. xxxiv).

physician, returning to Holland with him in 1644. Fr. Manuel Calado declares that the two men quarrelled and became irreconcilable enemies, but he must be exaggerating if he is not entirely mistaken.[1] At any rate, Piso continued to be the count's physician after his return home, and the doctor's studies were published with Johan Maurits's approval and financial support, as Marcgraf's had been ten years before. Piso contributed a lengthy section 'De Medicina Brasiliensi' to the *Historia Naturalis Brasiliae* of 1648, which remained an authoritative work on tropical medicine and hygiene until well into the nineteenth century. We owe to Piso, among other things, the first knowledge of ipecacuanha as a cure for dysentery. Piso's interests were not purely scientific. He was a member of the celebrated 'Muiden-circle', which comprised the cream of Dutch literary and intellectual society, as well as twice dean of the Collegium Medicum at Amsterdam.

Many of the woodcuts which illustrate the works of Barlaeus, Marcgraf, and Piso are derived from the paintings and sketches of Frans Post and Albert Eckhout. These were two of the six artists whom Johan Maurits maintained in Brazil, as he explained to Louis XIV in 1678, when offering the Roi Soleil some specimens of their work—'ayant eu dans mon service le temps de ma demeure au Brasil, six peintres, dont chacun a curieusement peint a quoy il estoit le plus capable'.[2] Albert Eckhout (*fl.* 1637–64) specialized in depicting men and animals, and the quality of his work can be judged from the sketches reproduced by Thomsen, and from his lifelike (and life-size) portraits in oils which are preserved in the National Museum at Copenhagen. Better known than Eckhout is his colleague, the landscape-painter Frans Post of Leiden (1612–80), examples of whose charming paintings of the Brazilian rural scene are to be found in several public and private collections. Both these artists have been the subjects of intensive study within recent years, but nothing has yet been discovered about their four colleagues mentioned in Johan Maurits's letter to Louis XIV.

Johan Maurits was not content with bringing six painters from the Netherlands, but encouraged local talent when he

[1] 'Another with whom the Prince showed himself aggrieved was Dr. Piso, his physician, and one of his household, with whom he ate, drank, and talked familiarly by night and day. Him he likewise ordered out of his house and never trusted him again' (Calado, *Valeroso Lucideno*, p. 62).

[2] Letter of Johan Maurits to Louis XIV, d. Cleeves, 21 Dec. 1678.

found it. Noticing that a German soldier from Dresden named Zacharias Wagener was a clever draughtsman, he made him his steward and gave him the opportunity of developing his talents. Wagener evidently worked closely with Eckhout, as many of the lively sketches in his *Thierbuch*, or album depicting Brazilian men and beasts, are miniature copies or adaptations of Eckhout's work. Wagener later entered the service of the Dutch East India Company, where he rose to be successively envoy to Canton, chief of the Dutch factory at Nagasaki in Japan, and governor of Cape Colony before his death at Amsterdam in 1668.[1]

It is a thousand pities that Johan Maurits dispersed his magnificent Brazilian collections before his death in 1679. Always a lavish spender and, it must be admitted, avid for titles and other marks of regal or princely favour, he began to dispose of his treasures in 1652, when he handed over a large section to the elector of Brandenburg in exchange for some lands along the Rhine. Two years later he presented several of Eckhout's great pictures and other 'curiosities' to the king of Denmark, who acknowledged this gift with the bestowal of the coveted Order of the White Elephant. Finally, a twelvemonth before his death, he offered a large number of pictures to Louis XIV, with the suggestion that they would make excellent designs for a series of Gobelin tapestries. The subjects of these *peintures des Indes*, as they came to be known, included Chilean and Peruvian themes, as well as Brazilian and Angolan. The tapestries, although long in the making, were so successful when finished that they were repeated at intervals on the same looms for the next 120 years. In addition to the surviving pictures of Post and Eckhout, Johan Maurits originated many other paintings and frescoes inspired by the Brazilian scene, some of which survived until lately in Saxony. Unfortunately, most of them have become war casualties, or were accidentally destroyed by fire, such as those at Christiansborg in Denmark and the interior decorations of the Mauritshuis at The Hague. Perhaps the most interesting picture which perished in this way was Eckhout's

[1] There are two excellent monographs which deal fully with Eckhout, Wagener, and Post: T. Thomsen, *Albert Eckhout, Ein Niederländischer Maler und sein Gönner Moritz der Brasilianer. Ein Kulturbild aus dem 17. Jahrhundert* (Copenhagen, 1938), pp. 61–78 of which also deal with Zacharias Wagener; J. de Sousa Leão Filho, *Frans Post* (Rio, 1948). Cf. also the richly illustrated catalogue, *Maurits de Braziliaan, Tentoonstelling 7 April–17 Mei 1953* (The Hague, 1953).

life-size portrait of Johan Maurits in the midst of a group of Tapuyas.

Johan Maurits's lasting monument remains the sumptuous folio volumes of Barlaeus, Marcgraf, and Piso, which were published under his auspices and which opened a new world to the European ken. This is not to say that they had no precursors, or that the works of the earlier Spanish savants, such as Hernández de Oviedo, Joseph de Acosta, S.J., and Fr. Francisco Ximenez, O.P., were not in themselves extremely valuable.[1] They were, and the same can be said of some Portuguese contributions, such as Brandão's *Diálogos*, and Fr. Christovão de Lisboa's work on the natural history of the Maranhão, both of which, however, remained unpublished for centuries.[2] But the work of Johan Maurits's scientific and artistic team, conducted and co-ordinated under his personal supervision, was less hampered by Aristotelian preconceptions and was inspired by a more rigorous idea of scientific exactitude. This was expressed by Marcgraf when he wrote, 'I will not write about anything which I have not actually seen and observed.'

Naturally enough, these books had a great and lasting success. We find King John IV writing to his envoy in Holland for a copy of Barlaeus's work within a few weeks of its publication. On the other side of the Atlantic, the Jesuit chronicler Simão de Vasconcellos, writing at Bahia in 1659, refers repeatedly to the books of Marcgraf and Piso which he calls 'hũa cousa grande'.[3] Two centuries later, Lichtenstein, Maximilian prince of Neuwied, Spix, Martius, and many other savants who made South America their field of study frequently drew attention to the accuracy and importance of the pioneer labours of Marcgraf and Piso. In 1912 the American scientist, Dr. E. W. Gudger, observed that the *Historia Naturalis Brasiliae* of 1648 was 'probably the most important work on natural history after the revival of learning, and, until the explorations of the prince of

[1] Gonzalo Hernández de Oviedo, *Historia general y natural de las Indias* (Seville, 1535); José de Acosta, S.J., *Historia natural y moral de las Indias* (Seville, 1590); Fr. Francisco Ximenez, O.P., *Quatro libros de la naturaleza y virtudes medicinales de las plantas y animales en la Nueva España* (Mexico, 1615).

[2] Ambrosio Fernandes Brandão, *Diálogos das grandezas do Brazil* (ed. Rio, 1943). The work of Fr. Christovão de Lisboa, O.F.M., 'Historia dos animaes, e avores do Maranhão', written about 1625–31, is still unpublished.

[3] Francisco de Sousa Coutinho, *Correspondência Diplomática*, ii. 286; Simão de Vasconcellos, S.J., *Noticias curiosas e necessarias das cousas de Brasil* (ed. Lisbon, 1668), pp. 21, 113, 175, 243, 257, 269, 279, 282, 284.

Neuwied were made known, certainly the most important work on Brazil'. Nor are modern Brazilian historians and scientists backward in their acknowledgements of the debt which their country owes to Johan Maurits and his collaborators in the first purely scientific researches carried out in the New World.[1]

I have already hinted that neither Johan Maurits's lavish patronage of the arts and sciences, nor his feverish building activities, met with the unqualified approval of the directors of a commercial company who were avid for sugar and dividends. The Heeren XIX obviously found their governor-general very expensive; but his popularity and prestige with all races and classes in the colony were so high, and the respect he inspired in his adversaries was so great, that for several years they did not dare to replace him. Johan Maurits on his side was continually irked by the directors' unwillingness or inability to send out adequate supplies of provisions, money, and men, and he more than once proffered his resignation. Since he took care to forward, at the same time, representations from all the communities at Recife asking for his continuance in office, it is most unlikely that he really wished to leave Brazil, where his position was in many ways that of a ruling prince.[2]

The spontaneity of these flattering testimonials may be doubted; but even if (as the Heeren XIX maintained) they were inspired by him or by someone in his entourage, they nevertheless reflected the feelings of the Portuguese and Jews, who realized that once his protection was withdrawn the Calvinist zealots would find it easier to clamp down on them. On the other hand, some of the Dutch burghers evidently resented his patronage of the hated Papists and despised Jews, which, in the case of the former at least, went far beyond mere toleration. The one thing which was generally resented about his conduct was his close association with the unscrupulous Gaspar Dias Ferreira. This arch-collaborator (as he would be termed nowadays) was bitterly hated by Catholics and Calvinists alike; and he was in fact a traitor to both sides, as everyone in the colony save Johan Maurits realized.[3]

[1] J. H. Rodrigues, *Bibliografia e Historiografia*, nos. 816-42, lists the titles of relevant European and American works.

[2] Barlaeus-Naber, *Nederlandsch Brazilië*, pp. 310-11, 371; *Kron. Hist. Gen. Utrecht*, xxv. 534-9; Aitzema, *Saken van staet en oorlogh*, ii. 899, 909.

[3] Calado, *Valeroso Lucideno*, pp. 55-57, 59, 61, 65-68, 121-2, 126-8, 130-4; *Journael ofte kort discours nopende de rebellye der Portugeesen in Brasil* (Arnhem, 1647), pp. 176-8.

After the conclusion of the truce with Portugal the directors felt that they need no longer truckle to Johan Maurits nor maintain a large garrison in Brazil, but could safely economize on both these expensive items. They therefore resolved in October 1641 drastically to reduce the garrison and to accept Johan Maurits's proffered resignation. The States-General and the prince of Orange protested that these moves were premature, but neither protests nor arguments could convince the Heeren XIX, although the final decision was thereby delayed for a few months. On 18 April 1642 the directors wrote to Johan Maurits, informing him that he was to reduce the garrison to eighteen companies forthwith, and that he could return to Europe in the spring of 1643. This decision was obviously an unpleasant surprise to the governor-general, who wrote to the States-General on 24 September asking whether they were of the same mind as the Heeren XIX, and warning them of the dangers of reducing the garrison. The directors countered this move by sending a deputation to the States-General in May 1643 asking them to agree to the recall of Johan Maurits. Their High Mightinesses did so with great reluctance, but resolved on 9 May 'to write to the Count Maurice of Nassau in discreet terms, asking him to come home and do the nation further service here'.[1]

Johan Maurits received this intimation in September 1643, but he postponed his departure from his beloved Brazil until May 1644. He did not leave unnoticed or unmourned. The popular acclaim which he received when he rode out from Recife to take ship at Paraíba makes impressive reading. Accompanied by a hundred burghers on horseback, he found the road thronged with people of all races, classes, and conditions who testified their sorrow at his going. The rich and powerful sought to shake him by the hand, the poor and lowly to touch the hem of his coat. As long as Recife and Mauritsstad were still in sight, Johan Maurits reined in his horse from time to time, and turned to look longingly at the city which he had built, 'while his trumpeters lustily sounded the old air, "Wilhelmus van Nassouwen" '. When he finally reached the shore, a mob of Brazilian Indians pushed all the white men aside, and

---

[1] Documents printed in *Bijdr. Hist. Gen. Utrecht*, iii. 352–62, where the date of the first one should be corrected to October 1641. Cf. also Barlaeus-Naber, *Nederlandsch Brazilië*, pp. 310–11, 371–3; Netscher, *Les Hollandais au Brésil*, pp. 126–32; Bouman, *Johan Maurits*, pp. 73–76.

carried him shoulder-high through the surf to the waiting boat. Only with difficulty could several hundreds of them be dissuaded from embarking in the ships next day; and he took along with him half a dozen Tapuyas out of twenty-three who had been sent by their chief, Nhandui, to beg him not to desert them.[1]

On handing over the reins of the government to his three colleagues of the High and Secret Council, Johan Maurits again stressed the necessity for tact and tolerance in ruling the jarring and ill-assorted racial groups which comprised the inhabitants of the colony. Strict discipline, but prompt payment and adequate rations for the soldiers; courtesy, respect, and toleration for the Portuguese inhabitants, with relative freedom for the exercise of the Roman Catholic religion; due consideration for the planters in exacting the repayment of their debts, now amounting to over two million florins; strict justice, tempered with mercy in so far as the use of torture was concerned; reform of the principal abuses in the local administration, even envisaging the abolition of the bailiffs who were so unpopular with the *moradores*; proper upkeep of the fortifications, stores, and magazines; maintenance of friendly relations with the Portuguese authorities at Bahia, without trusting either them or the *moradores* of Pernambuco too far. Such were the principal points of Johan Maurits's celebrated 'political testament' of May 1644, which has already been quoted more than once.

The voyage home was a speedy one, although Johan Maurits as usual suffered much from sea-sickness. Back at The Hague, he made no great haste to report to the Heeren XIX; but he found time to entertain his friends at an unconventional party in the Mauritshuis where many of his Brazilian treasures were now installed. On this occasion he caused his Tapuyas to do a war-dance, stark-naked in the true savage fashion, 'ceci a causé beaucoup de raillerie et risée parmi toute sorte de gens', as one of the guests reported. Others, however, were not amused: 'the dominies, who had come to have a look with their wives, did not find this at all nice', wrote another and more critical eyewitness.[2]

In a lengthy report of his stewardship to the States-General,

---

[1] Barlaeus-Naber, *Nederlandsch Brazilië*, pp. 395–8; Calado, *Valeroso Lucideno*, pp. 131–2; J. Nieuhof, *Gedenkweerdige Braziliaense Reize* (1682), p. 57.
[2] *Briefwisseling van Constantijn Huyghens*, iv. 52.

Johan Maurits again expounded his ideas of tolerance and moderation as regards the Portuguese of Pernambuco and their religion. He reviewed the condition of the colony, explaining the reasons for the great indebtedness of the planters, the fall in the price of slaves, and other symptoms of economic *malaise*, for which he suggested remedial measures. He openly criticized the directors for what he considered their shortcomings, although he admitted that lack of money was the chief trouble. 'A great empire and little minds go ill together' was the burden of this part of his speech; and he complained that too often the Heeren XIX had paid more attention to the spiteful gossip of underlings than to the official reports and requests of their governor-general and his council. Nevertheless, he concluded on a note of optimism, envisaging a fusion of the East and West India Companies, whose combined resources would enable the Dutch to wrest from the king of Spain all his colonial possessions from the Philippines to Peru.[1] Once again Johan Maurits was living up to his motto, *Qua patet orbis*, 'As wide as the world's bounds'.

Perhaps this vision of a brave Dutch New World seemed rather chimerical to his stolid listeners, even at a time when the tricolour of the United Provinces was the most familiar flag on the seven seas, and when Amsterdam was the commercial capital of Europe. But Johan Maurits was not alone in his conviction that a great future lay before the Dutch in South America, if only they would make full use of their resources and their opportunities. Whatever the admitted weaknesses of their own position in north-east Brazil, the difficulties and perplexities of their antagonists were still greater—or so it seemed to many sober minds in the young colony. Contrast, for instance, Padre Antonio Vieira's bitter reproaches to God in his sermon at Bahia in 1640, with the following resolution of the Calvinist consistory at Recife in June 1644: 'As we are living in these conquests enjoying peace and quiet, whereas the commonalty in Germany, England, and elsewhere groan under bloody wars, ought we not to hold a public thanksgiving-day to thank God for his mercy to these conquests, and to pray for the suffering Christendom of Europe?' Carried unanimously.[2]

---

[1] Barlaeus-Naber, *Nederlandsch Brazilië*, pp. 399–411.
[2] 'Classicale Acta van Brazilië', 18 June 1644 (*Kron. Hist. Gen. Utrecht*, xxv. 417).

V

THE 'WAR OF DIVINE LIBERTY'

1645–8

B Y recalling Johan Maurits and drastically reducing the strength of their garrison in Brazil, the directors had staked the security of the colony on the maintenance of peaceful relations with Portugal. We must therefore consider how far this assumption was warranted, and to what extent the Portuguese had reconciled themselves to the loss of the fairest part of their most prosperous overseas dominion. At first sight, it must be admitted that the directors had some excuse for their optimism. Apart from their unchallenged maritime supremacy, the Dutch were strongly posted on both sides of the South Atlantic. They had a couple of castles at Cape Verde (Goeree), and a chain of forts and factories along the Gulf of Guinea and Angola, where the Portuguese maintained only a precarious foothold in the hinterland of Angola and the island of São Thomé. On the other side of the Atlantic the Dutch held six or seven out of the fourteen captaincies into which Brazil and the Maranhão were divided. Even leaving out of account their possessions in the Caribbean and North America, which were of greater potential than actual importance, their empire in the South Atlantic must have seemed too solidly based to be seriously threatened by so weak and upstart a power as Portugal appeared to be in 1641–5. Indeed, the position of Portugal was so critical in the years following the accession of King John IV that this insecurely established monarch had no wish to involve himself in hostilities with the strongest sea power in the world. As Padre Antonio Vieira, S.J., was never tired of pointing out, since the combined efforts of Spain and Portugal had signally failed to stem the tide of Dutch colonial aggression, what could Portugal hope to achieve by herself when most of her efforts must necessarily be concentrated against Spain? This line of reasoning naturally was not overlooked in the United Provinces, where the East and West India Companies literally made the best of both worlds by enjoying peace with Portugal in Europe while waging war 'beyond the line', until the belated proclamation of the truce at Recife (July 1642) and at Goa (November 1644) respectively.

King John IV, through his ambassadors at The Hague, made repeated demands for the return of the colonial territories conquered from the Portuguese in 1641–4, whether these were in Brazil, West Africa, or Ceylon, but, as noted previously, these diplomatic protests were so much 'preaching to deaf men's ears'. Admittedly, the States-General, or some of them, were not unsympathetic in principle; but they could do nothing without the unanimous consent of the seven provincial states, each of which was sovereign in its own territory. The two maritime (and most powerful) provinces, Holland and Zeeland, were naturally strongly influenced by their close connexions with the East and West India Companies, and consequently were firmly opposed to making any colonial concessions to the Portuguese. King John IV later tried to bring pressure on the Companies by persuading the States-General not to renew their respective charters, both of which were due to expire about this time, unless they would consent to at least a compromise agreement with Portugal. This move also failed, as might have been foreseen, but the king likewise had recourse to French mediation. In August 1644 the French ambassador strongly protested to the States-General at their failure to curb the Companies' aggression, which, as he pointed out, prevented King John IV from effectively pursuing the war against Spain in Europe. This remonstrance made more impression on the Dutch than any purely Portuguese representations; but the States-General were still unwilling or unable to go back on their resolution of June 1644, by which they had finally rejected the Portuguese demands.[1]

In fact, the two great corporations considered that they had the whip-hand of the Portuguese, and they were not averse from cracking the whip, whatever the States-General might say or do. In August 1643 the Heeren XIX threatened that if the Portuguese would not drop their demands for the restitution of Luanda, São Thomé, and the Maranhão, the West India Company would proceed to make further conquests at the expense

[1] Aitzema, *Saken van staet en oorlogh*, ii. 975–6; Arend, *Algemeene Geschiedenis*, iii (5), 372–4, 443–51.

of the Lusitanian crown.[1] The East India Company's representatives in Ceylon were still more outspoken a few years later. The viceroy of Goa 'having sent an ambassador to Galle to demand Negombo, according to the conditions made between the King of Portugal and the States of the Low Countries, Maetsuycker, General in Galle for the Hollands Company, told the ambassador plainly that it was true they had order from the States and Prince of Orange to deliver Negombo to the Portugals, but they were not servants to the Prince nor States, but to the Company, from whom (they said) they had received no such order; nor when they shall receive such order from their Company, will they surrender it but by force'.[2]

In view of the diplomatic intransigence of the Dutch, it would not be surprising if the Portuguese government had thought of fomenting a rebellion in north-east Brazil as a last desperate remedy, but there is no proof that they actually did so. Although King John IV was theoretically an absolute monarch, in practice he seldom made any major decisions without consulting his senior councillors. Unfortunately, the proceedings of the Council of State for this period have not been preserved (or at any rate have not been found), and the minutes of the *Conselho Ultramarino*, or Overseas Council, begin with its creation in 1643. In any event, even if King John IV decided that a general rising in Pernambuco was the only solution (something very unlikely in view of his pacific nature and the need he had of the Dutch alliance in Europe), it is probable that this decision would not have been set down on paper but would have been verbally confided to a few intimate advisers. This supposition is all the more likely in view of his excessively cautious character, and the difficulties which his subjects were experiencing with the Dutch from the Maranhão to Macao. In fact, it was the fate of the cinnamon lands of Ceylon rather than the sugar-plantations of Pernambuco which was uppermost in the minds of the king and his councillors for most of the years 1643–4.

This does not mean that there was no unrest in Pernambuco, or that there was no thought among the Portuguese on either

---

[1] Aitzema, *Saken van staet en oorlogh*, ii. 923, 976, and H. Haecxs, 'Dagboek', p. 159, for the truculent attitude of the two great companies.
[2] W. Foster [ed.], *English Factories in India, 1646–1650* (Oxford, 1914), p. 55, letter of M. Bowman, Colombo, 26 Nov. 1646.

side of the Atlantic of overthrowing the Dutch in north-east Brazil. But such plots or plans as may have been hatching were still in an embryo stage, and there is no proof that any of them had received the support of King John IV until after Johan Maurits had left; if, indeed, they received it then. It is true that João Fernandes Vieira alleged the contrary in 1671, but his unsupported testimony on this point does not carry great weight. In any event, an atmosphere of distrust and suspicion was never wholly absent from Pernambuco, despite the sincere and by no means unfruitful efforts of Johan Maurits to reconcile the *moradores* to Dutch rule. In December 1642 João Fernandes Vieira asked for an interview with Johan Maurits and his council. He stated that he and his father-in-law, Francisco Berenguer de Andrade, had been denounced to the Heeren XIX for plotting to restore Pernambuco to King John IV. He warmly affirmed his innocence and his unwavering loyalty to the Dutch government, advising them to deprive the *moradores* of the weapons which they had been allowed to carry by the assembly of September 1640. This was accordingly done, although many of them later secured their arms again on one pretext or another. If João Fernandes Vieira's protestations did not entirely convince his hearers, at any rate his actions partly lulled their suspicions, especially since the accusations of his treachery could be explained away as the slanders of jealous rivals.[1]

The successful revolt of the Maranhão and the departure of Johan Maurits had given the Portuguese of Pernambuco two powerful incentives to transform their smouldering resentment against the hated heretics into action. But it was obvious that, largely disarmed as they were, they could do nothing without the assurance of prompt and effective support from Bahia. That assurance was forthcoming in September 1644, when André Vidal de Negreiros called at Recife on the transparently flimsy pretext of saying good-bye to his old father, 'who was a poor carpenter living in Paraíba, and whom he was about as anxious to see as I should be the King of Congo', as a contemporary Dutch pamphleteer sarcastically noted.[2]

Vidal had already sounded Fernandes Vieira on a visit to

---

[1] For this and what follows cf. Nieuhof, *Gedenkweerdige Reize*, pp. 51–56, 63–64; Calado, *Valeroso Lucideno*, pp. 160–78; Gonsalves de Mello, biographies of *Antonio Dias Cardoso*, pp. 14–17, *Henrique Dias*, pp. 28–31, *D. Felipe Camarão*, pp. 36–37.

[2] *Brasilsche gelt-saeck* (1647).

Recife (ostensibly in connexion with the truce negotiations) two years previously, but this time more definite arrangements were made. After several secret meetings between Vidal, Fernandes Vieira, and other leading planters, it was agreed that Vieira should lead a general revolt of the *moradores* in the following June, while some soldiers would be sent overland from Bahia to give support and direction to the largely untrained planters. These arrangements were made at the instigation of the governor-general at Bahia, Antonio Telles da Silva, who had assumed office in August 1642, and who was the prime mover and planner of the revolt as it finally took shape.

At the end of the year 1644 Antonio Telles sent to Pernambuco an experienced officer named Antonio Dias Cardoso, with a body of forty veteran soldiers, to act as instructors and leaders when the *moradores* should revolt. Not unnaturally, Fernandes Vieira found this small force quite insufficient, and he refused to raise the standard of revolt until far more substantial reinforcements were sent. Varnhagen and other writers have blamed him for this, but it is hard to see why. The *moradores* had been largely disarmed, and most of them were quite untrained. Fernandes Vieira had been able to conceal some arms and munitions in caches on his own plantations, but these weapons would not be very serviceable after being buried for months in the tropical earth during the rainy season.[1] Without immediate, close, and effective support from well-armed and well-trained soldiers or guerrilla fighters, the rebellion had no chance of success, and Fernandes Vieira cannot fairly be blamed for asking for more men.

Telles da Silva endeavoured to meet Fernandes Vieira's demands and to avoid arousing the suspicions of the Dutch, by arranging that the Negro leader, Henrique Dias, should penetrate into the hinterland of Dutch territory, ostensibly having quarrelled with the Portuguese governor. He and his men would then be followed by D. Felipe Camarão and his Amerindian levies, nominally in pursuit of the fugitive Negroes from justice, but in reality with orders to support them, and to join with Fernandes Vieira and the *moradores* as soon as the rising began. The departure of Dias and Camarão took place in March and April 1645, respectively.

[1] The rainy season in Pernambuco usually begins in March–April and ends in July–August.

Meanwhile, the conferences between Vidal and the leading planters in August–September 1644, and the subsequent comings and goings between Bahia and Pernambuco, did not fail to arouse the suspicions of the Dutch. The High Council which governed Netherlands Brazil after the departure of Johan Maurits was unkindly characterized by João Fernandes Vieira as being composed of 'four Flemish knaves and four infamous Jews', but it really consisted of only three members, as the fourth, Dirk Codde van der Burgh, died in 1644. These were Hendrik Hamel, a merchant of Amsterdam, Pieter Bas, formerly a goldsmith at Haarlem, and Adriaan Bullestrate, originally a master carpenter of Middelburg. However plebeian their origins may have been, they were (so to speak) trained in Johan Maurits's school of colonial administration, and they were by no means so venal or so incompetent as is often alleged. They were informed as early as 13 October 1644 of what was in the wind, and they received several subsequent warnings not only from 'New-Christians' and orthodox Jews, but from local planters who considered that a rebellion would have no chance of success and had no wish to become involved in one. The councillors effected to pooh-pooh these reports in public, so as to avoid spreading alarm and despondency among their own nationals; but they took them very seriously in reality, as can be seen from the following extracts from an official dispatch to the Heeren XIX which this body received on 6 January 1645.

'The Portuguese in this country, because they are so deeply indebted, indeed most of them much more than they can hope to pay in their lifetime, ... scheme night and day to revolt like those in the Maranhão and in Portugal itself have done, so as to be freed thereby from our rule and to avoid paying what they owe us.' After enumerating many indications that the local Portuguese were ripe for revolt, the councillors added that it would be relatively easy for the rebels to seize the Dutch forts in Recife and elsewhere by a *coup-de-main*, as their compatriots had done with the Spanish garrisons in Portugal in 1640, for they well knew that the forts were ill provisioned and undermanned. Moreover, the Portuguese felt that they had much more reason to revolt against the Dutch than ever they had against the Spaniards, who treated them (as they thought) better than the Dutch did, 'and they were also people of the same religion, whereas we on the contrary make a mock of their belief . . . so that it is to be feared that they will shortly attempt some evil against us'. They wrote again in the same sense, but even more emphatically, on 13 February 1645, urgently appealing for men and munitions to be sent them.[1]

The Recife council dispatched two emissaries to Bahia in January 1645, ostensibly to protest against absconding debtors being given asylum in Portuguese territory, but in reality to find out whether anything unusual was going on at Bahia. The envoys, one of whom was Major Dirk Hooghstraten, commander of the key fortress of Pontal de Nazaré, returned to Recife in March with a report which was reassuring on the whole. Antonio Telles da Silva had been profuse with pacific assurances, and they had seen only two warships in the harbour. These were a couple of royal galleons under the command of Salvador Correia de Sá e Benavides, on their way to Rio de Janeiro to convoy home the sugar-fleet. In reality, however, Telles da Silva was trying to induce Salvador Correia to co-operate in the projected Pernambuco rebellion. The governor-general wanted him to call at Recife with the homeward-bound sugar-fleet in June or July. If the place had not yet fallen to the insurgents, he was to assure the Dutch that he had come to help them against the rebels, and would like to land troops for this purpose. If the Dutch were foolish enough to consent, he could then take Recife by this Trojan Horse method. If they refused, he was to attack or blockade the place from seaward. The Pernambuco rising was originally timed for Midsummer Day 1645, but some faint-hearted conspirators among the *moradores* anonymously betrayed the outlines of the plot to the High Council at Recife on the evening of 30 May.[2]

The Council realized that this was no mere irresponsible libel, and they at once took precautionary measures. Fernandes Vieira and most of the ringleaders escaped into the bush, since they had scouts and sentries out on all sides, and received timely warning. But among those who were arrested was Sebastião de Carvalho, who proved to be one of the signatories

---

[1] High Council's letters in JHMS, fols. 2–66. Relevant extracts from the letter of 13 Feb. 1645 are printed in Nieuhof, *Gedenkweerdige Reize*, pp. 64–66.

[2] Nieuhof, op. cit., pp. 58–73; Calado, *Valeroso Lucideno*, pp. 168–78, are the principal printed sources. For a list of the others cf. J. H. Rodrigues, *Historiografia e Bibliografia*, nos. 489, 502–13, 516–23.

of the anonymous denunciation of Fernandes Vieira, and who willingly gave the Dutch all the details which he knew. His evidence was confirmed by that of other deponents, some freely and some under torture.

João Fernandes Vieira, who had secretly circularized the *moradores* to prepare to revolt 'in the name of divine liberty' on 15 May, was still protesting on paper his unswerving loyalty and dedication to the Dutch a month later,[1] although the betrayal of his plans forced him to take the field openly on 13 June. About 150 men, mostly Mulattoes and Negroes, answered his summons on the first day, and others rallied to him daily; but the bulk of the *moradores* remained quiescent, evidently waiting to see who would win the first round before they irrevocably committed themselves. The Dutch, who had only received definite intelligence of the movements of the columns of Camarão and Dias in June, now withdrew some of their outlying garrisons and concentrated their forces round Recife. Flying-columns of soldiers and burghers were organized under the command of Colonel Haus (the acting commander-in-chief) and Captain Blaer, to scour the countryside for Fernandes Vieira and his roving bands. Vieira naturally sought to avoid battle until he could join forces with Dias and Camarão; so that although some petty skirmishes took place between different Dutch detachments and parties of the insurgents, no major clash occurred for several weeks. On 26 June a Dutch official wrote home that the rebellion appeared to have been nipped in the bud, adding that a general pardon had been proclaimed for all rebels who submitted voluntarily (certain leaders only excepted), since the garrison was not strong enough to employ thoroughgoing offensive measures.

The High Councillors writing next day to the Heeren XIX were less optimistic. They blamed the directors' drastic reduction of their military and naval strength for the revolt of the Portuguese: 'since that nation, being so different from our own in religion, language and customs, and being moreover heavily indebted owing to the losses they suffered in the former war, which debt they despair of ever being able to repay, cannot be kept in obedience by any other way' than by force. The Councillors added that the rebels were expecting thirty-five sail with reinforcements from Bahia, which made it all the more

[1] Letter of 13 June 1645, in JHMS, fols. 230–1.

necessary for the directors to send urgently the troops and munitions for which they had been so often asked.[1]

In July the High Council sent Major Hooghstraten, this time accompanied by Balthazar van de Voorde, back to Bahia, with orders to remonstrate with Telles da Silva for his obvious and culpable encouragement of the rebels. The Portuguese governor again emphatically disclaimed all connexion with the revolt, and countered by reminding the Dutch of the breaches of the truce which they had committed in Angola and elsewhere. He added that he would send a detachment of soldiers from Bahia to recall Dias and Camarão to their obedience, and to pacify the rebellious *moradores* by force if necessary. During his short stay at Bahia, Hooghstraten had been sounded by Telles da Silva about the possibility of surrendering the fort of Pontal de Nazaré on a suitable occasion and in return for a lavish reward. Hooghstraten revealed this discussion to the High Council on his return to Recife, assuring them that he had no intention of doing anything of the kind, but he had given the Portuguese governor-general quite the contrary impression.[2]

Feeling assured of the co-operation of Hooghstraten, Telles da Silva now ventured on a step which otherwise he might have hesitated to take. The Dutch had asked him to send orders to stop the revolt of Pernambuco, but he seized on their request as a pretext for dispatching troops, not by devious paths through the bush (as with the levies of Dias and Camarão), but openly by sea. Two Portuguese regiments from the garrison at Bahia, one commanded by the elderly Indian-fighter, Martim Soares Moreno, and the other by the Paraíban-born colonel,[3] André Vidal de Negreiros, were shipped in sixteen caravels, under the command of Jeronimo Serrão de Paiva, to the roadstead of Tamandaré, where they landed at the end of July. Their ostensible orders were to co-operate with the Dutch in pacifying the *moradores* of Pernambuco, but their secret instructions were to assist João Fernandes Vieira. A few days after Serrão de Paiva's departure from Bahia, Salvador Correia entered the port with the Rio de Janeiro detachment of the homeward-

[1] Letter of Van de Voorde, 26 June, and High Council, 27 June 1645, in JHMS, fols. 170–205.
[2] Nieuhof, *Gedenkweerdige Reize*, pp. 87–98; *Bijdr. Hist. Gen. Utrecht*, iii. 362–78; Calado, *Valeroso Lucideno*, pp. 185–7.
[3] *mestre-de-campo* in the original. This rank corresponded to the contemporary English 'Colonel of Foot'.

bound sugar-fleet. Telles da Silva at once urged him to join Serrão de Paiva with his sixteen caravels and attack Recife from seaward in accordance with the prearranged plan. Salvador was most reluctant to comply, but he finally agreed to do so, although he made no secret of his dislike of the whole business in conversation with other people after his departure from Bahia.[1]

The month of July passed without a major clash between the insurgents and the Dutch, although it was marked by an event which greatly embittered the existing ill-feeling between the two races. The premature discovery of Fernandes Vieira's plot led to what was intended as a general rising being virtually limited to the *várzea*; but the Dutch were naturally very nervous of its spreading elsewhere, and they called on their cannibal Tapuya allies for help. These savages responded only too readily, and a band of them under their German-Jewish leader, Jacob Rabbe, who was 'married' with a Tapuya woman, massacred a number of the *moradores* of Rio Grande of all ages and both sexes. The High Councillors disclaimed all responsibility for this atrocity, but the Portuguese naturally assumed that it was done with their connivance if not on their orders, particularly since the perpetrators went unpunished. The insurgents resolved to repay their enemies in kind, and thus a cycle of mutual atrocities was begun for which each side blamed the other.

On 3 August the combined columns of Colonel Haus and Captain Blaer located João Fernandes Vieira and his men on a rocky hillock some thirty miles from Recife. This natural stronghold was called the Monte das Tabocas, after some thorny bushes of that name with which its slopes were covered. Fernandes Vieira did not refuse battle, as he could no longer afford to wait for Dias and Camarão, since some of his men were becoming discouraged and most of the *moradores* in the *várzea* were still holding back. A victory was urgently needed to give confidence to his men and to encourage the waverers; and although João Fernandes Vieira had many faults, cowardice was not one of them. The Dutch advanced to the attack with confidence, as the flower of their soldiery was present, and their opponents were described as being 'mostly a bunch of *canaille* who know nothing of war'. The attackers were inferior in

---

[1] *Claer Vertooch* (1647); documents printed in the *RIAGP*, nos. 32–35; and in the *RIHGB*, lxix. 87–98.

numbers, as they only totalled about 400 white soldiers and 300 Amerindians, whereas their opponents were about a thousand strong. But the numerical inferiority of the Dutch was more than offset by the fact that their opponents had relatively few firearms, most of them being equipped with pikes, swords, scythes, and other makeshift weapons. On the other hand, João Fernandes Vieira and Antonio Dias Cardoso (who acted as the former's chief of staff and directed most of the defenders' dispositions) had chosen a defensive position of great natural strength which afforded excellent concealment.

Haus launched four determined attacks on the hillock during the hot August day, but each time his men were repulsed with loss, although twice they very nearly broke through. At one of the most critical moments, when the Portuguese had begun to give way, João Fernandes Vieira promised a band of his Negro slaves their freedom if they could stem the Dutch attack. The onslaught of these men, most of whom were Minas and Ardras from Guinea, did indeed save the situation. When the action ceased at sundown both sides were completely exhausted, and the insurgents had almost finished their slender stock of ammunition. Fortunately for them, Haus beat a precipitate retreat during the dark and stormy night which followed; but the victors did not realize the extent of their success until the day broke and they found him gone. Estimates of the casualties varied widely, but those of the Dutch were probably a little over 200, whereas the defenders, who fought behind cover, evidently lost less than half that number.[1]

Whatever the respective casualties, the battle of Tabocas entirely changed the aspect of the campaign. The Dutch were now on the defensive, and could not prevent the junction of the insurgents with the various forces from Bahia which were converging on the *várzea*. The Negro levies of Henrique Dias and the Amerindians of D. Felipe Camarão joined João Fernandes Vieira's men ten days later, and their combined forces then went in search of the two Portuguese regiments commanded by Martim Soares Moreno and André Vidal de Negreiros. In the meantime, these latter, after disembarking their men at

---

[1] The best account of the battle of Tabocas is in Gonsalves de Mello, *Antonio Dias Cardoso*, pp. 18–21, which includes Haus's official report, d. 4 Aug. 1645, previously unpublished. Other details are taken from Nieuhof, *Gedenkweerdige Reize*, p. 104; *Journael ofte Kort Discours, 1645–1647*, Aug. 1646; *Kron. Hist. Gen. Utrecht*, xxv. 402.

Tamandaré, had occupied the district of Serinhaem without serious opposition, the local Dutch garrison surrendering on 6 August. Those of the Dutch colonists in this region who wished to remain under Portuguese rule were at first allowed to do so, although this tolerant attitude of the victors did not last long. Roeland Carpentier, the principal Dutch sugar-planter who accepted Portuguese protection, was charged with high treason in January 1646, and summarily executed, and others of his countrymen apparently shared his fate.[1]

Having occupied Serinhaem, Vidal and Moreno then advanced on the roadstead of Cabo de Santo Agostinho, which, with its commanding fortress of the Pontal de Nazaré, was surrendered to them by Hooghstraten on 13 August, after a token resistance. Hooghstraten not only took service with the Portuguese himself, but induced or compelled many officers and men in the garrison to do likewise. Some of these did so with the secret intention of deserting back to their compatriots at the first opportunity, as, in fact, a number of them were eventually able to do. This naturally caused the Portuguese to distrust the remainder, who were then disarmed and sent to Bahia. Hooghstraten was aided and abetted in his treachery by a number of senior Dutch officers who were married to local ladies, and whose affection for their wives was evidently stronger than their love for their country. Prominent among these turncoats was the *ritmeester*, Jasper van der Ley, whose descendants, under the name of Wanderley, are prominent in public life in Brazil today.

Having thus secured a fortified roadstead where they could receive supplies from Bahia by sea, Vidal and Moreno now marched inland to join forces with Fernandes Vieira, Dias, and Camarão. Their junction took place on 16 August, and Vidal at first went through the farce of pretending to arrest the rebel leader; but he immediately dropped this pose when the soldiers who had come from Bahia broke their ranks and shouted that they would join the insurgents whatever their commanding officers did. The combined forces then advanced to attack the Dutch punitive column commanded by Haus and Blaer, which was billeted in a neighbouring sugar-mill known as the Casa

---

[1] For the mistreatment of the Dutch who stayed in Serinhaem and the murder of Roeland Carpentier cf. *Journael ofte Kort Discours, 1645–47*, 4 Feb. 1646; Gonsalves de Mello, *Tempo dos Flamengos*, pp. 165–6; *Bijdr. Hist. Gen. Utrecht*, iii. 378–84.

Forte. The defenders, who numbered about 270 Europeans apart from Amerindians, offered a vigorous resistance when they were invested and attacked next day (17 August), but were eventually compelled to surrender at discretion. André Vidal insisted on giving the Dutch quarter, despite the protests of Fernandes Vieira; but he raised no objection to the massacre of the Amerindian auxiliaries by the infuriated Pernambucan insurgents.[1]

Had the united Portuguese forces attacked Recife immediately after the victory of the Casa Forte, they would in all probability have taken the place without much difficulty, as the defenders themselves later confessed. The position of the latter could hardly have been more critical, and the few remaining troops were badly demoralized by the desertion of so many of their senior officers. At the very hour when Hooghstraten was negotiating the final surrender of Pontal, Salvador Correia appeared off Recife with his homeward-bound convoy and the caravels of Serrão de Paiva, anchoring in the outer roadstead with thirty-seven sail. The High Councillors were greatly perturbed by his appearance, but they naturally refused to let him land his men to 'help' them as he requested. They asked him to continue his voyage, and ordered Admiral Lichthart to attack the Portuguese fleet (which only included a couple of warships) if they remained in the offing. Finding the Dutch on their guard, and being ignorant of the reverses which they had suffered elsewhere, Salvador Correia used the excuse of a squall which sprang up on the afternoon of 13 August, to resume his voyage next day, leaving Serrão de Paiva to his own devices. Seeing himself thus abandoned, the latter returned with his transport-caravels to Tamandaré, where his squadron was cornered and destroyed by Lichthart on 9 September.[2]

Lichthart's victory undoubtedly saved Netherlands Brazil and did much to restore the morale of its remaining defenders, but it could not prevent the loss of the *várzea* and most of the hinterland. The successive victories of Fernandes Vieira and André Vidal naturally gave those of the *moradores* who had hitherto sat on the fence (and they were the great majority)

---

[1] Mattheus van den Broeck, *Journael ofte Historiaelse Beschrivinge* (Amsterdam, 1651), *Journael ofte Kort Discours, 1645–47*, 3 Aug. 1645; Nieuhof, *Gedenkweerdige Reize*, pp. 133–4; Calado, *Valeroso Lucideno*, pp. 212–30.

[2] C. R. Boxer, *Salvador de Sá*, pp. 206–10, and sources quoted in footnotes.

every inducement to join the revolt, which spread like wildfire after the capitulation of Haus at the Casa Forte. The *moradores* of Paraíba rose against the Dutch on 2 September, and at the other end of the colony the garrisons of Porto Calvo and Fort Maurits (on the river São Francisco) surrendered on 17 and 18 September, respectively. Sergipe del Rey followed suit on the 22nd, and by the end of the month the Portuguese were masters of nearly all the country between Rio Grande do Norte and the Rio Real. The Dutch were able to repulse with heavy loss a determined attack on the island of Itamaracá (20–24 September), and their Tapuya allies carried out another atrocious massacre of the unfortunate colonists of Rio Grande do Norte on 3 October; but the year 1645 ended with the Dutch closely besieged in Recife, and with most of Netherlands Brazil in the hands of their opponents. Apart from the capital and the semicircle of outlying forts which protected it on the landward side, only the islands of Itamaracá and Fernão de Noronha, together with the coastal forts of Cabedello (Paraíba) and Ceulen (Rio Grande do Norte) remained in Dutch hands. These places were, however, of little economic importance in comparison with the loss of the *várzea* and the southern captaincies.

The conduct of the campaign was greatly embittered by the true and false stories of atrocities which were freely bandied about by both sides. The Dutch firmly believed that most of the prisoners captured at the Casa Forte and Pontal, who had been sent overland to Bahia, had been foully murdered on the way. In point of fact, Captain Blaer, who was one of the worst oppressors of the *moradores* in peacetime, was killed in cold blood on the march, as were a few others, but the vast majority of the prisoners reached Bahia safely. From here many of them were shipped to Europe, and some of them, including Colonel Haus, were back again at Recife within a twelvemonth. They naturally suffered greatly from hunger and other hardships on the way to Bahia; but as the victors themselves had very little to eat, the horrors of this 'death-march' (as it would be termed nowadays) were to a great extent unavoidable. Conversely, the Portuguese believed that the Dutch turned over all their prisoners to the cannibal Tapuyas; although the worst offender, Jacob Rabbe, was himself assassinated in April 1646, by order of Major Garstman, the commander at Rio Grande do Norte, whose wife was a Portuguese and many of whose relatives had perished in the massacres. The details of this affair are obscure, but it resulted in many of the Tapuyas forswearing their alliance with the Dutch, though not, it would appear, for very long. It may be added that these stories of mutual atrocities lost nothing in the telling by the deserters on both sides, who naturally strove to palliate their own behaviour by painting as black as possible the side which they had just deserted.[1]

The first vague reports of the outbreak of the revolt reached Holland at the end of August. They caused a great sensation, but it seemed at first as if the rebellion, having started prematurely, would be scotched by prompt and resolute action.[2] Nevertheless, the revolt could hardly have come at a more awkward time for the West India Company. After several years of disappointing sugar harvests, a record crop of cane was ripening in June 1645, and local optimists even thought that it would be large enough to enable the Portuguese planters to pay off all their debts. This would have been unlikely in any event; but in the expectation of a bumper harvest in 1645-6, the governing council at Recife had entered into a series of contracts with many of the principal (and most indebted) planters, whereby the Company assumed responsibility for the debts which they owed to private traders, on the security of their mills, equipment, plantations, and sugar crop. The deep indebtedness of the planters was largely due, as the Council recognized, to the excessively high rates of interest charged by their private creditors, monthly rates of 3 per cent. being very common. Indeed, if Vice-Admiral Witte de With is to be believed, interest at 20 per cent. a month was sometimes charged when harvest-time was near, and the yearly interest usually charged by the Dutch on their loans ranged from 36 to 48 per cent.[3]

Moreover, the Heeren XIX were in the middle of reorganizing the government of Netherlands Brazil, and their new and stronger team of four councillors and a president was still in process of formation. Their first choice for president was the

---

[1] Lichthart's letter of 28 Feb. 1646 to the Heeren XIX in JHMS; M. van den Broeck, *Journael ofte Historiaelse Beschrivinge* (1651); *Journael ofte Kort Discours, 1645-47*, 1-5 Sept., 14 Oct., 16 Dec. 1645 and 2 Feb. 1646; Nieuhof, *Gedenkweerdige Reize*, pp. 104, 147-9, 153, 164-5; Calado, *Valeroso Lucideno*, pp. 214-15, 277-80.

[2] 'Brieven van Doedens' in *Kron. Hist. Gen. Utrecht*, xxv. 400-12.

[3] Witte de With's journal d. 16 Sept. 1649, in JHMS; *Journael ofte Kort Discours*, June 1645; Nieuhof, *Gedenkweerdige Reize*, pp. 47-53; Aitzema, *Saken van staet en oorlogh*, iii. 31-32.

Gueldersman, Alexander van der Capellen, and when he declined the honour they selected Walter van Schonenburgh, an ex-burgomaster of Groningen and a deputy of that city in the States-General. The other councillors were Michiel van Goch, pensionary of Flushing; Simon van Beaumont, an ex-director of the Zeeland Chamber and the advocate-fiscal of Dordrecht; and two Amsterdam merchants, Abraham Trouwers (another ex-director) and Hendrik Haecxs. This last-named individual had previously lived for some years in Recife as a private trader, and he was the only one of the ruling five with personal experience of the colony.[1]

The new council took the oath at the hands of the States-General on 18 November, two days after Balthazar van de Voorde arrived from Recife with the local council's urgent appeal for help. Although he had sailed from Brazil the day before the battle of Tabocas was fought and lost, the news which he brought was disturbing enough. His report indicated pretty clearly that the authorities at Bahia were behind the rebellion, but the real Job's tidings came a week later. On 24 November two ships arrived from Recife bringing dispatches dated 17 September, wherein the successive Dutch disasters on land and Lichthart's solitary (if encouraging) victory at sea were related in detail. There could now be no doubt that the revolt was supported, if it was not directly organized, from Bahia; and the correspondence captured on board Serrão de Paiva's flagship at Tamandaré (9 September) indicated that the king of Portugal himself was involved.[2]

The weakness of the Dutch governmental system and of the West India Company's organization was clearly evinced in the ensuing months. As regards the former, the self-styled United Provinces were in most respects merely allied provinces; and, as allies are apt to do, they frequently fell out with each other. If they were united in anything, it was in the jealousy with which six of the provinces regarded the seventh, Holland, which was by far the richest and most powerful. On other occasions the five land provinces were frequently at odds with the two

---

[1] Van der Capellen, *Gedenkschriften*, ii. 111–13; H. Haecxs, 'Dagboek', pp. 149–54; P. Moreau, *Histoire*, pp. 37–38, 103–5. Moreau signed on as Van Goch's secretary.

[2] Van de Voorde's report printed *in extenso* in Aitzema, *Saken van staet en oorlogh*, iii. 30–32. Cf. also the *Claer Vertooch* (1647), and Francisco de Sousa Coutinho, *Correspondência Diplomática*, i. 336.

maritime provinces of Holland and Zeeland. The States-General was merely a common governing body of delegated and limited powers, and its members were bound to refer any new problem to the provincial authorities who had appointed them. Any resolutions which concerned the 'Generality', or the Union as a whole, had to be voted unanimously in order to be valid. All the resolutions of their High Mightinesses had to be referred back to the provincial assemblies for implementation, and no province considered itself under an obligation to obey unless it had consented. Combined action was obviously difficult to secure under such a government as this, where each province regarded itself as sovereign and independent, and where their interests by no means always coincided. In a way, the system of government might be described as government by committees appointed by the principal parties concerned. The position of the prince of Orange as commander-in-chief of the armed forces, and as a potential monarch in an oligarchic republic, complicated matters still further.

As regards the West India Company, both Arciszewski and Johan Maurits had cogently criticized the delay and inefficiency caused by the Company's cumbersome constitution. The regional chambers, like the different provinces in which they were situated, were both independent and jealous of each other, trading with their own capital, managing their own shipping, and struggling with their own loads of debt. The Heeren XIX were supposed to co-ordinate general policy, but the directors' authority was circumscribed by the chambers who appointed them, and the orders of the former could not be obeyed without the concurrence of the latter. The rule whereby the directors retired in rotation after three years' service, although not always strictly enforced, meant that many men had to resign just as they were getting thoroughly familiar with the business, being replaced by greenhorns who had everything to learn. This did not make for administrative efficiency nor for continuity of policy, and few of the Heeren XIX had ever been in Brazil. Their position was further aggravated by acrimonious disputes over the renewal of the Company's charter in 1644-5, and the uncertainty which its frequent postponement engendered. The Company's methods of book-keeping mystified even contemporaries, and its chronic indebtedness paralysed swift action. By the time the most urgent questions had been referred back and forth between the provincial assemblies, their High Mightinesses and the prince of Orange on the one hand, and the regional chambers and the Heeren XIX on the other, it was usually too late to do anything effective, and so in the upshot nothing was done.

It is, therefore, not altogether surprising that although the High Council at Recife had given repeated warnings of the coming storm in their dispatches of January–March 1645, and that although news of the outbreak of the revolt had been received at the end of August, nearly nine months passed before any substantial help left the Netherlands for Brazil. Under the impression of the dire news received in the last week of November, the representatives of the States-General and of the West India Company agreed that a subsidy of 500,000 florins (increased to 700,000 in December) should be given to the Company to enable it to send ships and troops to Brazil. At one stage they envisaged a fleet of thirty-six sail (including fifteen or twenty States' warships) with an expeditionary force of 6,000 men, including 1,800 volunteers from regiments in the pay of the States-General. These grandiose projects were no sooner set down on paper than they assumed much more modest dimensions in practice. The provinces having voted the money were, as usual, either very slow or altogether remiss in supplying their quotas. Both soldiers and sailors were very reluctant to volunteer for service in Brazil, and recruiting was further impeded by Venetian agents who were enlisting troops in the Netherlands to fight the Turks. Last not least, an exceptionally severe frost which began early in December 1645 rendered most of the ports icebound for many months. Some ships which left from Zeeland in February and March remained stormbound in the English Channel for weeks on end. The bulk of the expedition did not leave until May 1646, when the new president and Colonels von Schoppe and Henderson (who were then on leave in Holland) finally left the Scheldt. Of the thirty-six sail and 6,000 men which were originally envisaged, a total of twenty sail and 2,000 men eventually sailed at one time or another in the first five months of 1646. These included three warships (*Middelburg*, *Vlissingen*, and *Veere*) which were furnished by the admiralty of Zeeland under a special arrangement with the West India Company.[1] The troubled waters of Dutch

[1] For the mobilization and voyage of the expedition of 1645–6, cf. P. Moreau,

domestic politics afforded good fishing to the Portuguese envoy at The Hague, Francisco de Sousa Coutinho, although his remonstrances and intrigues were less responsible for the delay in the sailing of the expedition for Recife than were 'Generals January and February' and the cumbersome Dutch administrative system.

The news of the rebellion, when it reached Lisbon in August, embarrassed King John IV and many of his leading advisers as much as it annoyed Their High Mightinesses at The Hague. Even if the Portuguese monarch knew something of its antecedents, his subsequent behaviour indicated that he was not prepared to support or condone it, unless presented with a *fait accompli* in the form of the immediate and total expulsion of the Dutch from Brazil.[1] King John IV was above all things anxious to be included in the negotiations for a general peace which were then in the preliminary stages of the Congress of Munster, and the support of the United Provinces was essential to him in this and other vital respects. The rebellion having been launched prematurely, he first adopted his usual policy of masterly inactivity; and then, when he could no longer avoid saying something, he emphatically disclaimed all connexion with the rebels—to whom indeed he gave no help for a whole year.

Sousa Coutinho received no information or instructions from his master until mid-November; but he meanwhile hastened to assure the States-General, and anyone who would listen, that the king had nothing whatever to do with the revolt and regarded João Fernandes Vieira and his followers as traitors. Neither the ambassador's fervid denials nor the king's belated disclaimers impressed the States-General, while the West India Company's

Histoire, pp. 105–27; 'Brieven van Doedens', in *Kron. Hist. Gen. Utrecht*, xxv. 400–31; H. Haecxs, 'Dagboek', pp. 155–82; Nieuhof, *Gedenkweerdige Reize*, pp. 177–8; Arend, *Algemeene Geschiedenis*, iii (5), pp. 599–601, 691–4. For the arrangements concerning the three Zeeland warships, cf. Hoboken, *Witte de With*, ch. 1. Moreau claims that as many as forty-five sail eventually reached Recife, seven ships and about 500 men being lost on the voyage, but his figures seem to be exaggerated. The three Zeeland warships were under Admiral Banckert.

[1] This was categorically stated by Padre Antonio Vieira, S.J., in his famous (or infamous) *Papel Forte* of 1648–49. 'Responde-se que não consta de tal promessa de Vossa Magestade, e, em caso que a houvesse, não tem Vossa Magestade obrigação de a cumprir, com pôr a risco toda a monarquia; principalmente que essa promessa, se a houve, foi fundada na que os homens de Pernambuco fizeram, de haverem de tomar logo o Arrecife, e em outras informações e esperanças falsas . . .' (ed. Cidade e Sérgio, *Obras Escolhidas*, iii. 35–36).

friends incited the populace at The Hague to make hostile de-
monstrations against Sousa Coutinho's house and person. The
States-General informed him in December that King John IV
could prove his sincerity only by ordering the immediate restitution of the lost territory, the exemplary punishment of the
rebels, and the surrender of the traitor Hooghstraten. They also
rejected the renewed Portuguese proposals for the purchase of
Netherlands Brazil, which Sousa Coutinho submitted on the
instructions of his master, and which were largely based on the
suggestions of the versatile Gaspar Dias Ferreira. King John IV's
refusal to support the rebels at this juncture was quite genuine,
although the Dutch naturally did not realize this. His overseas councillors strongly advised him (23 October 1645) to
maintain peace with the United Provinces at any price. They
pointed out that if the combined strength of Spain and Portugal
had failed to check the tide of Dutch conquest in Brazil in
1630–40, Portugal could not conceivably hope to expel the
Dutch from Pernambuco at a time when she was fighting Spain.
It seemed clear to them that the revolt was ill advised and
doomed to failure. Not knowing of the capture of Pontal de
Nazaré, they thought that the Dutch still held all the ports and
harbours, and could pour in reinforcements while preventing
help arriving for the insurgents from Lisbon and Bahia.[1]

More effective than Sousa Coutinho's protestations of his
master's innocence was the press-campaign which he organized
against the West India Company and its supporters. Plentifully
supplied by disgruntled employees from Recife with inside information about the misdeeds and mistakes of the Company in
Brazil, he sponsored the publication of a series of pamphlets
denouncing (and exaggerating) both real and alleged abuses.
These were naturally published under fictitious imprints, and
they included a Dutch translation of the manifesto issued by the
insurgents in October 1645, justifying their resort to arms and
appealing for help to King John IV. I cannot say exactly how
much influence these pro-Portuguese pamphlets exercised; but
that they had some effect on public opinion is clear from the
fact that the Company felt compelled to reply to them with a

---

[1] 'Cartas e pareceres de Gaspar Dias Ferreira', in *RIAGP*, xxxi (1886),
pp. 323–52; ibid., xxxii (1887), pp. 73–117; AHU, 'Consultas Mixtas', Codice 13,
fols. 253–7ᵛ, *consulta* of 23 Oct. 1645; Sousa Coutinho, *Correspondência Diplomática*,
i. 231 ff.

rival series, vehemently denouncing King John IV's duplicity and Portuguese treachery. The States-General issued edicts against the publishers of the pamphlets defaming the West India Company; but apparently they did not succeed in identifying either the printers or the Dutch renegades who composed these pamphlets for the Portuguese ambassador. After the publication of the incriminating correspondence found in Serrão de Paiva's flagship at Tamandaré, in the *Claer Vertooch* of 1647, no unprejudiced person could doubt that the governor-general of Bahia was one of the prime movers of the revolt, whatever the attitude of the Portuguese king. Nevertheless, Sousa Coutinho's inspired scurrilities undoubtedly helped to undermine the Company's position at home, since many of the abuses exposed in these pamphlets were proved with chapter and verse from official documents, and were related with a convincing wealth of local colour.[1]

Sousa Coutinho also tried the time-honoured methods of bribery and corruption, but his promises in this sphere invariably outran his performance. His boast that all state secrets in the United Provinces could be bought with money was true enough, and was later repeated in more or less the same terms by Sir George Downing, the unscrupulous English envoy at The Hague.[2] Sousa Coutinho gives us an amusing glimpse of the preliminary stages in 'softening up' (as one might say nowadays) a selected individual. He explains that many of the members of the States-General and of the provincial assemblies were not wealthy and had several children. In paying a courtesy call on such a person, and discussing the matter in hand, 'one lets fall, as if by accident, a jewel worth about a thousand *cruzados* more or less (according to that person's relative standing and position) into the hand of one of the children'. The father would not make the child return the jewel, and so honour and 'face' were saved. The ambassador adds that this preliminary gift was in earnest of greater things to come; but this is where his system broke down through no fault of his own. The Portuguese treasury was nearly always empty, and Sousa Coutinho's own pay and allowances were correspondingly in

[1] Cf. Asher, *Bibliographical Essay*, pp. 186–99; Sousa Coutinho, *Correspondência Diplomática*, ii. 325, 339–40.

[2] Cf. Downing's letters of 1661 quoted in N. Japikse, *De Verwikkelingen tusschen de Republiek en Engeland, 1660–1665* (Leiden, 1900), p. 183 n.

arrears, as were those of his colleagues at London and else-where.[1] Consequently, although he kept begging for ample funds so that he could bribe really influential people (such as Amalia van Solms) on an adequate scale, he never received them. The result was that people soon ceased to take the specious offers of the impecunious Portuguese diplomat very seriously, and paid him with polite nothings or vague assurances of future co-operation. This is what Johan Maurits did when Sousa Coutinho interviewed him under rather theatrical circum-stances one dark and rainy night in a wood on the outskirts of The Hague. It is perfectly clear from Sousa Coutinho's own correspondence that his efforts to delay the sending of help to Netherlands Brazil were less effective than the great frost of 1645–6, and the clogged wheels of the Dutch administrative machinery.

The defenders of Recife were naturally perturbed at the slow-ness with which help arrived, despite the urgent and repeated appeals they had sent to Europe. A diarist in the beleaguered capital records the arrival of only eleven Dutch ships from home (a few others came from West Africa) between July 1645 and June 1646; and one of these vessels was an East-Indiaman, *Zas Van Gent*, which had been forced off her proper course. He noted despondently on 28 May 1646: 'We cannot understand why we have received during the ten months which this siege has lasted, only a few or no ships with provisions from the fatherland, whereas before the war we were plentifully supplied with pro-visions from Holland, wherewith we could furnish the whole country.' At this date the burgher's bread-ration was reduced to two ounces daily, all kinds of food sold at famine prices, and both garrison and burghers were suffering severely from beri-beri and other forms of malnutrition. Soon after the siege began the defenders had razed Johan Maurits's palaces and parks to the ground and levelled many of the buildings in his beloved Mauritsstad, in order to give a better field of fire to the forts protecting Recife, and to prevent the enemy from fortifying himself in the new city. Recife and Mauritsstad had been closely invested from the landward side since 17 August 1645. The besiegers had no artillery worth mentioning, and the Dutch had complete command of the sea, but the colonial capital was

---

[1] Sousa Coutinho, *Correspondência Diplomática*, ii. 49. For Portuguese penury cf. the diplomatic dispatches quoted by A. Pena Junior, *Arte de Furtar*, i. 248–58.

only saved from being starved into surrender by the providential arrival of two Dutch ships, the *Golden Falcon* and *Elizabeth*, on 22 June 1646, at a time when there was

> *no human help, no hope, no thought of relief in sight,*
> *the water was up to our lips, and we had no strength to fight,*

as our diarist recorded in doggerel verse. These ships not only brought provisions, without which the 8,000 souls cooped up in Recife could not have survived for more than a few days, since they were down to their last four barrels of flour, but the welcome news that the rest of the succour-fleet was close at hand. The bulk of this fleet arrived in July and August, although the stragglers only reached Recife in November.[1]

The rejoicings of the besieged, who saw themselves delivered at the last minute of the eleventh hour, are graphically related by Johan Nieuhof and other eyewitnesses. None were more delighted than the members of the Jewish community, who fully realized that the victorious besiegers would show them no mercy. Their leader, the celebrated Rabbi, Aboab da Fonseca, wrote a long Hebrew poem, *Zekher asiti leniflaot El* ('I made a memorial unto God's miracles') in which he celebrated this crowning mercy in terms reminiscent of the Psalmist.[2] He was particularly embittered against Fernandes Vieira, but denunciations of the Mulatto leader of the insurgents were not confined to the Dutch and the Jews. João Fernandes Vieira's conduct of the campaign provoked the most bitter criticism from several of the *moradores*, who appealed to the governor-general at Bahia to remove him from the command. He was accused of starting the rebellion solely on account of his great indebtedness to the Dutch, and not out of any patriotic or religious sentiments. His accusers depicted his moral character in the blackest colours, accusing him of murder, rape, and seduction. They alleged that he and many of his cronies, as also the senior officers from Bahia, were making fortunes out of the war by levying forced contributions on the *moradores*, and by keeping for themselves the slaves, oxen, and other booty taken from the Dutch.[3] Whereas Fernandes Vieira claimed that he was

---

[1] *Journael ofte Kort Discours*, 26 May and 5, 10, 22 June 1646; Nieuhof, *Gedenkweerdige Reize*, pp. 175–6; H. Haecxs, 'Dagboeck', pp. 183–4.

[2] A. Wiznitzer, *Records*, p. 3, for information concerning the provenance of the *Zekher asiti leniflaot El*.

[3] For partial confirmation of this particular point, cf. the *processo* of Manuel de

freely spending his own (admittedly large) private fortune on the war, his accusers stated that he was waging it 'with the blood of the poor'. One need not be a Marxist historian to observe that this has been the normal method of waging war ever since class divisions existed, but there was more force in some of the other allegations. It seems certain that João Fernandes Vieira used his position to pay off old scores, although on the other hand more than one attempt was made to assassinate him. In any event, Antonio Telles da Silva felt there was sufficient substance in the allegations against Fernandes Vieira to forward them to the government at Lisbon.[1] King John IV, as usual, procrastinated for months on end, but in March 1647 he directed that the accusations against João Fernandes Vieira should be filed 'somewhere where they cannot be seen'. Meanwhile, he resolved in December 1646 to appoint a commander-in-chief with the title of *mestre-de-campo-general*, to co-ordinate the operations of the insurgents and the expeditionary force from Bahia. This step had long been urged by the Overseas Council, but it was several months before their pleas and remonstrances overcame the king's native caution. The appointment was not noised abroad, but it meant in effect that the king was intervening directly, if secretly and tardily, in the struggle for Pernambuco.

In view of the precarious position of his throne, King John's hesitation is at least understandable, if not justifiable. An open break with the Dutch was something he was determined to avoid if it was humanly possible; and so long as no substantial reinforcements left the Netherlands for Recife, King John for his part refrained from sending any help to Pernambuco. Indeed, it was not until March 1646 that he decided to send substantial reinforcements to Bahia, although Telles da Silva had been begging for these for some time, being in fear of a Dutch counter-attack by sea. After receiving news of the revolt, the king first toyed with the idea, originally suggested by the Overseas Council in October 1645, that the rebellious *moradores* should be advised to emigrate *en masse* to Bahia, together with their slaves and what goods they could carry, destroying the

Moraes in the Inquisition (1647), in *RIHGB*, lxx. 27–28. Cf. also the *moradores* letter in *RIAGP*, no. 35 (1888), pp. 32–34.
[1] The relevant documents were first printed by A. Lamego in *RIHGB*, lxxv 23–50. Summarized in C. R. Boxer, *Salvador de Sá*, pp. 219–20.

sugar-plantations as they departed. The Dutch would be left with a devastated region which would be economically value-less to them; and they might then (so the wishful-thinkers argued) be prepared to sell their Brazilian possessions to the Portuguese crown. The first part of this plan was soon dis-carded as impracticable, since the insurgents were too numerous to move overland, and exodus by sea was out of the question. The *moradores* asked the king to send them 2,000 soldiers and a corresponding quantity of arms and amunition; but although the Overseas Council, reversing their original stand, strongly urged King John IV to send what help he possibly could, that cautious monarch replied, after considering the problem for three weeks, 'the terms of the peace [= truce] with Holland do not permit any action in these matters'. In July 1646, in response to further appeals by the Overseas Council, he first envisaged the possibility of sending direct help of some kind. This change of front was presumably due to the fact that the *moradores* of Porto Calvo and other places in Pernambuco had stated cate-gorically that unless King John IV would help them they would apply for assistance and protection to 'another Christian Prince'.[1]

The king's choice for the post of *mestre-de-campo-general* was Francisco Barreto de Menezes, who was born at Callao in Peru in 1616, the natural son of a Portuguese father and a Spanish Creole mother. He had participated in Torre's expedition, and in the epic march of Luiz Barbalho from Rio Grande do Norte to Bahia in 1640; but at the time of his selection for the com-mand in Pernambuco, he was only a cavalry regimental com-mander in the Alemtejo. It is not clear why the king selected him when more experienced senior officers were available; but the result fully justified his choice, although the beginning of Barreto's command was most unfortunate. The newly appointed *mestre-de-campo-general* left Lisbon for Bahia on 26 March 1647, with a squadron of five caravels and two pinnaces, carrying money, arms, and ammunition, besides some soldiers. The latter included a contingent supplied by the city of Oporto, 'including ninety-six raw recruits, most of them delinquent youths from lock-ups in the surrounding district'. When about ninety miles

[1] AHU, 'Consultas Mixtas', Cod. 13, *consultas* of 23 Oct. 1645; 14 Apr. 1646; 18 July 1646; 9 Sept. 1646; *Cartas de D. João IV para diversas autoridades do Reino*, pp. 41–45, 51, 54–56, 63, 142, 159–63.

from Bahia, the squadron was attacked by two Zeeland privateers, on 6 May. The caravels fled without further ado, and
the two pinnaces were taken after a short but sharp action in
which Francisco Barreto was severely wounded, as was his
second-in-command, Felipe Bandeira de Mello. The prisoners
were taken to Recife, where their assertions that they were
bound only for Bahia and had no intention of subsequently
going overland to Pernambuco were regarded with justified
suspicion.[1]

The situation at Recife had undergone comparatively little
change since the arrival of the relieving fleet in June–August
1646. The garrison was in such poor condition, and the newly
arrived soldiers were likewise so unfit, that no major operation
could be undertaken, and the sorties which were attempted
proved abortive. On the arrival of the Dutch fleet, the insurgents resolved to concentrate their strength in the *várzea*, and
they abandoned the districts of Paraíba, Goiana, and Itamaracá. João Fernandes Vieira ordered these regions to be
devastated by the inhabitants as they left, in order to render
them useless to the Dutch; but although these orders increased
his unpopularity with a section of the *moradores*, they were not
properly carried out.[2] The sugar-mills were destroyed, but the
Dutch found much of the manioc, tobacco, and fruit crops in
good condition, which afforded timely relief to the defenders of
Recife. Finding the insurgents too strongly posted in the immediate vicinity of Recife, Von Schoppe reverted to the strategy
which had proved so successful in 1633–5, attacking them at
other points with a view to severing their communications with
Bahia. His first efforts were unsuccessful, and although Fort
Maurits, on the Rio São Francisco, was reoccupied in November
by Colonel Henderson, the garrison was so roughly handled in
ill-conducted sorties that the place was abandoned in the following April. Even more serious was the death of Admiral
Lichthart in November 1646. His loss was a most grievous blow
to the defenders of Netherlands Brazil, and a corresponding
encouragement to the enemy, whose most dreaded opponent
he was.

[1] AHU, 'Consultas Mixtas', Cod. 13, 14 Apr., 2 May, 18 and 26 July 1646;
Gonsalves de Mello, *Filipe Bandeira de Melo*, pp. 21–27.

[2] João Fernandes Vieira's letters to the Prince Regent and Feliciano Dourado,
May 1671, in C. R. Boxer, *Salvador de Sá*, p. 219 n.; *Journael ofte Kort Discours*,
25 Sept. and 12 Nov. 1646.

Both sides made great efforts to seduce the Amerindian allies of the other, and their respective native champions, D. Felipe Camarão for the Portuguese and Pieter Poty for the Dutch, exchanged acrimonious letters in Tupí on the subject. Poty reminded Camarão that the Dutch treated the aborigines far better than did the Portuguese, and indignantly rejected the latter's reproach to him as a heretic. 'I am a Christian, and a better Christian than you', retorted Poty, 'since I believe in Christ alone, without polluting myself with the idolatry which you practise.' Declaring that 'the sea dominates Brazil', Poty reminded Camarão of the overwhelming strength of Dutch sea power, with which King John IV could not hope to contend. Poty had visited Holland in his youth, and knew that 'ships, men, money and all things are as numerous there as are stars in the heaven'. He concluded by urging Camarão to change sides, but the latter's loyalty to his Catholic allies was as firm as that of Poty to his Protestant friends. This correspondence does not seem to have effected any important change in the attitude of the Amerindian tribes; and despite the temporary defection of some of the Tapuyas after the murder of Jacob Rabbe, most of the tribes in the northern regions remained friendly to the Dutch.[1]

Since the reoccupation of Fort Maurits on the Rio São Francisco did not have the effect which had been hoped, the Council at Recife determined on a bolder stroke, which had long been advocated by Von Schoppe and which had been sanctioned by the Heeren XIX in April 1646. This was the occupation of the island of Itaparica in the Bay of All Saints, where Von Schoppe thought to found 'a new Dunkirk' which would completely paralyse Bahia's trade and would force Telles da Silva to recall the troops which he had sent to Pernambuco. The expedition under Von Schoppe, Banckert, and Beaumont, comprising twenty-six sail carrying 2,400 men, left on 4 February 1647. The initial occupation of the north-east point of the island (*Punta das Baleias*, or whaling-point) was effected without opposition, the Portuguese being taken completely by surprise, but the reaction was not exactly what had been anticipated. Telles da Silva launched two determined counter-attacks on the island (24 February and 10 August), but although they were both

[1] Poty's letter of 31 Oct. 1645, in JHMS, fols. 347–51; 'Cartas Tupís dos Camarões', in *RIAGP*, xii. 281–305.

repulsed with heavy loss to the assailants, the governor-general did *not* withdraw the troops and levies which he had sent to Pernambuco. Moreover, the local defence measures which he took proved so effective that Von Schoppe found himself confined to the tip of the island, and he was not able to ravage the *reconcavo* or even seriously hinder the maritime trade and communications of the city of Salvador.[1]

On the other hand, the threat posed by the Dutch landing on Itaparica was so grave that King John IV was at last forced to intervene openly in the Brazilian campaign, and to do something more than dispatch a few odd caravels with scratch collections of men and munitions. The king was prepared, if needs be, to sacrifice Pernambuco; but he could not afford to lose Bahia, for the loss of the colonial capital would inevitably mean the collapse of the rest of the colony. Without the sugar of Brazil, Portugal could not find the wherewithal to pay for the armies which kept the Spaniards at bay along the frontier; and hence the loss of Brazil would involve the disappearance of Portugal as an independent nation. Even the advocates of what might be termed 'peace with Holland at any price' realized this full well; and it was accordingly with the approval (if not, indeed, at the suggestion) of Padre Antonio Vieira, that King John IV resolved on the drastic step of sending the *Armada Real do Mar Oceano*, or High-seas Fleet, to Bahia.

The king's decision was taken early in May, and preceded by over three months the resolve of the States-General to take a similar step by equipping a powerful expedition which would suppress the revolt of Pernambuco for good and all. The West India Company had been agitating for this step since December 1646, when it was already apparent that the expeditionary force which had left to relieve Recife early in that year had failed to restore the situation in the hinterland. The Company was now a shuttlecock between the provincial interests of Holland and Zeeland, and consequently nine months elapsed before a decision was reached. Zeeland insisted that effective state help should be given to the West India Company in Brazil, and refused to contemplate signing a peace treaty with Spain unless Holland consented to assist the Company with men and money

---

[1] H. Haecxs, 'Dagboek', pp. 159, 217–18; Telles da Silva's dispatch of 15 Dec. 1647, in *Cartas del-Rey D. João IV ao Marquês de Niza*, i. 203–7; High Council's letter of 26 Feb. 1647 in JHMS.

on an adequate scale. Holland, on the other hand, did not wish to involve herself in a war with Portugal for the sake of the semi-bankrupt West India Company, but wanted to reap unhindered the profits of peaceful trade with the Iberian peninsula. The city of Amsterdam was mainly responsible for this attitude, since its merchants had a larger stake in the trade with Spain and Portugal than they had in that with Brazil, even though the Amsterdam chamber of the West India Company was the largest and most important. Moreover, many of the Amsterdam merchants hoped that if the Company collapsed, they could get the lion's share of the trade in ivory, gold, and slaves with West Africa, which they had enjoyed before the formation of the Company and which was still that body's profitable mono-poly. Most of the other provinces sided with Zeeland, although Holland was eventually able to talk them round, with the ex-ception of Utrecht, which opposed the projected peace out of loyalty to the French alliance, and Friesland, which spitefully refused to help the West India Company in any way, since this province had no chamber in the profitable East India Company.

Another reason for the delay was the argument which raged over the renewal of the two great trading Companies' charters. This problem was finally settled in March 1647 by an agree-ment that they should remain independent as hitherto, and that the wealthy East India Company would give her Cinderella sister a subsidy of 1,500,000 florins for the projected Brazilian expedition. Three hundred thousand florins of this subsidy were to be paid forthwith in cash, as much in merchandise, and the remainder in annual instalments of 300,000 florins in 1649–51. After five months of further discussion, the States-General resolved on 10 August 1647 to equip an expedition of twelve States' warships, and 6,000 troops, to be financed partly from the East India Company's subsidy and partly from an addi-tional provincial subsidy of 600,000 florins. In addition to this national contingent, the West India Company was to furnish thirty transports, nine yachts or frigates, and 1,350 soldiers on its own account. The consent of Amsterdam (and hence of the states of Holland) to this armament was only obtained with great difficulty on 16 August, and then on the express stipula-tion that the Dutch delegates to the Congress at Munster should press forward the conclusion of peace with Spain. It was confidently anticipated that this powerful expeditionary force, the strongest which had hitherto left for Brazil, would suffice, not merely to reconquer the lost captaincies, but to take Bahia and Portuguese Brazil if need be.[1]

Command of this expedition was first offered to Johan Maurits, but he declined the position unless he was given full powers not merely as commander-in-chief of the armed forces but as governor-general as well, together with a truly princely salary and emoluments, and an expeditionary force of 12,000 men. In stating his conditions Johan Maurits also told the States-General's deputies some home-truths concerning 'several strange and wholly improper, not to say atrocious misdeeds' committed by the Company's employees, particularly against the Portuguese in the Maranhão during the Dutch occupation of 1642–4.[2] The count's conditions being (perhaps designedly) too hard for the Company to accept, the project of a combined naval and military high command was dropped. The command of the naval forces was then given to Witte Corneliszoon de With, one of the finest of the pleiad of Dutch fighting admirals. He had seen much service in both hemispheres, but was notorious for his violent temper and overbearing manner. The command of the land forces, on Johan Maurits's suggestion, was given to Von Schoppe at Itaparica, who was promoted to lieutenant-general. The co-ordination of the military and naval high commands was left to the civilian High Councillors at Recife, none of whom had any experience of such matters. Active preparations for this expedition began in August, but recruiting and mobilization progressed very slowly, owing to the usual unpunctuality of the provincial subsidies, and the reluctance of the East India Company to provide its forced contribution. Moreover, Holland, the richest province, was hampered by the opposition of Amsterdam. This city made its agreement conditional on Zeeland's consenting to the continuance of the peace negotiations at Munster, which had reached a critical stage.

[1] Van der Capellen, *Gedenkschriften*, ii. 188–90; Arend, *Algemeene Geschiedenis*, iii (5), 149–50; 'Brieven van Doedens', in *Kron. Hist. Gen. Utrecht*, xxv. 481–92; *Resolutien Staten Holland*, Aug.–Nov. 1647.

[2] *Resolutien Staten Holland*, 5, 11, and 12 Sept. 1647; Aitzema, *Saken van staet en oorlogh*, iii. 212. According to the Resolutions of the States of Holland, 3 Sept. 1647, Johan Maurits also pleaded 'his natural aversion and indisposition to the sea' as a reason for his reluctance to return to Brazil.

Meanwhile, the High Council at Recife, finding themselves hardly any better off than when they arrived in June 1646, and having given a valuable hostage to fortune in Von Schoppe's force at Itaparica, resolved to send Hendrick Haecxs to report the seriousness of the situation direct to their High Mightinesses and the Heeren XIX. He left Recife on 4 August 1647, in company with Colonel Henderson and Admiral Banckert, the latter of whom died on the voyage home. Haecxs reached Zeeland on 5 November, and a week later he made his report to the States-General and the prince of Orange. This report claimed that with Von Schoppe's occupation of Itaparica, 'the time has now come, not only to revenge ourselves on the rebellious Portuguese for the loss we have suffered from them, but also to capture Bahia for good and all, from which place they have done us the most harm, and without which Brazil is quite useless to us. For unless we take Bahia, we have to expect at any time such ravage and desolation as the Portuguese nation chooses to inflict on us (as now), since henceforth we neither may nor can trust or believe any Portuguese again'.[1] Additional urgency was lent to his plea by the fact that on 16 October he had spoken a Hamburg ship from Oporto, whose skipper told him that the Portuguese Armada Real was on the point of sailing for Bahia.

Haecxs' informant spoke the truth. Having finally made up his mind to help Brazil, King John IV had resolved to risk virtually the whole of his navy (save three warships detached for service with the French in the Mediterranean) in a determined effort to relieve Bahia. The perennial penury of the royal treasury was overcome by arranging a loan from Duarte da Silva and other wealthy Marranos engaged in the Brazil trade, through the intermediary of Padre Antonio Vieira. An embargo was placed on all foreign shipping in Portuguese ports in June, and work on the armada went forward day and night with an enthusiasm recalling the 'expedition of the vassals' in 1624. Volunteers came forward in large numbers, and press-gangs were active everywhere, forcibly enlisting countrymen, sailors, and jail-birds. It may be added that, as some of the supporters of the West India Company sourly noted, the fitting-out of the armada was only rendered possible by the fact that much of

---

[1] H. Haecxs, 'Dagboek', pp. 216–21; 'Brieven van Doedens', in *Kron. Hist. Gen. Utrecht*, xxv. 445; Van der Capellen, *Gedenkschriften*, ii. 213–35.

the necessary naval stores and equipment were supplied, directly or indirectly, from Holland.[1]

When he had decided to commit the Armada Real at the end of May, King John IV envisaged its departure for Bahia at the beginning of September. This estimate proved too optimistic, but thanks to an unwonted display of energy by all concerned, the Armada Real left the Tagus on 18 October 1647, under the command of Antonio Telles de Menezes, created count of Villa-Pouca de Aguiar and governor-general of Brazil. The king himself accompanied the armada to the mouth of the river and distributed largess among the soldiers and crews. He ordered that daily services of prayer and intercession should be held in all churches throughout the country, until such time as the news of its arrival should be received. This news was awaited with the greatest expectation, as everyone realized that the existence of Portugal as an independent nation hinged upon the delivery of Bahia.

The count of Villa-Pouca's orders were to drive the Dutch from Itaparica and relieve Bahia, but otherwise to remain strictly on the defensive, and in particular to take no hostile action whatsoever against Recife. He was to place Antonio Telles da Silva under arrest for contravening the royal orders by assisting the rebels; but a secret paragraph of his instructions (which is left blank in the surviving copy) probably ordered him to arrange for the escape of the ex-governor-general to France after a discreet interval. The Armada Real consisted of eight galleons, two frigates, three armed merchant-ships, and two caravels, or fifteen sail in all, carrying 462 gentlemen-volunteers, 2,350 soldiers, and 1,000 sailors.[2]

On 7 November another squadron of seven sail, including several English ships on charter, left the Tagus bound for Rio de Janeiro with 600 soldiers. This squadron was commanded by Salvador Correia de Sá e Benavides, whose orders were to mobilize an expedition in Rio de Janeiro for the relief of

[1] 'Brieven van Doedens', in *Kron. Hist. Gen. Utrecht*, xxv. 481; Van der Capellen, *Gedenkschriften*, ii. 193; *Cartas del-Rei D. João IV para diversas autoridades do Reino*, pp. 172–220.

[2] Affonso Barbosa's letter of 13 Dec. 1647, printed in *Congresso Historico*, Recife, 1954; *Cartas de D. João para diversas autoridades do Reino*, p. 220; the *Regimento* for the count of Villa-Pouca, d. Lisbon, 8 Oct. 1647, is printed in *Anais do IV Congresso de Historia Nacional* (Abril 1649), edited by the Instituto Historico e Geografico Brasileiro, vol. v (1950), pp. 335–44. It furnishes additional proof that at this time King John IV was resigned to ceding Pernambuco to the Dutch.

Angola, where the Portuguese in the interior were on the point of succumbing to the combined attacks of the Dutch and their Negro allies. Salvador Correia was further instructed, either by a verbal assurance from the king or by secret written orders which have not survived, to avoid attacking the Dutch if he found them too strong, but to expel them from Luanda if a favourable opportunity presented itself.[1]

While the Portuguese preparations for the relief of Bahia were thus going forward with exceptional speed and efficiency, the mobilization of 'Double-With's' expedition was being hampered by the cross-purposes of Dutch domestic politics. It was only at the end of October, two weeks after the Portuguese armada had sailed, that any of the money voted in August was actually forthcoming and could be given to the admiralty boards responsible for fitting out the warships. Nor was finance the only problem.[2] As with the fleet of 1645-6, it proved very difficult to raise sufficient soldiers and sailors for service in Brazil, mainly for want of ready money to pay them, but partly because of the ill repute which the colony enjoyed. The troops were to be raised by voluntary enlistment from among eighty companies which had hitherto been maintained by an annual subsidy from the French government, recently withdrawn in consequence of the Dutch negotiations for a separate peace with Spain at Munster. Those men who were enlisted soon had cause to repent. None of the thirty transports intended for the expedition were ready by 8 October, and the soldiers had to remain packed on board lighters in the most insanitary conditions, while the deputies of Holland and Zeeland argued whether the sailing of the fleet should precede the conclusion of peace with Spain or vice versa. The arrival of Haecxs, with his first-hand news of the critical situation in Brazil, helped to speed up matters in November. It was in this month that Holland and Zeeland clinched a definite bargain, whereby the former province agreed that the expedition should sail at the earliest possible moment, while the God-fearing Zeelanders reluctantly consented to sign the peace with Popish Spain.

Seriously alarmed by the preparations for 'Double-With's'

---

[1] For details of the organization of this squadron see C. R. Boxer, *Salvador de Sá*, pp. 246-9.

[2] Full details in Hoboken, *Witte de With*, ch. 2. Cf. also 'Brieven van Doedens', in *Kron. Hist. Gen. Utrecht*, xxv. 481-96.

expedition, and still more by the exclusion of the Portuguese representatives from the peace negotiations at Munster, King John IV and his envoy at The Hague made frantic efforts to reach a peaceful agreement with the States-General over Brazil before the fleet sailed. Sousa Coutinho's renewed proposals for the purchase of Pernambuco having been rejected, he offered in desperation to accept whatever terms the Dutch might impose. The final Portuguese offer amounted to the restoration of Netherlands Brazil to the limits it had attained on 1 December 1640; the payment of the *moradores*' debts to the West India Company; and the use of force by the crown against the insurgents of Pernambuco if they should refuse to submit to the Dutch. Guarantees for the enforcement of these exceptionally onerous conditions were to be afforded by the appointment of Francisco de Sousa Coutinho as governor-general at Bahia with full powers to enforce them, and by the surrender of a 'cautionary town' into the hands of a Dutch garrison. This was to be none other than Oporto, the second city in the kingdom. At any time in the second half of the year 1647 the Dutch could have reached an agreement about Brazil on terms most favourable to themselves, had the ruling burgher-oligarchy been generally and genuinely desirous of doing so. But they were not.

Egged on by the directors of the West India Company who had their eyes fixed on Bahia, and against the opposition of Amsterdam and the better judgement of some of the provincial deputies, such as Alexander van der Capellen, the Dutch negotiators steadily raised their demands as the Portuguese raised their offers. Whereas Sousa Coutinho had originally offered to pay three million *cruzados* for the ransom of north-east Brazil, Angola, and São Thomé, the West India Company's representatives demanded 28 million florins for Brazil alone. When the Portuguese ambassador finally agreed that the Dutch should virtually dictate their own terms, the Dutch demanded Bahia as a 'cautionary town', in addition to an outrageously high indemnity. As indicated above, some better informed or less greedy individuals concurred with Alexander van der Capellen, who advocated serious discussion of the final Portuguese offer, on the grounds that 'it is folly to seek with the sword what one can obtain and enjoy in peace', but the exigencies of domestic politics forbade counsels of moderation. Zeeland would only consent to the peace with Spain if Holland would agree to support the West India Company to the utmost. Since the advantages of peace with Spain outweighed the drawbacks of a possible war with Portugal in the eyes of the latter province, the advocates of a 'tough' policy had their way, and Amsterdam reluctantly agreed to let force be the ultimate arbiter in Brazil.[1]

Some modern writers, including Portuguese, have argued that Sousa Coutinho's offers were not seriously meant, but were merely specious pretexts to gain time; and this argument was, of course, advanced by the West India Company's supporters in the years 1646–8. These latter were never tired of denouncing Portuguese treachery and bad faith, but they conveniently overlooked the fact that Dutch colonial aggression in 1641–4 was mainly if not entirely responsible for the Portuguese having reacted in kind in the Maranhão and elsewhere. It need hardly be added that this distrust was mutual. If the Dutch stigmatized the Portuguese as 'perfidious traitors who keep their word as do dogs conjugal fidelity',[2] the Portuguese denounced the Dutch as 'pirates and *canaille* from Hell'.[3] But much as they disliked and distrusted the Dutch, King John IV and his confidential advisers realized that 'peace with Holland is absolutely necessary, and war obviously impossible'.[4] It was to prove this point that Padre Antonio Vieira wrote his celebrated *Papel Forte* ('The strong paper') in the winter of 1648, when Portugal's fortunes appeared to be at their lowest, and the power of the United Provinces at their highest.

As we shall see in the next chapter, the cogency of the Jesuit's arguments confirmed King John IV in his desire to come to a peaceful arrangement with the United Provinces at almost any price, but there were two grave errors in Vieira's reasoning. Firstly, he made insufficient allowance for the hatred of the *moradores* of Pernambuco for the Dutch, and their resolve not to

---

[1] Sousa Coutinho, *Correspondência Diplomática*, ii. 157–277; *Cartas de D. João IV ao Marquês de Niza*, ii. 180–1, 209–16; Aitzema, *Vredehandeling* (1671), p. 318; Van der Capellen, *Gedenkschriften*, ii. 188–95, 201, 206, 213–35, 250–4; Arend, *Algemeene Geschiedenis*, iii (5), pp. 750–1; 'Brieven van Doedens', in *Kron. Hist. Gen. Utrecht*, xxv. 484–96; J. Poelkekke, *Vrede van Munster*, pp. 456–7; *Resolutien Staten Holland*, Aug.–Dec. 1647.

[2] J. Rosenberg to the Zeeland Chamber, Recife, 27 June 1645, in Wätjen, *Holländische Kolonialreich*, p. 147.

[3] Antonio de Sousa de Macedo, quoted in A. Pena, *Arte de Furtar*, i. 276.

[4] Quoted in P. Antonio Vieira, S.J., letter d. Bahia, 23 May 1689 (Azevedo, *Cartas*, iii. 568).

submit to the heretic yoke, whatever the king might ordain. Secondly, when the Jesuit wrote: 'Finally, the Dutch have their energy, their diligence, their covetousness, their love for each other and the common weal; we have our disunity, our jealousness, our presumption, our carelessness and our perpetual concern for private interests', he ignored the bitter rivalry between Holland and Zeeland, the ill-feeling between the two great India Companies, and, most important of all, the almost unbelievable clumsiness of the Dutch government's financial machinery.

Thanks to the delays imposed by these causes (and not the intrigues of the Portuguese ambassador), the fleet of Witte de With, which should have sailed in October, only left on the day after Christmas. On that date the count of Villa Pouca had already reached Bahia, where he found that Von Schoppe had evacuated Itaparica on 14 December, eight days before his own arrival.[1] Nor was 'Double-With's' fleet in good shape when it did sail. The admiral observed that 'pigs and dogs in our country are given better lodging' than were the soldiers packed into freighters, many of which had not been properly cleaned or fitted out as transports. A high proportion of weapons issued to the men proved to be unserviceable at the last moment, and had to be left behind in the hope that better types would be forthcoming later. Food, drink, medical supplies, and provisions were mostly insufficient or unsatisfactory, or both, and the evil results of the directors' cheese-paring economy were evident in many ways. When the fleet (or most of it) finally did get away, it was delayed for nearly three weeks by contrary winds in the English Channel, and then had to weather a severe storm off the coast of Portugal which scattered the ships to the four winds. Witte de With himself, after a stop at Cape Verde, reached Recife with twelve sail on 18 March 1648; but although most of his vessels reached Brazil by the end of that month, the last stragglers did not arrive until the end of August.[2]

Although in some ships as many as twenty or thirty soldiers had died on the voyage, and the great majority of the survivors reached Recife in very poor shape, the High Council was

[1] Cf. his dispatches of Jan. and Feb. 1648 in *Cartas de D. João IV ao Marquês de Niza*, ii. 238–40.
[2] Detailed account in Hoboken, 'Een troepentranspoort naar Brazilie in 1647' (*Tijdschrift voor Geschiedenis*, 1949, pp. 100–9), and *Witte de With*, chs. 2 and 3.

clamouring for speedy action and insisted on some major operation being attempted forthwith. It was generally agreed that
Bahia was too strong to be attacked, but the senior military
officers suggested an assault on Rio de Janeiro, probably not
uninfluenced by the hope of finding a good booty there. The
civilian councillors, however, preferred that a determined effort
should be made to inflict a decisive defeat on the besiegers of
Recife. After further discussion, Lt.-General Von Schoppe and
his colonels allowed themselves to be persuaded against their
better judgement. At a final council of war on 4 April 1648 it
was decided 'in God's name to bring the troops out into the
field against the enemy' in the hope of routing the besiegers in
a decisive battle. There was much talk of giving a substantial
payment to the troops before making the sortie; but in the
upshot, and with singular ineptitude, the council decided to
pay only the officers of the newly arrived regiments, and the
soldiers, whether new or old, got nothing. This naturally
adversely affected the men's morale, and many of them said
openly, 'let those who have been paid do the fighting; we won't
fight without pay'.[1]

A couple of months before the arrival of the relieving fleet,
Francisco Barreto and his two principal companions escaped
from prison at Recife by bribing the son of the jailer, who
absconded with them one dark January night. They made
their way 'through sea and rivers, past sentinels, ships, launches
and enemy-held forts' to the insurgents' lines, where they
arrived on the morning of 23 January 1648. Barreto found that
the senior colonel, Martim Soares Moreno, had returned to
Bahia some time before; and if Calado is to be credited, his
colleagues and subordinates were not sorry to see him go. After
his departure, the command was exercised jointly and amicably
by João Fernandes Vieira and André Vidal de Negreiros, who
duly recognized Francisco Barreto as *mestre-de-campo-general*
when they received instructions from the count of Villa-Pouca
to do so on 16 April. Barreto was now in command of about
3,000 men in the immediate vicinity of Recife, where the insurgents had concentrated their strength on the appearance of
the Dutch relieving fleet. Their force comprised the regiment

[1] The fullest and best-documented account of the deliberations of the Dutch
civilian and military authorities in Mar.–Apr. 1648 is in Hoboken, *Witte de With*,
ch. 3, on which the foregoing is based.

of João Fernandes Vieira, mostly consisting of Mulattoes and men recruited locally in Pernambuco; the regiment of Portuguese infantry which André Vidal had brought from Bahia; the Petiguar Indian regiment of D. Felipe Camarão, and a regiment of Negroes, Mulattoes, and freed slaves under the veteran Negro, Henrique Dias. What happened to Martim Soares Moreno's regiment of Portuguese infantry after his return to Bahia is not certain. Either the men were temporarily distributed among the regiments of Vidal and Fernandes Vieira, or they retained their identity and were used as a tactical reserve. It may be added that the majority of the *moradores* were not serving in these regiments, save perhaps in the case of João Fernandes Vieira's *terço*, which was a purely local unit and may have contained a fair number. But most of them remained on their plantations in the *várzea*, supervising their sugar-crops, although they could be called upon if necessary to do guard duty when the troops had to leave their quarters for the fighting-line.[1]

On the night of 17–18 April 1648 Von Schoppe led his men out to battle, marching southwards along the shore for some distance and then turning inland to find the enemy. His force, which comprised virtually all the fit men in the Dutch garrison and the Amerindian auxiliaries, totalled about 5,000 men. It was organized in two columns, the first of which was led by Von Schoppe himself, and the other by Colonel van den Brande, another veteran of Johan Maurits's campaigns. All the troops carried rations for eight days in their haversacks. An advanced detachment of the enemy was surprised and overrun on the 18th, the Tapuyas killing forty Portuguese at a cost of two casualties to themselves. When the survivors brought Barreto the news of this disaster, he at once held a council of war, at which it was decided to go and meet the Dutch, despite the fact that his force numbered only 2,200 men, since another 300 had to be left to man the makeshift defences of the camp.

The two sides met between seven and eight o'clock on the rugged hillocks known as the Guararapes, on the morning of Low Sunday, 19 April. A confused action ensued for some four hours, the preliminary musketry battle being followed by severe

---

[1] High Council's letter of 26 Feb. 1648 in JHMS; Francisco Barreto and Felipe Bandeira de Mello's own reports in Gonsalves de Mello, *Filipe Bandeira de Melo*, pp. 26–28, 34–35, and *RIHGB*, lvi. 71–75.

fighting at close quarters, when 'nothing was heard on both sides but cries of "Kill the dogs"'. A Dutch officer noted that the Portuguese were dressed 'after the manner in which the ancient Romans are described, with top-boots to below their knees, stockings above their knees, and their sleeves tucked up'. The same officer also noted that 'the general of the enemy was mounted on a white horse, showing great courage in front of his men'. Von Schoppe was severely wounded in the foot early in the action and carried off the field, leaving the command to Colonel van den Brande. This officer's regiment and that of Colonel Haulthain did their duty, but many of the other soldiers who had said they would not fight without pay proved as good as their word, and they were badly cut up in consequence. The action was broken off about midday by mutual exhaustion, the Portuguese not having eaten for over twenty-four hours, and most of the Dutch soldiers being unused to tropical warfare.

Both sides remained facing each other just out of musket-shot until nightfall, when the Dutch beat a precipitate retreat to Recife, which they reached unmolested next day. A rainy night prevented the Portuguese patrols from discovering that they had gone, just as had happened after the battle of Tabocas. Not until next morning did the Portuguese realize the extent of their victory, when they found the field littered with abandoned Dutch equipment, arms, and ammunition. The Dutch left 500 dead behind them, including 48 officers, and they had another 556 wounded, including 30 officers. Two of their six colonels, Haus and Van Elst, were among the dead; a third, Kerweer, was a prisoner, and a fourth, Haulthain, was wounded. In addition, they lost seventeen flags, including their principal colours with the arms of the States-General and the prince of Orange, as also one field-piece. The Portuguese only admitted to a loss of 80 killed (including the detachment overrun on the previous day) and nearly 400 wounded, which seems to be a suspiciously disproportionate amount. But whatever their real casualties, they had all the marks of victory on their side, and the moral effect was undisputed. When Barreto detached Henrique Dias to reoccupy Olinda (which they had temporarily abandoned in order to concentrate their forces for the battle), the Dutch garrison fled precipitately after offering only a token resistance. The High Councillors wrote to their superiors at home on 23 April that 'a brave major sorrowfully told us today that he would not dare to attack a hundred Portuguese with a thousand such soldiers'.[1]

Great though the moral effect of the victory was, it did not essentially change the existing situation. The Portuguese were greatly heartened by this success, and the Dutch were correspondingly depressed—even after the High Council had made a belated issue of pay to the soldiers. Olinda was left unoccupied by both parties, but the close investment of Recife continued on the landward side as before, and the Dutch could not venture beyond range of the guns of their forts. At sea, on the other hand, they continued to be the undisputed masters, as the count of Villa-Pouca, in accordance with his instructions, made no attempt to use the Armada Real against Witte de With's fleet. Even after receiving the unexpected news of the victory of Guararapes, he confined his support of the insurgents to detaching from the garrison of Bahia a regiment of infantry recruited in the Azores and Madeira, under the command of Francisco de Figueroa, which joined the besiegers of Recife in August. It seems likely that the remains of Soares Moreno's old regiment were incorporated in this new unit.[2]

The passivity of the count of Villa-Pouca was a sore trial to Witte de With, whose one idea was to bring the Armada Real to action. After much prodding of the High Council, he induced them to send him southwards in May to cruise off Bahia and see what damage he could do the enemy. He found that Villa-Pouca had moored his galleons close inshore, where they were too strongly defended to be attacked with any chance of success. He cruised off the Bay of All Saints for several weeks, during which time he captured a few prizes, but the homeward-bound sugar-fleet from Rio de Janeiro, which he had hoped to intercept off Bahia, escaped him by sailing direct to Portugal. He learnt later from prisoners that it had been convoyed for some distance by Salvador Correia, who had left Rio de Janeiro on 12 May for Angola with fifteen sail carrying about 2,000 men, 'in order to beat up our people there'. Alarmed at this news,

[1] For the first battle of the Guararapes cf. the contemporary accounts listed in J. H. Rodrigues, *Historiografia e Bibliografia*, nos. 541–5, 549–50, to which should be added the High Council's letter of 23 Apr. 1648 in JHMS, and Felipe Bandeira de Mello's accounts first printed in Gonsalves de Mello, *Filipe Bandeira de Melo*, pp. 26–37. Of the numerous secondary accounts the best seems to me that in Hoboken, *Witte de With*, ch. 3.

[2] Gonsalves de Mello, *Francisco de Figueroa*, pp. 27–28.

he sent word at once to the High Council at Recife, and after his return there to refit in July, he offered to go to Angola in pursuit of Salvador Correia. He felt sure that even if he was not in time to save Luanda, he could easily destroy Salvador's squadron and possibly recapture the place.

Much to his disgust, the Council (although fully aware of the great danger to Angola) refused to let him go, partly because they could not victual his ships for such an expedition, and partly because they feared that in his absence the galleons of the Armada Real might emerge from their refuge and attack Recife. This last fear, it may be added, was quite unfounded. Taking his orders to remain on the defensive very literally, Villa-Pouca moored his galleons up the river Matoim in the *reconcavo*, where they were further protected by strongly-garrisoned earthworks which were thrown up at the entrance to that river. Witte de With's forebodings were justified. News reached Recife in November that Salvador Correia had retaken Luanda from the Dutch. This bold stroke came only just in time to save the Portuguese based on Massangano, in the interior of Angola, from almost certain annihilation. Contrary to what was happening in Brazil, the Dutch were masters of the field in Angola, having inflicted a severe reverse on the Portuguese in the hinterland only a fortnight before Salvador Correia's arrival.[1]

On de With's return to Recife from his abortive cruise, he found that the military force at the disposal of the High Council totalled about 6,000 white soldiers and 600 Amerindian and Negro levies. About one-fifth of the Europeans were on the sick-list, and others were serving as sailors afloat, so that the effective strength amounted to some 5,100 men. Roughly half of these were needed for garrisoning the permanent defences, and 200 time-expired veterans had been shipped home for want of money to pay them. Since the defeat at the Guararapes the Dutch at Recife had attempted no further offensive action, save an abortive expedition by Colonel Haulthain to Alagoas.

At a council of war held in Von Schoppe's house on 15 and 16 September, the High Council pressed for another sortie in

[1] For the reconquest of Angola by Salvador Correia de Sá cf. C. R. Boxer, *Salvador de Sá*, pp. 253–69; Hoboken, *Witte de With*, ch. 4; High Council's letters of 27 Oct. and 19 Dec. 1648, in JHMS, fols. 236–79; Cadornega, *História Geral das guerras Angolanas*, i. 488–538; ibid. ii. 1–41.

force, 'because something must be risked in this war', and they were anxious to revenge the defeat of 19 April. The senior military officers were unanimously opposed to the suggestion, and argued that even a victory would probably bring no decisive result against an enemy who could always resort to guerrilla warfare. They again suggested an attack on Rio de Janeiro, or alternatively on the roadstead of Cabo de Santo Agostinho whence the insurgents shipped the sugar which they harvested in the *várzea*. The High Councillors in their turn opposed this suggestion on the grounds that 'all conquests are but burdens and foster-children for the Company unless they can be enjoyed in peace'. No major decisions had been taken when on 18 September news came that three of the Portuguese galleons had ventured out and were cruising off Bahia to protect local shipping. It was at once agreed that Witte de With should go and attack them. His chance had come at last.[1]

The admiral left Recife with seven sail on 22 September, and fell in with two of the galleons, *Nossa Senhora do Rosario* and *São Bartholomeu*, six days later. A short but exceedingly sharp action ensued, in the course of which the captain of the *Rosario* blew up his vessel when she was boarded and in danger of being captured by two of the Dutch ships, the *Utrecht* and the *Huys Nassau*. The *Utrecht* was also blown 'into a hundred thousand pieces' by the explosion, and the *Huys Nassau* was so severely damaged that she was abandoned by her surviving crew as a sinking derelict. This ship drifted on to the island of Itaparica, where she was subsequently salvaged and repaired by the Portuguese, to the intense chagrin of 'Double-With' when he eventually discovered this fact. Both sides suffered severely in this action, but the Portuguese loss was naturally much the heavier, over 400 casualties as compared with about 150.[2]

On 28 October two Dutch ships captured an English blockade-runner, the *Concordia*, twenty-eight guns and fifty-four men, which was carrying naval stores for the armada at Bahia. Nothing further of note occurred until 7 December, when Witte de With was joined by an expeditionary force of 2,000 men in

---

[1] Hoboken, *Witte de With*, ch. 5.

[2] Hoboken, ibid., gives the only detailed and reliable account of the naval action off Bahia on 28 Sept. 1648. All previous versions, whether Portuguese or Dutch, are hopelessly confused and wildly inaccurate.

thirty sail from Recife, under the command of Councillor Michiel van Goch and Colonels van den Brande and Haulthain. The object of this expedition was to ravage the sugar-plantations of the *Reconcavo*, burning and destroying what could not be carried away. The expedition attained its aim, for between 11 December 1648 and 11 January 1649, landing-parties burnt a total of twenty-three sugar-mills and carried off 1,500 chests of sugar besides other booty. No resistance was encountered, as the Portuguese galleons had taken refuge again in the river Matoim. In strong contrast to Telles da Silva's aggressive attitude during Von Schoppe's occupation of Itaparica, the count of Villa-Pouca inexplicably made no attempt to harass the raiders during their month's stay in the bay. Witte de With, to his annoyance, was employed on convoy duties during this time, and thereby had the mortification of seeing a richly laden Portuguese East-Indiaman, the *Santa Catarina*, enter Bahia to the windward of him on the morning of 15 December. Although the admiral criticized this expedition as having been ordered mainly to fill the pockets of Van Goch and the other leaders, there is no doubt that it did much to restore the morale of the troops, who returned to Recife 'courageous and cheerful'.[1]

'The sea dominates Brazil', as Poty wrote to Camarão in 1645, and the ravaging of the *Reconcavo* merely underlined a fact which was causing King John IV and his advisers the greatest anxiety. The outbreak of the insurrection in 1645 had naturally and immediately revived Dutch attacks on Portuguese shipping in the South Atlantic. Nor was this activity restricted to the West India Company's cruisers. The chief damage was done by vessels equipped by the Zeeland Privateering Board (*Zeeuwsche kaper-directie*), whose headquarters were at Middelburg. This privateering company had originally been formed to cope with the Dunkirk corsairs, but after the fall of that 'Algiers of the North' in 1646, the Zeelanders seized the opportunity of transferring their activities to Brazilian waters, and a branch of the board was established at Recife under Huybrecht Brest. 'A turd for trade if there is booty to be had!' was a popular Zeeland motto; and 'the New Sea-beggars' as these redoubtable

---

[1] Hoboken, *Witte de With*, ch. 6, for a detailed and fully documented account of the operations in and around the Bay of All Saints, Oct. 1648–Jan. 1649. For the escape of the *Santa Catarina* cf. the account of her captain, Antonio Pereira, in Frazão de Vasconcellos, *Pilotos das navegações portuguesas dos séculos XVI e XVII* (Lisbon, 1942), p. 15.

privateersmen were called, had no difficulty in filling their ranks
from the seamen of Middelburg and Flushing. The West India
Company received a percentage on prizes taken by the Zeelanders, and it is clear that some of the directors of the Company at Middelburg were more interested in the prosperity of
the privateering board than they were in their own concern.
But the two bodies were completely separate entities, and the
Zeeland privateers maintained their own magazines, stores,
and equipment, which were, incidentally, far better managed
and supplied than were those of the Company.[1]

The damage these privateers did to Portuguese maritime
trade with Brazil was enormous. Padre Antonio Vieira wrote
from The Hague, whither he had gone on a diplomatic mission
in May 1648, that between 1 January and 7 March 'the Dutch
captured twenty-two ships from Lisbon, Oporto, Vianna and
the Atlantic islands; Recife being full of their cargoes and
supplies, to its great benefit'. It was reckoned that more than
half of the caravels which left the roadstead of Cabo de Santo
Agostinho laden with sugar were taken by the Dutch, and it is
not surprising that the *moradores* of Pernambuco ruefully termed
themselves 'husbandmen of Holland'. A large proportion of the
vessels bound from Portugal and the Azores with men, arms,
and ammunition for Bahia and Pernambuco were also intercepted by the Dutch. Between 1 January 1647 and 31 December
1648 some 220 Portuguese Brazil-traders were lost by enemy
action, the vast majority being taken by the Zeeland privateers.
This represented a very high proportion of the vessels engaged
in the Brazil trade, and although caravels were relatively cheap
to build and easy to man, it was obvious that replacements
could not keep pace with losses at this rate. Thanks to the
number of prizes which they took, the Dutch were not only
able to maintain themselves in Recife, but to ship substantial
quantities of sugar to the United Provinces.[2]

---

[1] For the organization of the Zeeland privateers cf. Hoboken, *Witte de With*,
ch. 3. For instances of the jealousy between their representatives at Recife and the
Company's employees, and for the illicit interest of the Middelburg directors of
the West India Company in the privateering board's profits, cf. H. Haecxs,
'Dagboek', pp. 190–8, 232–5, and Hoboken, *Witte de With*, ch. 3.

[2] Antonio Vieira, S.J., letter of 19 May 1648 (*Cartas*, i. 196); *Journael van de
Reyse* (1648); list of Portuguese shipping losses translated in Appendix III below.
As will be seen, the total given there of 249 vessels lost includes over twenty dupli-
cates. The figure given in C. Boxer, *Salvador de Sá*, p. 181, and Gustavo de Freitas,
A Companhia Geral do Comercio do Brasil, p. 20, should be corrected accordingly.

By the end of 1648 it was clear that if this state of affairs continued much longer, all the victories of the insurgents on shore would be of no ultimate avail. Brazil had no arms industry of her own, and the insurgents could not rely indefinitely on captured weapons. If they could neither send their sugar for sale in Portugal, nor receive essential arms, ammunition, and military supplies from the mother-country, then sooner rather than later they would have to abandon the struggle, and either submit to the Dutch or else retire into the distant hinterland and lead a half-savage life. The problem was not a new one, but it was never so acute in 1630–40 as it was in 1646–8. The crisis was reached in this last year, and the Portuguese government had either to do something drastic or else succumb to the stranglehold of superior Dutch sea power.

VI

'THE SEA DOMINATES BRAZIL'

1649–54

IN the days before air power achieved its present predominance, it was regarded as axiomatic that the possession of sea power always gave the ultimate victory, whatever the inevitable vicissitudes of a war between two nations which were otherwise more or less evenly matched. This may have been so, as a general rule, but the closing years of the struggle for north-east Brazil form an interesting exception to this widely accepted proposition. This exception is all the more striking since the two contestants were not evenly matched, and resembled a giant and a dwarf rather than a whale and a lion. As we have repeatedly had occasion to observe, both the actual and potential resources of the United Provinces were far greater than those of Portugal. Nowhere was this disparity more obvious than in a comparison of their relative naval strengths; and nowhere was this comparison more clearly enunciated than in Padre Antonio Vieira's *Papel Forte* of February 1649.[1]

As he pointed out in this famous (or infamous) document, the strongest and richest kingdom in Europe was France, and France had been most careful to avoid antagonizing Spain and Holland simultaneously. How could Portugal, the weakest and poorest kingdom in Europe, hope to contend successfully with these two great powers? The Dutch alone, he argued, could crush Portugal by demolishing her colonial empire, if they vigorously exercised their overwhelming maritime preponderance. Men and money were the two main sinews of war. Portugal was very short of both, whereas the United Provinces possessed them in abundance. He estimated that the Dutch owned over 14,000 vessels which could be used as warships, whereas Portugal did not have thirteen sail of this kind. The Dutch, he claimed, had a quarter of a million sailors, whereas Portugal had less than

---

[1] Modern writers state that the *Papel Forte* was written in 1648, but since Vieira refers to the news of the reconquest of Luanda as having been received two months previously, it must have been given its final form early in 1649. The news of the recapture of Luanda reached Lisbon on 25 Nov. 1648.

4,000. He stigmatized the armada of the count of Villa-Pouca as the most deplorable example of Portugal's maritime weakness. Portugal had to be deprived of all her warships in home waters in order to find thirteen galleons and transports for the relief of Bahia. So short was the nation of sailors, that even this modest armada could not sail until mariners had been impressed from the newly arrived sugar-fleet of Rio de Janeiro. Sufficient soldiers were only found by taking veteran troops from the exposed provincial frontiers, and sufficient artillery was only secured by taking cannon from the forts defending the Tagus.

The great Jesuit never hesitated to use the multiplication table on the figures wherewith he clinched his arguments, and the *Papel Forte* is no exception to this rule. Reliable statistics for Dutch shipping at this period are not forthcoming, although wild guesses, such as Vieira's, abound. A well-informed Dutch pamphleteer of 1644 claims some 'two or three thousand yardarm ships', about 6,000 fishing-boats and inland craft, and 80,000 sailors, although he adds that these mariners were the best in the world.[1] Whatever the real figures, there can be no doubt that Dutch superiority in ships and sailors was crushing. Even those who disagreed with Padre Vieira about the impossibility of fighting Spain and the United Provinces simultaneously, agreed with his contention that the Portuguese Armada Real could not face Witte de With's fleet on the open sea. Pedro Fernandes Monteiro, one of the champions of resolute action, and against whose arguments Vieira's *Papel Forte* was more specifically directed, had to admit that the Armada Real which had been sent to Bahia with such effort and sacrifice was now mewed up in the river Matoim and begging for help.[2]

In view of this crushing Dutch superiority at sea, how could

---

[1] *Aenwysinge: Datmen vande Oost ende West-Indische Compagnien een Compagnie dient te maken* (The Hague, 1644). On 4 April 1648 Francisco de Sousa Coutinho wrote to his master that the maritime strength of the United Provinces was greater than that of all the other European powers put together, since the former could muster 'quatorze mil embarcações de duas gaveas' (*Correspondência Diplomática*, ii. 342). Vieira reduced his figure to 11,000 in later years (letter to the count of Ericeira dated 23 May 1689), and for other estimates cf. W. Vogel, 'Zur Grösse der Europäischen Handelsflottenim 15., 16. und 17. Jahrhundert: Ein historisch-statistisch Versuch', in *Forschungen und Versuche zur Geschichte des Mittelalters und der Neuzeit: Festschrift Dietrich Schäffer* (Jena, 1915).

[2] '... pois vemos que ainda hoje estando só o poder da Companhia tão atenuado, mandando Vossa Magestade huma armada tão poderoza com gente tão luzida, está temendo a Bahia, metendo os galiões em hum Rio sem ouzarem a sahir ao inimigo, e pedindo socorros' (BNRJ, Cod. I-6-2, No. 39).

Portugal prevent the catastrophic shipping losses which she was suffering in the South Atlantic? The most obvious suggestion was the organization of a convoy system, similar to that employed by the Spaniards in their trade with Mexico and the West Indies. Such a measure had been seriously discussed at Lisbon many times, and had even been half-heartedly implemented at the end of 1644, but it broke down within a twelvemonth. Conditions in the trade of Spain with her American colonies were very different from those prevailing in the trade between Portugal and Brazil. Whereas Spanish maritime commerce with the Indies had been centralized for over a century under the direct control of the House of Trade (*Casa de la Contratación*) at Seville, Portuguese vessels bound for Brazil sailed not only from Lisbon but from many smaller ports in Portugal, Madeira, and the Azores. Concentration of this commerce at Lisbon would inevitably ruin these subsidiary ports, several of which owed such importance as they possessed to their share in the Brazil trade.

Moreover, the organization of an effective convoy system presupposed the existence (or the acquisition) of well-gunned 'tall ships', together with an adequate supply of experienced seamen to man them. Portugal, for all her importance as a maritime power, was singularly deficient on both these counts. She had indeed a few well-built and heavily gunned galleons, such as the *Bom Jesus*, flagship of the Armada Real, which in themselves were admittedly superior to any Dutch vessel. But nine-tenths of her merchant shipping engaged in the Brazil trade consisted of defenceless caravels, or poorly armed pinnaces, whose only resource was flight when attacked by the Dutch privateers or Barbary corsairs. These vessels seldom exceeded 100 tons each, and many of them were even smaller. Padre Antonio Vieira, and those who thought like him, stigmatized these caravels as 'schools of cowardice' for the sailors who manned them; and even their allegedly good sailing qualities seldom saved them from capture by the nimble Zeeland privateers. Vieira was neither the first nor the last to demand legislation forbidding the construction of these puny caravels and encouraging the construction of bigger and better-gunned vessels. Suggestions to this effect were made from 1612 onwards, but nothing concrete had come of them, and little more of the legislation framed in this sense in 1644. Finance was of course another great obstacle. The construction of a navy or of a merchant marine could not be undertaken without more capital and more resources than the crown itself possessed. The marquis of Montalvão suggested (in December 1643) that the English precedent of the 'ship-money' fleet should be followed, but there was no large middle class in Portugal to bear the brunt of such a tax. Portugal was a poor country, and the small merchants and owner-skippers who formed a large proportion of those engaged in the Brazil trade had not sufficient capital to build large vessels or to operate them when built. The wealthy 'New-Christian' merchants who traded to Brazil apparently preferred, as did the crown on many occasions, to freight well-armed foreign shipping to carry their cargoes—originally Dutch vessels and later Hansa, English, and Genoese.[1]

This dependence on foreign shipping originated other proposals that the convoy problem should be solved by chartering foreign vessels to act as escorts for the poorly armed Portuguese ships. At one time during the union of the two Iberian crowns, it had been suggested that Dunkirk frigates should be used for this purpose; but although the Flemings were keen enough, the Portuguese were opposed to it. One proposal, ventilated in the Overseas Council in March 1647, envisaged the chartering of eight well-gunned English ships to give convoy to the Brazil fleets. The advocates of this proposal pointed out that it offered the additional advantage that England might thereby easily become embroiled in a war with the United Provinces, a consummation devoutly to be wished from the Portuguese point of view. Others, however, while admitting the courage and maritime skill of the English sailors, denounced their piratical proclivities,[2] and argued that it would be most unwise to give these ambitious and enterprising heretics the opportunity of firmly establishing themselves in Brazil and the Maranhão. An alternative proposal to use Hansa vessels for escorts to convoys found more supporters, as it was argued that German merchants and shipowners had no colonial ambitions or ulterior designs on

[1] AHU Lisbon, 'Consultas Mixtas', Codice 13, fols. 15ᵛ–20; cf. also the sources summarized in C. R. Boxer, *Salvador de Sá*, pp. 182–4, 290–2 (where, however, the *parecer* of Salvador referred to on p. 292, n. 113, should be dated 15 Dec. 1645, and not ascribed to the year 1652), and Gustavo de Freitas, *A Companhia Geral do comércio do Brasil, 1649–1720* (São Paulo, 1951), pp. 16–21.

[2] Instancing the case of the East-Indiaman *John*, whose master piratically seized her for King Charles I, and embezzled the goods of Portuguese passengers from Mozambique, after setting their owners ashore in Sept. 1644. Cf. W. Foster, *English Factories in India, 1642–1645* (Oxford, 1913), pp. xiii–xiv, 238–46, 261–5.

the Portuguese colonies. The use of Swedish ships was advocated by others for similar reasons; but all the councillors were agreed that for policy, prestige, and economy alike, it would be far more satisfactory to enforce the legislation framed in 1644 to discourage the use of caravels, and to organize the Brazil fleets in convoys under the escort of Portuguese warships.

King John IV hesitated a whole year before finally making up his mind to act on the advice of his Overseas Council, but the increasingly critical shipping situation eventually forced his hand. On 7 March 1648 he ordered his highest legal authority to draft two new laws for immediate promulgation. The first prohibited the construction, charter, or purchase of any ship, whether Portuguese or foreign, of less than 350 tons for use in the Brazil trade. An exception was made for vessels already on the stocks. The second enacted that three years after the promulgation of the first law, no vessel of less than 350 tons and sixteen guns (of 8 lb. shot) would be allowed to navigate to Portuguese overseas possessions. During the three-year interim period, however, foreign shipping could be chartered on the prevailing terms and under the usual safeguards.[1]

Ten months before this decision was taken, news reached Lisbon of the Dutch occupation of Itaparica, which was followed by the king's decision to send the Armada Real to the relief of Bahia. This meant that there were no Portuguese warships left available for convoy duties, and some other and urgent means had to be found of raising a new armada. Once more the ever-resourceful Padre Antonio Vieira came to the rescue, this time with a scheme which he had suggested four years previously, but which he had not pressed so hard as his alternative proposal to purchase peace by abandoning north-east Brazil to the Dutch.

This scheme was the formation of a powerful chartered trading company, organized on the lines of the great Dutch and English India companies which had wrought such havoc in the Portuguese colonial empire. Vieira's original plan envisaged the formation of two companies, one for the East and one for the West, but the former never progressed beyond the paper stage. His main idea was that the capital for these two chartered com-

[1] AHU, 'Consultas Mixtas', Codice 14, fols. 26v–32v, for the *consulta* of 17 Mar. 1647. The law was not, apparently, promulgated until 15 Mar. 1648. Cf. G. de Freitas, *A Companhia Geral do comércio do Brasil*, p. 71.

panies should be furnished by the New-Christian (or crypto-Jewish) financiers of Lisbon, and by the Portuguese Sephardic Jews who had settled in France, the United Provinces, and Germany, in order to avoid the rigours of the Iberian Inquisitions. The chief stumbling-block was Vieira's proposal to attract Jewish capital to his projected Brazil Company by specifically exempting subscribers therein from the penalty of having either their property or their capital confiscated if they were arrested (or even convicted) by the Inquisition for the crimes of 'heresy, apostasy, and Judaism'. This concession of the *izenção do fisco* as it was called, for the money came to the Holy Office by way of the Crown Fiscal, was bitterly opposed by the Inquisitors. They stated categorically that they could not continue to function without the funds which they derived from this source. Moreover, the Inquisitor-General of the powerful Portuguese branch of the Holy Office pointed out that the penalty of confiscation was the one most dreaded by crypto-Jews; for the formal stigma of Judaism meant little to them, and they could avoid the death penalty by an outward recantation.' And if with such a heavy penalty, Judaism has continued to flourish recently for our sins', wrote Dom Francisco de Castro, 'what will happen when it sees itself free and immune therefrom?' By the end of 1648, however, the situation was so critical that Vieira finally succeeded in convincing the king that the Holy Office of the Inquisition must be overruled, and the Brazil Company was formally incorporated three months later.[1]

The statutes of the Brazil Company (*Companhia Geral para o Estado do Brazil*), as set forth in the printed *alvará* of 8 March 1649, make interesting reading when compared with those of its rival body, the Dutch West India Company. The preamble, which is addressed to the king, clearly reflects Vieira's original conception. The Company's sphere of activity is given as extending from Rio Grande do Norte to São Vicente inclusive, thus including Dutch-occupied territory. Investors of all classes and nationalities would be eligible to become shareholders in the Company with a minimum subscription of twenty *cruzados*, for a term of twenty years beginning on Easter Day 1649.

[1] I have relied chiefly on the British Museum, Add. MS. 20951, which codex contains seventeenth-century transcripts of many of the relevant documents for the years 1645–54. Cf. also J. L. Azevedo, *História dos Christãos Novos portugueses* (Lisbon, 1922), pp. 244–57; G. de Freitas, *A Companhia Geral do comércio do Brasil*, pp. 21–28.

Option of a ten-year extension on the same terms was stipulated. The Company promised to fit out a fleet of thirty-six warships, each with a minimum of twenty to thirty guns, and to find crews for the same. This fleet was to be divided into two squadrons of eighteen warships, each squadron making an annual voyage to Brazil. All merchant ships sailing from Portugal and the Atlantic Islands would have to make the round voyage convoyed by one of these two squadrons. The subscription list for investors in the new Company was to remain open to all and sundry for one calendar month in Lisbon, three months for the remainder of Portugal, seven months for the Atlantic Islands, and for a year in Brazil, after which the lists would be closed. All subscribers would have to pay one-third of their investment in ready cash, and the balance in two instalments of four months each.

The governing board was composed of nine directors (*deputados*), eight of them merchants, with a representative of the Lisbon municipality, who was likewise to be taken from the Lisbon mercantile community. All directors were to have a minimum individual investment of 1,000 *cruzados*, and could serve for three consecutive years. Eight were to be elected by a majority vote of the shareholders, the ninth being nominated by the judge and senate of the Lisbon municipality. In addition, the Lisbon mercantile community (mainly composed of New-Christians or crypto-Jews) were to nominate another seven councillors who could be co-opted for board meetings whenever necessary, when they would have the same voting powers as the remaining nine. All the Company's officials were to be selected and appointed by the directors, and could be dismissed or removed at their pleasure. Appointments were normally to be triennial. The treasurer's accounts were to be audited by the board accountant and two directors. This meant that the shareholders had not even the semblance of control over the Company's finances, and in this respect the Brazil Company differed from its Dutch prototype. Board meetings were to be conducted at a large round table, in order to avoid wrangles over place and precedence.

It was categorically stipulated that the governing board was to be completely independent of all the crown courts and tribunals, as also from interference by the Inquisition. The triennial governing board would have to account only to the king and to the succeeding board for its doings. In this respect it enjoyed much greater freedom of action than did the Heeren XIX—or rather it would have done had its statutes been properly enforced. Its legal affairs were to be handled by a Judge-Conservator (*Juiz Conservador*), a peculiar official with far-reaching powers, who could deal summarily with most cases. Lawsuits involving large sums of money were to be handled by him in a special court nominated by the king from judicial officials selected by the directors—a packed court if ever there was one. A procurator-fiscal was appointed on similar terms.

Special facilities were accorded the Company for securing ship-building supplies and labour, and it was allowed to charter foreign shipping under the usual safeguards.[1] The Company's sea-service was recognized as being on a par with that of the crown, and the resources of the royal dockyards and magazines were made available to it. No vessel of any kind was to leave Portugal, Madeira, or the Azores for Brazil, and vice versa, unless she sailed in one of the Company's biannual convoys. Dispatch-boats with urgent naval or military intelligence formed the only exception to this rule. The sailing of a convoy had to be announced two months previously, by posting up notices of the sailing-date in all the principal ports. Originally, Lisbon was the only European terminal port, while those of Brazil were listed as Cabo de Santo Agostinho (in place of Dutch-occupied Recife), Bahia, and Rio de Janeiro, but this arrangement soon had to be modified. The master of any vessel sailing to or from Brazil other than in the regular convoys would have his licence endorsed and his ship confiscated. The Brazil Company was awarded a special flag, having the royal arms on one side and the representation of Our Lady of the Immaculate Conception on the other, with two inscriptions, *Sub tuum praesidium* and *Pro fide pro patria mori*—a somewhat ironical choice in view of the almost exclusively Jewish origin of the Company.

[1] For the extensive use of English shipping by the Portuguese in their Brazil trade see my article in the *Mariner's Mirror*, xxxvii. 197–230. To the sources quoted therein should be added Secretary Thurloe's classic appreciation of Anglo-Dutch rivalry, first printed in the *English Historical Review*, xxi. 319–27. Thurloe explained that in the abortive negotiations for an Anglo-Dutch alliance in 1650, the Dutch proposed that 'all the goods of an enemy found on the ships of a friend should be free, and all the goods of a friend found upon an enemy's ship should be prize . . . only they would except the goods belonging to Portugals that are carried out of Europe into Asia, Africa, and America, or è contra, because that trade is used to be driven by English ships' (ibid. p. 326).

The Company's commercial privileges included the monopoly of supplying Brazil with the colony's four most essential imports (other than slaves), viz. wine, flour, olive-oil, and codfish, and these at rates fixed by itself. As regards the return cargoes of sugar, tobacco, cotton, hides, &c., the Company was entitled to levy taxes on every chest, bag, or bale imported, in accordance with a sliding-scale ranging from 100 *reis* for a hide to 3,400 *reis* for a chest of white sugar. It was accorded a monopoly of all Brazil-wood exports from the four captaincies of Rio de Janeiro, Bahia, Ilheus, and Pernambuco, but paid an import tax at Lisbon on this commodity.

Capital once invested in the Company could never be withdrawn, but shareholders could sell or transfer their shares to others, in whole or in part, at the prevailing market price. Only shareholders with an investment of over 5,000 *cruzados* could vote in the triennial election for the eight directors. Capital invested in the Brazil Company by both Portuguese and foreign nationals was specifically exempted from confiscation by the Inquisition or by any other tribunal. Even in the event of war between Portugal and the country of a foreign investor, the latter would not forfeit either his investment or his dividends.[1] All the leading foreign merchants in Portugal were urged to subscribe liberally to the Company, on pain of not being allowed to participate in the trade with any of the Portuguese colonies. It is uncertain how far these foreigners did participate, but the bulk of the money subscribed (1,255,000 *cruzados*) came from the leading New-Christian merchants of Lisbon, much of it apparently in the nature of forced loans. It may be added that in the long run the Brazil Company proved no more profitable to its investors than did its Dutch prototype. Whereas the older West India Company only declared two or three dividends between 1623 and its dissolution in 1674, the Brazil Company only paid one dividend (of 15 per cent.) before its reorganization in 1662–4.

The organization of the Brazil Company coincided with a

---

[1] The summary of the 1649 statutes of the Brazil Company is taken from the very rare *Instituiçam da Companhia Geral para o Estado do Brazil*, dated 8 Mar. 1649, together with the *alvará de confirmação* of King John IV, dated 10 Mar. 1649, published at Lisbon by António Alvares, Mar. 1649, of which B.M. Add. MS. 20951 contains an example. Cf. also *HAHR*, xxix. 487–90; G. de Freitas, *A Companhia Geral do comércio do Brasil*, pp. 29–36; Andrade e Silva, *Collecção chronologica, 1648–1656*, pp. 31–41.

second trial of strength between the besiegers and besieged of Recife, the result of which had a decisive effect on the further course of the war. Greatly encouraged by the easy success of the expedition which had ravaged the *reconcavo* unopposed at the end of 1648, the High Council at Recife immediately pressed for another sortie in force on the return of the troops. They were the more anxious for this, since the Heeren XIX had repeatedly urged them to make such a move. Von Schoppe and his colonels would still have preferred an attack on Rio de Janeiro, but on 4 February 1649 a council of war finally agreed 'to sally out in God's name, bid defiance to the enemy by offering them battle, and hope for God's blessing thereon'.[1] The force mustered for the sortie comprised 3,060 white soldiers, 250 sailors, and 200 Amerindians; a total of some 3,500 men, as compared with 4,500 in the previous April. Colonel van den Brinck was in command, since Von Schoppe's leg-wound was not yet properly healed. His orders were to occupy the Guararapes and to bring the enemy to battle wherever found. The soldiers carried eight days' rations in their knapsacks, and five or six small field-pieces were taken along by the sailors.

The Dutch force left Recife on 17 February, and the Guararapes were occupied without difficulty on the following day. Francisco Barreto struck camp when he heard of the enemy's advance and marched with about 2,600 men to accept the challenge. He did not reach the scrub and swamps at the foothills of the Guararapes until after nightfall on the 18th, but he kept the Dutch under arms all night by disturbing them with false alarms. On the morning of 19 February the Dutch sent out a strong fighting-patrol to bring the Portuguese to action; but Barreto, having carefully reconnoitred their position, refused to be hustled into attacking prematurely. He kept his men in the shade of the scrub in the valley, while the thirsty Dutchmen panted on the barren hill-top in the tropical sun. At midday the heat became insupportable, and a hurriedly convened council-of-war decided, after much discussion, to retire on an outlying dairy-farm near Recife. The withdrawal of the main body began at about 3 p.m.,[2] Colonel van den Brande remaining on top of

[1] Quoted from the original proceedings in Hoboken, *Witte de With*, ch. vii.

[2] According to the Dutch accounts. The Portuguese versions give 2 p.m. or thereabouts. For the second battle of the Guararapes, I have relied chiefly on Michiel van Goch's report of 22 Feb. in JHMS. The principal Dutch and Portuguese accounts are collated and printed in Varnhagen, *História Geral*, iii (3rd ed.),

the hill with his own regiment, that of Van der Elst and the sailors with the artillery, to act as a rearguard and cover the retreat. This was the movement for which Francisco Barreto had been waiting.

When the main body reached a narrow path or defile at the foot of the hill, the Portuguese charged out of the scrub and fell upon its rear. The Dutch at first fought well, but eventually became demoralized and withdrew up the slopes in confusion, closely followed by the Portuguese. Van den Brande's rearguard now came into action but they, too, soon fell into confusion, the fight became a general mêlée, and the Dutch retreat turned into a precipitate rout. The officers vainly tried to rally their men who fled in all directions. Those who escaped from their pursuers made their way after dark to the dairy-farm, whence the beaten remnants returned along the beach to Recife next day. Fortunately for them, the victors fell to plundering the dead and wounded, and did not press the pursuit as hard as they might have done, although João Fernandes Vieira and some horsemen cut down many of the fugitives. If the pursuit had been pressed home, the whole Dutch force would have been annihilated, as Councillor van Goch frankly admitted in his eyewitness report of the disaster.

Even as it was, the defeat was more severe and demoralizing than that of the previous year. On that occasion, the Dutch had at least maintained their position on the field, and only retreated after nightfall. On this occasion, they acknowledged a loss of 957 killed and 89 captured, the casualties including about 100 officers. Among the slain were Colonel van den Brinck and the naval captain Matthijs Gillissen, who was Witte de With's second-in-command. The prisoners included the Calvinist Petiguar chief, Pieter Poty. He was most inhumanly treated by his captors, but steadfastly refused to change his side and his religion. He was finally sent in chains to Portugal, but died on the voyage. The Portuguese admitted a total casualty-list of 250, of which the great majority were wounded.[1]

pp. 91–95, 128–39. Cf. also J. H. Rodrigues, *Historiografia e bibliografia*, nos. 548–54*a*; Hoboken, *Witte de With*, ch. vii.

[1] For the mistreatment of Pieter Poty cf. *Twee verscheydenen Remonstrantien . . . door Antonio Paräupába* (The Hague, 1657), pp. 11–13. For João Fernandes Vieira's outstanding conduct and courage in the second battle of the Guararapes, see Francisco Barreto's citation ('. . . o vio proceder com assinalado valor, sendo o primeiro que rompeo o inimigo pelo lado esquerdo, indo matando nelle distancia

The disastrous result of the second battle of the Guararapes convinced even the Heeren XIX that the Portuguese were formidable opponents, something which they had hitherto refused to concede. The original plan of the West India Company for the conquest of Brazil in 1624, had been largely based on the assumption that the Portuguese were poor soldiers in comparison with the Spaniards, and on the knowledge that they had no experience of warfare against disciplined European troops. This belief persisted for a long time in the United Provinces. Even after the first battle of the Guararapes, a Dutch pamphleteer scornfully wrote that the Portuguese were a byword for cowardice and that 'their enemies have never considered them as being better than hens'.[1] The Recife Councillors, and for that matter Admiral Witte de With, explicitly contradicted this assertion. They strongly resented the fact that their repeated warnings of 'the strength and courage of the Portuguese' were scouted by their superiors in Europe, to whom they wrote as follows after the first defeat at the Guararapes.

'The Portuguese have become so experienced in this war that they can face the most veteran soldiers, as is shown by the encounters we have previously had with them, as also in our daily skirmishing. They now obstinately hold their ground after receiving a volley, and then fall on our men. They also know how to take full advantage of the ground, and to lay ambushes, charging out of the woods on our men and inflicting heavy casualties on them. They are well provided with weapons and well know how to use them. In bodily strength, self-control and character, they are the equals of our veteran soldiers. They also know how to live on very short commons much better and easier than our men, who must either go about always burdened with their knapsacks or else have their rations continually sent after them.'

Michiel van Goch's eyewitness report of the defeat at the second battle of the Guararapes is even more emphatic. 'The enemy's men are naturally agile and surefooted, able to advance or retreat speedily. They are also formidable from their natural ferocity, consisting as they do of Brazilians, Tapuyas, Negroes,

de duas legoas . . .') discussed in the Overseas Council on 9 July 1649 (AHU, 'Consultas Mixtas', Cod. 14, fols. 175ᵛ-6).
[1] *Brasilsche Oorloghs Overwegingh* (Delft, 1648). Cf. the seventeenth-century English saying, 'who so cowardly as a Portugal?' (W. Foster [ed.], *The voyage of Thomas Best to the East Indies 1612-14*, London, 1934, p. 120).

Mamelucos, etc., all natives of the country; as also Portuguese and Italians,[1] whose constitution enables them to adapt themselves very readily to the terrain, so that they can range the woods, cross the swamps, and climb or descend the hills (all of which natural obstacles are very numerous here), and that with remarkable speed and agility. Our men, on the contrary, fight ranged in serried ranks, after the manner of the fatherland, and they are sluggish and flabby, unsuited to this kind of country.'[2]

While these events were taking place in Portugal and Brazil, the confusion in the United Provinces over the policy to be adopted towards the West India Company and its prized possession, became worse than ever confounded. Sir William Temple wrote admiringly of the provincial assemblies in his classic *Observations upon the United Provinces*,[3] 'that united by one common bond of interest, and having all one common end of public good, they come after full debates to easy resolutions, yielding to the power of reason where it is clear and strong; and suppressing all private passions or interests, so as the smaller part seldom contests hard or long, what the greater agrees of'. This particular observation certainly does not hold good for the Brazilian problem of 1648–52, when the stubbornness of Zeeland was matched by the obstinacy of Holland, and 'easy resolutions' were very far to seek.

The provincial assemblies wrangled fiercely with each other, while public opinion was likewise sharply divided on the question of war or peace with Portugal. There were those who advocated an all-out offensive war, if necessary in alliance with Spain, and with a view to the capture of Bahia and all Portuguese Brazil. This was the policy most warmly favoured by the directors of the West India Company, but critics were not wanting who accused them of overreaching themselves.[4] Then there were those who advocated standing on the defensive in Brazil, while relying on a greatly intensified privateering war at sea to bring Portugal to heel by completely disrupting her maritime trade. This suggestion was particularly popular in Zeeland, where it

[1] These Italians were presumably veterans of Bagnuoli's Neapolitan levies.

[2] High Council's dispatch of the 9 July 1648, and Van Goch's report of 22 Feb. 1649 (JHMS). Cf. Braddock's defeat by the French and Red Indians in the forest near Fort Duquesne (July 1755), apart from more modern comparisons which suggest themselves.   [3] p. 107 of the 1676 edition.

[4] '. . . de begeerlicheyt van de Bewinthebbers soodanigh, dat sy alles wilden begapen ende bedingen, ofte verliesen' (Van der Capellen, *Gedenkschriften*, ii. 251).

was estimated that over a fifth of the inhabitants of the three leading towns of Middelburg, Flushing, and Veere were shareholders in the West India Company, and where (as previously mentioned) privateering was a major industry. Yet others, and particularly the powerful city of Amsterdam, were in favour of reopening peace negotiations with Portugal, on the basis of formal Portuguese recognition of Netherlands Brazil within its boundaries of July 1641, and an assured supply of slaves from Angola.[1]

The news of the loss of Luanda, which was received at the end of 1648, caused a major sensation and gave added (if only temporary) strength to the war-party—with whom, incidentally, the young stadtholder William II was apparently numbered, despite his close and cordial connexion with Portugal's French ally. In January 1649 five of the provinces (with Friesland still abstaining, and Zeeland advocating an intensified privateering war) agreed that Sousa Coutinho should be presented with an ultimatum demanding immediate Portuguese recognition of Netherlands Brazil and West Africa within the boundaries of late 1641, that is, including Angola and São Thomé. If this was refused, as was to be expected, then the five provinces urged that action should be taken in accordance with the following six-point resolution. The East India Company should recoup itself, at the expense of the Portuguese in Asia, for the 1,500,000-guilder subsidy paid to the sister company in 1647; privateers would be allowed to operate against all Portuguese shipping plying between Portugal and Brazil wherever found, and not merely south of the Line, as (theoretically) hitherto; the troops in Brazil, totalling some 3,500 men, would be paid wholly by the States-General; all arrears of the provincial subsidies to the West India Company, now amounting to over 6,500,000 guilders, would be paid up in regular instalments; shareholders in the Company would contribute another 12 per cent. on their investment; the Company would overhaul its finances and book-keeping, and institute certain drastic economies previously recommended by a commission of the States-General.[2]

[1] *Amsterdams Dam-praetje, van wat outs en wat nieuws en wat vreemts* (Amsterdam, 1649), p. D3; Aitzema, *Saken van staet en oorlogh*, iíi. 297; Van der Capellen, *Gedenkschriften*, ii. 250–2.

[2] For this and what follows cf. Aitzema, *Saken van staet en oorlogh*, iii. 297, 338–40, 415, 646–9, 684.

Sousa Coutinho did not reject the ultimatum outright, but gave a temporizing reply, pleading that certain articles, such as the cession of Angola and São Thomé, could not be granted without the authorization of his king. Nevertheless, the agressive six-point resolution was not enforced, since provincial unanimity was not attainable, the provincial arrears were not forthcoming, and Amsterdam remained steadfastly opposed to war with Portugal. News of the second Guararapes disaster was followed by the return of Councillor Beaumont and Colonel Haulthain from Recife in July, with detailed information of the desperate state of Netherlands Brazil. Highly pessimistic reports were also received from the High Council at Recife and Admiral Witte de With concerning the rapidly deteriorating condition of his warships, and the alarming shortage of all supplies and provisions. They indicated clearly that, unless the States-General were prepared to send out an expeditionary-force of 12,000 men and a fleet of forty sail (as Johan Maurits had originally suggested), nothing decisive could be achieved in Brazil without drastic action against Portugal in Europe.

In July 1649 the States-General resolved to send out twelve warships to relieve Witte de With's unseaworthy squadron, and to blockade the Tagus with another fleet of twenty-five sail, if the Portuguese crown would not consent to restore what the West India Company had lost in Brazil and West Africa since 1645. Amsterdam, however, refused to consent to this resolution save on a number of exacting conditions. The chief of these was that prior agreement should be reached with Denmark over a treaty then being negotiated on the redemption of the tolls which were levied on Dutch shipping passing through the Sound.[1]

The Danish 'redemption-treaty' was signed in October 1649, and six States' warships and six yachts were duly sent to Brazil, where they arrived in April and May 1650. Amsterdam and the towns of North-Holland, however, continued to oppose the sending of a fleet to the Tagus, since they were most reluctant to sacrifice their valuable trade with Portugal. The Amsterdamers pointed out that an average of about a hundred Dutch

---

[1] A 'precipitant ende scadelick contract', according to Alexander van der Capellen, *Gedenkschriften*, ii. 269. For a full account of the Danish redemption-treaty negotiations see G. W. Kernkamp, *De Sleutels van de Sont* (The Hague, 1890).

merchant-ships were always to be found in Portuguese ports, and that these would all be seized by King John IV if he was provoked too far. Zeeland consequently refused to ratify the Danish treaty of 1649, unless Holland first agreed to the dispatch of a fleet to the Tagus. Holland, egged on by Amsterdam, flatly refused to do this until Zeeland ratified the treaty. A deadlock developed, similar to that which had arisen over Holland's insistence on securing Zeeland's agreement to peace with Spain before the dispatch of Witte de With's fleet to Brazil in 1647. This time the deadlock lasted much longer, as the political crisis in the summer of 1650, which culminated in William II's abortive attempt to seize Amsterdam, pushed Brazil and the West India Company's affairs into the background. The sudden death of the young stadtholder in November 1650 was followed by the accession to power of the States or anti-stadtholder party; and the province of Holland seized the opportunity to reassert its predominance in the Union. Finally, in March 1651, Zeeland agreed to ratify the Danish treaty in return for Holland's reluctant consent to the mobilization of an effective naval expedition against Portugal.

No sooner had Zeeland ratified the treaty than Holland played its trump-card. The richest province now refused to pay its share of the projected expedition, unless all the other provinces first paid up their contributions *and* the arrears they owed on their Brazilian subsidies as well! This they could not do; and as Zeeland no longer had a *quid pro quo* to offer Holland, the stalemate continued until the outbreak of war with England in May 1652 made further drastic action against either Lisbon or Bahia impracticable.[1]

This inter-provincial bickering, and the resultant lack of any resolute policy regarding Netherlands Brazil, naturally had unfortunate repercussions in the miserable colony. The Company's servants and free-burghers alike felt themselves forgotten by the home government; and the soldiers and sailors were even worse off, with their pay continually in arrears and their rations frequently cut. Admiral Witte de With complained in August 1649 that he had received only one letter from the States-General since his arrival at Recife fifteen months previously—and that

---

[1] Elias, *Voorspel*, ii. 148–50, has a short and clear account of the dispute between Zeeland and Amsterdam over the Brazilian and Danish questions in 1649–52, but the best and fullest account is in Hoboken, *Witte de With*, ch. vii.

was a purely formal notification of the conclusion of peace with Spain.[1] He did not get on well with his civilian colleagues of the High Council, partly because he despised them as amateur strategists, partly because they did not keep him properly informed of their plans, but mainly because he regarded himself as primarily responsible to the States-General and the prince of Orange, whereas the Councillors considered he should obey their orders and those of the Heeren XIX.[2]

The difficulties of the situation at Recife did not prevent the Dutch from reoccupying Ceará, which had been a no-man's-land since the massacre of the garrison by Tapuyas at the end of 1643. An expedition under Mathias Beck which landed there in April 1649 founded a new fort called Schonenburgh without opposition; but although Beck made several journeys into the hinterland, he failed to find the rich deposits of silver-ore whose reported existence was the principal motive for this move.[3] Nevertheless the Dutch remained here unmolested until the capitulation of Recife five years later. In May 1649 Admiral Witte de With undertook a blockade of Rio de Janeiro, with a view to intercepting the homeward-bound sugar-fleet; but these ships did not venture out of the inner harbour, so the admiral was compelled to return empty-handed to Recife at the end of June.[4]

The chronic lack of supplies and provisions of all kinds in the beleaguered stronghold, prevented the Dutch from making full use of their naval superiority. Both admiral and council, much as they disliked each other, were agreed that the situation at Recife was so bad 'that no pen can describe it'.[5] The High Council wrote that the soldiers of the garrison went about 'quite bare and unclad', while the admiral reported that they were

[1] Witte de With to the States-General, 26 Aug. 1649, in Hoboken, *Witte de With*, ch. x.

[2] The admiral's disputes with the High Council are very fully documented in Hoboken, *Witte de With*, chs. ix and x.

[3] Elias notes (*Voorspel*, ii. 130 n. (4)) that the date of the reoccupation of Ceará is nowhere stated by Dutch historians. This may be so, but the episode is fully documented from the original records in the Rijksarchief, by the Barão de Studhart in the *Revista do Instituto de Ceará*, xvii. 325 ff. The fort founded there by Mathias Beck in April 1649 was called Schonenburgh or Schoonenborch after the president of the High Council.

[4] For a detailed account of Witte de With's abortive cruise off Rio de Janeiro see Hoboken, *Witte de With*, ch. viii.

[5] High Council's letters of 23 July, 2 and 11 Nov. 1649 (JHMS); Hoboken, *Witte de With*, ch. x and sources there quoted.

'like earthworms, a pitiful sight to see. I verily believe that if one cut their ears, no blood would ooze out.' The Council further stated that the soldiers were deserting in groups of ten or twelve by broad daylight, which indicates that the men agreed with the admiral's description of Recife as 'starvation corner'. This despite the fact that the besiegers themselves were on exceedingly short commons, and that desertions from their side were likewise relatively frequent. The sailors in Witte de With's ships were in slightly better condition, but only because the admiral insisted that they should be rationed on the home-fleet's scale and not (as the Council maintained) on the West India Company's meaner allowance. In June 1648 a ship inaptly named the *Getrouwen Herder*, or *Faithful Shepherd*, which was bound with reinforcements for Luanda, was seized by the mutinous soldiers and crew and carried into Rio de Janeiro. Other vessels absconded to the Antilles on one pretext or another, and in May 1649 one of Witte de With's warships, the *Dolphijn*, was also seized by her mutinous crew who sailed her back to Holland.[1]

The provisioning of Recife had to be done almost entirely from the United Provinces, since efforts to grow adequate manioc and other crops in Paraíba, Itamaracá, Rio Grande do Norte, Ceará, and the rat-infested island of Fernão de Noronha, proved abortive. In an effort to alleviate the consequent strain on their disordered finances, the West India Company made further concessions in their regulations regarding trade and navigation with Netherlands Brazil. It will be remembered that the actual trade had been partly freed in 1638; but only merchants who were also shareholders in the Company were supposed to participate, and all cargoes had to be carried in ships owned or freighted by the Company. Under the revised regulations promulgated in August 1648, the Brazil trade was thrown open (on payment of certain dues to the Company) to all Dutch merchants and shipping in general, with the exception of the commerce in munitions and Brazil-wood which remained the Company's monopoly.[2] The slave-trade, which had formerly been another, was now relinquished, since with the loss of the plantations in the *várzea*

---

[1] For the mutiny of the *Dolphijn* cf. Hoboken, *Witte de With*, ch. ix.

[2] *Reglement bij de West-Indische Compagnie . . . over het open-stellen van den hande op Brazil* (The Hague, 1648). Cf. *Groote Plakaatboek*, i. 614–18.

the demand for Negro slaves in Netherlands Brazil was greatly diminished.

The results of throwing open the trade were disappointing but might have been foreseen. There were no longer the actual achievements or the even more alluring prospects of Johan Maurits's relatively golden days, to tempt traders to throw good money after bad. Recife was closely besieged by land, and the other places still in possession of the Dutch had little or nothing to attract merchants or investors. The provisioning of Recife continued to be carried out almost entirely by the Company, and the chronic indebtedness of this once mighty corporation was the chief reason why there were never enough stores or supplies in the beleaguered capital. Amsterdam also used its influence to have the Guinea trade thrown open, but here it was less successful, although some concessions were made. In any event, a marked decline in the profits of this trade set in after 1645, although gold from Guinea more than once helped Recife in the hour of utmost need.[1]

When Witte de With left on his abortive cruise to Rio de Janeiro, he took a gloomy view of the outlook for Netherlands Brazil. The Tapuya and Petiguar allies of the Company were becoming discontented with their treatment, or so he alleged. The fortifications, being mostly made of earth, were crumbling and deteriorating fast, whereby the enemy, 'who are very bold', were still further encouraged. The garrison consisted of four regiments under Von Schoppe, Van den Brande, Haulthain, and Kerweer, totalling about 4,000 men, 'mostly inferior and untrained fellows', including four companies at Paraíba and one in Rio Grande do Norte. The Company had only three sizeable ships of its own, two of which were shortly due to sail for Holland, and the third to Guinea. None of its yachts would be fit for further service in a year, and his own warships were very short of tackle and stores. It may be added that the High Council had noted in February that the admiral would not have been able to put to sea at all, but for using the sails captured in the English ship *Concordia*. As regards the enemy, there were sixteen or eighteen sail at Cabo de Santo Agostinho;

---

[1] For the decline in the Guinea trade at this period see Ratelband, *Vijf Dagh-registers*, pp. xxvii, xxviii, xl, xcvi. For the (unauthorized) coinage of Guinea gold at Recife see Alfredo de Carvalho's excerpts from the 'Dagel. Notulen' in *RIAGP*, xii. 160–8 ('Moedas Obsidionaes cunhadas no Recife em 1645, 1646, 1654').

five or six royal galleons, eight English ships, the Indiaman
Santa Catarina, and eight or nine smaller ships in Bahia; and
about thirty sail, mostly the caravels of the homeward-bound
sugar-fleet, in Rio de Janeiro.[1]

The High Councillors, writing home about six weeks later,
were equally pessimistic. They dreaded the return of Witte de
With's warships 'which will stand in want of everything, and
since there are no supplies here, they will have to stay in harbour
without doing the least service'. They accused the Heeren XIX
of wanton neglect in sending the money and supplies for which
they had so often asked, stressing the resultant demoralization
and dissatisfaction of all the Company's employees. They themselves wanted nothing better than to be relieved of the crushing
burden of their office and allowed to repatriate.[2] Beaumont
had resigned his seat on the Council as soon as he was back
in Holland, and no successor could be found to replace him.
His three luckless colleagues at Recife proffered their resigna-
tions every time they wrote home; but since nobody could be
found willing to take their places, they had perforce to stay
where they were. All those who could do so, left the colony in
whatever ship was available, over 250 leaving in the *Coning
David* at the end of August 1649. The lucky ones included the
chronicler Johan Nieuhof, and the veteran Colonel van den
Brande; but the High Council forestalled the great bulk of
military applications by ordering the field-officers to reject all
such requests automatically. With typical short-sightedness, the
Heeren XIX had also ordained that nobody who owed any
money to the Company should be allowed to return home until
his debts were paid. This merely increased the number of useless
mouths which the harassed High Council had to feed at Recife.

In response to Witte de With's urgent and repeated representations, the High Council reluctantly agreed at the end of
July 1649 to let the admiral return home with three of his best
ships (*Brederode*, *Guelderland*, and *Coning David*), leaving the
remaining six at Recife; although the Council considered that
on his departure the fate of Netherlands Brazil would hang 'as
on a silken thread'. Early in August, however, they heard from

---

[1] Witte de With, MS. 'Journael', 23 Apr. 1649 (JHMS). For the use of the
Concordia's sails see 'Dagel. Notulen' of 26 Feb. 1649 in Hoboken, *Witte de With*,
ch. viii.

[2] High Council's letter of 7 June 1649 (JHMS).

prisoners and deserters that Francisco Barreto had written to Bahia, asking for the galleons of the Armada Real to be sent up to relieve the English ships blockaded in the roadstead of Cabo de Santo Agostinho, and perhaps attack Recife in conjunction with them. Alarmed at this intelligence, they reversed their previous decision and decided to let the *Coning David* sail alone at the end of the month, retaining the admiral with the other two vessels for some time longer. Witte de With protested strenuously at this change of front, arguing (correctly enough) that the galleons at Bahia were in an even worse condition than his own ships, and that they would 'keep themselves from getting scorched by the fire for so long as ever they can'. The Council rejected his protests, and their attitude hardened still further when they received a letter from the Heeren XIX telling them that another fleet of twelve sail was being prepared to relieve the admiral's squadron, and until the arrival of these fresh vessels they were on no account to let his ships return home.

As mentioned previously, Admiral Witte de With did not regard himself as the West India Company's servant, but as directly responsible to the States-General and the prince of Orange for the safety and condition of his warships. When he found that all his arguments failed to convince the Recife Councillors, he resolved to return home with the *Brederode* and *Guelderland* despite their opposition. If these two warships stayed any longer in Brazil, he wrote, they would serve only as firewood for bakers' ovens. After provisioning them from the other warships which were blockading Cabo de Santo Agostinho, he left Recife roads on 8 November, and reached Holland in the *Brederode* at the end of April 1650, after many weeks of misadventure in the Irish Sea and St. George's Channel. The example of the flagship was soon followed by her consorts. Indeed it had been anticipated by some of them, as, apart from the mutinous *Dolphijn*, both the *Overijssel* and the prize *São Bartholomeu* had already sailed for home, without awaiting orders from either the admiral or the High Council at Recife. After their admiral's departure the crews of the five remaining States' warships (*Witte Eenhoorn, Haerlem, Eendracht, Zutphen,* and *Wapen van Nassau*) mutinied and forced their captains to sail for Holland in November and December 1649.[1] Within

---

[1] For details see Hoboken, *Witte de With*, chs. x and xi, and the sources there quoted.

these two months, the whole strategic situation in the South
Atlantic Ocean was completely reversed. The Portuguese were
left in unchallenged command of the sea, without having fired
a single gun or moved a single ship to secure it.

The consternation of the High Council can easily be imagined,
and was shared by all ranks and classes at Recife. Even Von
Schoppe, who had always remained on good terms with his
naval colleague, joined with the civilian Councillors in demanding that exemplary (and preferably capital) punishment should
be meted out to the absconding admiral and his captains after
their return home. Otherwise, everyone else in the colony would
follow their example as soon as the opportunity occurred. When
the warships had gone, the Council were left with one ship and
three unseaworthy yachts; and although there were also a few
Zeeland privateers operating on the coast, they had no hope of
being able to resist an attack by the Portuguese from seaward.
The Council considered that this was a danger not only from
the royal galleons at Bahia and the powerful English ships at
Cabo de Santo Agostinho, but from the expected arrival of the
Brazil Company's first armada. They had been warned about
this possibility in a dispatch of the Heeren XIX dated 17 July
1649, and also from intercepted letters. Acknowledging receipt
of the Company's warning, the Council retorted that what they
wanted was not stale news but fresh warships to enable them
to cope with the superior Portuguese power; 'for the enemy
here is not lacking in either men, ships, or courage which will
enable him to take the offensive against us'. They further complained that Witte de With was much better supplied than he
had alleged when he left, as some of his sailors had been selling
their surplus bread-ration ashore.[1]

The Brazil Company's first armada left the Tagus for Bahia
on 4 November 1649. It comprised sixty-six sail of merchantmen convoyed by eighteen galleons and warships. At least ten
of these eighty-four sail were English ships on charter, apart
from others which the Company or the private traders who
sailed in its convoy had bought outright. The General, or
commander-in-chief, was the count of Castel-Melhor, who flew
his flag in the new Oporto-built galleon *São Paulo*. The admiral,
or second-in-command, was Pedro Jacques de Magalhães, in
another new Oporto-built galleon *São Pedro*. On arrival at Bahia,

[1] High Council's letters of 17 July, 2, 11, 29 Nov., and 13 Dec. 1649 (JHMS).

the count of Castel-Melhor was to take over the government
of the colony from the count of Villa-Pouca, who was to return
to Lisbon next year with the Armada Real and the Brazil
Company's homeward-bound armada in convoy.[1] The count
of Villa-Pouca was evidently a lax disciplinarian, as numerous
complaints were received by the home government of the undisciplined state of his soldiers and sailors at Bahia, and the
outrages which they had perpetrated against the local *moradores*.
As had happened during the lengthy stay of the count of
Torre's armada at Bahia in 1639, the exasperated citizens declared they would rather endure another Dutch occupation than
the excesses of the brutal and licentious Portuguese soldiery.[2]

Castel-Melhor's voyage proved a long and difficult one, his
unwieldy convoy taking twice the usual time for the Brazil
voyage, owing to the contrary winds and currents experienced
after leaving Madeira, which was the only official port of call.
Due to these fortuitous circumstances, an unexpected landfall
was made just north of Recife on 19 February 1650. Hendrick
Haecxs describes in his *Journal* how three large English ships
from the convoy 'mounting, as it was said, forty guns each, with
red English flags flying at the stern and a pennant from the
forestay', made 'a great bravado' against the six Dutch ships
in Recife roads. The Anglo-Dutch fight which followed seemed
to be a very fierce one to the anxious onlookers from the shore,
but we do not hear of any casualties on either side. The Dutch
squadron, under Commander Goevertsz. Cop,[3] not only failed
to prevent a contingent of the armada from entering the haven

[1] Full details of the armada, and Castel-Melhor's orders for his captains, will
be found in the documents transcribed in BNRJ, Cod. I-4-1-62, and printed in
IV Congresso da Historia Nacional, 317-22, 354-59. Unfortunately, Castel-Melhor's
own orders from the crown, d. 14 Oct. 1649 ('Regimento que trouxe o Conde de
Castel-Melhor sobre a Armada da Companhia Geral de que veyo por General')
which are contained in the same codex, were inadvertently omitted from this
publication.

[2] AHU, 'Consultas Mixtas', Cod. 14, fol. 282ᵛ. Cf. also the reports from the
count of Castel-Melhor for the years 1650-2, which are embodied in numerous
other *consultas* of this codex, and his correspondence for those years in 'Bahia,
Papeis avulsos', *passim*.

[3] Cop had assumed command of the West India Company's warships, as distinct
from those of the States-General and the Zeeland privateers, after the departure
of Banckert for Zeeland (High Council's letter of 28 Aug. 1647, in JHMS). For
details of the actions of 19-23 Feb. 1650, cf. High Council's letter of 26 Feb. 1650
(JHMS); *Dagboek van Hendrik Haecxs*, pp. 284-6; *Relaçam dos successos da armada que
a Companhia Geral do Brazil expedio o anno passado de 1649* (Lisbon, 1650); *HAHR*,
xxix. 492-3.

of Cabo de Santo Agostinho, and so relieving the English and other ships lying there, but failed to take a Portuguese frigate, the *Santa Luzia*, which became separated from the armada, but beat off all attacks on her for two successive days. The Dutch ships dogged the rest of the convoy for about a week on its voyage to Bahia, but the Portuguese station-keeping was so good that they captured only one straggler. The rest of Castel-Melhor's armada reached Bahia on 7 March 1650.

In the same month as the Brazil Company's armada made its unwelcome appearance off Recife, the High Council wrote another series of their pessimistic dispatches to the States-General and the prince of Orange, evidently in the hope that those august authorities would do more for them than their own directors. The picture they drew of local conditions was the now familiar one of unrelieved gloom. The garrison numbered about 3,000 ill-clad and famished men, of whom less than 1,200 were fit for duty in an emergency. Many of the soldiers were literally in rags, 'and some have not the wherewithal to hide their private parts, . . . slouching along the streets like beggars and eating offal from the gutters'. Soldiers and civilians alike would all return to Europe forthwith, if there were only sufficient ships and provisions to take them. The unpaid soldiers even forced their way into the Councillors' bedrooms, demanding their back-pay. It is not surprising that these worthies wrote 'we are all here stretched on a perpetual rack'.

Apart from this demoralized garrison, there were about 4,000 white civilians of all ages and both sexes, including a sizeable Jewish community of about 600 souls. There were also about 3,000 or 4,000 Amerindians and Negroes. All of these 10,000 souls were living on meagre rations from the Company's stores, which would be completely exhausted within seven weeks. If no relief arrived from Holland during that time, they would have no option but to surrender unconditionally 'into the enemy's bloodthirsty hands'. If this happened, they would probably all be massacred, despite promises of good quarter, as so many other Dutch prisoners had been on their way to Bahia. With the 'desertion' of Witte de With, and the arrival of the Brazil Company's armada, 'we all stand now like sheep in the slaughter-house, defenceless before our bloodthirsty foes'. The enemy, on the other hand, were very 'strong, bold, proud and courageous' after their two successive victories at the

Guararapes, and confident that they could continue the siege of Recife indefinitely, even if they had to depend on local resources and received no further help from Portugal. Moreover, 'they are of such a nature that they can and will get along on little scraps from the land or sea, quite unlike our nation'.[1]

Even after allowing for deliberate exaggeration in these reports, it is clear that Recife was in a most critical position in February 1650; but Castel-Melhor's orders, like those of the count of Villa-Pouca, limited him to a strictly defensive attitude regarding the Dutch. King John IV was as anxious as ever to avoid any extension of the existing unofficial and purely American war with the United Provinces. Apart from anything else, he feared that the expansion of the conflict would involve the loss of his ill-defended Asian possessions, which were completely at the mercy of the greatly superior maritime power of the Dutch East India Company. Moreover, although the *moradores* of Pernambuco did not know it, King John IV and some of his principal advisers were still prepared to envisage the surrender of Pernambuco to the Dutch, even after the two victories of the Guararapes and Witte de With's withdrawal. In such an event, they hoped to persuade João Fernandes Vieira and his followers to emigrate to Angola.[2] The Brazil Company's armada therefore made no attempt to attack the tottering Dutch stronghold from seaward, and the immediate crisis was relieved by the arrival of Colonel Haulthain with a number of warships from Holland in April and May. Like the fleets of Von Schoppe and Witte de With, the ships of Haulthain had experienced inordinately bad weather on their voyage. Although his ships had been provisioned for sixteen months when they left Dutch ports, most of them averaged five months on the voyage and had less than a year's supply on board when they arrived.[3]

The High Council's statement that the besiegers were confident of capturing Recife, even without receiving further help from Portugal, was either a great mistake or else a deliberate

---

[1] High Council's letters of 15 and 26 Feb. 1650 (JHMS). The figure for the Jewish community is taken from A. Wiznitzer, 'The Number of Jews in Dutch Brazil, 1630–1654', reprinted from *Jewish Social Studies*, xvi (1954), pp. 107–14.

[2] *Parecer* of the count of Odemira, 11 Nov. 1650, in the Cadaval archives (kindly communicated by D. Virginia Rau).

[3] *Graef Willem, Princes Amelia, 't Huis Nassau, Westfriesland, Nimegen, Breda, Tertholen, Hollantsen Tuyn, Wapen van Hoorn, Vergulden Dolfijn*, according to the High Council's letters of 1 Apr., 9 May, and 8 June 1650 (JHMS).

exaggeration. In point of fact, Bahia was little better off than Recife; and the besiegers of the Dutch capital were as ragged and famished, though not as disheartened, as were the defenders. The Brazil Company's convoy system undoubtedly prevented the Dutch from taking as many prizes as previously,[1] but the arrival of over eighty sail at Bahia created famine conditions in that port, which was already unable adequately to provision the Armada Real, still anchored in the bay. A two-year drought further worsened a highly critical situation (although the effects of the drought were felt in Netherlands Brazil as well), while the Brazil Company's monopoly of flour, olive-oil, wine, and codfish imports created immense dissatisfaction. As the marquis of Niza had written to King John IV from Paris when the formation of the Company was still under discussion: 'Monopolies of those articles which form the necessaries of life always proved to be highly prejudicial to those monarchs who authorized them, for even though some benefit is derived by the royal exchequer therefrom, the harm suffered by the common people far outweighs that strictly limited advantage.' The *moradores* of Portuguese Brazil were soon deluging the crown with complaints that the Company imported totally insufficient quantities of the four principal commodities, and charged excessive prices for those that it did bring. Their complaints were described by the count of Castel-Melhor as being perfectly justified; and it is clear from their correspondence that neither the governor-general nor the Overseas Council approved of the Brazil Company.[2]

Moreover, the besiegers of Recife, courageous and determined as they undoubtedly were, were also desperately short of munitions, clothing, and food-stuffs, and kept bombarding Bahia and Lisbon with appeals for speedy assistance. Soon after receiving news of the first victory of the Guararapes, the Overseas Council reminded King John IV that the Dutch had recently taken thirty caravels, many of which were laden with munitions and

---

[1] 'alsoo den vijant niet als in vlooten sijne schepen af ende toebrengt, om welcke tegens te gaen geen gecombineerde suffisante scheepsmacht connen uijtbrengen' (High Council's letter of 1 Apr. 1650, in JHMS).
[2] For the situation in Bahia and complaints against the inefficiency and greed of the Brazil Company, cf. AHU, 'Consultas Mixtas', Cod. 14, fols. 229[v], 240, 242-5, 265[v], 266[v], 268[v], 272-4, 293[v], 301[v], 309-11, 351[v], 353; G. de Freitas, *A Companhia Geral do comércio do Brasil*, pp. 38-39, 73-79. Niza's *consulta* of 26 Nov. 1648 was printed in *IV Congresso da Historia Nacional*, v. 310-15.

supplies for the victors. The Council stressed the urgent need to send them fresh supplies 'in English ships if it is possible'. A couple of months later the Overseas Council interviewed an eyewitness of the battle. He reported that although the victory was greater than had at first been realized, and the soldiers were in good heart, 'they are so short of clothing and so ill-provided with the necessaries of life, that they live as by a miracle, for the majority have no clothes to cover them, and when a ration for three days is issued to them, this consists only of a small porringer of flour and half a pound of codfish when there is any, which is seldom'. So desperate were the men after the second battle of Guararapes that they actually mutinied, having been told that some clothing and money which had come for them in the recently arrived English ships had been retained by their commander-in-chief. Francisco Barreto (who at first blamed João Fernandes for this fracas, although he later retracted this allegation) suppressed the mutiny and hanged the seven ringleaders out of hand; but he did not deny that his men were sorely in need of supplies of all kinds.[1]

This stalemate, punctuated by periodic crises at Recife and Bahia, lasted from after the second battle of the Guararapes until the Capitulation of Taborda five years later. During most of this period neither side in Brazil was strong enough to give the knock-out blow to the other; and both sent repeated appeals to their respective home governments, imploring them to send sufficient help to enable the *coup de grâce* to be given to their opponents. The Councillors at Recife described the situation as they saw it as follows. There were only two ways of putting Netherlands Brazil on its feet again: either by waging a vigorous offensive war, or else by making a firm and lasting peace. The latter course being obviously impossible, since Portuguese promises could never be relied upon, only the former alternative remained. This would have a good chance of success, 'particularly if coupled with the refusal of quarter by land or sea, which would undoubtedly bring the Portuguese to their senses'.[2]

This was not the first time that a reversion to the *lex talionis* which had prevailed in 1640 was suggested, nor was it the last. The Councillors subsequently proposed that the same treatment

---

[1] AHU, 'Consultas Mixtas', Cod. 14, fols. 122, 132^v, 177, 203, 204. Francisco Barreto's dispatch of 28 Feb. 1649, in Varnhagen, *História Geral*, iii. 139.

[2] High Council's letter of 20 Nov. 1651 (JHMS).

should be meted out to the crews of English and other neutral ships which were freighted by the Portuguese for the Brazil trade. The directors and the States-General were reluctant to authorize such a drastic procedure officially, although they made it clear that they had no objection to the Councillors at Recife giving such orders on their own responsibility. The latter, however, wished the formal order to come from their lawful superiors, with the result that although the proposal was seriously discussed, it was never actually enforced.[1] The Portuguese do not seem to have contemplated a general refusal of quarter to their opponents, although the Dutch genuinely believed the contrary. The contemporary chronicler, Diogo Lopes de Santiago, admits that their senior officers had great difficulty in preventing the Negro levies of Henrique Dias from killing all their prisoners or from mutilating them when dead[2]—and it is possible that they did not always try very hard to do so.

Although the besiegers of Recife had established a definite ascendancy over their opponents in the field by 1650, this did not mean that the Dutch position in Brazil was quite hopeless. The situation in South America might yet be dramatically reversed by developments in Europe, where Portugal's position was more critical than ever before. King John IV's hospitality to the fugitive Royalist princes, Rupert and Maurice, involved Portugal in hostilities with the Commonwealth of England for most of 1650. This unlucky war was only ended by King John's abject submission to the harsh terms imposed by Cromwell and the Parliament, which were of unexampled severity.[3] Admiral Blake inflicted great damage on Brazil shipping during his blockade of the Tagus from May to October 1650. He first stopped the outward-bound armada of the Brazil Company, and detained nine chartered English ships which composed the bulk (if not all) of its convoy. In September he intercepted the homeward-bound sugar-fleet from Rio de Janeiro, which, contrary to the orders originally given to Castel-Melhor, had not called at Bahia on the return voyage for convoy. Blake destroyed one and captured seven sail of this squadron, while his colleague, Popham, and some Zeeland privateers cruising off the Tagus took another

---

[1] Directors' letters of 8 Feb. and 20 July 1648, 8 May 1653; High Council's letters of 21 Nov. 1650, 20 Nov., and 5 Dec. 1651 (JHMS).

[2] Lopes de Santiago, *História da guerra de Pernambuco* (ed. 1943), p. 651.

[3] E. Prestage, *Diplomatic Relations*, pp. 111-27.

three, only nine of the Portuguese ships reaching Setúbal and Lisbon in safety. Luckily for the Portuguese, the homeward-bound armadas of the count of Villa-Pouca and the Brazil Company, which had left Bahia together in July 1650, were forced back by contrary winds and tides some two weeks later, and so escaped interception by Blake. When they resumed their voyage in September they were later scattered by a severe storm off the Azores, in which four of the royal galleons were wrecked, mostly with great loss of life. The remainder of the combined armadas reached Lisbon safely in January 1651, the sea being temporarily clear of the English. Their arrival probably saved Portugal from complete collapse, as the seventy-odd sail which reached port were very richly laden.[1]

The rupture with England in 1650 forced the Brazil Company temporarily to abandon its preference for chartering English ships, and to freight Genoese, French, and even Dutch vessels instead. Moreover, the arrival of Haulthain's fleet, together with the purely defensive attitude maintained by the Portuguese at Bahia, gave the command of the sea once more to the Dutch in the second half of 1650. Both Haulthain's warships and the Zeeland privateers operating on the Brazilian coast picked up a fair number of prizes, including a large chartered French ship named *Villeroy*.[2] But the bulk of the Brazil Company's armadas eluded them, and their pickings were small compared with the bumper years of 1647–8.

Despite the naval losses they sustained from both English and Dutch warships and privateers in 1650–1, the Brazil Company still managed to find the means of equipping an armada of sixty sail which appeared off Recife on 25 February 1652. Haulthain's eight warships formed the nucleus of a respectable fleet of twelve sail which was now dispatched to shadow the Portuguese armada, in order to cut off any stragglers, or to bring part of it to action if a favourable opportunity should occur. A running fight, or rather series of fights, took place between Haulthain's ships (only about seven or eight of which apparently came into action) and the Portuguese armada between 26 February and 3 March 1652. One of the largest Portuguese galleons accidentally

[1] C. R. Boxer, 'Blake and the Brazil Fleets in 1650', *Mariner's Mirror*, xxxvi. 212–28.

[2] High Council's letters of 21 Nov. 1650 and 21 Mar. 1651 (JHMS); Castel-Melhor's letter to the Camara of Rio de Janeiro, 25 Nov. 1651, in *Documentos Historicos, 1648–1711*, xxxiii. 261.

caught fire and blew up from the explosion of its own powder-magazine, 'not a splinter of wood being recovered'. According to some accounts, the Portuguese armada kept such close formation that the attackers were unable to do any further damage. Other accounts allege that the Portuguese fell into great confusion after the explosion of the huge galleon, but that Haulthain pulled out of the fight at this critical moment because his flag-ship had received a shot on the waterline. The Councillors considered that Haulthain had failed to make use of at least two good opportunities to press home the attack successfully, despite the fact that his men were in very good heart and wanted nothing better than to board the enemy.[1]

The States' warships which had come out with Haulthain two years previously, were now in as bad a condition as those of Witte de With had been when they took French leave. Although this admiral and his captains had been brought to trial after the return to Holland, when the public prosecutor demanded the infliction of the death penalty, the tedious legal proceedings had ended in a virtual acquittal for most of them. Possibly encouraged by this anti-climax, Haulthain's men now insisted on returning home, and the remaining States' warships left for Holland in March and April 1652, without the permission of the Council and without awaiting the promised reliefs from Europe. Haulthain himself did not go with them. Either out of loyalty to the Company, or else disillusioned with his experience as an admiral at sea, he reverted to his former military rank and became commandant of the fort at Paraíba. This second mass desertion of the States' warships was all the more annoying for the Council, since they learnt from escaped Spanish prisoners and other deserters that the situation at Bahia was once again exceedingly critical, and that the place was in no condition to withstand a determined attack.[2]

With the unauthorized departure of Haulthain's warships, the command of the sea passed for the second time to the

---

[1] 'Kort Verhael van 't geene gepaseert is omtrent de Portugese Vloote gedurende alhier op de kuste tusschen de Recife ende Cabo St. Augustijn sich heeft onthouden desen 25 Feb. 1652', and 'Verklaringen van de naervolgende Capiteinen van Oorloge', Recife, 11 Mar. 1652, both in JHMS; *Dagboek van Hendrik Haecxs*, pp. 287-90, 308-10.

[2] High Council's letters of 28 Mar. and 3 Apr. 1652; Declaration of Don Pedro de Vivera and Alexandre de Hinjosa, in Council's letters of 10 and 13 Apr. 1652 (JHMS).

Portuguese without their having taken any offensive measures to secure it, but once again they made no use of the opportunity. The High Council naturally felt that Portuguese passivity could not be relied upon indefinitely, and they reproached the States-General for neglecting to send them any ships at a time when 'a mighty enemy fleet is expected here from Portugal, consisting of a greater number of ships than the present total of the Company's sailors'.[1] In August and September 1652 provisions and stores were once again down to the bottom of the barrel. The Councillors wrote despondently that if the Brazil Company's homeward-bound fleet under Salvador Correia de Sá attacked Recife from seaward (as it was expected to do), they would have no option but to surrender unconditionally. Fortunately for them, Salvador had no orders to this effect, and his armada of over seventy sail passed Recife in August without attempting to close the port.[2] This particular crisis, which recalled the critical days of June 1646, was shortly afterwards relieved by the seasonable arrival of six ships from Holland, and by the unseasonable but welcome rains which ended the two-year drought in December and brought on the manioc crop.

Plucking up heart of grace, the Recife Councillors again wrote to their superiors, urging them not to abandon the colony to the 'idolatrous' king of Portugal. Striking a sternly Calvinist note, they averred that 'everyone knows that the kingdom of Portugal has always been the most fervent in upholding idolatry in Christendom, and that with all the strength of the Inquisition, burning at the stake etc., against the truth and clarity of God's holy word'. They added that no compromise peace was possible with the 'rebel Portuguese', who on their side were determined to fight the struggle to a victorious finish. Some Portuguese prisoners had told them that at a recent meeting of the Cortes or Three Estates at Lisbon, many of the deputies had been inclined to assent to a peace with the United Provinces on the basis of abandoning Pernambuco to the Dutch. This suggestion would have been carried but for the count of Penaguião, who, followed by the clergy, had advanced many weighty reasons against the same, amounting to the resolve that heresy should

---

[1] High Council to States-General, 18 May 1652 (JHMS).

[2] High Council to States-General, 12 Aug. and 5 Sept. 1652; Aitzema, *Saken van staet en oorlogh*, iii. 872–3; C. R. Boxer, *Salvador de Sá*, pp. 288–9.

never be allowed to keep a footing in Brazil; 'thus showing themselves', the Councillors reluctantly concluded, 'more zealous for
the honour of their idol, than we would be in matters concerning
our God and our religion'.[1] In this connexion the Councillors
urged that if all or part of Netherlands Brazil could be regained
for the Dutch by treaty or by war, on no account should freedom
of religion be permitted to the local Portuguese, as it had been
in the days of Johan Maurits. The most that should be granted,
they observed, was freedom of conscience, on the same conditions
as prevailed in the United Provinces. They regarded even this
limited concession with misgiving, and would have preferred
to ban Roman Catholicism altogether.

The Councillors went so far as to threaten that if the Republic
of the United Netherlands either could not or would not help
them, then they would find some other 'neighbouring poten-
tates' who would be able and willing to do so. Anything was
better than submission to the 'barbaric and cruel Portuguese
nation, under whom we cannot live (nor can any other nation
in the world) since they have a natural antipathy against each
and every nation whose way of life, whether in family, household or business, is in any point different from their own'. No
names were mentioned in this outspoken missive, which recalls
the threats of the Pernambucan patriots to place themselves
under French or Spanish rule if King John would not help
them in 1645–6, but it is obvious that it was Cromwellian
England and the Scandinavian monarchies which the Council
had in mind. The Councillors were also greatly worried at the
news of the outbreak of war between the United Provinces and
England, which had occurred as a result of Tromp's clash with
Blake off Dover in May 1652. They hoped that peace would be
made as soon as possible, since they realized that otherwise ships
and supplies originally destined for the relief of Netherlands
Brazil would be diverted to the more important theatre of the
North Sea.

In point of fact, the Anglo-Dutch war of 1652–4 did not
sever communications between the United Provinces and
Netherlands Brazil, as is often asserted. It is true that the

---

[1] High Council to Heeren XIX, 20 Dec. 1652. This would imply that the
Cortes was the one summoned after the death of Prince Theodosio in May, but
the count of Penaguião went as ambassador extraordinary to England in July.
Either there is a mistake in the name, or the anecdote may relate to the previous
Cortes of 1646.

English did capture a few ships bound to or from Recife, but the great majority escaped by going 'North about'. Even the crisis of the war in the North Sea did not prevent the Dutch from sending a total of twenty-one ships to Recife in 1653, as compared with sixteen in 1652, fifteen in 1651, and twenty-five in 1650, although the Council complained that some of these vessels were very ill found.[1] They also reiterated a grievance of long standing when they wrote that many of these ships arrived without bringing a single letter from either the States-General or the Heeren XIX, thus indicating that what was happening in Brazil was of little concern to the authorities in the mother country. On the other hand, the Councillors were well posted as to the enemy's situation, thanks not only to the reports of deserters, but to the more reliable information gleaned from intercepted dispatches in captured Portuguese shipping. From some of these they learnt, in June 1653, not only that Bahia and Rio de Janeiro were in a very bad way, but that the Portuguese in Angola were distracted by civil strife. The Recife Councillors considered that the whole of Portuguese Brazil might yet be conquered, if only a peace could be patched up with England; and that in any event an expedition from the United Provinces could recapture the great African slave-depot, 'with virtually no trouble or danger, and at very small expense'.[2]

Their High Mightinesses were far too preoccupied with the life-and-death struggle with England to think of attacking either Bahia or Luanda at this juncture, and the days of Netherlands Brazil were in fact now nearly numbered. After the expiration of the ten-year Luso-Dutch truce in June 1651, the States-General could, of course, have declared war on Portugal, as many of the Zeelanders and the supporters of the West India Company urged them to do. But, as explained above (pp. 218–19), Amsterdam was loath to jeopardize the valuable Setúbal salt-trade, and many of her merchants and ship-owners did not care whether they traded to Brazil under the Dutch or under the Portuguese flag. An Amsterdam ship in the Brazil

[1] High Council's dispatches of 17 Jan., 3 Mar., 21 May, 13 and 30 June, 10 and 21 Nov. 1653 (JHMS); shipping statistics in Wätjen, *Holländische Kolonialreich in Brasilien*, pp. 333–4.

[2] High Council to Heeren XIX, 13 June 1653 (JHMS); AHU, 'Consultas Mixtas', Cod. 15, fols. 35, 63^v, 82, 89; ibid., 'Angola, Papeis avulsos de 1653', containing correspondence from the authorities at Luanda and Massangano, March–May 1653, which provides confirmation of the Recife Council's allegation

Company's service was captured by Zeeland privateers off the Rio Formosa in November 1652, and seven months later four freighted Dutch *fluyt*-ships were among a squadron of eighteen sail which left Cabo de Santo Agostinho laden with sugar for Lisbon.[1] These typical instances of the traditional Dutch readiness to trade with the Devil in Hell if they could avoid burning the sails of their ships, naturally annoyed the Recife Councillors intensely, but there was nothing they could do about it. Apart from the opposition of Amsterdam, the States-General probably feared that if they declared war on Portugal, the Mediterranean and North Atlantic would soon be swarming with corsairs of all nations, pillaging Dutch shipping under cover of the Portuguese flag and letters-of-marque.[2]

On his side, King John IV, while steadily increasing his clandestine assistance to the Pernambuco patriots (mostly via Bahia), for some years shrank from authorizing the Brazil Company's armada to attack Recife from the seaward, as Francisco Barreto and João Fernandes Vieira had repeatedly advocated since 1648. He fully realized that if he took this step, Recife might indeed fall, but he would then almost certainly be faced with a strong Dutch blockade of the Tagus. For this reason (it may be presumed) he turned a deaf ear to the pleas of his commanders in Brazil, who more than once urged him to take advantage of the Dutch weakness at sea by sending a fleet to attack Recife.[3] This prudence can only have been strengthened by his disastrous experience with Blake's fleet in 1650. Both sides, therefore, resorted to temporizing and largely insincere diplomatic negotiations in Europe, while continuing to fight a purely colonial war in America and Asia after the expiration of the truce in 1651.

The outbreak of the Anglo-Dutch war in May 1652 helped to resolve the strategic deadlock in Brazil. There was now no possibility of the Dutch being able to blockade Lisbon, however much they might be provoked in America, and the Portuguese were not slow to see their opportunity. On 1 July the Overseas

---

[1] High Council's letters of 20 Dec. 1652 and 13 June 1653 (JHMS).

[2] E. Prestage, *Diplomatic Relations*, pp. 208, 210; Knuttel, *Catalogus*, no. 6473, p. 18. Dr. van Hoboken kindly drew my attention to this last source.

[3] Intercepted and deciphered letter of Antonio Telles da Silva, d. Bahia, 25 Nov. 1649, in the Archief der Staten-General no. 5777 (copy kindly supplied by Dr. W. J. van Hoboken); AHU, 'Consultas Mixtas', Cod. 14, fols. 175, 225, 352ᵛ, 355.

Council suggested to the king that the time had come to accept Francisco Barreto's repeated proposals for a combined attack upon Recife, by ordering the Brazil Company's next armada 'to close Pernambuco in order to attempt its recovery, or at least to cut out the ships which are lying laden there'.[1] The suggestion was not implemented that year, perhaps because King John IV thought that a peace might yet be patched up between England and the United Provinces.[2] A year later he apparently felt surer of his ground. At any rate, in October 1653 the Dutch envoys who were then at Lisbon, trying to negotiate a compromise agreement for the division of Nether- lands Brazil, warned their masters at The Hague that something was in the wind. It was credibly reported that the newly appointed governor-general of Bahia, Dom Jeronimo de Ataide, count of Atouguia, who was then preparing to sail with the Brazil Company's next armada, 'would besiege the Riff of Pernambuco by water and by land, and was resolved to storm the place and make a quick dispatch. And the better to effect this business, they write that the governor is to take with him great store of money, to corrupt the governor and soldiers of the said place therewith, who are already discontented, since they receive no money from hence.'[3]

When the Brazil Company's armada of seventy-seven sail appeared off Recife roads on 20 December 1653, the defenders were not unduly alarmed. The outward-bound Brazil fleets had made such appearances in 1650 and 1652, but on both occasions had contented themselves with landing supplies for the insurgents at Cabo de Santo Agostinho, and had then resumed their voyage southwards to Bahia. Their preliminary manœuvres indicated that the same procedure would be fol- lowed this year, and it was only when the bulk of the armada remained to blockade Recife roads, leaving twelve or fourteen ships to sail southwards, that the Dutch commanders realized that this time the enemy was in earnest. The classic Portuguese account, given by Dom Francisco Manuel de Mello in his

[1] AHU, 'Consultas Mixtas', Cod. 15, fols. 3ᵛ, 10.

[2] Although the first shots were exchanged between Blake and Tromp off Dover i n May, the Anglo-Dutch war did not start in earnest until Oct. 1652.

[3] 'A Letter of Intelligence from Holland, dated The Hague, 18–20 November 1653', in State Papers of John Thurloe, i. 594. The two Dutch envoys at Lisbon were G. Rudolfi and W. van de Hoeven, for whose abortive mission see Aitzema, Saken van staet en oorlogh, iii. 873–4, and Prestage, Diplomatic Relations, pp. 214–15.

Epanaphoras, states that Pedro Jacques de Magalhães and Francisco de Brito Freyre allowed themselves to be persuaded by Francisco Barreto and his colleagues into giving direct support to the land forces; but in view of what the Dutch envoys at Lisbon reported in October, it is much more likely that the two naval commanders had already received orders from the crown to co-operate with the besiegers. In any event, both the land and the sea commanders realized that this opportunity might never recur, and that if it was neglected now, the war-weary *moradores* of Pernambuco might give up the struggle and withdraw in disgust into the interior.[1]

There were seven Dutch ships in the roadstead, and a number of others along the coast, including the powerful East-Indiaman, *Westfriesland*, at Paraíba, where she had been detained owing to a mutiny on board when outward bound for Batavia. In June 1653 three Zeeland privateers had intercepted the homeward-bound Bahia sugar-fleet of some thirty sail, and taken four of them with 1,600 chests of sugar. If more warships had been available the whole convoy could easily have been taken, wrote the High Council, since the Portuguese offered virtually no opposition. The arrival of a number of supply ships from Holland within the last few weeks had given the Council the opportunity of replenishing their magazines and stores, which now contained supplies sufficient for ten or twelve months. This was in striking contrast with the previous crises of June 1646, February 1650, and August 1652, when the magazines were virtually empty; but by this time the will to fight had gone, and the garrison was not prepared to offer more than a token resistance. Most of the soldiers had served for two or three times the period of their original engagement, and their pay was so much in arrears that they were on the verge of mutiny before the Portuguese armada appeared. Of the High Councillors who had come out in 1647, only the aged Schonenburgh and the sickly Haecxs were left, as the energetic Van Goch had been sent home in March, to make urgent representations to the States-General and the Heeren XIX about the critical state of the colony. The conduct of the defence thus

[1] *Breve Relação dos ultimos successos da guerra do Brasil, restituicão da cidade Mauricia, Fortalezas do Recife de Pernambuco, e mais praças que os Olandeses occupavão naquelle Estado* (Lisbon, 1654). The war-weariness of the *moradores* of Pernambuco was also admitted in the 'Consultas Mixtas', Cod. 14, fols. 136, 309-11, 351^v-2, 355-6, 379^v, 391.

rested with these two civilians, and the veteran Von Schoppe, who was more feared than loved by his men. The behaviour of this triumvirate was bitterly criticized by hostile pamphleteers, who alleged that Recife could have been held with more determined leadership, as the free-burghers were in good heart and Huybrecht Brest offered the use of the Zeeland privateering board's local resources. These allegations notwithstanding, there is ample evidence that the garrison (or most of it) was so demoralized before the siege began that any very prolonged or determined resistance was out of the question.[1]

The besiegers, however, were not without their own difficulties. Apart from their total lack of a siege-train, they did not possess a single officer with engineering experience adequate to directing the work of the approaches. Fortunately for them, there happened to be a French engineer on board one of the Portuguese ships, and his services proved invaluable.[2] Under his direction and with the active participation of João Fernandes Vieira, André Vidal, and Henrique Dias, all of whom personally encouraged their men in the front-line trenches, the besiegers pressed the attack on the landward side with skill and determination. The blockade by the Brazil Company's armada, although efficient, was not so effective as to prevent a detachment of 150 men from reinforcing the garrison by sea from Paraíba under cover of darkness, but the moral effect on the disheartened soldiery was very great. The outlying defences were isolated and taken one by one, and on 22 January 1654 the High Council decided to ask for a parley. Francisco

[1] The last days of Recife and Netherlands Brazil are fully documented in the subsequent inquiry held at The Hague into the conduct of Schonenburgh, Haecxs, and Von Schoppe. These proceedings, together with those of the court martial of the last-named, are transcribed in JHMS. The allegations against the Council are contained in the *Cort, Bondigh ende Waerachtigh Verhael van't schandelijck overgeven van Brasil* (Middelburg, 1655). Cf. also Aitzema, *Saken van staet en oorlogh*, iii. 1116–25; *Dagboek van Hendrik Haecxs*, pp. 295–303; *Inventario das armas e petrechos belicos que os Holandêses deixaram em Pernambuco e dos predios edificados ou reparadas até 1654* (Recife, 1940); *Documentos Historicos*, xxi. 49–60. On the Portuguese side, more reliable than D. Francisco Manuel's polished rhetoric in his *Epananphora Triumfante* (first printed in 1660, and edited by E. Prestage, *Epanáforas de vária história Portuguesa*, Coimbra, 1933, pp. 372–418), are the narrative cited in the previous note, the *Relaçam Diaria do sitio e tomada da forte praça do Recife* (Lisbon, 1654), and the recently discovered account by Francisco de Brito Freyre in the Cadaval archives, kindly communicated by D. Virginia Rau. Cf. also Varnhagen, *História Geral*, iii. 100–6, 139–48, and J. H. Rodrigues, *Historiografia e Bibliografia*, nos. 680–9.

[2] V. Rau [ed.], 'Relação inédita de Francisco de Brito Freire sobre a capitulação do Recife', *Brasilia*, ix. 1–17; AHU, 'Consultas Mixtas', Cod. 15, fol. 95ᵛ.

Barreto was fully prepared to concede honourable terms of surrender, and after some preliminary palaver the Capitulation
of Taborda was signed on 26 January 1654.

This convention included not merely Recife and Mauritsstad, but all the places still occupied by the Dutch in Brazil;
that is to say the islands of Itamaracá and Fernão de Noronha,
and the captaincies of Paraíba, Rio Grande do Norte, and
Ceará. Barreto promised to supply sufficient shipping to eva-
cuate all those who wished to leave, and to allow them to do so
unmolested, after selling such goods and possessions as they had
to leave behind them. Any Dutch citizens who wished to stay
in Brazil would be allowed to do so, and they would be treated
as if they were Portuguese subjects. Those who were Protestants
would be subjected to the same restrictions on the public
exercise of their faith as were foreign Protestant traders in
Portugal. Even orthodox Jews were apparently allowed to remain if they wished, although naturally none of them did so.
An amnesty was declared for all offences and atrocities committed, or allegedly committed, by the Dutch during the whole
course of the war; and their persons were expressly guaranteed
from any reprisal by word or act on the part of the victorious
Portuguese. All Dutch subjects who wished to leave would be
given three months to settle their affairs, and during this period
all law-cases between Dutchmen would be conducted in their
own courts. Other clauses dealt with arrangements for shipping,
and the conditions specially accorded to the garrison. The bulk
of the artillery was to be handed over to the Portuguese, but
Von Schoppe was allowed to take twenty assorted bronze guns
with him, and sufficient iron cannon for the defence of his ships
on their voyage home.[1]

Francisco Barreto made his triumphal entry into Recife on
28 January 1654. He treated the vanquished with the utmost
courtesy and consideration, personally accompanying Von
Schoppe back to his house after receiving the keys of the city
from the veteran German soldier. Barreto must have felt satisfied if he recalled, as surely he did, the last time that he had
trod the streets of Recife—escaping as a fugitive from jail on
that January night six years ago. He was, like Von Schoppe,

[1] The terms of surrender are printed in full in J. H. Rodrigues, *Historiografia e
Bibliografia*, nos. 680–1. The Capitulation of Taborda was so called because the
field where it was signed once belonged to a fisherman of that name.

a harsh disciplinarian, and clearly his men stood in awe of him. Hendrik Haecxs noted in his journal when the vanguard of the victors under João Fernandes Vieira entered the suburbs on the previous day: 'They were all terrifying men to look upon, marching in such good order and so well armed, as have ever been seen.' Another and more hostile eyewitness was constrained to admit: 'The *Mestre de Campo General*, Francisco Barreto, enforced such strict discipline in everything, that none of the burghers were harmed or insulted in the smallest degree, which was a most astonishing thing, considering that there were so many different races, Whites, Mulattoes, Brazilians [=Tupís], Negroes and Tapuyas all mixed up together, and all as bare and needy as if they had been dropped from the gallows.'[1]

Although the Councillors' oft-expressed fear that the Portuguese would pitilessly massacre the whole population of Recife if ever they took the city thus proved baseless, the Dutch elsewhere were victimized by their own propaganda. An officer who escaped on a *jangada* (sailing-raft) from Recife on the night before the capitulation,[2] brought the news of what was happening to the northern settlements of Itamaracá and Paraíba, still strongly held by the Dutch. He added, presumably to justify his own behaviour, that the bloodthirsty victors would undoubtedly ignore whatever terms they agreed to, and would butcher every living soul in Recife. This caused such a panic among the northern garrisons that without waiting to be attacked, or to learn if they were included in the terms of capitulation, most of them hurriedly embarked in what shipping was available and fled to the West Indies. The example was set by the amphibious Colonel Haulthain, who handed over the strong and well-provisioned fortress of Paraíba to the Portuguese prisoners there, and set sail for the Caribbean, picking up the garrison of Rio Grande do Norte on the way.

[1] *Dagboek van Hendrik Haecxs*, p. 301; *Cort, Bondigh ende Waerachtigh Verhael* (1655), para. 78. In contrast to Hendrik Haecxs, this anonymous writer states that although the victorious besiegers had sufficient powder, they were very short of shot, most of their men having only three or four bullets left.

[2] Claes Claeszoon. He was one of those who had taken service with the Portuguese after Hooghstraten's treacherous surrender at Pontal, and who had later deserted back to the Dutch (*Journal ofte Kort Discours nopende de Rebellye, 1645–1647*, under 14 Nov. 1645, and *RIAGP*, no. 32, p. 159). He obviously thought that he was a marked man, and had already had one narrow escape from death or recapture by the Portuguese at the second battle of Guararapes, where he commanded Von Schoppe's regiment.

Francisco Barreto's rectitude was best shown in his treatment of the Jewish community at Recife, which more than any other had reason to fear the Portuguese reconquest, and could hope for no consideration at the hands of fanatical Roman Catholics. To their relief and surprise, Barreto's conduct towards them could not have been more correct. 'Almighty God in His infinite power protected His people and saved them from all imminent dangers by influencing the heart of Governor Barreto. The latter prohibited any person of the Hebrew nation from being touched or molested, and provided severe penalties against those acting contrary to this prohibition. And not only this, he also agreed to let the Jews sell their merchandise and he permitted to embark for Holland, the more than six hundred persons of our nation who were present there.'[1] Not all these Jews returned to the United Provinces. No doubt the majority did so; but some went to France (Nantes); some to the West Indies, where they gave an additional impulse to the rising sugar industry of the Caribbean colonies; and one shipload eventually reached New Amsterdam, thus becoming the Pilgrim Fathers of American Jewry.[2]

Francisco Barreto was even more chivalrous to the defeated Dutch leaders, allowing Von Schoppe and his wife to take away a quantity of Brazil-wood without paying any duty, and doing other personal favours for Schonenburgh and Haecxs.[3] When these worthies reached Holland in July they were placed under arrest pending a formal trial, but the proceedings petered out rather inconclusively. This was probably because the evidence clearly indicated (hostile pamphleteers notwithstanding) that it was the authorities in Holland rather than their subordinates at Recife who were primarily responsible for the loss of 'neglected Brazil' (*verzuimd Brazil*), as the colony later became known in Dutch literature. Von Schoppe was tried by a military court martial, and received a sentence similar to that given to Admiral Witte de With four years previously—the forfeiture of all his

[1] Saul Levy Mortera, 'Providencia de Dios con Ysrael, y Verdad y Eternidad de la Ley de Moseh y Nulidad de los demas Leyes', translated in A. Wiznitzer, *Jewish Social Studies*, xvi. 112–13.

[2] A. Wiznitzer, 'The exodus from Brazil and arrival in New Amsterdam of the Jewish Pilgrim Fathers', in *Publications of the American Jewish Historical Society*, xliv. 80–97.

[3] AHU, 'Consultas Mixtas', Cod. 15, fol. 98*v*; 'Dagboek van Hendrik Haecxs', p. 301.

pay and allowances as from the date of the surrender. As with the admiral, this was virtually tantamount to an acquittal, or to the award of a farthing damages in a modern libel case. The proceedings against his civilian colleagues seem to have been dropped eventually, although at one time the prosecution tried hard to make Hendrik Haecxs the chief scapegoat. Readers of his journal will be relieved to know that this evidently came to nothing, since we find him settled as a wealthy burgher in Amsterdam and married to a Dutch lady in 1658.[1]

As regards the victors, historians differ widely as to whom the chief credit is due. Contemporary chroniclers were unanimous in awarding the palm to João Fernandes Vieira, who served continuously from the first day to the last of the 'Pernambucan Iliad', and whose paid panegyrists publicized his achievements in his lifetime.[2] A reaction set in with Francisco Adolfo Varnhagen, who preferred the Brazilian-born André Vidal de Negreiros, 'so great a man that only a Plutarch could do justice to him', and Varnhagen's preference has steadily gained ground to the present day. One might argue that nothing could have been achieved without the armada of the Brazil Company, as Pedro Jacques de Magalhães pointed out at the time, and as Padre Antonio Vieira claimed many years later. It can also be urged that Francisco Barreto was the principal architect of victory, at any rate in the last six years of the struggle; but it is worth noting that the commander-in-chief himself wrote to his king in the hour of triumph (1 February 1654): 'Your Majesty well knows how the *mestre-de-campo* João Fernandes Vieira is the first cause of the happiness which the Crown of Portugal enjoys today in seeing itself adorned with the jewel of the captaincy of Pernambuco.'[3]

The Capitulation of Taborda evidently came as a surprise to most contemporaries, despite the pessimistic series of reports which had come from the High Council at Recife ever since the

---

[1] Hoboken, *Witte de With*, ch. 1.

[2] Fr. Manuel Calado, *O Valeroso Lucideno ou Triumpho da Liberdade* (Lisbon, 1648); Fr. Rafael de Jesus, *Castrioto Lusitano* (Lisbon, 1679).

[3] AHU, 'Consultas Mixtas', Cod. 15, fol. 94, '. . . bem prezente he a Vossa Magestade como o mestre de campo João Fernandes Vieira he a primeira causa do bem que hoje goza a Coroa de Portugal em se ver adornada com a joya da capitania de Pernambuco.' It is true that Francisco Barreto wrote in an equally eulogistic strain about André Vidal's services, 'Consultas Mixtas', Cod. 15, fol. 94ᵛ). His unstinted praise of his two chief subordinates is all the more creditable, as they had previously complained to the crown about him (Cod. 14, fol. 345).

revolt of June 1645, and despite the intense aversion with which service in Netherlands Brazil was regarded by all those who were there in that period. The strength of the fortifications of Recife and Mauritsstad was a good deal overestimated in Europe, possibly because of books like Pierre Moreau's *Histoire*, which described Recife as one of the strongest places in the world. In point of fact, most of the forts were built of tamped earth which deteriorated rapidly in the rainy weather. The Tapuya and Petiguar allies of the Dutch were particularly disgusted at the collapse of the colony, and reproached the Hollanders in bitter terms for so lightly abandoning their strongholds and leaving their Amerindian friends to the revenge of the Portuguese.[1] On the other side of the world, when the Dutch prisoners in Portuguese India were told this news at Goa, they refused to believe it, retorting that 'one day the Portuguese might take Amsterdam, but Recife never!'[2] Later generations in the Netherlands regarded this disaster as marking the turning-point in that golden age of Dutch colonial expansion which had begun with the foundation of Batavia by Jan Pieterszoon Coen on the site of the Javanese Jacatra in 1619:

> *From Jacatra of yore began the victory*
> *From the conquered Recife the defeat.*

[1] *Twee verscheydenen Remonstrantiën* (1657); cf. also Mathias Beck's letter from Barbados (8 Oct. 1654), cited in Varnhagen, *História Geral*, iii. 105 n.

[2] Fernão de Queiroz, S.J., *Conquista temporal e espiritual de Ceylão* (ed. Colombo, 1916), p. 968. Dom Braz de Castro, the acting governor-general of Portuguese India, wrote to the crown on 24 Jan. 1655: 'There is no convincing the Dutch of this event, and when we informed them of it through our nearest strongholds they still refused to believe it. Even those of them who were prisoners here, affirmed that it would be easier to conquer Holland than to capture Recife' (Arquivo Historico do Estado da India, Goa, 'Livros das Monções', tomo xxiv, fol. 228). The contemporary chronicler, Abraham de Wicquefort, when he heard of the capitulation of Recife, wrote: 'Cette place est dans une assiette si avantageuse que l'on peut dire que c'est la plus forte de toutes celles des deux Indes, comme elle est sans doute la plus importante de tout le Brésil' (*Histoire des Provinces Unies*, ed. Utrecht, 1864, ii. 324). Cf. also *Hollandtze Mercurius*, Feb. 1654 (ed. Haarlem, 1675), pp. 24–26.

VII

DIPLOMATIC EPILOGUE

1655–69

THE Capitulation of Taborda sealed the fate of Netherlands Brazil in fact as well as on paper, but this consummation was not obvious at the time. The collapse of the colony virtually coincided with the conclusion of the treaty of Westminster, which marked the end of the first Anglo-Dutch war. This meant that the States-General now had sufficient naval strength either to blockade the Tagus or to attack Brazil, if only the vast arrears of the provincial subsidies which had been voted for the navy and the West India Company could be collected. But finance, as usual, was the rub. Although the statement that grass was growing in the streets of Amsterdam by the end of the war with England may have been a picturesque exaggeration, that great city was in no mood to embark on another struggle, even with the hated and despised Portuguese. Peaceful and profitable trade was what her merchant-oligarchs sought above all things. They preferred the very present profits of the Setúbal salt-trade to the problematical benefits from a war of revenge on the 'false and faithless foe' for which Calvinist zealots in Zeeland and elsewhere kept clamouring.[1]

'The affairs of Portugal are detested in this country', wrote the chronicler Aitzema at The Hague in 1651, and they naturally became still more unpopular after the ignominious collapse of New Holland. Even before things had reached this climax, supporters of the West India Company complained that the king of Portugal was subjecting the United Provinces to more 'scorn, affronts, vituperation and shame' than they had ever received from any other power, including their Spanish arch-enemy, although King John IV owed the States-General 'more obligations than he had hairs on his head'.[2] The war-party was

---

[1] Aitzema, *Saken van staet en oorlogh*, iii. 1037, 1125. 'Trouwloose ende meyneedige' was the favourite Dutch term of abuse for the Portuguese.
[2] *Vertoogh over den toestant der West-Indische Compagnie* (Rotterdam, 1651).

too strong to be ignored altogether, even by Amsterdam in its most peaceful mood. The possibility of declaring war on Portugal and blockading the Tagus with a fleet of twenty-five or thirty sail (sixteen or seventeen to be supplied by Amsterdam and ten or twelve by Zeeland) if King John IV refused to restore all or most of Netherlands Brazil was therefore seriously, if intermittently, discussed in the States of Holland in 1654.[1] But the financial embarrassments of the provincial admiralty boards and the virtual bankruptcy of the West India Company prevented anything from being done before public attention was diverted to the Baltic, where one of the recurrent crises between Sweden and Denmark broke out in the summer of 1655. Whatever the value of the Dutch commercial stake in Portugal and Brazil, it was small in comparison with Dutch dependence on the Baltic trade. This was still the mainstay of the maritime prosperity of the United Provinces in general, and of that of Amsterdam and the ports of North-Holland in particular.

The Portuguese government was naturally apprehensive of what might befall them before Swedish aggression diverted Dutch warships to the Baltic. In June 1654 King John IV informed his governors in Brazil that England and the United Provinces now had fleets of over a hundred sail at their disposal. Both of these maritime powers had outstanding claims against the Portuguese government, and might be tempted to seek suitable employment for their fleets by attacking Brazil. Neither the count of Atouguia at Bahia nor Francisco Barreto at Recife received much comfort from the king's assurances that he would have liked to send them reinforcements at this critical juncture, but that unfortunately he had neither the time, the men, nor the money. This was all the more perplexing for them since their own local resources were already strained to the utmost.[2] Although some stalwarts, whom Padre Antonio Vieira described as the *valentões de Portugal*, were quite prepared to take on the English as well as the Dutch and the Spaniards,[3] the king

[1] *Secrete Resolutien van de Ed. Gr. Mog. Heeren Staten van Hollandt en West-Vrieslandt*, 7 and 9 May, 7 and 8 Aug., 28 Nov., and 4 Dec. 1654.

[2] AHU Lisbon, 'Consultas Mixtas', Cod. 15, fols. 120, 158, 162^v, 167, 225^v. Cf. also the correspondence between Lisbon, Bahia, and Recife printed in BNRJ, *Documentos Historicos*, iv. 237–42; ibid. lxvi. 57–63, 70–72, 84–87, 91.

[3] Dr. Antonio de Sousa de Macedo was the protagonist of this school of thought, no doubt owing to his unpleasant experiences as an envoy in England and Holland, 1641–51. Cf. the outbursts in his *Armonia Politica* (The Hague, 1651); A. Pena,

himself had no illusions about the folly of quarrelling with the maritime powers, and he tried earnestly to come to terms with them. Moreover, his efforts to mobilize an armada in 1656 were hampered by the opposition of the citizens of Lisbon. They refused to vote the necessary subsidies, on the grounds that money previously given for the armada had been squandered by the court on other things.[1] All the king's efforts to reach an accommodation with the Dutch failed; but as far as the English were concerned, Portuguese anxieties were relieved by the belated ratification (May 1656) of the treaty imposed by Cromwell two years earlier, and by the subsequent diversion of Blake's fleet against Spain.

The death of King John IV in November 1656, leaving his three-year-old heir to the care of the Queen-Regent, Dona Luisa de Guzman, and a temporary lull in the perennial Baltic crises of the sixteen-fifties, gave the war-party in the United Provinces fresh wind in their sails. The Dutch had made an astonishingly rapid recovery from the disastrous English war, and the increasing tide of commercial prosperity helped temporarily to overcome the opposition of Amsterdam. Intercepted dispatches taken by Zeeland privateers in the South Atlantic indicated that the situation in Brazil was critical. From these captured letters of João Fernandes Vieira and others, it seemed that the victors of 1654 had fallen out among themselves. The Mulatto, Negro, and Amerindian levies which had borne the brunt of the fighting and the hardships in 1645–54, were greatly discontented with their subsequent treatment and were seemingly ripe for revolt.[2] There was also widespread discontent with the exactions of the Brazil Company and its failure to fulfil

---

Arte de Furtar, pp. 273–6; E. Brazão, *Alguns documentos da Biblioteca de Ajuda sôbre a Restauração* (Lisbon, 1940), pp. 67–68.

[1] For the royal decree of 21 Feb. 1656, and the outspoken criticisms of the Lisbon guilds, see Freire de Oliveira, *Elementos para a historia do municipio de Lisboa*, v. 541–94. English reports from Lisbon in 1656–7 noted that the Portuguese Armada Real comprised thirteen 'gallant men of war . . . their ships are good, their soldiers ill-paid, their seamen few and unskilful' (Thurloe, *State Papers*, iv. 112–15, vi. 559–60).

[2] *Twee Verscheyden Remonstrantien . . . door Anthonio Paräupaba*, pp. 18–20. João Fernandes Vieira's letter of 22 Sept. 1655, which is there translated, was addressed to Marcos Rodrigues Tinoco, secretary of the Overseas Council at Lisbon. In an earlier letter, dated 6 Mar. 1652, he had already stressed the necessity of 'sobre tudo tratar bem os negros, indios e mais gentio, que com as suas vidas e fazendas sustentavam a guerra' (original in the Cadaval archives kindly communicated by D. Virginia Rau).

the terms of its charter. The convoy system was not working very satisfactorily, and Zeeland privateers blockaded Bahia with relative impunity on several occasions in 1655–8. It may be added that the Brazil Company's privileges were drastically curtailed in 1657, and in 1664 it was incorporated in the crown.[1]

Doubtless stimulated by these and other indications of Portuguese weakness, the States-General resolved, in the summer of 1657, to declare war on Portugal if that crown would not agree to the immediate restitution of Netherlands Brazil, Angola, and São Thomé. These harsh terms were a reversion to those which King John IV had been ready to accept in 1648; but they were much stiffer than those which the Dutch themselves had offered in 1653. At that time, under the influence of the English war, they suggested an indemnity, and a division of the disputed territory in Brazil. This would have left the West India Company in possession of Recife, Mauritsstad, Olinda, and the captaincies of Itamaracá, Paraíba, Rio Grande do Norte, and Ceará, but the negotiations were broken off, as the Dutch refused to restore any of the conquests they had made in Asia. The two envoys who brought the Dutch ultimatum to Lisbon in September 1657, sailed in the fleet of Wassenaer van Obdam, who was later joined off the mouth of the Tagus by De Ruyter's squadron from the Mediterranean. If the Queen-Regent rejected the Dutch ultimatum, the envoys were instructed to deliver a formal declaration of war, and the naval commanders were to institute a blockade of the Tagus and endeavour to intercept the homeward-bound Brazil fleet.[2]

Despite Portugal's admitted weakness and her critical international position, the Queen-Regent and her councillors courageously rejected the Dutch ultimatum, repeating the former Portuguese offers of a substantial indemnity and generous compensation for the West India Company. Their stand received the unanimous support of public opinion, as all classes were agreed that Portugal could not survive without Brazil,

---

[1] E. Prestage, 'O Conselho de Estado, D. João IV e D. Luisa de Gusmão', *Arquivo Histórico Português*, xi. 21–24; id., 'Tres Consultas do Conselho da Fazenda de 1656 a 1657', *Revista de Historia*, xi. 14–26. For the unpopularity of the Brazil Company see also G. de Freitas, *A Companhia Geral do comércio do Brasil*, pp. 51–54, 75–86; *RIHGB*, xxv. 459–64; *Documentos Historicos*, lxvi, 127–30; *Atas da Camara da Bahia*, iii. 90–91, 156–7, 163, 198–200, 288–90, 320–2, 378–83, 403–6.

[2] Aitzema, *Saken van staet en oorlogh*, iv. 107–9; *Hollandtze Mercurius*, August 1657, pp. 83–92 (ed. 1679).

and war therefore broke out at the end of October. De Ruyter intercepted a part of the homeward-bound Brazil fleet in the first week of November, taking twenty-one out of thirty-four sail, thus inflicting greater damage than Blake had done seven years previously.[1] Immediately afterwards, however, bad weather forced the return of the Dutch warships to their home ports, and the costs of the expedition considerably exceeded the value of the sugar captured in the prizes. Nevertheless, the Armada Real could not venture to challenge the Dutch fleet on the open sea, and it was on diplomatic pressure by France and England that the Portuguese government chiefly relied in this crisis. Both sides set forth their views in well-argued pamphlets, but the Portuguese case was certainly the stronger.[2]

When preparing for war against Portugal, the States-General had realized that the Portuguese government would be bound to seek French and British support against the United Provinces. They sought to forestall this move by giving Cromwell and Mazarin most emphatic assurances that the blockade of the Tagus was not intended to help Spain, directly or indirectly, but solely to obtain satisfaction over Brazil.[3] These assurances naturally failed to carry conviction. Both the French and the English governments remonstrated against the States-General's action and promptly proffered their mediation. France could not afford to see Spain strengthened by the collapse of Portugal, and England's stake in the Portuguese trade was so great that she could not tolerate any interference with this singularly profitable commerce. The States-General at first politely rejected the Anglo-French representations; but when these were renewed more emphatically, and when Amsterdam and the ports of North-Holland also renewed their former opposition to the war, they reluctantly consented to reopen serious negotiations for a settlement of all outstanding disputes with Portugal.

[1] Aitzema, *Saken van staet en oorlogh*, iv. 109–16. Other sources claim only fifteen prizes. Cf. P. J. Blok, *Michiel Adriaanszoon de Ruyter* (The Hague, 1928), pp. 142–5; J. de Graaf, *Scheepsjournal van Admiraal Jacob van Wassenaer van Obdam, betreffende een reis van Hellevoetsluis naar Lissabon en terug in 1657* (Deventer, 1923).

[2] *Razam da guerra entre Portugal e as Provincias Unidas dos Paizes Baixos: com as noticias da causa de que procedeo* (Lisbon, 1657), usually ascribed to Dr. Antonio de Sousa de Macedo, and the Dutch reply, *Manifest ofte Reden van den oorlogh tuschen Portugal ende de Vereenichde Provintien van de Nederlanden . . . Mitsgaders Manifestatie van de leugenen ende valsheden waermede het is vervult* (The Hague, 1659).

[3] *Secrete Resolutien Hollandt en West-Vrieslandt*, 8 and 6 Oct., 21 and 22 Nov. 1657.

These negotiations began in earnest when the Portuguese envoy, D. Fernando Telles de Faro, reached The Hague in July 1658, but they were complicated by the usual sharp differences of opinion between the various provinces. Holland was in favour of acquiescing in the loss of Brazil, in return for a large indemnity and extensive commercial privileges in Portugal and her colonies, similar to those secured by Cromwell in 1654-6. Friesland adopted the same line; but Zeeland, supported by Guelderland, Utrecht, and Groningen, continued to oppose a settlement which did not include the restitution of all or most of Netherlands Brazil. A fleet under De Ruyter was dispatched to cruise off the Portuguese coast this summer, but his blockade of the Tagus can only be described as half-hearted. The most visible result was to give a larger share of the Portuguese trade with Brazil to freighted English shipping.[1]

Portuguese efforts to secure peace with the United Provinces, and thus save their remaining Asian settlements from capture by the Dutch East India Company, were handicapped not only by the Calvinist intransigence of Zeeland, but by English commercial greed. Most seventeenth-century Englishmen regarded Dutch competition in a light very similar to that in which many people regard German or Japanese today. It was an article of faith with them that they could never compete with the Dutch on equal terms, as the latter would always either undersell or outbid them. They found a staunch and very vocal champion in George Downing, the unscrupulous English envoy at The Hague. His French colleague, Comminge, called him *un assez désagréable personage*. This characterization can only be described as a masterpiece of understatement; but although Pepys's description of him as 'so stingy a fellow', a 'perfidious rogue', and 'a most ungrateful villain' is nearer the mark, it cannot be denied that Downing was exceedingly capable and a very amusing letter-writer. His dispatches are among the raciest and most penetrating ever penned by any diplomat, and it requires a major effort of will-power to refrain from quoting them extensively.[2]

[1] Ibid., 26 Jan. and 16 Mar. 1658; P. J. Blok, *M. A. de Ruyter*, pp. 145-7; *Mariner's Mirror*, xxxvii. 212-15.

[2] Japikse, *Verwikkelingen*, pp. 115-27; K. Feiling, *English Foreign Policy, 1660-1672* (London, 1930), pp. 111-16, 121-3; Pepys's *Diary* (ed. Wheatley), under 28 June 1660, 12 and 17 Mar. 1661-2. Downing's dislike of the Dutch was notorious, but he had an even heartier contempt for some people nearer home: 'Pray what

In 1658 George Downing, the ostensible mediator, reported to London that he was doing his best to hinder the conclusion of a projected Luso-Dutch treaty, by the terms of which the Portuguese would be allowed to freight twenty Dutch ships for the Brazil trade. Cromwell's secretary of state, Thurloe, remarked in his ciphered reply: 'You do rightly observe that what the Portugal ambassador has propounded about their giving liberty for twenty ships to be hired for the trade of Brazil is quite contrary to our treaty with the King of Portugal and must not be permitted by you to be part of this treaty with the States-General, and what you write about representing it to the King of Portugal shall be done.'[1] Apart from this English interference, the Luso-Dutch negotiations were further hampered by the spectacular desertion of the Portuguese envoy at The Hague to the Spaniards in April 1659. He was not replaced until the end of the year, when the count of Miranda arrived from Lisbon to resume the discussions in January 1660.

The Restoration of Charles II to the English throne, and his subsequent betrothal to Catherine of Braganza, caused that king to take a personal interest in effecting a peace between Portugal and the United Provinces, but the English attitude to Dutch competition remained unchanged. Clarendon, despite his genuine gratitude to the House of Braganza for what King John IV had done to help the Stuarts in their need, was of the same mind as Thurloe when it came to denying the Dutch equal privileges in the Luso-Brazilian trade: 'I can say no more of the business of Portugal than the King our Master must never endure that the Hollanders should enjoy equal privileges with him in point of trade.' Downing, once again the ostensible mediator between the Dutch and Portuguese negotiators, but once again a source of discord rather than of conciliation, bullied Miranda into inserting a clause in the final draft of the treaty, stipulating that it should be of no effect wherever it ran contrary to the Anglo-Portuguese alliance concluded on the occasion of the marriage of Charles II with 'the Daughter of Portugal'.

As is often the case with eminent statesmen, Clarendon's

hath England lost by naturalizing the Welsh and Scots, and yet those are both poor nations which have nothing of art or ingenuity in them' (Downing to Bennett, 24 Jan. 1664 (o.s.).

[1] Thurloe, *State Papers*, vii. 18, 22, 30, 456–7; Japikse, *Verwikkelingen*, 122 n.

geographical knowledge was extremely hazy. During the marriage negotiations he was evidently under the impression that Bombay, which formed a part of Catherine's dowry, was 'within a very little distance from Brazil',[1] and that its acquisition would thus enable the English to get a greater share of the coveted Brazil trade.

Apart from this anything but disinterested English mediation, the violent squabbles between the different Dutch provinces formed another reason for the long-drawn-out nature of the negotiations at The Hague in 1660–1. Disregarding the provisions of the Union of Utrecht that all such matters must be settled unanimously, the deputies of Holland led by the Grand Pensionary, Johan de Witt, resolved to push the projected treaty through the States-General, despite the opposition of Zeeland, Guelderland, and Groningen, the hesitation of Miranda, and the intrigues of Downing. At the end of July 1661 Miranda was presented with an ultimatum requiring him to sign the treaty within ten days or leave the country. He signed on 6 August, to the undisguised fury of Downing. Owing to English opposition, the Queen-Regent at first refused to ratify the treaty; but Charles II subsequently received such pessimistic reports about Portugal's situation from his envoy at Lisbon, Sir Richard Fanshawe, that he withdrew his objections, reserving the right to claim compensation at the expense of the Portuguese elsewhere. This enabled the Portuguese crown to ratify the treaty on 24 May 1662, and the States-General, after overruling Zeeland's reiterated and wearisome protests, six months later.[2]

The main provisions of the treaty were as follows. Portugal was to pay the United Provinces 4 million *cruzados* in sixteen years as an indemnity for the loss of Netherlands Brazil, and to restore all the artillery taken there which bore the Dutch arms. The Dutch were to be granted trade and residence in Portugal and her overseas possessions on the same terms as those already enjoyed by the English, or which might be granted to the latter in the future. The claims of Dutchmen formerly resident in Netherlands Brazil were to be settled by a mixed commission, one member of which was to be elected arbitrator

---

[1] *Life of Clarendon* (ed. Oxford, 1842–3), pp. 1037, 1046.

[2] Dutch text of the 6 Aug. 1661 treaty in Aitzema, *Saken van staet en oorlogh*, iv. 774–80; Latin and Portuguese texts in J. F. J. Biker, *Collecção de tratados e concertos de pazes*, iv (Lisbon, 1884), pp. 80–117. Cf. also J. H. Rodrigues, *Historiografia e Bibliografia*, nos. 690–8.

with a decisive vote in case of disagreement among the others. The treaty was to be ratified within three months and published within six; but owing to the subsequent disputes and delays, the formal publication did not take place until March and April 1663.

In order to help pay the colossal indemnity and the generous dowry for Catherine of Braganza, the Portuguese government instituted a special tax for this purpose, nearly half of which was levied in Brazil. The collection of this tax lasted for much longer than the sixteen years envisaged in the treaty. Under one pretext or another, Brazilians were still paying it as late as 1830.[1] The payment of debts due to or claimed by former Dutch colonists in Pernambuco proved a simpler matter. Although João Fernandes Vieira had some serious misgivings that he might be called upon to repay Stachouwer or his heirs, there appear to have been only three or four claimants. These private debts were finally liquidated by payments made to the respective heirs in November 1692.[2]

Even with the belated publication of the treaty in the spring of 1663, matters were not finally settled, and each side subsequently accused the other of infringing the terms. The Portuguese claimed the return of their strongholds on the pepper-producing coast of Malabar, which had been taken by the Dutch East India Company in the interval between the signing and the publication of the peace. The Dutch complained that Portugal was defaulting on the payment of the indemnity and evading fulfilment of the commercial clauses. In 1667 the States-General threatened to renew the war, and although this was probably bluff, the threat caused great alarm in Portugal and Brazil.[3] Recourse was again had to Anglo-French diplomatic intervention, and partly as a result of this pressure, a supplementary treaty was signed at The Hague at the end of July 1669. By this treaty, payment of the indemnity was further secured by giving the Dutch the pre-emption on the revenue from the

[1] Varnhagen, _História Geral_, iii. 264. For the original imposition of this tax see _Documentos Historicos_, lxvi. 190–2, 242, 255–6, 337.

[2] AHU, 'Consultas Mixtas', Cod. 15, fols. 140ᵛ, 197ᵛ; _Documentos Historicos_, ix. 235–6; Varnhagen, _Historia das Lutas_, pp. 394–401. A claimant, not cited by Varnhagen, for whom special provision was made in a supplementary article to the 1661 Luso-Dutch treaty, was Huybrecht Brest, former Recife representative of the Zeeland privateering board (Aitzema, _Saken van staet en oorlogh_, iv. 781).

[3] AHU, 'Consultas Mixtas', Cod. 15, fols. 278, 297ᵛ; _Documentos Historicos_, ix. 284 ff.; ibid. lxvii. 17.

salt-duties at Setúbal. Even so, Portugal could not pay off the indemnity until the first decade of the eighteenth century, but she was at last left in unchallenged possession of Brazil.[1]

The Dutch West India Company never recovered from the loss of Netherlands Brazil. Already in 1655 creditors began to distrain the Company's property, but the States-General intervened and put a stop to this. The Company received another blow with the loss of its modest but promising settlement on Manhattan island to the English in 1664, although it had done little to develop its North American colony even after the loss of Pernambuco. A proportion of the revenue derived by the Dutch from the salt-duties at Setúbal was allotted to the Company in 1669, and this enabled it to pay some of its debts and keep afloat a little longer. In 1674, however, its condition was so hopeless that the States-General subjected it to a drastic reorganization under a new charter.[2] The Company now became primarily a slave-trading organization for the export of Negroes from West Africa to the West Indies, and its further vicissitudes do not concern us here.

Why did the Dutch fail to hold at least a part of Netherlands Brazil at a time when their resources were so much greater than those of Portugal, and when (save for a few fleeting interludes) they held command of the sea? The usual reason given for their failure, the semi-bankruptcy and inherent unsoundness of the Dutch West India Company, is not altogether convincing, although it was certainly a contributory factor. But from 1645 onwards, Netherlands Brazil (or what was left of it) was in practice the responsibility of the States-General, which bore the whole cost of the war and decided what policy should be adopted towards Portugal. If Their High Mightinesses had followed a clear and consistent policy in 1645–50, the outcome might well have been very different.

The fight for Pernambuco was fought to the finish, and the valour and tenacity of the besiegers of Recife must always rightly

[1] French and Dutch texts of the 30–31 July 1669 treaty in the undated pamphlet listed in Knuttel, *Catalogus*, ii (2), no. 9752; Portuguese and Latin texts in J. Biker, *Collecção de tratados e concertos de pazes*, iv. 140–69. Cf. also *Documentos Historicos*, lxvii. 123–6. For the working of the Dutch pre-emption of the Setúbal salt-revenues see V. Rau, *Os holandeses e a exportação do sal de Setúbal nos fins do século XVII* (Coimbra, 1950).

[2] O. van Rees, *Staathuishoudkunde*, ii. 218–20.

be assigned the first place in the victory. But they could not have fought on for as long as they did, without the arms and supplies which they received from Portugal and Bahia, even though much of those fell by the way. If the States-General had done what many people urged them to do—blockade the Tagus and attack Bahia—then it is difficult to see how the revolt could have been kept going. The besiegers of Recife, bereft of supplies, would perforce have had either to abandon the struggle or to retire into the backwoods. No outside power was in a condition to help them in 1645–50, even if any had been willing to do so (a most unlikely contingency). Spain abandoned her own Roman Catholic subjects in Brabant to heretic rule rather than imperil the negotiations for the treaty of Munster. She certainly would not have risked that priceless peace for the sake of the *mazombos* (as Francisco Barreto called them) of Brazil.[1] England was still hampered by the aftermath of the civil war, France by the troubles of the Fronde, and Sweden too deeply engrossed in Germany. What, then, prevented the States-General from taking drastic action against Portugal at a time when no other power in Europe could have interfered effectively? Answer: Amsterdam.

There can be no certainty about the might-have-beens of History, but it is probably correct to say that if Amsterdam had been willing to find the money, then a strong Dutch expeditionary force would either have blockaded Lisbon, or taken Bahia, or both, before the war with England broke out in 1652. In that event, it is all Lombard Street to a China orange that Portugal would have been forced to abandon the insurgents in deed as well as in word; as, in fact, we know that King John IV was (however reluctantly) prepared to do. This in turn would, in all probability, have led to the rebellion petering out through lack of supplies, disillusionment, and war-weariness—or at least the Dutch would have been able to contain it within bounds. After 1651 it was, of course, too late. When the States-General finally did decide to embark on a 'tough' policy towards Portugal

---

[1] Francisco Barreto to Pedro de Mello, Bahia, 29 Apr. 1662: 'a lastima de differença que ha de vencer Castelhanos, a lidar com Mazombos' (*Documentos Historicos*, v. 146). By articles 5 and 6 of the treaty of Munster, Spain explicitly recognized the whole of Netherlands Brazil as being Dutch territory, including the regions taken by the Portuguese since June 1645. The French envoy at The Hague in 1647 remarked that the Spaniards were so anxious for peace with the Dutch that 'if necessary they would crucify Christ again to obtain it'.

in 1657, England and France were again unified and first-class powers. They had designs of their own on Portugal, and they were not prepared to stand aside and see that kingdom crushed for the benefit of Spain and the United Provinces.[1]

Some historians, of whom the late Professor Prestage may be taken as the exemplar, have assigned the main reason for the Dutch failure to take drastic action against King John IV, at a time when they could have brought him to his knees, to the intrigues and machinations of the Portuguese envoy at The Hague.[2] This is, I am convinced, a great exaggeration. In denouncing and exposing the corruption and inefficiency of the West India Company, Sousa Coutinho was largely preaching to the already converted. There were plenty of influential people in Holland, and particularly in Amsterdam, who disliked the West India Company on principle, and they had no intention of rescuing it from the Brazilian morass.[3] It was not Sousa Coutinho's bribes, arguments, and protestations, but Amsterdam's view of its own interests, whether enlightened or self-centred, which exercised a decisive influence in the States-General. These interests were not, it will be recalled, precisely the same in 1647–8 as they were in 1649–51; but if Amsterdam chose (as she did) to 'drag her feet' at the critical moments, the States-General were hamstrung in their own policy.

The material resources of Portugal were admittedly far inferior to those of the United Provinces, but in one respect that little kingdom had a great advantage. King John IV did not have to worry about obtaining the concurrence of the Algarve and the Alemtejo before carrying out decisions which had been reached in his council of state. Contrast this unified form of

---

[1] Cromwell at one time contemplated a division of Brazil with the Dutch, but when his idea of a Protestant treaty of Tordesillas was rejected by them, England's main concern was the preservation of Portuguese independence, owing to her large stake in Portugal's overseas trade. Cf. the project submitted through Cornelis Vermuyden in 1653, and printed in Thurloe, State Papers, ii. 125–6; J. Elias, De Tweede Engelsche Oorlog als het keerpunt in onze betrekkingen met Engeland (Amsterdam, 1930), pp. 8–9, 20–21.

[2] Prestage, Diplomatic Relations, p. 209.

[3] The East India Company, very powerful in Amsterdam, certainly regarded the West Indian concern with a jaundiced eye, but the extent of their rivalry has evidently been exaggerated. Allegations that the directors of the former company deliberately sabotaged the latter were widely believed at the time, but probably rest on little or no foundation. For an example of these tales, see Duarte Ribeiro de Macedo's anecdote reproduced in A. Sérgio, Antologia dos Economistas Portugueses (Lisbon, 1924), pp. 379–81.

government with the chaotic situation in the self-styled United Provinces. As Downing wrote from The Hague to his own government in 1664: 'You have infinite advantages upon the account of the form of the government of this country which is such a shattered and divided thing; and though the rest of the provinces give Holland their votes, yet nothing is more evident and certain than that Holland must expect to bear the burden. Even Zeeland can do very little, for that it is very poor, and for the other provinces they neither can nor will.'[1] The province of Holland itself depended on Amsterdam almost as much as did the other provinces on Holland. In the last resort, it was Amsterdam which paid the piper and called the tune.

What the Dutch would have done with north-east Brazil, if they had been able to retain all or part of it, is another question. Johan Maurits had pointed out how suitable immigrants could have been obtained in his day, and others echoed his opinions later on. Whether the States-General would have had the ability to implement this vision is very doubtful. As Violet Barbour has written, views such as these received small attention at Amsterdam, where the great merchant houses preferred an empire of trade and the expectation of quick profits to the uncertain and more distant returns from colonization.[2] As things turned out, this emigration policy could hardly have been effectively tried in the war years which constituted most of the life of the colony. A Dutch empire in the south Atlantic, which seemed on the verge of realization in 1644, did not come to fruition. But that failure was not a foregone conclusion, as is so often alleged. The epic struggle for Pernambuco, like the battle of Waterloo, was a 'demmed close-run thing'.

[1] Downing to Bennett, 24 Jan. 1664 (o.s.), in Japikse, *Verwikkelingen*, p. liv.

[2] V. Barbour, *Capitalism in Amsterdam in the seventeenth century*, pp. 139–40. The directors of the Amsterdam Chamber of the WIC were not, however, invariably unreceptive to more enlightened views. Cf. p. 145, above.

PERSONALIA

I. DUTCH

DE WITH, WITTE CORNELISZOON (*1599–1658*). Born near Den Briel of pacifist Mennonite parents in March 1599, he entered the service of the East India Company in 1616. He soon became the steward and halberdier of the famous governor-general, Jan Pieterszoon Coen, participating in the defence of Jacatra and the foundation of Batavia in 1618–19. Returning to Holland in 1620, he entered the States-General's naval service, cruising in the Mediterranean and off the coast of Portugal in 1621. In 1623–6 he made the circumnavigation of the world with the Nassau fleet, as captain of the *Delft* (50), flagship of Vice-Admiral Schapenham; and in 1628 he was Piet Heyn's flag-captain at the capture of the Mexican silver-fleet in Matanzas Bay. In 1630–2 he was commander of the escort to the 'great fishery' in the North Sea; and in 1637 he became vice-admiral to M. H. Tromp, with whom he soon became and remained on terms of bitter personal enmity. He greatly distinguished himself in the fighting with Oquendo's armada in the English Channel and the subsequent destruction of the Spanish fleet off Dover, in September and October of 1639. In 1640 he captured Matthias Rombout, vice-admiral of Dunkirk and one of the most dreaded of those famous corsairs. In 1641 he convoyed Prince William II over to England for his marriage with Mary Stuart, and cruised in the channel against the Dunkirkers during the following two years. In 1644 he led a convoy of 42 warships and 900 merchant ships through the Sound into the Baltic, repeating this performance with 800 merchant ships in the following year. He was knighted by King Louis XIV for his share in the capture of Dunkirk in 1646, and sailed for Brazil at the end of 1647. After his virtual acquittal in February 1651 he resumed his service in the navy, and fought in all the great battles of the first English war, 1652–4. He was killed at the battle of the Sound (8 November 1658), being mortally wounded in defending his ship against overwhelming odds. He died on board a Swedish flagship, breathing defiance to the last, somewhat after the manner of Sir Richard Grenville. From 1616 to 1654 Witte Corneliszoon de With had served in over fifty actions by land and sea, and had crossed the Equator twenty-four times. Although many sailors detested him as a harsh disciplinarian, he was popular with his own fellow provincials from the Maas region, and was undoubtedly one of the greatest admirals of Holland's golden century.

MARCGRAF, GEORG (MARCGRAVE) (*1610–44*). Born 10 September 1610 at Liebstadt, he studied botany and medicine at the University of Rostock under Professor S. Pauli (1603–80), and astronomy under L. Eichstadt at the University of Stettin. Owing to the ravages of the Thirty Years War, Marcgraf, like so many of his countrymen, later pursued his researches in the more peaceful atmosphere of the United Provinces. In September 1636 he enrolled at the University of Leiden, where he studied medicine, botany, astronomy, and mathematics for fifteen months. Here he became a friend of the learned Johannes de Laet, through whose influence he was able to embark for Brazil and join Johan Maurits's scientific entourage. He sailed on New Year's Day 1638, and reached Recife on the eve of Johan Maurits's departure for the attack on Bahia. Marcgraf lost no time in learning Portuguese, and he was already addressing notes in that language to Johan Maurits during the siege of Bahia, in which he likewise participated. As mentioned previously, Johan Maurits built for Marcgraf the first astronomical observatory in the New World, which was located in one of the towers of the palace of Vrijburg. The prince also provided Marcgraf with an escort of soldiers, commanded by Colonel Mansvelt, who accompanied him on all his botanical and zoological expeditions into the interior. The living specimens which he secured were preserved in Johan Maurits's spacious park, and the dead were carefully dissected, or dried, pressed, and catalogued by Marcgraf.

Johannes de Laet explains in his preface to the *Historia Naturalis Braziliae* of 1648, that Marcgraf had assembled his mathematical and astronomical observations in a massive work entitled *Progymnastica Mathematica Americana* which was divided into three parts. The first section dealt with astronomy and optics, and included a list of all the stars observed between the Tropic of Cancer and the South Pole; numerous miscellaneous observations of all the planets and of solar and lunar eclipses; 'new and true theories' concerning Venus and Mercury, based on his own observations; theory of refractions and parallaxes; observations of sunspots, and many other astronomical data. The second section, comprising geography and geodesy, also contained a discussion of the theory of longitude and methods of calculating it, together with a refutation of 'the errors of ancient and modern geographers'. The third section comprised a set of astronomical tables entitled *Tabulae Mauritii Astronomicae*. Unfortunately this work did not survive in a completed form, and only some fragmentary notes and memoranda which had been used in compiling it were left for De Laet and Golius to decipher.

Of Marcgraf's numerous botanical and zoological excursions into the hinterland, we only have the dates of those which were undertaken in 1639–40, but it is known that he made many more. The material which he collected on these trips, and which was subsequently brought to Europe by Johan Maurits, served for over a century and a half as the scientific basis for the study of Brazilian fauna, flora, and anthropology. Marcgraf had originally intended returning to Europe with Johan Maurits in May 1644, but his plans were changed at the last minute and he went instead to Angola. There he died from an attack of fever shortly after his arrival at Luanda, in July or August 1644. For further details of his surviving works, and the very high opinion of him held by modern scientists who have worked in the same fields, the reader is referred to Taunay's 'Escorço Biografico'.

JOHAN MAURITS, *of Nassau-Siegen (1604–79)*. His early military service in the Low Countries and his governorship of Brazil have been described above (Chs. III and IV), and his career after his return to Europe in 1644 may be resumed as follows. He was soon appointed lieutenant-general of cavalry and commander of the Dutch garrison at Wezel, besides participating in the Flanders campaigns of 1644–6. The fighting on this front in the last years of the war with Spain was carried on rather half-heartedly by the Dutch, many of whom were growing increasingly nervous of their powerful French ally. Johan Maurits was able to spend much of his time at The Hague and in Germany, where family disputes with his Roman Catholic relations called for his presence at Siegen.

He was asked to return to Brazil as military and naval commander-in-chief in the summer of 1647, but the proposal came to nothing, as explained in Chapter V above. It may be added that Francisco de Sousa Coutinho doubted the genuineness of Johan Maurits's professions of goodwill towards the *moradores* of Pernambuco, but we know from the count's own correspondence and his statements to the States-General in September 1647 that the Portuguese envoy was wrong on this point. Sousa Coutinho had previously tried to win over Johan Maurits in 1644–5, but he took refuge in polite generalities. This annoyed Sousa Coutinho, who, not understanding that Johan Maurits had no wish to betray his adopted country, reported irritably to King John IV (16 January 1645): 'I realized that we had little to hope from Count Maurice ever since the first time I met him, and each day that passes strengthens my conviction on this point. For even though he was not born in Holland, he was brought up among the Hollanders, and he has absorbed a great deal of their character.' As for the idea that Johan Maurits might be persuaded to enter the Portuguese service, 'once returned home and back to the drinking-parties of this country, he thought no more about it'. This low opinion of Johan Maurits's character did not prevent Sousa Coutinho from claiming great credit for inducing the count not to return to Brazil two years later. In September 1647 he wrote: 'It is most important that this man should not go, because he is so greatly beloved in these provinces and in those of Brazil, that he would have taken from here the best officers, who originally volunteered to go and withdrew after he declined. On the other side of the Atlantic he might cause a revolution in the attitude of the *moradores*, if not in all of them at least in those who are already weary of the war.' A month later he wrote: 'My diverting him from this enterprise was the greatest service made to your majesty.' As noted above, the real reason for Johan Maurits's disinclination to return to Brazil was that he was not given the full powers and the full number of men for which he asked. He may, however, have been speaking from the heart when he assured Sousa Coutinho that he would willingly go back to Pernambuco as governor and end his days there in time of peace, but added that he had no wish to return to a war-torn colony.

The Brazilian project having fallen through, Johan Maurits gladly accepted the offer of Friedrich Wilhelm, the Elector of Brandenburg, to become Stadtholder of Cleves, one of the Hohenzollern possessions along the Rhine. For the next twenty years he spent most of his time in this territory, although he paid frequent and extended visits to The Hague, Berlin, and other places. In 1652 he was created a prince of the Holy Roman Empire by Ferdinand III, and invested as Grand Master of the Brandenburg bailiwick of the Order of St. John of Jerusalem. While in Germany, he spent much of his time in his favourite pursuits of architecture and landscape-gardening, and he sold part of his Brazilian collections to the Great Elector in return for some landed property. He also took a lively interest in the foundation of the Protestant University of Duisburg. In 1651 he rejected another tentative suggestion that he might return to Brazil; and it would seem that next year he was seriously considered for the supreme command at sea, during the temporary disgrace of Lieut.-Admiral M. H. Tromp in the course of the war with England. At any rate, the well-informed Abraham de Wicquefort, writing to Queen Christina of Sweden at the end of July 1652, reported: 'Mesme ont esté en deliberation de faire election d'un General de mer et conferer cette charge a M. le Comte Maurice, mais puisque S.E. ne peut pas bien souffrir la mer, ie crois qu'elle s'en excusera: aussi l'affaire n'a pas esté portee encore a l'Assemblee des Estats Generaux.' In 1658 he acted as the Brandenburg representative at the election and coronation of the Emperor Leopold at Frankfurt.

While in Germany, Johan Maurits still retained his rank and emoluments as lieutenant-general of the Dutch cavalry and garrison-commander of Wezel, but he was most anxious to secure the post of field-marshal which fell vacant with Brederode's death in September 1655. He indulged in rather unseemly rivalry with his cousin, the

Frisian Stadtholder, Willem Frederik, over this vacancy, reminding the States-General that the latter had played a prominent part in Prince William II's abortive attempt on Amsterdam five years previously. Neither of these two Nassau princes secured the coveted dignity then, since the province of Holland under the leadership of Johan de Witt was against the post being filled, and blocked all efforts to do so for the next twelve years. It may be added that although Johan Maurits took a keen practical interest in military affairs, personally superintending artillery tests on the beach at Scheveningen and even inventing a new type of gun-carriage for horse-artillery, he was not a great commander.

When Charles II was invited to resume the throne of England in the summer of 1660, he was lodged in the Mauritshuis during his stay at The Hague. Johan Maurits was wont to boast in later years, 'it was in my house that Charles II became a king', and its splendours attracted the admiration of the English courtiers. They were particularly impressed with the main staircase, 'one of the finest and costliest of all Europe, because it is double, most large, and all built of a most rare Indian [= Brazilian] wood', as Sir William Lower reported in his contemporary *Relation*. Moreover, in his capacity of Brandenburg representative, Johan Maurits was the first person of princely rank or status to congratulate Charles on his accession, and so he was received in the most flattering manner by that monarch. Possibly in the hope of utilizing this favourable impression, Johan Maurits was sent as chief Brandenburg envoy on a mission to England in the spring of the next year, his colleague being the Great Elector's closest adviser, Daniel Weimann. This embassy had the triple object of discussing the guardianship of the young William of Orange, the possibility of a match between Charles II and Mary of Orange (the last unwed daughter of Amalia Von Solms), and the conclusion of an alliance with England to curb Swedish aggression. The marriage project was rendered still-born by Charles II's betrothal to Catherine of Braganza, and no great change was made in the guardianship of the Prince of Orange, but a defensive alliance between Brandenburg and England was concluded in July 1661.

The outbreak of the second Anglo-Dutch war and the bellicose bishop of Munster's attack on the United Provinces, led to Johan Maurits's appointment as commander-in-chief on the eastern frontier in 1665. His purely defensive and unenterprising leadership in the brief campaign which followed was severely criticized by Johan de Witt. But the Grand Pensionary was himself largely to blame for the poor showing of the Dutch army in 1665-6, since his fear of the monarchical tendencies of the House of Orange-Nassau had led him deliberately to neglect the army. Moreover, Johan Maurits's initiative was curbed by the presence of field-deputies from the States-

General at his headquarters, whose sanction had to be obtained for all moves. In any case, Johan Maurits later received a grant of 10,000 guilders for his participation in this campaign, and was finally promoted to field-marshal in January 1668.

Johan Maurits made a much better showing in the critical campaigns of 1672–4, when the very existence of the United Provinces was at stake. He particularly distinguished himself at the battle of Senef (11 August 1674), where, as the Prince of Orange under whom he served subsequently told Sir William Temple, 'he had with the greatest industry that could be, sought all occasions of dying fairly at the battle, without succeeding, which had given him great regrets. And I do not wonder at it', added the English ambassador, 'considering his age of about seventy-six and his long habits both of gout and stone.' His shattered health prevented him from taking any further active part in the French war, and although he was appointed governor of Utrecht, he spent most of his time at The Hague. In 1676 he returned for good to his Rhineland territory, where he designed and superintended the construction of his own grave in idyllic rural surroundings. A broken man physically, but in full possession of all his mental faculties, he passed away peacefully on 20 December 1679.

VAN DEN BRANDE, CORNELIS (VAN DER BRANDEN, VAN BRANDT, &c.). I have not found the date of his birth, death, nor when he came to Brazil, but he was one of the veterans of this colonial war. He had evidently been some time in the country when he was stationed as a captain in the garrison of Fort Frederik Hendrik on the outskirts of Mauritsstad in 1634. He distinguished himself at Arciszewski's victory of the Mata Redonda, and again in Johan Maurits's siege of Bahia, where he captured the outlying fort of São Felipe in the opening stages of the campaign. In 1639 he was major commanding Fort Maurits on the River São Francisco; but he was defeated and captured by Dom Francisco de Moura in an ill-judged foray along the Rio Real in the following year. He remained for some time a prisoner at Bahia, and presumably was released after the declaration of the truce in 1642. He returned to the United Provinces at some unascertained date, and in September 1647 he was commissioned as one of the colonels of the five regiments raised for service in Brazil. He fought with great distinction at the first battle of the Guararapes, and if the *Journael van de Reyse* written by someone in his own regiment is to be trusted, it was largely due to his leadership after Von Schoppe had retired wounded that the defeat was not worse than it was. Owing to his knowledge of the terrain around Bahia, he was associated with Van Goch in the command of the expedition which ravaged the *Reconcavo* in December 1648. He fought in the second battle of the Guararapes, but this time he was unable to prevent a complete débâcle, and was lucky to escape with his life. Evidently feeling that there was no future in Netherlands Brazil, he resigned and repatriated later in 1649, but I have not been able to find out what became of him subsequently.

From the wording of his dispatches and reports, which are among the most readable of those from Netherlands Brazil, he would seem to have been a zealous Calvinist, but he was not without his detractors. The *Brasyls Schuytpraetjen* (1649) accuses him of peculation, cowardice, and incompetence, adding: 'In the official memorandum of Count Maurits he is registered as a liar; and although the Zeelanders would make a saint of this man, that cannot be done, for his cowardly and dissembling deeds are too well known to the common man.' Needless to say, the self-styled 'impartial' compiler of this scurrilous pamphlet was anything but open-minded, though it may perhaps be deduced from this outburst (and from Haecxs' *Journal* of 7 November 1647) that Van den Brande was a Zeelander. A contemporary portrait of him is reproduced in Dr. J. van Hoboken, *Witte de With in Brazilië*.

VAN DER DUSSEN, ADRIAEN JACOBSZ. (*1585–1642*). Born at Delft in 1585, he may have gone out to the East Indies as early as 1602 in the fleet of Wybrant van Warwijck; and he certainly went out there as assistant in the East India Company's fleet which left at the end of 1607, under the command of Admiral P. W. Verhoeff. Van der Dussen was stationed for two years in Banda and the Moluccas, but was then sentenced to be dismissed from the Company's service for criminal adultery (Governor-General Both wrote that young Van der Dussen was *abondomatissimo mette hoererije*). Having promised amendment, he was re-employed almost immediately, partly on account of his influential connexions at Delft, and partly because of his outstanding administrative abilities. Being a good Malay speaker, he was posted to Johore in 1614, and subsequently served in many other places in the Indonesian archipelago, becoming lieutenant-governor of the Banda islands in May 1616. Just over a year later he was again sentenced for 'adultery and whoring', but once again soon re-employed and sent back to Banda. He commanded a company in the capture of Jacatra (Jakarta) at the end of May 1619, and two months later he was appointed *opperhoofd* or chief of the Company's agency at Jambi in Sumatra, where he remained until the end of 1623. He returned to Holland in 1624, and settled at Rotterdam, where he filled various important municipal posts between 1629 and 1636. I do not know what relation he was to 'the traitor Van der Dussen of Rotterdam', whose proposals for reducing the Dutch to the King of Spain's allegiance in 1628 are printed in the *Kron. Hist. Gen. Utrecht*, xxv. 159–66. I do not think, however, that he was identical, as the writer of the 1628 proposals came home (at least temporarily) in 1618. In July 1632 Adriaen van der Dussen was appointed a director of the Rotterdam Chamber of the West India Company, and after his return from Brazil in 1640 he again settled at Rotterdam, where he died in 1642.

VAN GOCH, MICHIEL (*1603–68*). He was born at Flushing in 1603, and studied (but apparently did not graduate) at Leiden University. He also travelled extensively in Europe to complete his education, and seems to have been a good linguist. At the time of his appointment to the High Council at Recife in 1645, he was already a magistrate and the Pensionary of Flushing, and a deputy of the province of Zeeland in the States-General. As mentioned above (p. 176), his voyage to Brazil in 1645–6 was a singularly stormy and difficult one. If the testimony of his secretary, Pierre Moreau, is to be believed, Van Goch behaved very well on this voyage. He suppressed two mutinies on board his flagship, one in the English Channel and another off the coast of Portugal, with an admirable mixture of tact and firmness. He also had a quarrel about precedence with his Hollander colleague, Simon van Beaumont, which reflects the typical and continual jealousy between Holland and Zeeland, but he had the satisfaction of being the first member of the new government to reach Recife.

During the next six years Michiel van Goch was by far the most active and conspicuous member of the High Council in Brazil. Schonenburgh was an old man and never ceased to regret having come to Brazil at all. Haecxs was much younger, but was mainly employed on commercial and financial affairs, and was often prostrated by long bouts of illness. Van Goch, on the other hand, was always to the fore in time of trouble. It was he who organized and led the expedition which sacked the *reconcavo* in December 1648, and it was he who acted as field-deputy at the second battle of the Guararapes in February 1649. When the High Council had to send someone to remonstrate with the prickly Admiral Witte de With at Paraíba, it was Van Goch who was selected. When the same Council had to select someone to try to pacify the mutineers in the States' warships and prevent them from returning to Europe, it was again Van Goch who volunteered for this difficult task; and one which, on the second occasion at least, exposed him to great personal danger. It was also Van Goch who was sent home in June 1653 to make a last desperate appeal for assistance before it was too late, and to point out that the whole situation might yet be retrieved and reversed if adequate help was sent to Recife in time, or if drastic action was taken against Portugal. The complications caused by the English war and the opposition of Amsterdam prevented anything from being done until news came of the collapse of the colony. From Aitzema's references to this mission we learn that Van Goch was particularly embittered against the Portuguese, whom he described as 'the falsest, cruellest, and most knavish nation in the world'.

Being unable to return to Recife, Van Goch resumed his position as Pensionary of Flushing in 1655, and he later became auditor-general of Zeeland. He was a member of the delegation from the States-General which congratulated Charles II on his accession, and in 1664 he was appointed Dutch ambassador to England. Professor Keith Feiling calls him 'the weak and vapouring Van Goch', but this characterization seems to me to be unfair. Van Goch had a very difficult if not an impossible task, since neither government could nor would yield over the main points that were in dispute. 'Coûte que coûte', honest George Monk, Earl of Albemarle, told Van Goch, 'England must be allowed its share in world trade.' Another and still more honest sea-captain put the fundamental issue still more bluntly: 'The trade of the world is too small for us two, therefore one must down.' Van Goch stayed on in England for a twelvemonth after the outbreak of war, sending reports on the situation to his own government, just as Downing was doing in so racy a fashion from The Hague. He finally returned home in December 1665, resuming his post as auditor-general of Zeeland, and became a councillor of Flushing in January 1667. He died in 1668.

II. LUSO-BRAZILIAN

DE MORAES, MANUEL (*c. 1596–c. 1651*). Born at São Paulo about 1596, probably with a good deal of Amerindian blood in his veins, Manuel de Moraes, like most children of that region, spoke fluent Tupí. After studying at the Jesuit College of Bahia, he became an ordained priest, taking the ordinary vows of the Society, and was superior of one of the Indian mission-villages in Pernambuco at the time of the Dutch invasion. His superiors had every reason to be satisfied with him so far, and a confidential report of 1631 highly commends his intellectual abilities. As related in the text, he fought at the head of his savage parishioners against the heretic invaders until January 1635, when he was captured near Paraíba. To the great embarrassment of his compatriots and co-religionists, and for no readily ascertainable reason, he now threw in his lot openly with the Dutch. He dressed as a layman, outwardly professed Protestantism, and jeered at Portuguese prisoners who would not eat meat on Good Friday. Just before his desertion to the Dutch, disquieting reports had reached his superiors at Bahia concerning his disregard of the sixth (R.C.) commandment. He was accordingly expelled from the Society for these misdemeanours, and in due course burnt in effigy at an *auto-da-fé* at Lisbon (6 April 1642). The Paulista enemies of the Jesuits called him 'the greatest heretic and apostate which the Church of God has nowadays', and alleged that he was directly responsible for the deaths of thousands of innocent men, women, and children at the hands of the heretic Hollanders and their cannibal Tapuya allies. His name became a hissing and a reproach to the Society of Jesus. This spectacular apostasy was compared with that of the Jesuit Provincial in Japan, Christovão Ferreira, who, after apostatizing under torture in 1633, married a Japanese wife and acted as adviser to the anti-Christian Inquisition.

After spending some time at Recife, Manuel de Moraes was sent to Holland, where he married twice, both times with Calvinist women, by whom he had three children. After the death of his first wife at Harderwijk, he married 'one of the most beautiful women in the country', who 'lived next door to the library of Leiden University'. He was a familiar figure to the students and the faculty at this university, and was patronized by Johannes de Laet, to whom he gave much valuable information about Brazil. He also began to compile a work of his own on that country, but it does not seem to have got very far. During his years in Holland he frequently met Portuguese prisoners at Amsterdam, some of whom thought that he was a crypto-Catholic, while others maintained that he was a genuine Calvinist convert. Whatever he was, he was still in one respect a son of Loyola. In the course of a heated argument with a Brazilian Capuchin friar, he told the latter that 'a cook in the Company of Jesus knew more than a Franciscan scholar'.

Abandoning his second wife and children (according to his own account), he returned to Pernambuco at the end of 1643, and engaged in the Brazil-wood business, felling trees in the interior for transportation to Recife. He was captured by João Fernandes Vieira's men a few days after the revolt broke out, but saved his skin by changing sides again without delay. He acted as self-appointed chaplain at the battle of Tabocas, but was later arrested by Martim Soares Moreno and sent to Bahia, whence he was shipped to Lisbon for examination and trial by the Inquisition. During these proceedings he took the line that he had always remained a genuine Roman Catholic at heart, and had never more than outwardly conformed to Calvinism; nor did he regard his formal expulsion from the Society of Jesus as binding. He admitted that he had attended Calvinist services occasionally, but pleaded that he knew no Dutch, and had never understood a single word of what was said. As for his marriages, he did not regard either of them as a state of holy matrimony, but merely as carnal concupiscence with heretic women, for which 'fleshly sins' he professed repentance and pleaded forgiveness. His statements were substantially accepted by the Inquisitors, and although sentenced to a term of imprisonment, he was soon released on the grounds of chronic ill health in March 1648. He apparently died in 1651, and his case is certainly one of the most singular that ever occurred in the annals of the Holy Office.

FERREIRA, GASPAR DIAS (*c. 1595–c. 1656*). Born at Lisbon about 1595, he emigrated to Brazil in 1618, and is variously reported as having been (*a*) a wealthy planter, and (*b*) only a poor shopkeeper, at the time of the Dutch invasion in 1630. According to Calado, whose allegations in the *Valeroso Lucideno* are of course subject to caution, he was of New-Christian origin, the bishop of Bahia declining to ordain one of his relatives in 1643 on those grounds. Gaspar Dias Ferreira indignantly denied that he was a Marrano, but his denial is just as suspect as Calado's allegation. The spiteful but well-informed friar further alleges that Gaspar Dias Ferreira was the first *morador* who voluntarily passed over to the invaders, taking up residence in Recife with his wife and family, and giving the Dutch the most detailed information about his compatriots. This may well be true, although it was only after the arrival of Johan Maurits that he really came into his own as an arch-collaborator. Francisco de Sousa Coutinho later termed him the *Nayre* of Johan Maurits, and he speedily became what would nowadays be called the governor-general's principal 'contact-man'. He acted as the latter's adviser during the expedition to Bahia in 1638, and Johan Maurits seems often to have sought his opinion on questions concerning the Pernambuco *moradores*. He was a town councillor of Olinda and Mauritsstad from 1637 to 1640, and was associated with the construction of the bridge between Mauritsstad and Recife in 1644. Thanks to his whole-hearted collaboration with the invaders, he became a very wealthy man, and the owner of at least two sugar plantations. Calado alleges that he used his position to extort sugar and money from the *moradores* and Roman Catholic clergy, ostensibly for bribing Johan Maurits and the members of the High Council, although he retained for himself most of what he acquired in this way. These allegations are largely confirmed from independent sources, including the formal complaints of Benedictine and Carmelite friars. He also organized a contraband slaving venture to Cape Verde, in collaboration with Johan Maurits, which earned the latter a dignified rebuke from the Heeren XIX when this scandal came to light.

Gaspar Dias Ferreira accompanied his protector back to Holland in 1644, being about the most hated man in the colony, according to both Dutch and Portuguese accounts. He continued to be Johan Maurits's trusted adviser on Brazilian affairs, and it was doubtless through his patron's influence that he was officially naturalized as a citizen of the United Provinces in February 1645. On the instructions of Johan Maurits he offered to help Caspar Barlaeus in the compilation of the *Rerum per Octennium*, but it is not clear whether he actually did so. Notwithstanding all the grace and favours which he had received from the Dutch, Gaspar Dias Ferreira was at this time carrying on a treasonable correspondence with both Seville and Lisbon. Unfortunately for him, a ship with some of these compromising letters on board was captured by Barbary rovers and taken to Algiers in August 1645. A local Jewish merchant who read the missives was struck by their importance and sent them to a coreligionist at Amsterdam, who promptly handed them over to the Heeren XIX. Gaspar Dias Ferreira was arrested on a charge of high treason on 20 October 1645, and brought to trial some months later. He was lucky to escape a death-sentence, being condemned to forfeit his recently acquired nationality, to pay a fine of 30,000 florins, and to serve a seven-year prison sentence to be followed by banishment. His sojourn in jail did not prevent him from protesting his innocence to the Dutch, nor from sending Francisco de Sousa Coutinho periodic advice and information about the Dutch in Brazil from his cell.

He effected a spectacular escape from prison on the night of 17/18 October 1649, leaving an elegant Latin letter addressed to the States-General in justification of his actions. Successfully evading the hue and cry which was raised after him, he made his way to Portugal where he was well received, although Calado's *Valeroso Lucideno* which denounced him in such unmeasured terms had only been published a twelvemonth previously. The marquis of Montalvão had always warmly advocated his cause at the Portuguese court; and although Sousa Coutinho had at first denounced him as an unscrupulous traitor to both sides, he later changed his opinion, 'for there is nobody more experienced in the affairs of Brazil'. King John IV accepted his lying assurances that only through his influence had Johan Maurits tolerated the friars and secular clergy in Pernambuco, and Calado's aspersions against him were silenced. Despite his real or alleged Jewish blood, he was awarded a knighthood in the Order of Christ and another was conferred on one of his sons, and he himself received the *foro* (patent) of a *fidalgo-cavalheiro* in 1652-4. Regardless of his denunciation of João Fernandes Vieira as a perfidious Mulatto in 1645, he had the effrontery to write to the insurgent leader in September 1652, asking to be appointed the latter's official representative at Lisbon. He was still alive and flourishing in 1655; but I cannot trace what subsequently became of this adventurer who showed such singular skill in hunting with the Dutch hounds and running with the Portuguese hare. It is worth noticing that although Fr. Rafael de Jesus in his *Castrioto Lusitano* of 1679 reproduced (without mentioning his source) some of Calado's

allegations against Gaspar Dias Ferreira in the *Valeroso Lucideno* of
1648, the Benedictine chronicler carefully avoided specifying this
collaborator by name, merely referring to him as a Jew.

VIEIRA, ANTONIO, *S.J.* (*1608–97*). Born at Lisbon on 6 February
1608, of humble ancestry, his paternal grandmother being a Mulatto
serving-woman in the household of the counts of Unhão, and his
maternal grandfather an armourer. Six years later he went with his
parents to Bahia, where his father, Christovão Vieira Ravasco, had
been given the post of secretary to the high court of justice. The
young Vieira was educated at the local Jesuit college, where he soon
made his mark as a brilliant pupil, entering the Society as a novice
at the age of fifteen. He was an eyewitness of the Dutch invasion in
1624–5, of which he wrote the best and fullest account, subsequently
spending some time at Olinda, where he lectured on rhetoric at the
Jesuit college. Returning to Bahia before the Dutch attack in 1630,
he was already renowned as an eloquent preacher at the time of his
ordination in 1635. His fervour inspired the defenders of the colonial
capital against Johan Maurits in 1638, and it was he who was chosen
to preach the victory sermon after the Dutch withdrawal. He went
to Portugal in 1641 with the emissaries who brought the news of the
colony's adhesion to King John IV, whose interest and patronage he
at once secured, and whose court-preacher he speedily became. The
king was obviously fascinated by Vieira's many-sided genius, and
considered him to be in some ways 'the greatest man in the world'.
Vieira returned the compliment by his whole-hearted devotion to
the new monarch, in whose person he saw the fulfilment of the
Sebastianist prophecies which were so widely spread in Portugal,
and whose resurrection after his death in 1656 he confidently
expected for many years.

The king sought Vieira's advice on all questions of major importance, particularly those connected with Brazil, being so impressed
by the Jesuit's knowledge of the colony that he assumed that he was
born there. From February to July of 1646 he was employed (dis-
guised as a layman) on a confidential diplomatic mission to France
and Holland, principally in connexion with the abortive attempt to
reach an agreement with the Dutch over the purchase of Pernambuco. Despite the failure of this effort, he was employed on another
similar mission in the following year (August 1647–October 1648),
which this time envisaged the outright cession of Pernambuco to the
Dutch. He was also ordered to ascertain the possibility of arranging
a suitable French marriage for the Infante Dom Theodosio, but both
projects fell through. On his way to Holland, Vieira spent a few
weeks in England, visiting London and Dover in September 1647,
and while in Holland he arranged for the purchase of warships and

naval stores for the Portuguese navy. From January to July 1650 he was employed on a secret mission to Rome, partly with the object of putting out feelers for a Spanish marriage with Dom Theodosio, and partly to try to add fuel to the flames of the revolt at Naples against the suzerainty of Spain. In neither respect was he able to achieve anything, and he was forced to leave Rome precipitately, in order to escape being assassinated on the orders of the Spanish ambassador. These successive failures evidently blunted the keenness of his inclination for diplomacy, since two years later he rejected the invitation of the count of Penaguião to accompany him as his chaplain on his embassy to England.

At the end of 1652 Vieira was sent by his superiors to the Maranhão mission-field, where he remained for the next nine years, with the exception of a brief visit to Portugal (June 1654–April 1655). He had already learnt Tupí when catechizing the Amerindians of the mission villages near Bahia in his younger days, and he now studied the local dialects as well. Although he had left Lisbon for the Maranhão with considerable reluctance, once arrived in the colony he displayed as much energy, zeal, and ardour in the pursuit of souls as he had previously employed in the exercise of worldly wisdom. He travelled extensively in the interior, and has left us graphic accounts of several of the tribes along the Amazon and some of its tributaries. Owing to his outspoken criticism of the colonists for their endeavours to enslave the Amerindians, he aroused the intense hostility of the local *moradores*, by whom he was arrested and deported, together with all the other Jesuits in Pará and the Maranhão, in September 1661.

On his enforced return to Lisbon, Vieira was at first received with sympathy and favour by the court, but the palace revolution which brought the count of Castel-Melhor to power in June 1662 likewise resulted in the exile or disgrace of Vieira and his friends. He had long been an object of dislike and suspicion to the Inquisition, partly on account of his unorthodox Messianic and Sebastianist beliefs, but mainly because of his outspoken advocacy of toleration for the hated Marranos or New-Christians. He was arraigned by this dreaded tribunal on various charges, and after a lengthy legal process, in which he defended himself with great skill and pertinacity, he was finally sentenced to be deprived of his licence to preach and to be imprisoned in a monastery, in December 1667. The final stages of his trial coincided with another palace revolution which resulted in the disgrace of Castel-Melhor, the deposition of King Affonso VI, and the accession of the Prince-Regent, Dom Pedro, and his friends to power.

Vieira was speedily released from his confinement, but not being as fully reinstated at court as he had hoped, he shook the dust of

Lisbon off his feet and left for Rome in August 1669, partly to plead his own cause there, and partly to forward that of the Marranos which he had so much at heart. He obtained from the Pope a personal safe-conduct which protected him from any further interference by the Portuguese Inquisition; but his efforts to secure a degree of toleration for the Marranos proved abortive in the long run, although his activities caused the Portuguese branch of the Holy Office much anxiety. He enjoyed a great success as a preacher in Rome, where he was the favourite orator of both Queen Christina of Sweden and the Jesuit General, Oliva. He remained in Rome until May 1675, when he returned to Portugal; but, to his unconcealed disappointment, he never secured the same degree of influence with Dom Pedro as he had had with the Prince-Regent's father. Finally disillusioned with court politics, he returned to Bahia in 1681, where he remained until his death sixteen years later. He died a complete physical wreck but mentally active and alert to the last.

Apart from his feverish diplomatic and missionary activity, Vieira's place in Portuguese and Brazilian history is secure for all time. As Southey observed long ago, better Portuguese has never been written than that penned by this remarkable man. His letters and sermons are still as readable today as they were 300 years ago, and of how few writers of any age and country can that be said. All the most competent literary critics are agreed that Antonio Vieira is the finest exemplar of Portuguese prose, and that he and Luis de Camões are the two writers who have extracted the most from the genius, style, and structure of the Portuguese language.

VIEIRA, JOÃO FERNANDES (16??–81). The arguments concerning this highly controversial figure begin with his birth at an uncertain date and place in the island of Madeira. His official biographer, Fr. Rafael de Jesus, states in the *Castrioto Lusitano* (1679) that Vieira was born at Funchal in 1613, but Vieira himself gives two different dates for this event. Giving evidence before a representative of the Inquisition in 1647, he stated that he was then 'a little more or less than thirty-seven years old'. Writing to the Misericordia at Funchal in 1672, he then stated that he was born there in the year 1602. His parentage is even more dubious, since both Vieira himself and his three contemporary panegyrists, Fr. Manuel Calado, Fr. Rafael de Jesus, and Diogo Lopes de Santiago, all carefully avoid mentioning the names of his parents, and content themselves with vague and totally unsubstantiated statements that he was of noble birth. Official *alvarás* of 1649–52 give his father's name as Francisco de Ornellas Moniz; but the *moradores* who petitioned for his removal from the command in 1646 imply that this man was merely his putative father, and they state categorically that his mother was a Mulatto prostitute with a shapely figure ('filho de hũa mulata Rameira a quem chamão a bemfeitinha e de hũ homem que lhe dão por pay'). The fact that he was a Mulatto is also attested by several contemporaries who knew him well, including the Rabbi Isaac Aboab da Fonseca in his epic poem *Zekher asiti leniflaot El*, and by several well-informed Dutch pamphleteers. Gaspar Dias Ferreira, who was the rival of João Fernandes Vieira for the position of the most trusted collaborator of the Dutch, terms him 'scelere et perfidia illius mulati Vieira' in a letter written to their mutual patron, Johan Maurits, in November 1645. On the other hand, the wording of an application by one of his natural sons for a knighthood in the Order of Christ in 1683 implies that João Fernandes Vieira himself had the requisite purity of blood; but as his own *processo* has disappeared from the records of the Order, this isolated testimony is of no great weight among the numerous sworn depositions to the contrary.

The date on which he left Madeira and emigrated to Pernambuco is also the subject of vague and conflicting statements, but it is clear that he was in very poor and humble circumstances at the time of the Dutch invasion in 1630. He seems to have fought in the guerrilla warfare of the next five years, but at the time of the surrender of the *arraial* in 1635 he was only a butcher-boy in the camp, 'from whom one could get anything for a sop, or a puff of tobacco', if the writer of the *Brasylsche Breedebyl* (1647) is to be believed. From this point onwards, however, his rise was astonishingly rapid.

Probably through showing Stachouwer where the riches of the luckless Marrano, Pantaleão Monteiro, were hidden, João Fernandes Vieira now became the trusted confidant of this influential member of the local government. Within a few years he was not merely Stachouwer's protégé but his partner, and the Dutchman left him with full powers of attorney over all his interests when he returned to Holland. Vieira actively collaborated in the establishment and functioning of Dutch rule, being a town councillor of Mauritsstad in 1641–3, a contractor for the collection of sugar-tithes and Brazil-wood, an official hunter of runaway slaves, and (most remarkable of all) captain of a squadron of the local yeomanry which was mainly if not exclusively composed of Dutchmen. By 1645 he was the owner of at least five sugar plantations, although it must be added that these had not been paid for. Vieira was the second largest debtor to the Dutch in the colony, his outstanding debts of 321,000 florins being only exceeded by the sum owed by Jorge Homem Pinto which amounted to over a million. Despite the claims of Calado and Rafael de Jesus, and despite Vieira's own allegations in later life, there is no reliable evidence that he actively plotted a rebellion against the Dutch before pressure was brought to bear on the West India Company's debtors in 1643–4. On the other hand, he was probably not influenced exclusively by financial considerations. There is no reason to doubt the sincerity of his religious convictions, or the fact that once he had agreed to lead the revolt he never wavered in his determination to expel the heretics from Brazilian soil. I have given sufficient authorities in the footnotes to the text for refuting Varnhagen's view that João Fernandes Vieira's role in 1644–54 was much less important than that of André Vidal de Negreiros. It is quite clear from the Dutch records and from the minutes of the Overseas Council at Lisbon that Vieira's military leadership was no whit inferior to that of André Vidal, and that as the richer and more influential man locally, he bore an even greater share in the burden of the campaign.

Vieira was governor of Paraíba from 1655 to 1658, being then transferred to Angola. His governorship of the West African colony (1658–61) was chiefly remarkable for a violent quarrel which he had with the local Jesuits. Unlike the great majority of his countrymen, Vieira clearly was no admirer of the sons of Loyola, and it is significant that he got on much better with the friars. Writing to the crown from Luanda on 20 September 1659, Vieira argued that it was unnecessary to make a large annual grant to the Jesuit mission in Angola. According to him, there were only five Jesuits who said mass in their college, although they had fifty large estates up-country, from which they drew huge profits each year. He alleged that they had over 10,000 Negro slaves and owned much housing property and shipping. He estimated their capital at over a million *cruzados*, and claimed that they were far too busy supervising their farms, ranches, and estates, to trouble themselves about converting the heathen. He concluded his denunciation by alleging that in addition to their numerous slaves, the Jesuits 'had many freemen whom they employed without paying, and who would be better employed in serving the King in the wars'. As Vieira was excommunicated by the Jesuits of Luanda in the course of an unedifying dispute over some stray pigs from their college, there is no need to take his allegations too seriously; but other evidence indicates that Angola was not one of the Jesuits' most creditable mission fields.

After his return to Brazil, João Fernandes Vieira resided mainly on one or another of his plantations at Paraíba, although he possessed much property elsewhere, including some fine houses at Recife which he had occupied in 1654 and subsequently refused to restore to their rightful owners. A document of 1668 affirms that he was the greatest plantation-owner and rural landlord in Brazil, 'where he owns sixteen mills for making sugar'. The same source states that he applied for, and received, extensive grants of crown land (*sesmarias*) for raising cattle and oxen in hitherto uncultivated districts. From other documents of 1675–8 we learn that he was very active in promoting emigration from Madeira and the Azores to Brazil, frequently supporting the new arrivals from his own purse until they were well established. He maintained a princely establishment on his plantations, including a band of musicians and a couple of skilful painters, although unfortunately neither the works nor the names of the latter have survived. As a reward for his services in 1644–54 he had been made an absentee member of the Council of War at Lisbon, and had been granted two commanderies or bailiwicks in the Order of Christ. After his return from Angola he was also appointed superintendent and overseer of all fortifications along the Brazilian coast from the Alagoas to the Maranhão. Despite these and other marks of royal favour, he never ceased to pester the crown for bigger and better rewards, comparing his services to those of Duarte Pacheco Pereira in India, and claiming that he was the original and sole cause 'of the happiness which Portugal now enjoys'. He died at Olinda on 10 January 1681, after making a lengthy last will and testament which makes very interesting reading. His frank, one might almost say complacent, confessions of his sexual irregularities and other misdeeds, clearly show that there was more truth in some of the allegations of his personal enemies than in the panegyrics of Calado and Rafael de Jesus, who depict him as a very perfect gentle knight. But whatever his shortcomings, the rebellion of 1645 could hardly have succeeded without him, and his name is an imperishable one in Luso-Brazilian history.

TENTATIVE BALANCE-SHEET OF NETHERLANDS BRAZIL AND WEST AFRICA IN 1644[1]

Calculation of the revenues and charges of Brazil and of the revenues now actually available

	guilders
Brazil gives a yield from the revenues farmed-out[2] .	400,000
From freight on goods exported from the fatherland .	400,000
From dues[3] on the sugar exported from Brazil, *viz* approximately 3,000 chests at 200 guilders a chest .	600,000
From dues on the goods exported to Brazil, on the basis of what has been received recently . . .	250,000
From freight, convoy-tax, and the new freight duty imposed on sugars exported from Brazil by private traders, and on the basis of what has been received hitherto in this way	1,000,000
From the profit on Brazil-wood exported thence . .	50,000
Total	2,700,000

The above is exclusive of what is derived from the tenures by long lease, renting of houses and agricultural land, and the balance due on the *engenhos*, lands, &c., previously auctioned,[4] and some other outstanding debts, all of which amount to a great sum, apart from the tax of 40 pence on the sale of real estate.

Now follow the charges thereon

	guilders
36 ships outward and homeward bound, which can bring over 18,000 chests at 15,000 guilders a ship .	540,000

[1] *Hollandtze Mercurius*, January 1669, pp. 8–10, where the document is wrongly dated 1634. From the context, the real date must be shortly after the departure of Johan Maurits in May 1644. The original contains some other obvious misprints which I have corrected with the aid of Professor Engel Sluiter.

[2] The *dizimos* or tithes were the most important of these.

[3] *recognitie* (lit. 'recognition') in the original. These dues were paid by private traders and independent merchants to the Company in recognition of being allowed to trade in an area which was originally reserved for the Company's monopoly. They varied in category, time, and place, but might amount to 10 or 20 per cent. on certain commodities.

[4] Principally in 1637–8.

                                                              guilders
12 ships on ordinary freight at 6,000 guilders a ship   .   72,000
2,700 common soldiers, including sergeants and cadets,
    at 15 guilders each a month, including expenses   486,000
50 officers at 100 guilders each a month, including board   60,000
200 maintenance-personnel[1] at 80 guilders a month   .   192,000
Salaries of the High Council   30,000
Consumption and wastage of ammunition and expenses   50,000
                                                             ─────────
                                                             1,430,000
                                    Credit balance 1,270,000
                                                             ─────────
                                        Total 2,700,000

The foregoing are the revenues which Brazil was estimated to yield,
but which were expected to increase yearly as a result of the greatly
increased importation of Negroes.[2]

Revenues on the West Coast of Africa

Guinea can take yearly goods to the value of 600,000   *guilders*
    guilders, so that the Company may estimate to enjoy
    therefrom on imports and exports   150,000
Advance on freights on imports and exports   .   .   50,000
Some 2,000 slaves can be traded yearly at Arder (Ardra)
    and Calabar, and dues on the goods exported thither
    can be reckoned at 50 guilders at 10% with convoy-tax   6,000
And dues on the 2,000 slaves at 40 guilders   .   .   80,000
Advance for exporting to Brazil at 40 guilders a head,
    whereof at least half paid in advance, so calculated
    here at 20 guilders a slave   40,000
The Grain-Coast is frequented by one or two ships yearly
    which yields in dues for each year   20,000
Cape Verde, Sierra Leone, Cacheu, Arguin, Senegal
    and the River Gambia, can yield altogether in ad-
    vances on freight, dues and convoy-taxes   .   .   100,000
Loango, from the trade in ivory, copper and slaves,
    dues on imports and exports, advance on freight and
    convoy charges   50,000
São Thomé produces about 100 *arrobas* of sugar yearly,
    on which dues, taxes on goods exported thither, ad-
    vance on freight and convoy charges   .   .   .   100,000

---

[1] *trains-persoonen*. These were artificers, armourers, storemen, and other personnel employed on duties which are nowadays carried out by men of the army
service corps and ordnance corps or their equivalents.

[2] But which did not do so owing to the revolt of June 1645.

São Paulo de Luanda has formerly produced 15,000   *guilders*
    Negroes yearly, but nowadays estimated only 1,200,
    at 49 guilders each in dues[1]   480,000
Advance on exporting slaves at 20 guilders a head   .   240,000
Dues and convoy-taxes on the goods exported thither
    assuming the value at 600,000 guilders .   .   .   66,000

                                      1,382,000

Charges on the West Coast of Africa

Garrison of 400 men at São Paulo de Luanda, with
    130 in Guinea and 30 men at Cape Verde; together
    560 men plus 40 maintenance-personnel, totalling
    600 men at 20 guilders a month on the average, with
    the officers   144,000

                      Credit balance   1,238,000

[1] These figures do not seem to fit in with the total.

LIST OF PORTUGUESE SHIPPING IN THE BRAZIL TRADE TAKEN BY THE DUTCH IN 1647 AND 1648[1]

List of the ships which were lost going to and coming from the State of Brazil, from the beginning of the year 1647 until the end of the year 1648

	From	To	Type[2]	Name	Master
1.	Lisbon	Rio de Janeiro	navio	N.S. da Conceição	Leonardo Rodrigues
2.	Lisbon	Pernambuco	caravela	N.S. de Nazaré	Antonio Gonsalves Quaresma
3.	✠Bahia	Portugal	navio	Jesus	João Luis Brabo[3]
4.	✠Bahia	Lisbon	navio	[blank]	José Gomes Branco
5.	Lisbon	Pernambuco	[blank]	N.S. da Piedade	João Franco
6.	Viana	Pernambuco	navio	N.S. do Carmo[4]	Simão Gonsalves Fiuza
7.	Terceira	Rio de Janeiro	navio	As Almas	Gaspar Affonso
8.	Viana	Bahia	navio	Anjo da Guarda[5]	Domingos Gonsalves da Costa
9.	Lisbon	Pernambuco	navio	N.S. do Rozario	João Martins Guedes
10.	Viana	Pernambuco	caravela	[blank]	Gaspar Marques
11.	Lisbon	Cape St. Agostinho	navio	N.S. do Rozario e Santo Antonio[6]	Simão Jacome
12.	✠Pernambuco	[blank]	caravela	Santo Christo	Salvador Louzado
13.	Lisbon	Pernambuco	caravela	Spirito Santo e N.S. de Nazaré[7]	Manuel Cardozo
14.	Lisbon	Pernambuco	caravela	N.S. do Bom Sucesso	Salvador Pereira
15.	Lisbon	Pernambuco	não	Santa Catarina	Manuel André Vareiro
16.	Lisbon	Bahia	não	N.S. do Rozario	Pantalião Jacome
17.	✠Bahia	Portugal	navio	N.S. do Rozario	Manuel Ferreira
18.	Viana	Bahia	navio	N.S. da Piedade	Gaspar Alvares
19.	✠Bahia	Lisbon	caravela	[blank]	Agostinho Franco Grojão[8]
20.	Lisbon	Cape St. Agostinho	caravela	Santo Antonio	Antonio Gomes Bocanegra

21. Lisbon	Pernambuco	caravela	N.S. da Graça	Braz Affonso
22. Mondego	Pernambuco	caravela	N.S. do Rozario e Almas	Gaspar de Mattos
23.✠Bahia	Portugal	caravela	[blank]	Agostinho Francisco
24.✠Bahia	Lisbon	caravela	Porto Santo	Luis Nunes
25. Lisbon	Pernambuco	caravela	Santo Sacramento e N.S. do Rozario	Jorge Pinheiro
26. Villa do Conde	Pernambuco	navio	N.S. da Conceição e Bom Despacho	João Pestana
27. Lisbon	Brazil	caravela	N.S. da Conceição	Antonio do Valle
28. Madeira	Rio de Janeiro	caravela	N.S. do Rozario	Manuel Velho
29. Lisbon	Pernambuco	navio	N.S. da Vida	Manuel de Brito
30. Lisbon	Pernambuco	navio	N.S. da Conceição	Manuel Lopes Anginho
31. Viana	Bahia	navio	Anjo da Guarda[9]	Domingos Gonsalves
32.✠Pernambuco	Portugal	caravela	S. Antonio e Fieis de Deus[10]	Pedro Carvalho
33. Lisbon	Pernambuco	navio	N.S. do Amparo[11]	João Lopes
34. Lisbon	Pernambuco	navio	N.S. de Nazaré	Thomé Correia
35. Lisbon	São Thomé	navio	N.S. do Rozario	Antonio Machado
36. Lisbon	Bahia	navio	N.S. da Ajuda	Miguel Alvares
37. Porto	Bahia	navio	N.S. da Piedade[12]	Miguel Alvares Figueira
38.✠Pernambuco	Portugal	caravela	N.S. da Boa Viagem	Francisco Fernandes
39. Porto	Bahia	navio	N.S. da Piedade	Miguel Figueira

1 Arquivo Historico Ultramarino, Lisbon: 'Bahia, papeis avulsos, 1651', document annexed to the minutes of the meeting of the Conselho Ultramarino, 2 May 1651.

2 The overwhelming majority of these vessels were *navios* and *caravelas*, small ships of less than 150 tons. The list includes very few *náos* or 'great ships' (*anglice* 'tall ships'), and even those few were probably small of their kind, say 400 or 500 tons. The few odd pinnaces and frigates were likewise small vessels, the Portuguese *fragata* being at this period a much smaller and feebler vessel than the celebrated Dunkirk frigates which became the prototypes of the warships of that name. *Pataxos* (pinnaces) were probably about 150–300 tons.

3 Either there is some confusion over this man's name, or else he was taken three times by the Dutch in two years. Cf. nos. 4 and 52 under 1648.

4 Duplicated in no. 50 below.

5 Ship and master appear in triplicate. Cf. nos. 31 and 103 below.

6 Duplicated in no. 24 of 1648.

7 Duplicated in no. 5 of 1648.

8 Duplicated in no. 72 of 1647. Cf. also no. 54 of 1648.

9 Cf. nos. 8 and 103 for duplication.

10 Ship and master appear in quadruplicate. Cf. nos. 1, 69, and 84 of 1648.

11 Duplicated in no. 113 below.

12 Ship and master appear in triplicate. Cf. nos. 39 and 54 below.

APPENDIX III—*continued*

From	To	Type	Name	Master
40. Porto	Bahia	navio	*São Francisco Xavier*	Francisco Luis Sol
41. Lisbon	Bahia	navio	*N.S. das Neves*	Pedro Pires
42. Porto	Bahia	navio	*São João*	Luis Alvares
43. Lisbon	Maranhão	caravela	*São Pedro*	Manuel Alvares
44. Porto	Bahia	navio	*N.S. da Penha de França*	Miguel Affonso
45. Lisbon	Brazil	caravela	[*blank*]	Antonio Martins
46. Lisbon	Bahia	caravela	*N.S. da Piedade*	Miguel Francisco
47. Porto	Bahia	navio	*São Francisco*	Francisco Luis
48. ✠Pernambuco	Portugal	caravela	*N.S. da Boa Hora*	João Affonso
49. ✠Bahia	Lisbon	caravela	*N.S. dos Remedios*	Francisco Madeira
50. Viana	Bahia	navio	*N.S. do Monte do Carmo*	Simão Gonsalves Fiuza[1]
51. ✠Rio de Janeiro	Lisbon	navio	*N.S. da Piedade*	Manuel Velho
52. Lisbon	Maranhão	caravela	*N.S. dos Remedios e Santo Antonio*	João Luis
53. Viana	[Pernambuco]	navio	*São João Baptista e Almas*[2]	Manuel Fernandes Sequeiros
54. Porto	Bahia	navio	*N.S. da Piedade*[3]	Miguel Alvares
55. ✠Bahia	Portugal	caravela	*N.S. de Nazaré*	Domingos Branco
56. Lisbon	Bahia	caravela	*N.S. do Rozario e S. Nicolao*	Antonio Ribeiro
57. ✠Bahia	Portugal	caravela	*São Francisco*	Antonio Francisco
58. ✠Rio de Janeiro	Lisbon	navio	*N.S. do Rozario*	Manuel Ribeiro Maya
59. Viana	Bahia	navio	*São João Baptista*	Pedro Francisco
60. Lisbon	Pernambuco	caravela	*N.S. do Rozario*	Antonio Mendes
61. Terceira	[Pernambuco]	navio	*N.S. da Ajuda*	Estevão Caiado
62. ✠Bahia	Portugal	caravela	*N.S. do Livramento*	Manuel de Moraes
63. ✠Bahia	Portugal	caravela	*N.S. dos Remedios e S. Boaventura*	Agostinho Francisco Madeira
64. ✠Bahia	Portugal	caravela	*São Francisco Xavier*[4]	Francisco Fernandes Rios
65. ✠Bahia	Portugal	caravela	*Santo Antonio*	Manuel Monteiro
66. Viana	Bahia	navio	*N.S. da Boa Hora*	Simão Alvares
67. Madeira	Rio de Janeiro	caravela	*N.S. dos Remedios*	Manuel Vaz

68. Madeira	Bahia	caravela	*Spirito Santo*	Agostinho Francisco
69. ✠Bahia	Portugal	caravela	*N.S. dos Remedios*	André dos Santos
70. ✠Bahia	Portugal	caravela	*São Francisco Xavier*[5]	Francisco Fernandes
71. Lisbon	Bahia	caravela	*São Francisco*	Antonio Mendes
72. ✠Bahia	Portugal	caravela	*N.S. dos Remedios*	Antonio Francisco Grojão[6]
73. Viana	Bahia	navio	*São João Baptista*	Manuel Fernandes
74. ✠Bahia	Portugal	caravela	*As Almas*[7]	Clemente Pires
75. ✠Rio de Janeiro	Portugal	navio	*N.S. das Angustias*	Manuel Godinho
76. Porto	Bahia	navio	*São Francisco*	Francisco Vaz
77. Lisbon	Bahia	navio	*N.S. dos Remedios*	Antonio Ribeiro
78. Lisbon	Bahia	navio	*N.S. da Piedade*	Francisco Affonso
79. ✠Bahia	Lisbon	caravela	*São João*	Manuel Martins de Moraes
80. ✠Rio de Janeiro	Lisbon	caravela	*Santo Antonio*	Alberto Machado
81. ✠Rio de Janeiro	Lisbon	caravela	*Santo Antonio*	Antonio Alvares
82. ✠Maranhão	Lisbon	navio	*As Almas*	Gaspar Gonsalves
83. ✠Rio de Janeiro	Lisbon	não	*Santíssimo Sacramento*	Manuel Dias de Figueiredo
84. ✠Rio de Janeiro	Portugal	não	*N.S. dos Remedios*	Manuel Lourenço
85. Porto	Bahia	caravela	*N.S. do Rozario e Almas*	João Rodrigues Taborda
86. Lisbon	Rio de Janeiro	navio	*Santo Antonio das Chagas*[8]	João Domingues 'o fole'
87. Lisbon	Rio de Janeiro	navio	*Santo Antonio das Chagas*[8]	João Domingues
88. Lisbon	Brazil	caravela	*N.S. da Assumpção*	Manuel Lourenço Franco
89. Lisbon	Pernambuco	caravela	*São Martinho*	Antonio Luis the younger
90. Fayal	Rio de Janeiro	navio	*São João*	Manuel Godins
91. Porto	Bahia	navio	*N.S. da Piedade*	Miguel Gonsalves
92. Porto	Brazil	navio	*N.S. da Ajuda*	Miguel Alvares
93. ✠Bahia	Portugal	navio	*S. Antonio e N.S. da Boa Viagem*	Manuel Martins
94. Lisbon	Rio de Janeiro	caravela	*São João*	Lourenço Affonso

1 Duplicate of no. 6 above.
2 Duplicated in no. 10 of 1648.
3 Duplicated in nos. 37 and 39 above.
4 Duplicated in no. 70 below.

5 Duplicated in no. 64 above.
6 Cf. nos. 19 of 1647 and 54 of 1648.
7 Duplicated in no. 85 of 1648.
8 Duplicates.

APPENDIX III—*continued*

	From	To	Type	Name	Master
95.	Lisbon	Rio de Janeiro	não	*N.S. do Rozario*	Francisco Neto
96.	Lisbon	Bahia	caravela	*São Francisco*	Antonio Ribeiro
97.	Lisbon	Pernambuco	caravela	*S. Bento e S. Antonio*	Antonio Martins 'mil ameixas'
98.	✠Bahia	Portugal	caravela	*N.S. do Rozario e S. Leonardo*	Vicente Jorge Caria
99.	Cape Verde	Portugal	caravela	*Bom Jesus*	Felipe Gomes
100.	✠Bahia	Portugal	navio	*N.S. do Rozario*	Manuel Rodrigues Serrabodes
101.	Lisbon	Pernambuco	caravela	*N.S. de Nazaré e S. Francisco*	Francisco Luis Calvo[1]
102.	Porto	Pernambuco	caravela	*Bom Jesus e Almas*	Salvador de Leão
103.	Viana	Pernambuco	navio	*Anjo da Guarda*[2]	Domingos Alvares
104.	Porto	Pernambuco	caravela	[*blank*]	Ambrosio Carneiro
105.	Lisbon	Pernambuco	caravela	*Spirito Santo*	Affonso Louzado
106.	✠Spirito Santo	Bahia	caravela	*Jesus Maria Joseph*	Francisco Fernandes
107.	Lisbon	Rio de Janeiro	navio	*N.S. da Conceição*	Leonardo Rodrigues
108.	Aveiro	Brazil	caravela	*N.S. do Rozario*	Manuel Ribeiro Lemos
109.	Villa do Conde	Cape St. Agostinho	navio	*N.S. da Conceição*	João Pestana
110.	Lisbon	Rio de Janeiro	navio	*N.S. do Rozario*	Francisco Rodrigues
111.	Lisbon	Rio de Janeiro	navio	*N.S. da Conceição*	Francisco Affonso
112.	Lisbon	Rio de Janeiro	navio	*N.S. do Rozario*	Simão dos Santos
113.	Lisbon	Pernambuco	navio	*N.S. do Amparo*[3]	João Lopes
114.	Lisbon	Rio de Janeiro	caravela	*N.S. da Conceição*	Lourenço Affonso Penso
115.	Terceira	Pernambuco	navio	*N.S. da Ajuda*	Estevão Cazado
116.	✠Bahia	Portugal	caravela	*N.S. de Nazaré*	Francisco Fernandes
117.	✠Pernambuco	Portugal	caravela	*São João*	Francisco Baptista
118.	✠Bahia	Lisbon	navio	*N.S. da Ajuda*	Simão dos Santos
				1648	
1.	✠Pernambuco	Portugal	caravela	*Santo Antonio*[4]	Pedro Carvalho
2.	✠Cape St. Agostinho	Portugal	caravela	*Sacramento*	Francisco Vicente Aleixo

No.		Port	Type	Ship name	Captain
3.	Lisbon	Pernambuco	caravela	S. Jorge do Spirito Santo	Affonso Louzado
4.†	Bahia	Portugal	navio	N.S. da Penha de França e S. Sacramento	João Luis Bravo[5]
5.	Lisbon	Pernambuco	caravela	N.S. de Nazaré e Spirito Santo[6]	Manuel Cardozo
6.	Lisbon	Pernambuco	caravela	N.S. da Encarnação	Antonio Anes do Valle
7.†	Rio de Janeiro	Lisbon	navio	S. Spirito do Monte de Piedade e S. Antonio	Manuel de Sousa
8.†	Pernambuco	Portugal	caravela	São Leonardo	Pedro Simoens da Costa
9.	Terceira	Brazil	navio	S. Antonio e Almas	Gaspar do Valle
10.	Setubal	Brazil	navio	São João e Almas[7]	Manuel Fernandes Sequeiros
11.	Viana	Pernambuco	navio	N.S. da Esperança	Amador de Araujo
12.	Arrabida	Pernambuco	caravela	Santo Antonio e Almas	Francisco Lopes
13.	Porto	Bahia	navio	N.S. do Rozario	Manuel Rodrigues
14.†	Maranhão	Lisbon	navio	N.S. da Ajuda e Almas do Purgatorio	Pascoal da Silva
15.	Lisbon	Bahia	navio	São João Baptista	Francisco Jorge
16.†	Bahia	Portugal	caravela	São Mattheus	Diogo das Povoas
17.	Lisbon	Bahia	navio	N.S. da Visitação e S. Boaventura	Sebastião Francisco
18.	Lisbon	Pernambuco	navio	S. Antonio e Almas	Manuel Francisco Migueis
19.	Aveiro	Pernambuco	pataxo	N.S. do Rozario e Almas	Gaspar de Mattos
20.	Lisbon	Brazil	caravela	N.S. do Bom Sucesso	Salvador Pereira
21.†	Bahia	Lisbon	navio	N.S. da Ajuda	João da Costa Lima
22.	Arrabida	Brazil	caravela	Santo Antonio	Antonio Pires
23.	Lisbon	Bahia	caravela	N.S. do Rozario	Pedro de Lemos
24.	Lisbon	Pernambuco	navio	N.S. do Rozario[8]	Simão Jacone
25.	Lisbon	Bahia	navio	São João	Francisco Fernandes
26.†	Bahia	Lisbon	caravela	Almas	Manuel Velho
27.	Lisbon	Bahia	caravela	N.S. de Nazaré	Jorge Rodrigues
28.	Lisbon	Bahia	não	Jesus Maria e Almas	Luis da Silva
29.†	Bahia	Portugal	caravela	N.S. da Graça e Corpo Santo	Manuel de Freitas

1 Cf. no. 86 of 1648.
2 Cf. nos. 8 and 31 above.
3 Duplicate of no. 33 above.
4 Cf. no. 32 of 1647 and nos. 69 and 84 below.
5 Cf. nos. 3 of 1647 and 52 of 1648.
6 Duplicate of no. 13 of 1647.
7 Duplicate of no. 53 of 1647.
8 Cf. no. 11 of 1647.

APPENDIX III—*continued*

From	To	Type	Name	Master
30.✠Bahia	Portugal	caravela	*N.S. da Penha de França*	Rodrigo Migueis[1]
31.✠Bahia	Portugal	caravela	*N.S. da Graça*	Manuel Fernandes
32.✠Bahia	Portugal	caravela	*N.S. do Rozario*	André Luis Parola
33. Porto	Bahia	não	*N.S. da Boa Hora*	Bernardo da Fonseca
34.✠Pernambuco	Portugal	caravela	*São Lourenço*	Pedro de Christo
35.✠Bahia	Portugal	caravela	*N.S. das Neves*	Pedro Peres
36. Lisbon	Pernambuco	navio	*N.S. da Estrella e Almas*	João Nunes
37. Porto	Bahia	navio	*N.S. do Rozario*	Manuel Loucano
38.✠Pernambuco	Portugal	caravela	*Santo Antonio*	Pedro Carneiro
39. Lisbon	Pernambuco	navio	*N.S. do Rozario*	João Martins Bezerra
40.✠Maranhão	Lisbon	navio	*Fieis de Deus*	Paschoal Coelho
41. Lisbon	Pernambuco	caravela	*São Francisco Xavier*	Braz Franco
42. Lisbon	Cape Verde	caravela	*N.S. dos Remedios*	Paschoal Francisco
43.✠Bahia	Lisbon	caravela	*São Francisco*	Domingos Affonso
44.✠Pernambuco	Portugal	navio	*N.S. do Rozario*	Marinho Dias Pereira
45.✠Cape St. Agostinho	Lisbon	caravela	*Santo Antonio*	Pedro Simoens
46.✠Bahia	Portugal	caravela	*Santo Antonio e Almas*	Rodrigo Affonso
47.✠Bahia	Portugal	pataxo	*Santa Maria*	Joseph Gomes
48.✠Porto Calvo	Portugal	navio	*N.S. do Rozario e Santas Almas*	Gaspar Gonsalves
49.✠Bahia	Portugal	caravela	*São Matthias*	Mathias de Sousa
50.✠Bahia	Portugal	navio	*N.S. da Boa Hora*	Domingos de Torres
51. Lisbon	Bahia	não	*N.S. de Nazaré*	Jorge Rodrigues
52. Madeira	Bahia	não	*Santo Sacramento*	João Luis Bravo[2]
53.✠Bahia	Portugal	navio	*Santa Maria Maior*	João Gomes Branco
54.✠Pernambuco	Portugal	não	[*blank*]	Antonio Franco Grojão[3]
55. Lisbon	Bahia	navio	*N.S. do Rozario*	Manuel Rodrigues
56. Porto	Bahia	navio	*N.S. do Rozario*	Pedro Fernandes
57.✠Bahia	Portugal	navio	*N.S. das Neves*	Pedro Fernandes

58. ✠Bahia	Portugal	caravela	*Santo Antonio*	Rodrigues Migueis[4]
59. ✠Bahia	Porto	caravela	*São Bento*	Antonio Moniz
60. ✠Bahia	Portugal	navio	*N.S. da Penha de França*	João Lopes
61. ✠Bahia	Portugal	caravela	*N.S. do Rozario e S. Antonio*	André Luis of Alfama
62. ✠Bahia	Portugal	caravela	*N.S. de Nazaré*	Mathias Rigau
63. ✠Spirito Santo	Portugal	navio	*Santo Antonio*	Affonso Verga
64. ✠Porto Calvo	Portugal	navio	*N.S. do Rozario e Almas*	Gaspar Figueira
65. ✠Bahia	Portugal	navio	*São Pedro*	Joseph Gomes
66. ✠Pernambuco	Lisbon	navio	*N.S. da Estrella*	Lourenço Domingues Durão
67. Porto	Bahia	navio	*Jesus Maria Joseph*	Luis da Silva
68. ✠Bahia	Portugal	navio	*N.S. do Rozario*	Lopo Simões
69. ✠Pernambuco	Lisbon	caravela	*Santo Antonio*	Pedro Carvalho
70. Porto	Bahia	não	*Jesus Maria Joseph e Almas*	Luis da Silveira
71. Arrabida	Pernambuco	caravela	*N.S. do Socorro*	João Lopes
72. Lisbon	Pernambuco	navio	*N.S. da [Boa] Hora*	João Martins
73. ✠Rio Fermoso	Portugal	caravela	*N.S. da Boa Hora*	Ambrosio Carneiro
74. Lisbon	Bahia	caravela	*N.S. das Candeas*	Domingos Franco
75. ✠Bahia	Portugal	caravela	*N.S. da Graça*	Manuel de Froes
76. ✠Bahia	Portugal	caravela	*S. Francisco Xavier*	Braz Dorta
77. ✠Bahia	Portugal	fragata	*Nazaré*	Antonio Ferreira
78. ✠Bahia	Lisbon	caravela	*N.S. da Guia*	Manuel de Freitas
79. Viana	Bahia	navio	*N.S. da Ajuda*	João da Costa
80. Porto	Rio de Janeiro	caravela	*S. Antonio e S. Boaventura*[5]	João da Costa
81. ✠Bahia	Portugal	navio	*N.S. do Rozario*	Pedro Fernandes
82. ✠Bahia	Portugal	caravela	*São Francisco*	André Dias
83. ✠Spirito Santo	Portugal	não	*Santo Antonio*	Affonso Dias
84. ✠Cape St. Agostinho	Portugal	caravela	*Fieis de Deus*	Pedro Carvalho
85. Porto	Brazil	navio	*Almas*[6]	Clemente Perez

1 Cf. no. 58 below.
2 Cf. no. 4 of 1648 and no. 3 of 1647.
3 Cf. no. 94 below and no. 19 of 1647.

4 Cf. no. 30 above.
5 Duplicate of no. 93 below.
6 Duplicate of no. 74 of 1647.

APPENDIX III—continued

From	To	Type	Name	Master
86. ✠Pernambuco	Portugal	caravela	N.S. de Nazaré[1]	Francisco Luis Calvo
87. ✠Cape St. Agostinho	Lisbon	caravela	[blank]	Diogo de Pax
88. ✠Pernambuco	Portugal	navio		Domingos Fernandes Pedra
89. Porto	Bahia	navio	N.S. da Ajuda	Manuel Cardia
90. Cape Verde	Lisbon	caravela	N.S. da Conceição	Manuel de Araujo
91. Porto	Bahia	navio	N.S. dos Remedios	Antonio Dias Picão
92. ✠Pernambuco	Portugal	navio	N.S. da Conceição	Gaspar Marques
93. Porto	Rio de Janeiro	caravela	N.S. da Ajuda	João da Costa Carvalho
94. Madeira	Bahia	caravela	S. Antonio e S. Boaentura[2]	Antonio Franco Grojão
95. ✠Pernambuco	Portugal	navio	Spirito Santo[3]	Marinho Dias
96. ✠Bahia	Lisbon	navio	N.S. do Rozario	Pedro de Seixas
97. ✠Rio de Janeiro	Portugal	navio	N.S. das Neves	Francisco Alvares
98. Porto	Bahia	navio	Bom Jesus	Luis Nunes
99. ✠Bahia	Portugal	caravela	N.S. da Assumpção	Mattheus Rodrigues
100. ✠Bahia	Portugal	caravela	N.S. dos Remedios e S. Antonio	Diogo Netto Ponçe
101. ✠Rio de Janeiro	Portugal	não	N.S. da Conceição	Manuel Lopes
102. Porto	Rio de Janeiro	caravela	Santo Antonio	João de Carvalho
103. ✠Spirito Santo	Lisbon	navio	Santo Antonio	Manuel da Veiga
104. Porto	Pernambuco	não	Santa Maria	João Diniz
105. ✠Bahia	Lisbon	caravela	[blank]	Affonso Louzado
106. ✠Bahia	Portugal	caravela	N.S. do Rozario e São Vicente	Manuel de Paiva
107. Angola	Rio de Janeiro	navio	N.S. do Rozario e São João de Deus	Antonio Vaz de Oliveira
108. Madeira	Bahia	caravela	N.S. das Necessidades	João Rollão
109. Lisbon	Bahia	caravela	N.S. dos Remedios e S. Joseph	André Leitão
110. ✠Bahia	Portugal	navio	São Pedro	Gaspar Rodrigues
111. ✠Bahia	Portugal	caravela	São Joseph	Pedro Gonsalves
112. ✠Pernambuco	Portugal	caravela	belonging to the Mercenarian Friars	[blank]
113. ✠Bahia	Portugal	navio	N.S. dos Remedios	Antonio Fernandes

114.	Porto	Bahia	*N.S. do Rosario*	navio	Francisco Alvares
115.✠	Rio de Janeiro	Portugal	[blank]	caravela	Gonçalo Pires de Carvalho
116.✠	Rio de Janeiro	Portugal	[blank]	navio	Roque Garcia
117.	Lisbon	Bahia	*São Pedro*	caravela	Francisco Domingues
118.	Porto	Bahia	*N.S. do Rozario*	navio	Manuel Gonsalves Tojeiro
119.	Porto	Rio de Janeiro	*Bom Jesus de Boucas*	navio	Francisco Alvares
120.	Porto	Bahia	*S. Antonio e N.S. do Rozario*	caravela	Manuel Pretto
121.	Lisbon	Bahia	*N.S. da Ajuda*	caravela	Jorge Rodrigues Calvo
122.	Madeira	Bahia	[blank]	caravela	Antonio Franco
123.	Porto	Bahia	*N.S. da Conceição*	navio	Antonio Dias Pousado
124.	Madeira	Bahia	*Santo Antonio*	não	Mathias Gomes
125.✠	Bahia	Portugal	*São Francisco*	caravela	Matheus Dias
126.	Lisbon	Bahia	*São João*	caravela	Francisco Fernandes Bonito
127.✠	Bahia	Portugal	*São Matheus*	caravela	Diogo Lopes
128.	Porto	Bahia	*N.S. da Conceição*	navio	Antonio Villela
129.	Lisbon	Maranhão	*N.S. da Ajuda*	fragata	Francisco de Pina
130.	Madeira	Brazil	*N.S. das Necessidades*	caravela	Antonio Dias Pereira
131.	Madeira	Bahia	[blank]	caravela	Antonio Farto
132.✠	Bahia	Portugal	[blank]	navio	Antonio Velho
133.	Madeira	Bahia	[blank]	caravela	Simão Farto
134.	Lisbon	Bahia	*N.S. da Boa Viagem*	caravela	Domingos Machado
135.	Porto	Bahia	*N.S. do Desterro*	navio	João da Rocha
136.✠	Pernambuco	Portugal	*Santissimo Sacramento*	navio	Antonio Barbosa
137.✠	Bahia	Portugal	*São Joseph*	caravela	Antonio Gomes
138.✠	Nazaré	Portugal	*N.S. de Nazaré*	caravela	Antonio Vaz Coresma
139.✠	Cape St. Agostinho	Portugal	*N.S. das Merces*	caravela	João Jorge
140.✠	Bahia	Portugal	*N.S. da Ajuda*	caravela	André da Fonseca
141.	Madeira	Bahia	*N.S. dos Remedios*	caravela	Manuel Leitão

1 Cf. no. 101 of 1647.
2 Duplicate of no. 80 above.
3 Cf. nos. 19 and 72 of 1647.

U

In the year 1647 there were lost   108 vessels
In the year 1648 there were lost   141 vessels

Total losses for 1647 and 1648   249 vessels

And of these vessels, there were lost in the year 1647, thirty-five vessels which were coming from Brazil and had gone thither from the kingdom. These are marked with a ✠ so that the names of the masters can be identified.

And in the year 1648, there were lost seventy-three vessels which were coming from Brazil and had gone thither from the kingdom, which are likewise marked with a ✠. Thus making a total of 108 vessels lost coming from Brazil in 1647 and 1648.[1]

[1] All these figures are erroneous. As can be seen from the notes above, many ships are recorded in duplicate, others in triplicate, and one in quadruplicate. The real total is probably that given by the directors of the Brazil Company, who estimated the total losses for 1647–8 as 220 sail. It is curious that the Overseas Councillors, in contravening this figure and putting forward the total of 249, should not have read carefully this list on which their claim was based and which contains such flagrant errors and obvious duplicates.

BIBLIOGRAPHICAL NOTE

There is no need to give a full bibliography of all the manuscript and printed material used in this book. As regards printed works in all languages, virtually all books and articles published prior to 1949 are listed (and usually evaluated) in the definitive critical bibliography of the subject by José Honorio Rodrigues, *Historiografia e Bibliografia do domínio Holandês no Brasil* (Rio de Janeiro, 1949). I can fairly claim to have read or at least glanced through practically all of the material listed there, and certainly all of prime importance. This bibliography is indispensable to anyone studying the subject seriously, and can be confidently recommended as a nearly infallible guide. The bibliographical survey and discussion of source material on pp. 1–24 of Wätjen's *Das holländische Kolonialreich in Brasilien* is also of great assistance, although as regards Luso-Brazilian works the judgement of Wätjen is not always so sound as that of J. H. Rodrigues.

In view of the adequacy of these two bibliographical surveys, I have limited myself here to briefly discussing and assessing the material on which I have more particularly relied, including works which have been published since 1949, and a couple which were inadvertently omitted by Rodrigues. As indicated in the Preface, I have assumed that most of my readers will have some knowledge of the seventeenth-century background on both sides of the Atlantic. Those who feel that their knowledge is insufficient may be referred to G. N. Clark, *The Seventeenth Century* (Oxford, 1929), and to the following more specialized works on Dutch history: P. Geyl, *The Netherlands Divided, 1609–1648* (London 1936); G. J. Renier, *The Dutch Nation. An historical study* (London, 1944); B. H. M. Vlekke, *Evolution of the Dutch Nation* (New York, 1945), pp. 124–240. For the Brazilian background, they should consult the works of the Pernambuco historian and sociologist, Gilberto Freyre, *Brazil. An interpretation* (New York, 1945), and *The Masters and the Slaves* (New York, 1946). Compare also Bailey W. Diffie, *Latin-American Civilization. Colonial Period* (Harrisburg, 1947), pp. 633–73.

(a) Manuscript Sources

The Dutch manuscript sources for the history of the West India Company in Brazil comprise those of its records which have survived and are now preserved in the colonial archives section of the Algemeen Rijksarchief at The Hague. It was formerly believed that nineteenth-century vandalism was responsible for the wanton destruction of virtually the whole of the West India Company's records. It is now known that, whereas many of those papers were apparently destroyed on the reorganization of the Company in 1674, a great number, particularly the Brazilian records of the Zeeland chamber from 1630 to 1654, escaped destruction. These surviving records are described by José Hygino Duarte Pereira in the *Revista do Instituto Archeologico e Geographico Pernambucano*, no. 30 (Recife, 1886), pp. 7–110, 131–70, and by H. Wätjen, *Das holländische Kolonialreich in Brasilien*, pp. 1–4, and are more briefly enumerated by M. A. P. Meilink-Roelofsz, 'A survey of archives in the Netherlands pertaining to the history of the Netherlands Antilles', pp. 1–2 of the reprint from *De West-Indische Gids*, xxxv (1954). There is therefore no point in my repeating this information here. I need only explain that where I quote documents from the colonial archives at The Hague, those citations are not taken direct from the originals (except where furnished to me by Dr. W. J. van Hoboken), but from the transcripts made by and for José Hygino Duarte Pereira in 1885–6, and whose peculiar interest and importance are explained by J. A. Gonsalves de Mello on pp. 19–27 of the preface to his *Tempo dos Flamengos* (Rio de Janeiro, 1947). I was able to consult these bulky transcripts during my visit to Recife in 1949, by courtesy of the director and officials of the Historical Institute where they are housed. My citations from these records are distinguished by the prefix JHMS; but since they are all dated, anyone interested can easily identify the originals in the Rijksarchief.

As regards documents in Portuguese archives, the principal depositories where relevant material is to be found are listed in the articles by Bailey W. Diffie and D. Virginia Rau, on pp. 181–213 of the *Proceedings of the International Colloquium on Luso-Brazilian Studies, Washington, October 15–20, 1950* (Vanderbilt University Press, Nashville, 1953). In the present work I have relied mainly on the series known as the 'Conselho Ultramarino, Consultas Mixtas', in the Arquivo Historico Ultramarino (formerly Arquivo Colonial) at Junqueira, Lisbon. Codices 13–15 of this voluminous series cover the years 1644–54, and thus coincide with the last decade of the Dutch colony. An excellent inventory of these documents is now in the course of publication in the Lisbon *Revista do Gabinete de Estudos Ultramarinos*, of which nos. 1–8 appeared in 1951–4.

Where documents or transcripts have been cited from the manuscript section of the Biblioteca Nacional at Rio de Janeiro, these have been prefixed by the initials BNRJ. The bulk of the documents cited from Brazilian archives are, however, taken from printed collections, such as the *Documentos Historicos*, published by the Biblioteca Nacional, Rio de Janeiro (1928 to date), and the *Atas da Camara da Cidade do Salvador* (3 vols., Bahia, 1944–9). For further information concerning relevant Portuguese and Brazilian source material see my *Salvador de Sá and the struggle for Brazil and Angola, 1602–1686* (London, 1952), pp. 407–11.

(b) Printed works

As regards Dutch printed works, the four main quarries for the historian or student of Netherlands Brazil are the contemporary narratives of De Laet, Barlaeus, Nieuhof, and Haecxs.

Johannes de Laet's *Historie ofte Iaerlyck Verhael van de West-Indische Compagnie* (Leiden, 1644) gives an almost blow-by-blow description of the campaigns in Brazil from 1630 to the end of 1636, inserting also a wealth of geographical and other information about that country. He also gives an excellent account of the preliminary operations of the West India Company from 1621 to 1630, so his work really comprises a history of that organization from its origin to the end of the year 1636. As one of the directors of the chamber of Amsterdam, and for some time a member of the council of the Nineteen, De Laet had exceptional opportunities for examining all the papers and documents which he required, and he made the most of them. The learned Antwerper was a man of astounding erudition, and his curiosity ranged over the Old World as well as the New. He participated in the Synod of Dordrecht, and in 1625 he published the *Nieuwe Wereldt of Beschrijvinghe van West-Indien*, which was several times reprinted, and translated into French and Latin. It remained for long a standard work on America and the West Indies. De Laet was exceedingly well read in both Spanish and Portuguese sources, and equally at home in compiling treatises on geography, natural history, or ethnology. Although he never left the Netherlands, he compiled a standard work on Mogul India, *De Imperio Magni Mogolis sive India vera commentarius* (Leiden, 1631), whose accuracy has earned high praise from so competent a critic as W. H. Moreland. As other instances of the range of his learning, I need only mention his voluminous annotations to Marcgraf's section of the *Historia Naturalis Brasiliae* (Leiden, 1648) and his celebrated controversy with Grotius on the origins of the American Indians. His *Iaerlyck Verhael* is written in a strictly chronological form, and his style, though readable, cannot be called lively. As noted previously, quotations from the *Iaerlyck Verhael* in my work are taken from the four-volume edition edited for the Linschoten Vereeniging by S. P. L'Honoré Naber and J. C. M. Warnsinck in 1931–7.

Caspar van Barle's *Casparis Barlaei, rerum per octennium in Brasilia et alibi nuper gestarum sub praefectura Illustrissimi Comitis I, Mauritii, Nassoviae &c. Comitis, nunc Vasaliae Gubernatoris e Equitatus Federatorum Belgii Ordd, sub Auriaco Ductoris, historia* (Amsterdam, 1647) begins where De Laet's work ends, and covers the whole period of the governorship of Johan Maurits (January 1637–May 1644), for which it must always remain the primary printed authority. Like De Laet, Barlaeus never left the Netherlands, but he likewise had access to original records; in this instance primarily to the papers and dispatches of Johan Maurits, although he supplemented them from other material as well. The work is avowedly eulogistic in tone, but Barlaeus was not altogether blinded by hero-worship. In his treatment of Johan Maurits's controversy with Arciszewski, for instance, he lets the aggrieved Polish colonel speak at length in his own defence, and implies pretty clearly that there was a good deal to be said on his behalf. A more serious defect is that he is very vague about dates. He often gives lengthy citations from original dispatches without dating them, or else combines dispatches of different dates into one connected whole without indicating that he has done so. For reasons best known to themselves, Edmundson and Wätjen both used the inferior German and Latin editions of 1659 and 1660 in preference to the original Latin. I have had the advantage of using S. P. L'Honoré Naber's superb Dutch translation, *Nederlandsch Brazilië onder het bewind van Johan Maurits Grave van Nassau, 1637–1644* (The Hague, 1923), which has the additional merit of incorporating much of the material which Barlaeus abridged or elided, in the original form. The artistic engravings of Brazilian scenery reproduced from sketches by Frans Post (some of which are now in the British Museum) make this book the first European work in which representations of tropical scenery were taken direct from drawings made by a professional artist on the spot.

Johan Nieuhof's posthumous *Gedenkweerdige Brasiliaense Zee- en Lant-Reize. Behelzende al het geen op dezelve is voorgevallen. Beneffens een bondige beschrijving van gantsch Neerlants Brasil* (Amsterdam, 1682) conveniently begins, to all intents and purposes, with the departure of Johan Maurits in May 1644, and covers the period down to Nieuhof's own departure from Brazil in July 1649. It is a work of curiously uneven value. For the years 1644–7, and more especially for 1645–6, it is very valuable indeed, being richly documented from the original sources and reproducing much of the official correspondence between the local Dutch and Portuguese authorities. This section also includes copious extracts from the minutes (*Notulen*) of the meetings of the High Council at Recife in that critical period. After the relief of Recife in June 1646 the work tends to become much more scrappy, and Nieuhof's account of events in the years 1648–9 is so superficial and inexact as to be worse than useless. He even confuses the two battles of the Guararapes, although he was still in Recife when they were fought. Presumably he had not given this section of his book the final form when he was killed on the island of Madagascar outward bound to the East Indies in 1672. His brother,

who edited his papers for publication, must bear part of the blame
for this. Nieuhof was a keen and intelligent observer, and his work,
with all its faults, forms no unworthy pendant to those of De Laet and
Barlaeus. It is certainly deserving of a far higher place than S. P.
L'Honoré Naber contemptuously accorded it in his review of the
relevant source material (*De West-Indische Compagnie in Brazilië en
Guinee*, p. 18).

Hendrik Haecxs's journal for 1645–54 published by S. P. L'Honoré
Naber under the title of 'Het Dagboek van Hendrik Haecxs, lid van
den Hoogen Raad van Brazilië', in the *Bijdragen en Mededeelingen
van het Historisch Genootschap gevestigd te Utrecht*, xlvi (Utrecht, 1925),
pp. 127–303, forms the last link in the chain of Dutch primary printed
sources for the history of Netherlands Brazil. This valuable source
was unknown to Netscher and Wätjen, which may help to account
for the rather superficial way in which they both dealt with the
colony's last years. Haecxs evidently kept his journal irregularly, and
there are no entries at all for some lengthy periods. From 19 August
1646 to 3 September 1647 is one blank, for example, and from
6 October 1650 to 25 February 1652 is another. By way of compensation, the journal is particularly detailed for the period from 3 September 1647 to the first battle of the Guararapes in April 1648.
Especially valuable is the account of Haecxs's stay in the homeland
(November and December 1647), where we are taken behind the
scenes and shown the rivalry between the various chambers of the
West India Company, the mutual dislike between civilians and
soldiers, the machinations of war-profiteers, and other things which
help to explain the decline of Netherlands Brazil. There is an
annotated Portuguese translation in the *Anais da Biblioteca Nacional*,
lxix (Rio de Janeiro, 1950), pp. 19–153.

The importance and interest of the contemporary Dutch
pamphlet-literature for the history of Netherlands Brazil has already
been pointed out by Asher, Wätjen, and, above all, by J. H. Rodrigues. Naber tended to underrate the value of these pamphlets
when he cavalierly dismissed them as 'mostly libellous tracts which
are not lacking in passion'. Certainly envy, hatred, malice, and all
uncharitableness are by no means absent from many of them,
although some of their accusations do not seem very deadly today.
When we read in the *Brasilsche Gelt-saeck* (1647), for instance, that one
of the crimes of the Councillors of Justice at Recife was that they
were in the habit of changing their clothes daily, this would nowadays be accepted as the normal procedure in a tropical country,
rather than as damning evidence of unbridled luxury. Cleanliness
and godliness have moved a good deal closer to each other than they
were in seventeenth-century Christendom, where preoccupation
with personal hygiene was looked upon as something either unduly

eccentric or downright sinful. Moreover, it is these glimpses of daily life and thought which help to bring vividly to the reader the atmosphere of the times. From this point of view, the pamphlets (or 'blue-books' as the Dutch called them from the fact that they were originally issued in blue paper wrappers), whether scurrilous or not, are a valuable as well as an entertaining source. Other 'blue-books', such as the *Claer Vertooch* (1647), are very important for the copious extracts from state papers, or from intercepted correspondence, which they reproduce. A third class, such as the *Journael ofte kort discours nopende de rebellye ende verradelijcke desseynen der Portugesen alhier in Brasil* (Arnhem, 1647), contain eyewitness accounts which must always be consulted by the historian, even though the information contained in them is not necessarily wholly reliable.

Leeuw van Aitzema's literally monumental compilation, *Saken van staet en oorlogh in ende omtrent de Vereenigde Nederlanden* (6 parts in 7 vols., The Hague, 1669–72), is well known to all students of Dutch history. The information concerning the West India Company to be found in this work is somewhat sporadic; but certain episodes, such as the Capitulation of Taborda, are very fully documented. A useful adjunct to Aitzema's work, and one of the rare omissions from J. H. Rodrigues's bibliography, is the *Gedenkschriften van Jonkheer Alexander van der Capellen ... beginende met den jaere 1621, en gaande tot 1654* (2 vols., Utrecht, 1777–8). Both Alexander van der Capellen and his brother were among the earliest investors in the West India Company, and the latter was for some time the chairman of the Heeren XIX. As noted on p. 174 above, Alexander was asked to go out to Recife as president of the new high council which was to take over the government of the colony after the return of Johan Maurits. Although he declined this embarassing honour, being clearly of a stay-at-home disposition, he retained his interest in the Company and frequently served on committees of the States-General (in which he was a member for Guelderland) which dealt with the affairs of that concern.

As regards the printed *Resolutien* of the provincial States of Holland and West Friesland, Asher has already listed those which are of importance for the history of the West India Company in Brazil on pp. 49–70 of his *Bibliographical and Historical Essay on the Dutch books and pamphlets relating to New-Netherland and to the Dutch West-India Company and its possessions in Brazil, Angola etc.* (Amsterdam, 1854–67). Unfortunately, the 'Secret Resolutions' only begin in February 1653, but this massive compilation of over 300 volumes is, of course, one which must be consulted by all students of the period. There is a collection in the state-paper room of the British Museum, which is complete for the years covering the West India Company's Brazilian enterprise. The printed *Resolutien* of the States-General only begin in 1721, and those of the provincial states of Zeeland for this period have not been published.

One work mentioned by Asher, but omitted by Wätjen and J. H. Rodrigues, is worth recalling here for the help it gives in understanding the Calvinist viewpoint which was so strongly represented in the West India Company. This is the Calvinist *predikant*, the Rev. Godfried Udemans's *'T Geestelick Roer*, whose long-winded title explains the scope of the work and may be rendered in English as follows: *The Spiritual Rudder of the merchant's ship. That is: True tidings how a merchant and trader must conduct himself in his dealings in peace and war, before God and men, on sea and on land, especially among the heathen in the East and West-Indies, to the honour of God, foundation of his congregation and the salvation of his soul; as also for the temporal welfare of his fatherland and of his family.* This work was evidently very popular in its day and generation, as it ran through three editions published at Dordrecht in 1638, 1640, and 1655 respectively. It was dedicated to the directors of the East and West India Companies, and intended principally as a manual of conscience for their employees. The book is anything but easy reading and fairly staggers under the weight of its biblical quotations, but it affords an excellent insight into the mentality of the Contra-Remonstrant party, and the application of their beliefs and theories to colonial affairs. Dutch activities in the East and West Indies are justified with chapter and verse from the Bible and other authorities. Udemans's work forms a Calvinist counterpart to the Roman Catholic treatises, such as *De Justo Imperio Lusitanorum Asiatico* of Fr. Serafim de Freitas, which claimed divine sanction for the Iberian colonial empires.

In concluding this brief survey of some of the principal Dutch sources, I would again draw attention to the thesis of Dr. W. J. van Hoboken, *Witte de With in Brazilië*, which appeared while my own book was in the press. As explained in the preface (p. ix), this well-documented survey is particularly important for the critical years 1647–9, when, to a great extent, the ultimate fate of the colony was decided.

As regards Portuguese (or rather Luso-Brazilian) printed works, apart from collections of published documents, I have relied principally on the following authors: Duarte de Albuquerque, Fr. Manuel Calado do Salvador, Padre Antonio Vieira, S.J., Francisco Adolfo de Varnhagen, and José Antonio Gonsalves de Mello, neto.

Duarte de Albuquerque Coelho kept a journal during his participation in the Brazilian campaigns of 1631–8, and from this and his brother's papers he compiled his methodical and invaluable narrative, *Memorias Diarias de la Guerra del Brasil, por discurso de nueve años, empeçando desde el de MDCXXX* (Madrid, 1654). Wätjen made no use of this book—he does not even refer to it—an omission which is all the more surprising as Varnhagen and Edmundson had already emphasized its importance. Duarte de Albuquerque, the fourth *donatário* of Pernambuco, took part in the Bahia campaign of 1625, and first arrived in Pernambuco with Oquendo's armada in September 1631. From then until the great retreat southwards in 1637, he served as a gentleman volunteer without holding any command, but being frequently asked for his advice. He was therefore well placed to write a detailed account of the Pernambuco campaigns, although his narrative is naturally biased in favour of his brother, Mathias de Albuquerque. He participated in the defence of Bahia against Johan Maurits (May 1638), returning to the Iberian peninsula at the end of that year. He subsequently settled in Madrid and remained loyal (whether voluntarily or otherwise) to the Spanish crown after the Portuguese revolution of 1640. His manuscript was ready for the press in 1644, but publication was postponed for a decade by the protests of hostile critics. One of the objections made to the work was that it glorified the character and military skill of Mathias de Albuquerque, who in 1644 was the commander-in-chief of the Portuguese forces on the Alemtejo front. I have used both the original edition and the Brazilian translation published at Recife in 1944. Since both these versions are very rare, I have given all citations under the date rather than by chapter and page, as the work is arranged in a strictly chronological order.

Fr. Manuel Calado do Salvador's *Valeroso Lucideno e Triumpho da Liberdade* (Lisbon, 1648) is an equally valuable work in its way. Wätjen made a serious error when he contemptuously dismissed this book as a boring and highly tendentious piece of writing, deserving only of a very low place among the contemporary authorities. Admittedly, Fr. Manuel Calado was no unprejudiced or dispassionate observer. He wrote at white heat, and often with the fighting raging within earshot of him, between September 1645 and July 1646. But his work is all the more vivid and graphic for that, and much of it reads very like the front-line dispatches of a first-rate war correspondent. Apart from his vivid account of the first year of the Pernambuco insurrection, with which he was so closely connected, he gives us a fascinating description of the colony in the days of Johan Maurits. He was on intimate terms with the tolerant governor-general, and knew Von Schoppe, Lichthart, Arciszewski, and other Dutch leaders very well. He was, in fact, what would nowadays be termed a collaborator, and a most successful one at that. He contrived to ingratiate himself with both sides simultaneously, and to change his allegiance at exactly the right times. His book, which was ready for the press in October 1647 (about a year after his return to Portugal), was intended to whip up popular and official support for the Pernambuco patriots, and it is naturally very one-sided. Under the circumstances it could not have been anything else, nor can complete objectivity ever be expected from anyone who considers himself as engaged in a holy war. When due allowance is made for wilful distortion (as in the account of Lichthart's victory at Tamandaré, in Book IV, ch. 3, p. 234 of the 1648 edition), for malevolent anti-Semitism (the incident of the two wretched Jews related ibid., ch. 4), and for the friar's exceptionally strong personal likes and dislikes, his work still remains absolutely indispensable. Moreover, despite Wätjen's strictures, the book is written in a very graphic and readable style, apart from some rather unnecessary outbursts of doggerel versification.

Calado can, on occasion, do justice even to the detested Dutch *predikants* (cf. his acknowledgement of their courtesy at the end of Book II, ch. 4), and he makes no attempt to hide his admiration for Johan Maurits, while not glossing over the prince's faults. His malicious pen-portraits of those whom he disliked, the Italian commander, Bagnuoli; the alleged Marrano merchant, Gaspar Dias Ferreira; and the luckless vicar of the *várzea*, Padre Gaspar Ferreira, are in a class by themselves as vivid masterpieces of spite. It is surprising how the book got past the censorship, as bishops and Jesuits alike come under his lash on occasion, something most unusual in so priest-ridden a country as seventeenth-century Portugal. The book was indeed placed on the Roman Index in November 1655, but a second edition was published in 1668. Contrary to what J. H. Rodrigues (evidently misled by a defective copy in the Biblioteca Nacional at Rio de Janeiro) states in his *Bibliografia* (item no. 540), there is no difference whatever between the text of the first and second editions, as both are printed from the same sheets. The only difference between the two editions is in their respective title-pages, and in the preliminary leaves which contain congratulatory odes, sonnets, and other trifles.

All my quotations and references are taken from the 1648 edition, and readers wishing to know more about the hard-hitting friar and his work are again referred to the definitive study by J. A. Gonsalves de Mello, neto, *Frei Manuel Calado do Salvador, Religioso da Ordem de São Paulo, pregador apostólico por Sua Santidade, cronista da Restauração* (Recife, 1954). From this model monograph they will see that both the other Portuguese chroniclers of the war, Diogo Lopes de Santiago in his *História da Guerra de Pernambuco*, and Fr. Rafael de Jesus in his *Castrioto Lusitano*, drew very largely on Calado for their own works, usually without making the slightest acknowledgement.

The sermons, the letters, and the miscellaneous works of the great Jesuit, Padre Antonio Vieira, form another very valuable source for the study of the period which was overlooked by Wätjen. The importance of Vieira's writings for our subject is threefold. Firstly, he lived in Brazil for many years, being an eyewitness of the siege of Bahia in 1624–5, and again in 1638. Secondly, he was one of the closest advisers of King John IV, and took an active part in formulating that monarch's Brazilian policy and in the diplomatic negotiations undertaken to implement it. Thirdly, his collected works form what is probably the best single source for the understanding of 'the climate of opinion' in seventeenth-century Portugal, Brazil, and the Maranhão. In an age when the pulpit occupied the place which is filled nowadays by the press as a moulder of public opinion, Vieira's sermons were among the most famous and influential, nor was their fame confined to Portugal and Brazil. The English consul, Thomas Maynard, wrote from Lisbon in 1666 that Vieira's sermons were 'bought up as fast as they were printed, and sent for out of all parts of Spain, Italy and France'. While I have consulted the original collected edition of Vieira's *Sermoens* published at Lisbon in 1679–1710, my references and quotations are taken from the selected edition by Hernâni Cidade and Antonio Sérgio in the *Clássicos Sá da Costa* (Lisboa, 1954). Quotations from the *Obras Varias* are likewise taken from this latest edition, but references to his correspondence are taken from the *Cartas* edited in three volumes by J. Lucio de Azevedo (Coimbra, 1925–8).

Francisco Adolfo de Varnhagen's *História das Lutas com os Hollandezes no Brazil desde 1624 a 1654* (1st ed. Vienna, 1871; 2nd ed. Lisbon, 1872) was for long the classic work on the subject and can still, like P. M. Netscher's *Les Hollandais au Brésil, Notice Historique sur les Pays-Bas et le Brésil au XVIIe siècle* (The Hague, 1853), be consulted with profit. A large portion of Varnhagen's *Lutas* was also embodied in his *História Geral do Brasil antes da sua separação e independencia de Portugal*, originally published in two volumes at Rio de Janeiro in 1854–7, and which had a total of four editions, all widely differing from each other. The third edition of the *História Geral*, with numerous notes and appendixes by two great Brazilian historians, Capistrano de Abreu and Rodolfo Garcia, was published by the Companhia Melhoramentos at São Paulo in five volumes; but unfortunately the publishers took great pains to prevent the reader from ascertaining the date at which these volumes were printed. A fourth edition was published at São Paulo by the same firm in 1948–9. My own copy of this work comprises volumes i and ii of the fourth edition, both of which are dated 1948, and volumes iii, iv, and v of the third edition. The preface to the fifth volume, by Affonso E. de Taunay, is dated 25 May 1936, so this volume was presumably published that year or shortly afterwards. There is no means of ascertaining when volumes iii and iv were published; but judging from the context of some of the notes, volume iii *may* have been issued in 1928, and volume iv some time in the early nineteen-thirties. Whatever the real dates of publication, citations from the *História Geral* in my book are taken from the fourth edition (1948) as regards volumes i and ii, and from the third edition (? 1928–36?) as regards volumes iii, iv, and v.

The *História Geral* does not entirely supersede the *Lutas*, for if the former contains much additional matter, particularly in the form of copious quotations from translated Dutch documents, there are also some important omissions. Both works must therefore be consulted by the serious student. The additional notes and documentation provided by Capistrano de Abreu and Rodolfo Garcia for the third and fourth editions of the *História Geral* tend to pile Pelion on Ossa in some places; but nevertheless the venerable old cliché 'a veritable mine of information' can be applied to their editions of this work.

José Antonio Gonsalves de Mello, neto, *Tempo dos Flamengos, Influência da Ocupação Holandesa na Vida e na Cultura do Norte do Brasil* (Rio de Janeiro and São Paulo, 1947), is the standard work on the social history of the Dutch colony and is likely to remain so. Based largely on the daily minutes of the meetings of the High Council at Recife (*Dagelijksche Notulen der Hooge Raden in Brazilië*), this book is built upon contemporary Dutch records which neither Netscher, Varnhagen, nor Wätjen used, or used only most inadequately. Just as Wätjen's book is the definitive work on the economic and financial history of Netherlands Brazil, so the *Tempo dos Flamengos* is the definitive work on how the colonists lived, moved, and had their daily being. Not, it may be added, the Dutch colonists only, but the Portuguese *moradores*, the Jewish community, the Amerindians, and the Negro slaves all come under the microscope of Dr. Gonsalves de Mello. All the minutiae of social life in Recife, whether in times of bust and boom or of siege and famine, are here meticulously recorded and set down for posterity. As Dr. Gonsalves de Mello states in his introduction, he has used this material for its social and human interest, 'looking with myopic eyes at what may be of merely political, administrative, or purely chronological interest'. Within these admitted limits, however, the book could hardly be bettered, and must always remain required reading for anyone concerned with the history of Netherlands Brazil.

SELECT LIST OF AUTHORITIES

As explained in the Bibliographical Note (p. 291), there is a full and critical survey of the literature relating to Netherlands Brazil in J. H. Rodrigues, *Historiografia e Bibliografia do domínio holandês no Brasil* (Rio de Janeiro, 1949). This list is therefore limited to those works which have been cited in the footnotes in an abbreviated form.

Aenwysinge: dat men vande Oost- en West-Indische Compagnien, een Compagnie dient te maken. Mitsgaders twintich consideratien op de trafyque, zeevaert en commertie deser Landen. The Hague, 1644.

AITZEMA, Leeuw van, *Saken van staet en oorlogh, in ende omtrent de Vereenigde Nederlanden, 1621–1668.* 6 vols. The Hague, 1669–72.

—— *Verhael vande Nederlandsche Vrede-handeling. Op nieuws gecorrigeert, en met eenige stucken vermeerdert.* The Hague, 1671.

ALBUQUERQUE, Duarte de, *Memorias Diarias de la guerra del Brasil, por discurso de nueve años, empeçando desde el de M.D.C.XXX.* Madrid, 1654.

—— *Memórias Diárias da guerra do Brasil, 1630–1638.* Recife, 1944.

Amsterdams Dam-Praetje van wat outs en wat nieuws en wat vreemts. Amsterdam. 1649.

Anais da Academia Portuguesa de História. Ciclo da Restauração de Portugal. 11 vols. Lisbon, 1940–9.

Anais do IV Congresso. . . . See under *IV Congresso.*

Anais do Museu Paulista. São Paulo, 1922 to date.

ANDRADE E SILVA, José Justino, *Collecção Chronológica da legislação portugueza, 1603–1674.* 8 vols. Lisbon, 1854–6.

ARCISZEWSKI, Crestofle d'Artischau, 'Missive van den kolonnel Artichofsky aan Graaf Maurits en den Hoogen Raad in Brazilië, 24 Juli 1637', *Kroniek Historisch Genootschap Utrecht,* xxv (1869), pp. 222–48.

—— 'Memorie door den kolonnel Artichofsky, bij zijn vertrek uit Brazilië in 1637 overgeleverd aan Graaf Maurits en zijnen Geheimen Raad', op. cit., pp. 253–349.

— 'Apologie van Artichofsky tegen de beschuldiging van den Raad van Brazilië, ingeleverd aan de Staten Generaal in Augustus 1639', op. cit., pp. 351–92.

AREND, J. P., *Algemeene Geschiedenis des Vaderlands, 1581–1795,* IIIᵉ Deel, 5ᵉ Stuk. Amsterdam, 1874.
Based almost entirely on the Resolutions of the States-General and the provincial States of Holland.

ASHER, G. M. *A Bibliographical and Historical Essay on the Dutch books and pamphlets relating to New Netherland and to the Dutch West-India Company and its possessions in Brazil, Angola etc.* Amsterdam, 1854–67.

AZEVEDO, João Lucio de, *História dos Christãos Novos Portugueses.* Lisbon, 1922.

—— *Cartas do Padre António Vieira.* 3 vols. Coimbra, 1925–8.

BAHIA, Prefeitura Municipal do Salvador, *Documentos históricos do Arquivo Municipal. Atas da Camara, 1625–1659.* 3 vols. Bahia, 1949.
There is a fourth volume, covering the years 1660–4, but I have not seen it.

BARBOUR, Violet, *Capitalism in Amsterdam in the seventeenth century.* Baltimore, 1950.

BARLAEUS, Caspar [and S. P. L'Honoré Naber, editor and translator], *Nederlandsch Brazilië onder het bewind van Johan Maurits Grave van Nassau, 1637–1644. Historisch-Geographisch-Ethnographisch. Naar de Latijnsche uitgave van 1647 voor het eerst in het Nederlandsch bewerkt door S.P.L'H.N.* The Hague, 1923.
A Dutch translation, with some additional matter, of C. Barlaeus, *Rerum per octennium in Brasilia,* Amsterdam, 1647.

Bijdragen en Mededeelingen van het Historisch Genootschap gevestigd te Utrecht. Utrecht, 1878 to date.
Prior to 1878, title began with *Kroniek,* q.v. Vols. ii (1879), iii (1880), x (1887), xxi (1900), xxvii (1906), xlvi (1925), xlvii (1925), and xlviii (1926) are particularly useful for the documents they contain.

BOUMAN, D. J., *Johan Maurits van Nassau, de Braziliaan.* Utrecht, 1947.

BOXER, C. R., 'Blake and the Brazil Fleets in 1650', *The Mariner's Mirror,* vol. xxxvi (1950).

—— 'English shipping in the Brazil Trade 1640–65', *The Mariner's Mirror,* vol. xxxvii (1951).

—— *Salvador de Sá and the struggle for Brazil and Angola, 1602–1686.* London, 1952.

Brasilia. Revista de assuntos brasileiros. Coimbra, 1942 to date.
Vol. ix (1954/5) is particularly rich in relevant documents.

Brasilsche Gelt-Sack, Waer in dat klaerlijck vertoont wort, waer dat de participanten van de West-Indische Compagnie haer geldt ghebleven is. n.p., 1647.

Brasyls Schuyt-praetjen, gehouden tusschen een officier, een Domine, en een coopman, noopende den Staet van Brasyl : Mede hoe de officieren en soldaten tegenwoordich aldaer ghetracteert werden, en hoe men placht te leven ten tyde doen de Portogysen noch onder het onverdraeghlijck Iock der Hollanderen saten. n.p., 1649.

Briefwisseling van Constantijn Huyghens, 1608–1687, vols. ii–iv. The Hague, 1913–15.

BROECK, Matheus van den, *Journael ofte Historiaelse Beschrijvinge van Matheus vanden Broeck. Van 't geen hy selfs ghesien ende waerachtigh gebeurt is, wegen 't begin ende revolte van de Portugese in Brasiel, als mede de conditie en het overgaen van de forten aldaer.* Amsterdam, 1651.

CADORNEGA, Antonio de Oliveira de, *História Geral das guerras Angolanas.* 3 vols. Lisbon, 1940–2.
    Vols. i–ii edited by José Matias Delgado, vol. iii by Manuel Alves da Cunha. The original was written at Luanda in 1680–1.

CALADO DO SALVADOR, Manuel, *O Valeroso Lucideno e triumpho da Liberdade. Primeira Parte. Composta por o P. Mestre Frei Manoel Calado da Ordem de S. Paulo primeiro Ermitão, da Congregação dos Eremitas da Serra d'Ossa, natural de Villauiçosa.* Lisbon, 1648.
    A second part was never published.

CANABRAVA, Alice Piffer, *O Comércio português no Rio da Prata, 1580–1640.* São Paulo, 1944.

CAPELLEN, R. J. van der (ed.), *Gedenkschriften van Jonkheer Alexander van der Capellen, 1621–1654.* 2 vols. Utrecht, 1777–8.

CARDIM, Fernão, S.J., *Tratados da terra e gente do Brasil. Introducções e notas de Baptista Caetano, Capistrano de Abreu, e Rodolpho Garcia.* Rio de Janeiro, 1925. The originals date from 1584–1601.

Cartas de El-Rei D. João IV ao Conde da Vidigueira (Marquês de Niza) Embaixador em França. 2 vols. Lisbon, 1940.
    Covers the period May 1642–March 1649. Edited by P. M. Laranjo Coelho.

Cartas de El-Rei D. João IV para diversas autoridades do Reino. Lisbon, 1940.
    Covers the period October 1645–August 1651. Edited by P. M. Laranjo Coelho.

Claer Vertooch vande verradersche en vyantlijcke acten en proceduren van Poortugaal, in't verwecken ende stijven van de rebellie ende oorloghe in Brasil. Beweesen uyt de brieven en geschriften van het selve rijck ende hare ministers, door een lief-hebber by een versamelt, tot wederlegginge van de frivole excusen tot der Portugijsen onschult voort gebracht. Amsterdam, 1647.

IV Congresso de História Nacional, 21–28 Abril de 1949. Anais. 10 vols. Rio de Janeiro, 1950–1. Edited by the Instituto Histórico e Geográfico Brasileiro.
    Vol. v (1950) is particularly rich in relevant documents.

CUVELIER, J., & LEFÈVRE, J. [eds.], *Correspondance de la Cour d'Espagne sur les affaires des Pays-Bas au XVIIe siècle,* vols. ii–iii. Brussels, 1927–30.
    These two volumes cover the period 1621–47.

DEERR, N., *The History of Sugar.* 2 vols. London, 1949–50.

Documentos Históricos. Rio de Janeiro, 1928 to date. Published by the Biblioteca Nacional, Rio de Janeiro.

DOEDENS, H., 'Origineele Brieven van H. Doedens aan Ant. van Hilten, betreffende de West-Indische Compagnie, 1641–1648', *Kroniek van het Historisch Genootschap Utrecht,* vol. xxv (1869).

DUSSEN, Adriaen van der, *Relatório sôbre as capitanias conquistadas no Brasil pelos holandeses (1639)*. *Suas condições econômicas e sociais*. Tradução, introdução e notas de José Antonio Gonsalves de Mello, neto. Rio de Janeiro, 1947.

EDMUNDSON, George, 'The Dutch Power in Brazil, 1624–1654', *English Historical Review*, vol. xi (1896); vol. xiv (1899); vol. xv (1900).

—— 'The Dutch in Western Guiana', *English Historical Review*, vol. xvi (1901).

—— 'The Dutch on the Amazon and Negro in the seventeenth century'. *English Historical Review*, vol. xviii (1903); vol. xix (1904).

—— 'Early relations of the Manoas with the Dutch, 1606–1732', *English Historical Review*, vol. xxi (1906).

ELIAS, Johan, E., *Het Voorspel van den eersten Engelschen Oorlog. II, Het Britsch-Nederlandsch antagonisme buiten Europa*. The Hague, 1920.

FERNÁNDEZ DURO, Cesáreo, *Armada Española desde la unión de los reinos de Castilla y de Aragón*, vol. iii. Madrid, 1898.

FREIRE DE OLIVEIRA, Eduardo, *Elementos para a história do município de Lisboa*. 19 vols. Lisbon, 1882–1943.
    Vols. iii–iv cover the period 1621–69.

FREITAS, Gustavo de, *A Companhia Geral do Comércio do Brasil, 1649–1720*. *Subsídios para a história econômica de Portugal e do Brasil*. São Paulo, 1951.

GEYL, Pieter, *The Netherlands Divided, 1609–1648*. London, 1936.

GONSALVES DE MELLO, NETO, José Antonio, *Tempo dos Flamengos. Influência da Ocupação Holandesa na vida e na cultura do Norte do Brasil*. Rio de Janeiro, 1947.

—— *Francisco de Figueroa. Mestre de campo do Têrço das Ilhas em Pernambuco.* Recife, 1954.

—— *Antonio Dias Cardoso. Sargento-mor do Têrço de infantaria de Pernambuco.* Recife, 1954.

—— *Henrique Dias. Governador dos Pretos, Crioulos e Mulatos do Estado do Brasil.* Recife, 1954.

—— *D. Antônio Filipe Camarão. Capitão-mor dos Indios da costa do Nordeste do Brasil.* Recife, 1954.

—— *Filipe Bandeira de Melo. Tenente de Mestre de Campo General do Estado do Brasil.* Recife, 1954.

—— *Frei Manuel Calado do Salvador. Religioso da Ordem de São Paulo, pregador apostólico por Sua Santidade, cronista da Restauração.* Recife, 1954.
    See also under DUSSEN, ADRIAEN VAN DER.

HAECXS, Hendrik, 'Het Dagboek van Hendrik Haecxs, Lid van den Hoogen Raad van Brazilië, 1645–1654'. *Bijdragen en Mededeelingen Historisch Genootschap Utrecht*, vol. xlvi (1925). Edited by S. P. L'Honoré Naber.

Hispanic-American Historical Review. Baltimore and Durham (N.C.), 1918 to date. Edited by the Duke University Press.

Historia Naturalis Brasiliae, Auspicio et Beneficio Illustriss. I. Mauritii Com. Nassau. Leiden, 1648.
With contributions by Marcgraf, Piso, and De Laet. Cf. under TAUNAY below.

HOBOKEN, W. J. van, *Witte de With in Brazilië, 1648–1649.* Amsterdam, 1955.

Instituiçam da Companhia Geral para o Estado do Brazil. Lisbon, 1649.

JAPIKSE, N., *De Verwikkelingen tusschen de Republiek en Engeland, 1660–1665.* Leiden, 1900.

JONGE, J. K., de, *Oorsprong van Nederlands bezittingen op de kust van Guinea.* The Hague, 1871.

Journael ofte kort discours, nopende de rebellye ende verradelijcke desseynen der Portugesen, alhier in Brasil voorgenomen, 't welck in Junio 1645 is ontdeckt. Ende wat vorder daer nae ghepasseert is, tot den 28 April 1647. Beschreven door een Liefhebber, die selfs uit begin der rebellye daer te lande is gheweest, ende aldaer noch is residerende. Arnhem, 1647.

Journael van de reyse van de vlote uyt de Vereenighde Nederlanden na Brasilien, vervattende alles 't gene is voorgevallen; mitsgaders de batalie tusschen den Heere Ghenerael Sigismundus Schoppe, ende den Ghenerael van de Portugiesen. Beginnende van den 17 January anno 1648 tot den 17 May. Alles beschreven door een capiteyn-luytenant van het legher van den voorsz. Heer Generael Sigismundus Schoppe. Amsterdam, 1648.

Kort, bondigh ende waerachtigh verhael van't schandelijck overgeven ende verlaten vande voornaemste conquesten van Brasil, onder de regieringe vande Heeren Wouter van Schonenburgh, President, Hendrick Haecx, Hoogen Raet, ende Sigismondus van Schoppe, Luytenant Generael over de Militie, 1654. Middelburg, 1655.

KNUTTEL, W. P. C., *Catalogus van de pamfletten-verzameling berustende in de Koninklijke Bibliotheek, 1486–1688.* 4 vols., The Hague, 1889–95.

Kroniek van het Historisch Genootschap gevestigd te Utrecht. 31 vols. Utrecht, 1846–75.
Vols. xi (1855), xiv (1858), and xxv (1869) are especially useful. Title subsequently changed to *Bijdragen*, q.v.

LAET, Johannes de, *Iaerlyck Verhael van de Verrichtinghen der Geoctroyeerde West-Indische Compagnie . . . uitgegeven door S. P. L'Honoré Naber,* 4 vols. The Hague, 1931–7.
Vol. iv edited by J. C. M. Warnsinck. The original one-volume edition was published at Leiden, 1644.

LEITE, Serafim, S.J., *História da Companhia de Jesus no Brasil.* 10 vols. Lisbon and Rio de Janeiro, 1938–50.

LOPES DE SANTIAGO, Diogo, *História da guerra de Pernambuco e feitas memoráveis do mestre de campo João Fernandes Vieira, herói digno de eterna memória, primeiro aclamador da guerra.* Recife, 1943.
The original was written in the lifetime of João Fernandes Vieira, but nearly half of the work is a slavish copy of Calado's *Valeroso Lucideno.*

MOREAU, Pierre, *Histoire des derniers troubles du Brésil, entre les Hollandois et les Portugais*. Paris, 1651.

Usually bound up with a number of other relations forming one volume with a general title-page, *Relations véritables et curieuses de l'isle de Madagascar et du Brésil*. Paris, 1651.

NABER, S. P. L'Honoré, & WRIGHT, Irene A. [eds.], *Piet Heyn en de Zilvervloot. Bescheiden uit Nederlandsche en Spaansche archieven bijeenverzameld en uitgegeven*. Utrecht, 1928.

See also under BARLAEUS, LAET, and HAECXS.

NETSCHER, P. M., *Les Hollandais au Brésil. Notice historique sur les Pays-Bas et le Brésil au XVIIᵉ siècle*. The Hague, 1853.

NIEUHOF, Johan, *Gedenkweerdige Brasiliaense Zee- en Lant-Reize. Behelzende al het geen op dezelve is voorgevallen. Beneffens een bondige beschrijving van gantsch Neerlants Brasil . . . En inzonderheit een wijtloopig verhael der merkwaardigste voorvallen en geschiedenissen, die zich, geduurende zijn negenjarigh verblijf in Brasil, in d'oorlogen en opstant der Portugesen tegen d'onzen, zich sedert het jaer 1640 tot 1649 hebben toegedragen*. Amsterdam, 1682.

PENA JUNIOR, Afonso, *A Arte de Furtar e o seu autor*. 2 vols. Rio de Janeiro, 1946.

POELHEKKE, J. J., *De Vrede van Munster*. The Hague, 1948.

PORTO SEGURO, Barão de. See VARNHAGEN.

PRESTAGE, Edgar, *The Diplomatic Relations of Portugal with France, England, and Holland from 1640 to 1668*. Watford, 1925.

QUELEN, A. van, *Kort verhael vanden staet van Fernambuc, Toe-ge-eygent de E. Heeren Gecommitteerde ter Vergaederinghe vande Negentien inde Geoctroyeerde West-Indische Compagnie ter Camere van Amstelredam*. Amsterdam, 1640.

RAFAEL DE JESUS, Fr., O.S.B., *Castrioto Lusitano Parte I. Entrepresa, e Restauração de Pernambuco, e das capitanías confinantes. Varios e bellicos sucçessos entre Portuguezes e Belgas, acontecidos pello discurso de vinte e quatro annos, e tirados de noticias, relações, e memórias certas*. Lisbon, 1679.

Part II was never published, and this work is based almost exclusively on those of Fr. Manuel CALADO and Diogo LOPES DE SANTIAGO, q.v.

RATELBAND, K., *Vijf Dagregisters van het kasteel São Jorge da Mina (Elmina) aan de Goudkust, 1645-1647*. The Hague, 1953.

RAU, Virginia, 'A primeira batalha dos Guararapes descrita por André Vidal de Negreiros.' *Brasilia*, vol. ix (1955).

—— 'Relação inédita de Francisco de Brito Freire sôbre a capitulação do Recife.' *Brasilia*, vol. ix (1955).

REES, O. van, *Geschiedenis der Staathuishoudkunde in Nederland tot het einde der achttiende eeuw*. 2 vols. Utrecht, 1865-8.

Vol. ii has separate title: *Geschiedenis der koloniale politiek van de republiek der Vereenigde Nederlanden*.

Resolutien van de Staten van Holland en West Vriesland van het jaar 1524 tot het jaar 1795. 277 vols. n.d. n.p.
The relevant entries for Brazil during the years 1621–64 are calendared in G. M. Asher, *Bibliographical and Historical Essay*, pp. 40–69.

Revista de História. Publicação trimestral. 16 vols. Lisbon, 1912–28. Edited by Fidelino de Figueiredo.

Revista de História. Publicaçao trimestral. São Paulo, 1950 to date. Edited by E. Simões de Paula.

Revista do Instituto Archeológico e Geográphico Pernambucano. Recife, 1863 to date.

Revista Trimensal do Instituto Histórico e Geográphico Brasileiro. Rio de Janeiro, 1838 to date.

RODRIGUES, José Honorio, *Historiografia e Bibliografia do domínio Holandês no Brasil.* Rio de Janeiro, 1949.

Secrete Resolutien van de Edele Groot Mog. Heeren Staten van Hollandt ende West-Vrieslandt, beginnende met den jare 1653. 17 vols. n.d. n.p.

SÉRGIO, António, and CIDADE, Hernâni [eds.], *Padre António Vieira. Obras Escolhidas.* 12 vols. Lisbon, 1951–4.

SOUSA COUTINHO, Francisco de, *Correspondência diplomática de Francisco de Sousa Coutinho durante a sua embaixada em Holanda, 1643–1648.* 2 vols. Coimbra, 1920–6. Edited by E. Prestage & Pedro de Azevedo.

TAUNAY, Affonso de E. [ed.], *Jorge Marcgrave. História Natural do Brasil. Edição do Museo Paulista.* São Paulo, 1942.
A Brazilian translation of Marcgraf's section of the *Historia Naturalis Brasiliae*, Leiden, 1648.

THOMSEN, Thomas, *Albert Eckhout. Ein Niederländischer Maler und sein Gönner Moritz der Brasilianer. Ein Kulturbild aus dem 17. Jahrhundert.* Copenhagen, 1938.

Tijdschrift voor Geschiedenis, Groningen, 1886 to date.

THURLOE, John, *A Collection of the State Papers of John Thurloe.* 7 vols. London, 1742.

Twee verscheyden Remonstrantien ofte vertogen overgegeven aen de Heeren Staten Generael door Anthonio Paräupaba, in syn leven geweest Regidoor vande Brazilianen inde Capitania van Rio Grande. Ende met de laetste ongeluckigh verlies van Brazyl, vande gantsche Braziliaensche Natie afgesonden aen hare Ho: Mo: om derselver Natie erbermelijcken en jammerlijcken toestant te vertoenen ende met eenen hulp ende bystant te versoecken. The Hague, 1657.

UDEMANS, Godfried, *'T Geestelyck Roer van't Coopmans schip. Dat is : Trouw bericht hoe dat een coopman en coopvaerder, hem selven dragen moet in syne handelinge in pays ende in oorloge, voor Godt ende de menschen, te water ende te lande, insonderheyt onder de heydenen in Oost- ende West-Indien . . . Den derden druck, verbetert ende vermeerdert by den Autheur.* Dordrecht, 1655. Dedicated to the directors of the East and West India Companies.

VARNHAGEN, Francisco Adolfo de (also styled Barão de Porto Seguro), *História Geral do Brasil antes da sua separação e independência de Portugal.* 4 vols. São Paulo, 1928–48.
Citations from vols. i and ii are taken from the 4th edition (1948) and from vols. iii and iv from the 3rd edition (1928–36?), as explained in the bibliographical note.

—— *História das lutas com os Hollandezes no Brazil desde 1624 a 1654. Nova edição melhorada e acrescentada.* Lisbon, 1872.
Contains a *post facio* of xv pages, dated May 1874.

Vertoogh over den Toestant der West-Indische Compagnie, in haer begin, midden, ende eynde. Met een remedie tot redres van deselve. Rotterdam, 1651.

VIANNA, Helio, *Estudos de História Colonial.* São Paulo, 1948.

VICENTE DO SALVADOR, Fr., O.F.M., *Historia do Brasil por Frei Vicente do Salvador, natural da Bahia. Terceira edição. Revista por Capistrano de Abreu e Rodolpho Garcia.* São Paulo, 1931.
The original was written in 1627.

WARNSINCK, J. C. M., *Van Vlootvoogden en Zeeslagen.* Amsterdam, 1940.
Pp. 129–59: 'Een mislukte aanslag op Nederlandsch Brazilië'.
See also under LAET–NABER, *Iaerlyck Verhael.*

WASSENAER, Nicholas van, *Historisch Verhael aldaer ghedencwerdichste geschiedenisse, die hier en daer . . . van den beginne des jaers 1621 voorgevallen syn.* 21 vols. Amsterdam, 1622–32.

WÄTJEN, Hermann, *Das holländische Kolonialreich in Brasilien. Ein Kapitel aus der Kolonialgeschichte des 17. Jahrhunderts.* The Hague and Gotha, 1921.

WIZNITZER, Arnold, *The Records of the earliest Jewish Community in the New World.* New York, 1954.

GLOSSARY

Aldeia (P.):   Amerindian village, usually under control of Jesuit missionaries in Portuguese Brazil.

Almiranta (P.):   flagship of a Portuguese admiral (this latter was equivalent to a Dutch or English vice-admiral).

Alvará (P.):   a royal decree.

Armada Real do Mar Oceano (P.):   Atlantic High Seas Fleet of Portugal.

Arraial (P.)   camp, usually entrenched; also used in the sense of 'army'.

Arroba (P.):   Portuguese weight of 32 lb. avd.

Avaria (P.):   convoy-tax.

Camara (*Senado da Camara*) (P.):   municipal or town council (Spanish *Cabildo*).

Capitania (P.):   (1) Captaincy (a territorial division); (2) flagship of the 'General' (usually equivalent of a Dutch or English admiral) of a Portuguese fleet.

Carta-régia (P.):   a royal provision or letter.

Christão-Novo (P.):   lit., New-Christian; converted and/or crypto-Jew; same as Spanish *Marrano*.

Conde (P.):   Count.

Conselho (P.):   council; *Conselho Ultramarino*, Overseas Council, founded at Lisbon in 1643.

Consulta (P.):   Minutes or record of a council meeting with the relevant decision signed by those attending.

Cortes (P.):   Parliament of the three Estates of the realm (clergy, nobility, and people).

Creole (S.):   person born of white parents in a Spanish-American colony.

Cruzado (P.):   Portuguese coin worth about 4*s.* English, containing 400 *reis* (see *milreis* below).

Donatário (P.):   Lord-proprietor of a *capitania* in Brazil.

Dizimos (P.):   tithes.

Encomendero (S.):   a settler in Spanish America holding in trust from the crown a district with its Indian inhabitants by whose labour or tribute he was supported. *Encomienda*, a district so held or 'commended'.

Engenho (P.):   a sugar-mill; by extension, a sugar-plantation. *Senhor de engenho*, a mill-owner, or plantation-owner; a planter.

Farinha (P.):   flour, usually meaning manioc-flour in Brazil.

Fazenda (P.):   (1) Exchequer, Treasury; (2) farm, plantation; (3) any kind of property.

Festa (P.):   holiday or feast-day celebrations.

Fidalgo (P.):   lit. *filho d'algo*, 'son of somebody', and so 'gentleman'. Portuguese equivalent of the Spanish *Hidalgo*.

Florin (D.) : used interchangeably with *Guilder*; Dutch coin, and money of account, containing 20 *stuivers*, and equivalent to about 2*s*. English. Represented by the sign *fl.*

Flota (S.) : fleet, mostly in the sense of a silver-fleet or treasure-fleet.

Fluyt (D.) : Dutch merchant ship with great cargo capacity in relation to small number of crew.

Fumos da India (P.) : vapours of India; flattering hopes of quick riches in the East.

Heeren XIX (D.) : the nineteen directors of the central board of management of the Dutch West India Company. (The equivalent body for the Dutch East India Company numbered seventeen: *Heeren XVII.*)

hũa cousa grande (P.) : something great.

Kamer (D.) : chamber or board of a Dutch trading company, or of the provincial admiralty, &c.

Kaper (D.) : privateer or corsair provided with letters of marque.

Lavrador (P.) : copyholder: smallholder.

Lingua geral (P.) : The Tupí language which was the *lingua-franca* of the Tupí-Guaraní tribes in Brazil. *Linguas Travadas*, 'twisted tongues', languages spoken by the Tapuya and other tribes.

Mameluco (P.) : offspring of European father and Amerindian mother.

Maravedi (P.) : equivalent of the English farthing.

Marrano (S.) : converted and/or crypto-Jew. Cf. *Christão-novo* above.

Mazombo (P.) : person born of white parents in Brazil. Equivalent to the Spanish-American *Creole*, q.v.

Mestiço (P.) ⎫
Mestizo (S.) ⎭ : person of mixed white and Amerindian parentage; half-breed.

Mestre-de-campo (P.) : colonel of an infantry regiment. *Mestre-de-campo-general*, a field-force commander.

Milreis (P.) : a Portuguese coin, and money of account, worth about 12*s*. English. The *real* (pl. *reis*), one four-hundreth part of a *cruzado* and one-thousandth part of a *milreis*, existed only as a money of account.

Morador (P.) : settler, citizen; specifically, the head of a white family or household.

Muscavado (P.) : brown sugar cake.

Nayre (P.) : Nair.

Octroy (*octrooi*) (D) : charter.

Panela (P.) : low-grade sugar.

Parecer (P.) : considered opinion.

Partido plot of ground, allotment.

Pataca (P.) : money of account, calculated at 360 *reis* (cf. *milreis*).

Peça de Indias (P.) : standard measurement for the classification of Negro slaves, by which was meant 'a Negro from fifteen to twenty-five years old; from eight to fifteen, and from twenty-five to thirty-five, three pass for two; beneath eight, and from thirty-five to forty-five, two pass for one; sucking infants follow their mothers without accompt; all above forty-five years, with the diseased, are valued by arbiters', according to a definition of 1678.

Predikant (D.):   lit. preacher; ordained Calvinist minister.

Processo (P.):   legal proceedings: record of a court case.

Provincias Obedien- Southern Netherlands; Spanish Flanders.
tes (S.):

Reconcavo (P.):   hollow tract of cultivated land; applied primarily to the sugar-producing environs of Bahia.

Regimento (P.):   standing orders, set of instructions, regulations.

Ritmeester (D.):   cavalry captain.

Sertão (P.):   backwoods, bush, hinterland.

Schepen (D.):   Dutch sheriff, magistrate, or alderman.

Schout[en] (D.):   Dutch sheriff[s], or bailiff[s].

Sesmarias (P.):   grants of crown land.

Stuiver (Stiver) (D.): Dutch penny, twenty of which went to the guilder or florin, q.v.

Terço (P.) }
Terçio (S.) }   infantry regiment.

Valentões (P.):   bravoes or bully-boys.

Várzea (P.):   fertile sugar-producing region around Olinda and Recife.

Vrijluiden (D.):   free burghers, settlers, or traders in Netherlands Brazil not in the service of the West India Company.

Zekher asiti leniflaot 'I made a memorial unto God's miracles.'
El (Hebrew)

INDEX

Aboab da Fonseca, Isaac, first Rabbi in the New World, 181, 274.

Afogados, 51.

Aitzema, Leeuw van, diplomat and chronicler: value of his work, 296; cited, 49 *n.*–256 *n. passim.*

Alagoas, 59, 60, 62, 64, 85, 146, 199, 276.

Albuquerque, Mathias de (1590–1647): character, 38–39; acting governor-general of Brazil, 38 *n.*; sent to Pernambuco, 38; defence of Olinda and Recife, 40, 46; organizes resistance to Dutch invasion, 40–41, 49–50, 52, 54, 56, 298; recapture of Porto Calvo, 60, 63; recalled, 62; attitude of *moradores* towards, 48–49, 56, 62; c.-in-c. in Alemtejo, 298; correspondence of, 23 *n.*, 31 *n.*, 36, 37 *n.*

Albuquerque Coelho, Duarte de (1591–1658): value of his *Memorias Diarias*, 297–8; cited, 37–71 *passim.*

Almeida, Dona Jeronima, 126–7.

Amazon, 5, 13–14, 18, 136, 272.

Amerindians, types of, 18–19, 134–5; enslavement of, 18–19, 137, 272; Jesuits and, 18, 19, 57, 58, 267, 272; Dutch and, 27, 51–52, 64, 84, 85, 96, 134–7, 144; auxiliaries of Portuguese, 52, 62, 63, 64, 96, 196, 242, 248; auxiliaries of Dutch, 99, 107, 169, 171, 196, 199, 213, 222, 227, 245. *See also* Tapuyas, Tupís, Petiguares.

Amsterdam: attitude to the Brazilian question, 77–80, 103, 187–8, 192–3, 217–19, 236–7, 246, 248, 250, 256–8; and the Danish Redemption-Treaty, 218–19; and the Setúbal salt-trade, 218, 236; share in the WIC, 8, 9, 10, 13, 187; share in the Guinea trade, 187; tendency to trade with the enemy, 78, 236–7.

Angola: Negro slave-trade in, 19, 25–26, 106–7, 137–9, 279; abortive Dutch attack on, 26, 84; Dutch capture coast of, 107; Dutch–Portuguese fighting in, 146, 159, 190–1, 199; recaptured by Portuguese, 198–9, 217; Dutch treatment of Negroes in, 137; Dutch project for reconquest of, 236; criticism of Jesuits in, 275. *See also* Luanda.

Anobom, 107.

Antonio Vaz, island, 40, 49, 112, 115.

Arciszewski, Crestofle d'Artischau, Polish colonel (1592–1656): biographical sketch of, 49–50, 90; commander at Fort Oranje, 49; progress in bush-warfare, 53, 64, 130; captures the *arraial*, 59; in reoccupation of Porto Calvo, 60; and Fr. Manuel Calado, 60–61, 298; victory at Mata Redonda, 63; urges appointment of a governor-general, 65–66; returns to Holland, 75, 79; advocate of free-trade, 79–81; on good terms with Von Schoppe, 53; his opinion of *moradores*, 75, 79–80; disgraced by Johan Maurits, 90, 294; last years of, 90–91; criticizes WIC, 65, 175.

Ardra (Arder), Negro slaves from, 138, 169, 278.

Arguin, 278.

Armada(s), for the reconquest of Bahia in 1624–5, 25, 27, 42; for the recovery of Pernambuco, 42–45, 46–48, 55–56, 61–62, 86, 88–94; for the relief of Bahia in 1647, 186, 189–90, 205; and in 1648–9, 204–5; Portuguese in 1656, 248. *See also* Brazil Company.

Arraial do Bom Jesus, 40, 41, 46, 48; unsuccessfully attacked, 52; capitulation of, 59, 274.

Ataide, Dom Antonio de, count of Castro-Daire and Castanheira, 32 *n.*, 45 *n.*, 55.

Ataide, Dom Jeronimo de, count of Atouguia, 238, 247.

Atrocities and war-crimes, 172–3, 227, 230–1, 241, 242.

Aviary, built by Johan Maurits, 112, 115–16, 180.

Axim, 107.

Azores: hostility of population to Spaniards, 100–1; regiment recruited for Brazil, 198; and the Brazil trade, 202, 206, 210, 211; emigrants from, 101, 276.

ADDENDA TO BIBLIOGRAPHY

SINCE the first publication of this work fifteen years ago, a number of books and articles have appeared which modify or alter my own findings in some respects, and confirm or complement them in others. The following list is not exhaustive; but the serious student is advised to consult those which deal more specifically with certain aspects in which he may be interested.

Inadvertently omitted from the bibliography to the first edition (although in point of fact, actually consulted) was Gino Doria, *I Soldati napolitani nelle guerre del Brasile contro gli Olandesi, 1625–1641* Naples, 1932). Recent publications dealing with the military side of the Luso-Dutch struggle include Cleonis Xavier de Albuquerque, *A remuneração de serviços da guerra Holandesa* (University of Recife Press, 1968), and Francisco José Moonen, *Gaspar van der Ley no Brasil* (University of Recife Press, 1968).

We now have a superb definitive study of Frans Post by Erik Larsen, *Frans Post. Interprête du Brésil* (Colibris Editora, Amsterdam and Rio de Janeiro, 1962). Compare also Joaquim de Sousa Leão, *Os Pintores de Maurício de Nassau. Exposicão, 21 de Maio a 2 de Julho, Museu de Arte Moderna* (Rio de Janeiro, 1968). There is a good (but not faultless) history of the Jews in colonial Brazil by Arnold Wiznitzeı, *Jews in Colonial Brazil* (Columbia University Press, 1960). Well-documented work in this field is now being done by several Brazilian historians, typified by articles in *The Revista de História* of São Paulo, especially Vol. XLIIII (1971), and in progress. Recent books and monographs on this topic include Anita Novinsky, *Cristãos-Novos na Bahia* (São Paulo, 1972) and José Gonçalves Salvador, *Cristãos-Novos, Jesuítas e Inquisição 1530–1680* (São Paulo, 1969).

On a wider canvas, we have an excellent work whose scope can be deduced from its title and which has become a classic: Frédéric Mauro, *Le Portugal et l'Atlantique au XVIIᵉ siècle, 1570–1670: Étude économique* (Paris, 1960). Mauro's work has very recently been complemented by T. Bentley Duncan, *Atlantic Islands: Madeira, the Azores, and the Cape Verdes in seventeenth-century commerce and navigation* (University of Chicago Press, 1972), a richly documented book which is required reading for anyone interested in the Portuguese empire of the South Atlantic. More narrowly focused, but worth consulting despite the author's controversial "revisionist" views is Mário Neme, *Fórmulas Políticas no Brasil Holandês* (São Paulo, 1971).

On the Dutch side, W. J. van Hoboken, whose *Witte de With in Brazilie, 1648–1649* (Amsterdam, 1955) was a major source for my own work, subsequently published two relevant articles: "The Dutch West India Company; the political background of its rise and decline," in J. S. Bromley and E. H. Kossman (eds.), *Britain and the Netherlands,* Vol. I (London, 1960), pp. 41–61, and "Een wederwoord inzake de West Indische Compagnie," in the *Tijdschrift voor Geschiedenis,* Vol. LXXV (1962), pp. 49–53, with a postscript by J. C. van Dillen, *ibidem*, pp. 53–56.

I. CAPTAINCIES OF BRAZIL, 1630

2. NETHERLANDS BRAZIL, 1643

3. RECIFE AND NEIGHBOURHOOD, 1648

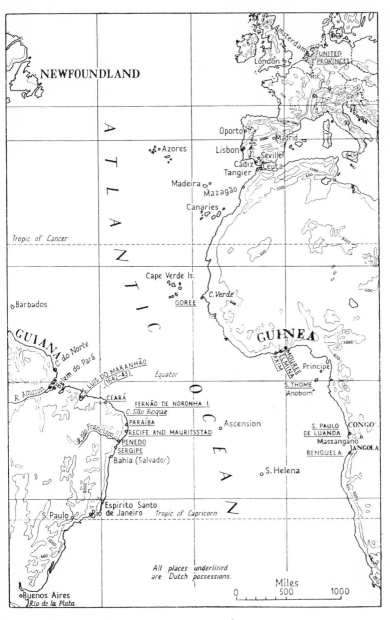

NEWFOUNDLAND

A T L A N T I C

Tropic of Cancer

Oporto
Lisbon
Madrid
Seville
Cádiz
Tangier
Ceuta

Azores

Madeira
Mazagão

Canaries

Cape Verde Is.

C. Verde
GOREE

Barbados

GUIANA

C. do Norte
Belem do Pará
LUIS DO MARANHÃO
(1642-43).

R. Amazon

Equator

O C E A N

GUINEA

MOUREE
ELMINA
AXIM

Principe

S. THOME
Anobom

CEARÁ
FERNÃO DE NORONHA I.
C. São Roque
PARAÍBA
RECIFE AND MAURITSSTAD
PENEDO
SERGIPE
Bahia (Salvador)

Rio S. Francisco

Ascension

S. PAULO
DE LUANDA
Massangano
BENGUELA

CONGO

ANGOLA

S. Helena

Espirito Santo
Rio de Janeiro
S. Paulo

Tropic of Capricorn

Amsterdam
London
UNITED
PROVINCES

All places underlined
are Dutch possessions.

Buenos Aires
Rio de la Plata

Miles
0   500   1000

4. THE WEST INDIA COMPANY'S EMPIRE IN THE
SOUTH ATLANTIC, 1643

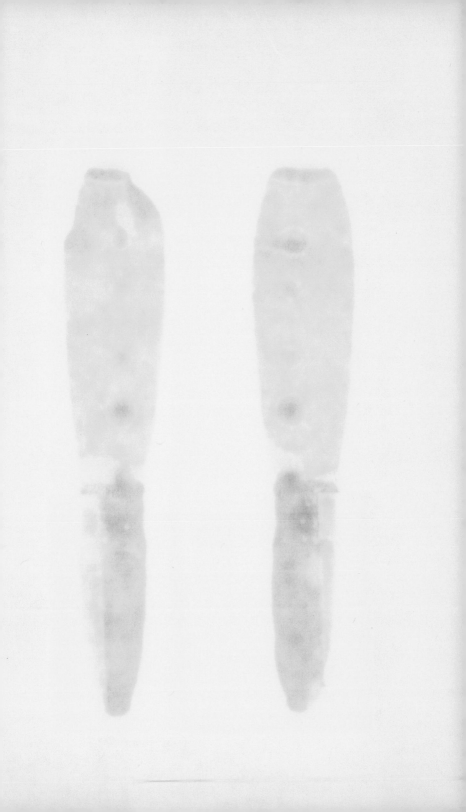

DATE DUE
